DATE DUE

APR 13 '00			
GAYLORD			PRINTED IN U.S.A.

S0-DGE-375

"THE HIGHER CHRISTIAN LIFE"

SOURCES FOR THE STUDY OF THE HOLINESS, PENTECOSTAL, AND KESWICK MOVEMENTS

*A forty-eight-volume
facsimile series reprinting
extremely rare documents for the study of
nineteenth-century religious and social history,
the rise of feminism, and the history of the
Pentecostal and Charismatic movements*

Edited by
Donald W. Dayton
Northern Baptist Theological Seminary

Advisory Editors
D. William Faupel, *Asbury Theological Seminary*
Cecil M. Robeck, Jr., *Fuller Theological Seminary*
Gerald T. Sheppard, *Union Theological Seminary*

A GARLAND SERIES

THE LIFE OF
CHARLES F. PARHAM
FOUNDER OF THE
APOSTOLIC FAITH MOVEMENT

Sarah E. Parham

Garland Publishing, Inc.
New York & London
1985

For a complete list of the titles in this series
see the final pages of this volume.

Library of Congress Cataloging in Publication Data

Parham, Sarah E.
THE LIFE OF CHARLES F. PARHAM,
FOUNDER OF THE APOSTOLIC FAITH MOVEMENT.

(The Higher Christian life)
Reprint. Originally published: Joplin, Mo. :
Hunter Print. Co., c1930.
1. Parham, Charles F. 2. Apostolic Faith
(Organization)—Clergy—Biography. 3. Pentecostalism—
United States—History. 4. United States—Church history
—20th century. I. Title. II. Series.
BX8766.Z8P37 1985   289.9 [B]   84-28743
ISBN 0-8240-6436-4 (alk. paper)

The volumes in this series are printed on
acid-free, 250-year-life paper.

Printed in the United States of America

EVANGELIST CHARLES FOX PARHAM

MRS. CHARLES FOX PARHAM

THE LIFE
of
CHARLES F. PARHAM

FOUNDER
of the
APOSTOLIC FAITH MOVEMENT

by
HIS WIFE

Press of
HUNTER PRINTING COMPANY
Joplin, Missouri

Preface

I shall not be able in this book to give a full account of Charles F. Parham's work for God, or a complete history of his busy life which was filled with so much joy and sorrow. While his life was crowned with many blessings, and victories in Christ, he also knew much of persecution and hardships. Though he did not complain, those who were with him knew he was often weary and exhausted through constant labor and traveling.

In his nearly forty years spent in the ministry, it would be impossible for me to tell now how many thousands of miles he has traveled over land and sea, and the number of meetings he has held; how many souls have been converted, sanctified and filled with the Holy Spirit; how many bodies have been healed through his prayer of faith, and are living witnesses to God's healing power. Scores of ministers and evangelists all over the United States, and missionaries in foreign fields, are now preaching the gospel, as a result of his faithful service for God. Eternity only can give a true record, when the books are opened, and our lives are read in the light of our Father's love; then shall all receive a just reward.

I will try, however, to give you a brief sketch of his consecrated life, trusting that it will be an encouragement to all who love God, to continue to preach the gospel to a sinful suffering world, that hungry souls may be satisfied, and their bodies healed by the power of God and that they may learn to trust in Christ as the Great Physician. As we who know God, look back over the years that are passed I am sure we will all acknowledge that the bright spots in our lives which ever remain fresh in our memory, are the experiences we have had with God, when He touched our hearts, and revealed Himself to our lives.

So in these pages, I have tried to tell you about some of the bright spots in his life, and the precious truths God revealed to him through His Word, which he ever held as a sacred trust. He counted no sacrifice too great that he might cause the gospel light to shine into darken lives, and bring the deeper truths to those who knew God. When amidst bitter persecutions, of dangers seen and unseen, we would often fear for his life, he would always assure us that "his life was immortal till his work was done."

It has been said, "He has achieved success who has lived well, laughed often and loved much; who has gained the respect of intellegent men, the trust of pure women and the love of little children; who has filled his niche and accomplished his task; who has left the world better than he found it, whether by an improved poppy, a perfect poem, or a rescued soul; who has never lacked appreciation for the earth's beauty or failed to express it; who has looked for the best in others and given them the best he had; whose life was an inspiration, his memory a benediction."

All of this can be said of his life and much more. Truly the world is better because of his life and the message he gave to the people. As he often said, we "must pour out our lives for humanity." He did this and "his labor was not in vain in the Lord." In his last days, he said many times that he felt that his work was finished. God said, "It is enough, come up higher."

January 29, 1929, he answered the call; and "rests from his labors, and his works do follow him."

I felt impressed that I should publish a sketch of his life and a selection of his sermons, but before I made this plan public several wrote me and said they had been praying that I would do this. I am publishing this book in loving rememberance of one who holds a place in the affections of many hearts, and praying that it may bring forth fruit for the glory of God. I do not consider this my work alone, for many have helped in different ways to make this book possible. I could not mention all the names, but I appreciate what each one has done, and I am sure that God will reward all who have assisted in this book. You will see that I have told his experiences in his own words as much as possible, and have earnestly endeavored to make my statements correct, to the best of my knowledge.

I am trusting that this book may be a blessing to many who have never heard these messages from his lips. Some who perhaps have been hindered before by false reports and prejudice may now through these pages receive light and truth. We know he has many precious sheaves to lay at the Master's feet, and we believe while he rests from his labors, other fields that he has planted will ripen and yield an abundant harvest. May God bless all who read this book and may each heart be encouraged to press on for God, "to occupy till He comes," or to be ready, clothed in His righteousness, when He calls us to meet Him.

Your Sister in Christ

SARAH E. PARHAM

Dedication

I am dedicating this book to our children; one daughter, Mrs. Esther Rardin and four sons, Claude, Philip, Wilfred and Robert, who, with their families all believe in and stand for the truths their father taught; also one grandson, Charles E. Rardin, who was named after his grandfather. I also dedicate it to his spiritual children everywhere, who looked to him for spiritual food and affectionately called him, "Daddy Parham."

SARAH E. PARHAM

Contents

Illustrations

Chapter 1

IN THE DAYS OF HIS YOUTH

HE Parham family is an old English family. In the geanology of the family, mention is made of Sir Edward Parham (1604) but connection is lost between him and Sir John Parham, who founded the Philadelphia family in the colonial period of American history. William M. Parham was born in Philadelphia, Penn., Dec. 24, 1846. He was married at Muscatine, Iowa to Ann Maria Eckel of Germantown, Penn, she being of German decent.

In 1878, the Parham family moved from Muscatine, Iowa, to Cheney, Kansas, and numbered themselves among the pioneer settlers in Sedgwick county. There were five sons, Harry Clayton, Edgar Eckel, Charles Fox, Frank and Arthur M. — Harry, Frank, and Arthur are still living.

Charles Fox Parham, of whom this book is written, was born in Muscatine, Iowa, June 4, 1873.

Their mother died at Cheney, Kansas, in December, 1885. Though Charles was only about twelve years old at the time of his mother's death, I have often heard him speak very affectionately of her while preaching, and tell of her death. They came to the school house for him one day, saying he must come at once if he would see his mother alive.

As the family surrounded her bed, his grief seemed double as he felt that he had been more care to her than the other children, as he had always been weak and sickly.

As the mother said good-by to the family she was leaving, she turned her beautiful brown eyes to him and lovingly said, "Charlie, be good." There, in the presence of God and his dying mother, he vowed that he would meet her in heaven.

The words, "Be Good" made a deep impression on his heart, and influenced him in later years to consecrate his life to God and the work of the ministry. She was buried at Wichita, Kansas. Only those who have been left thus, know the sadness of "a home without a mother."

The care of the new baby rested largely on Charles as he was not strong enough to do the heavy work of the farm. In 1886, William Parham was married to Harriet Miller. As the children witnessed their father's marriage, they welcomed the new mother who filled a needed place in the home and was a real mother to them. In the year 1879, Charles attended his first sunday school, in the home of Arthur Dibbens.

Charles F. Parham tells his experience as follows: "At six months of age I was taken with a fever that left me an invalid. For five years I suffered with dreadful spasms, and enlargement of the head, until my fore head became abnormally large. At nine years of age I was stricken with the first case of inflammatory rheumatism, virtually tied up in a knot; with other complication, I suffered much. Until, when the affliction left, I could count the bones in my hand by holding it up to the light. About this time I took medicines of various kinds to destroy a tape worm. One concoction was of such nature that it destroyed the lining of my stomach and dwarfed me so that I did not grow any for three years. Being very sick and weakly, my early days were spent at light-tasks, or when well enough, at herding the cattle.

"The earliest recollection I have of a call to the ministry was when about nine years of age, and though unconverted, I realized as certainly as did Samuel that God had laid His hand on me, and for many years endured the feeling of Paul, "Woe is me, if I preach not the gospel."

"As our parents had emigrated to Kansas in an early day in a prairie scooner the library was of small proportions. It contained, as I remember: "The letters from Hell, a natural history, a few antiquated school books, a dictionary, a history of all nations, recording facts from early historic times until 1878; and last, but not least the Bible. The last two books were the most valuable in preparing me for the work which has now developed upon me.

"The Bible was almost a constant companion, and though unconverted, time and again I used to round up the cattle and give them a rousing sermon on the realities of a future life, whether of the "minstrels of bliss, or the "wailing of the damned."

"Thus with no preconceived ideas, with no knowlegde of what creeds and doctrines meant, not having any traditional spectacles upon the eyes to see through, I scarcely knew anything about church and Sunday School. These facts are stated to show that any early Scriptures were entirely unbiased. I became thoroughly familiar with it, reading it just as it says. I don't remember to have ever heard but one or two preachers before reaching the age of thirteen years; and was then converted in a meeting held by Brother Lippard of the Congregational Church. Other scenes and memories may fade, but who shall ever forget the place where God spoke peace to the soul!

> "There is a spot to me more dear,
> Than native vale or mountain,
> A spot for where affections' tear
> Springs grateful from its fountain
> Tis not where kindred souls abound;
> Though that is almost heaven;
> But where I first my Savior found,
> And felt my sins forgiven."

"O sacred hour! O hallowed spot!
Where love divine first found me
Wherever falls my distant lot,
My heart still lingers round thee.
And when from earth I rise to soar
Up to my home in heaven,
Down will I cast my eyes once more
Where I was first forgiven."

"The preacher who was holding meetings in a school house, said, — on Thursday evening that unless some one made a start, the meeting would close on Sunday; so on the road home, I decided to start the next evening. There were several reasons why this decision was made; first and uppermost, was to keep the meeting running, as it was quite an innovation ,and enjoyable place to spend the long evenings, and although I had never decided in my mind when I should become a Christian, that was in the vague future, sometime. Yet, owing to sickness and always feeling thus inclined, it did not require much urging to decide; I stood up, and was immediately marked down as a convert. No interest seemed to be shown whether I was really converted or not, but the idea seemed to prevail that if a preson made a strong resolution and did the best they could, that was all to be required.

"On the road home that night, the Holy Spirit wrought deep and pungent conviction on my heart; and from the knowledge already obtained from the Scriptures, I knew it would be utterly impossible to live a Christian life, without a real conversion. Some people may try it, but in all the years of experience since, I have never known a single individual who made a success of the Christian life, who did not have deep and pungent conviction for sin, repenting with a godly sorrow for the same, with the restitution to fellow creatures of

all wrongs. Yea, and I have also learned that the blood of
Jesus Christ never blots out any sin between man and man
that they can righten; but if this is impossible, the blood of
Jesus Christ graciously covers. So on that night when
weighted down by mighty convictions, being unable to pray, I
tried to sing, (which was an impossibility to do until years
afterward, when in answer to prayer God supplied the need,
and gave me ability to lead the hymns in the meeting); so
humming that old familiar song,—"I am Coming to the Cross"
—had reached the third verse, when with face upturned, and
meaning every word of it;

"Here, I give my all to Thee,
    Friends, and time and earthly store,
Soul and body Thine to be;
    Wholly Thine forever more."

"While repeating the word, "wholly," there flashed from
the heavens a light above the brightness of the sun; like a
stroke of lightening it penetrated, thrilling every fibre of my
being; making me to know by experimental knowledge what
Peter knew of old, that He was the Christ, the Son of the
Living God. Though the devil has accused and thrown many
doubts and fears into my mind in regard to other things, yet
the experience of that night years ago, has ever been, "an
anchor to the soul, both sure and steadfast."

"Oh, happy day, that fixed my choice,
    On Thee, my Savior and my God."

"Nothing worthy of note happened in the following years.
I became a Sunday School teacher and worker and at the age
of fifteen, held the first public meetings, which were followed
with marked results. After teaching a short time I entered
college at sixteen; pursuing the religious work with more vig-
or than the studies, for which I was often severely reprimand-
ed and graded down in the examination.

"The Southwestern Kansas College was not then and is not now, a good place to back-slide, but for all that, I did backslide. The thought of the ministry, with no special abiding place, its many starvation stations and hard scrabble circuits, was not nearly so alluring as some other professions; especially when coupled with this the ministry seemed generally to be considered a great burden on society, which they don't seem to be able to get rid of, and which they are unwilling to support. Of whom it is often said, they demand more salary than the school teacher, and in return do the community little or no good; usually working about one-sixth of the time the teacher does. Having been a collecting steward and being thoroughly educated and trained in all the grafts and gambling schemes used to obtain money, until it seemed that it was absolutely necessary to put a poultice of oysters, strawberry short cake or ice-cream on the people's stomachs to draw or burst open their purse-strings.

"I became disgusted with the prospect; at the same time was seriously tormented with the promise I had made the Lord when converted, to go to Africa as a missionary. Having been an invalid for many years, the devil suggested that it would be a great philanthropic work to become a physician; to relieve suffering humanity, and then, by the by, have a nice home and some ease and comfort in this world. Accordingly, I chose my studies with this end in view; but the lamp of life faded. The devil tried to make me believe I could be a physician and a Christian too; losing ground, day after day, I became not only guilty of sins of omission, but sins of commission as well, until my associates failed to recognize me any longer as a Christian. Yet as certain as are God's mercies, so certain are His judgments, which are often-times mercies in disguise.

"For months I suffered the torments of hell, and the flames of rheumatic fever, given up by physicians and friends. While thus suffering many deaths, knowing I was in rebellion against

God, earnestly desiring and coveting to die (vainly expecting relief for soul and body by it) —yet realizing the fact that God was dealing with me, and I could not die. The preacher came to see me but I despised the sight of him. This is truly a fact that no one ever back-slides except they either blame the preacher of some other saint of God for it. So in the ministry, when enjoying the deep truths of God, I have preached a gospel of hearts,—or love; and when down in my experience, I preached a gospel of clubs.

"When the preacher came to see me, I put on a very sanctimonious air, and gave vent to a good many expressions I did not feel inside, so as to get rid of him.

"After many months of suffering in this manner, I became very much emaciated; one day when the physician called to see others in the house, he was brought in to see me. From weakness and an overdose of morphine (which I was privileged to eat as desired) I was in a semi-conscious condition, but heard the physician say I could last but for a short time. How I would have liked to have told him that I knew a good deal better. There was a consciousness within, that while I was suffering for disobedience and being sorely punished, some day I would have to surrender my arms of rebellion, and preach the everlasting gospel.

"The next morning there came to me so forcibly all those wonderful lessons of how Jesus healed; why could He not do the same today? All through the months I had lain there suffering, the words kept ringing in my ears, "Will you preach? Will you preach? WILL YOU PREACH?" I had steadfastly refused to do so, if I had to depend upon merchandising for my support. But on that morning when the physician said I would last but a few days, I cried out to the Lord, that if He would let me go somewhere, someplace, where I would not have to take collections or beg for a living that I would preach if He would turn me loose. Then I tried to pray.

With mind beclouded with drugs, I was unable to frame my thoughts satisfactorily, but soon began to repeat the Lord's prayer, "Our Father which art in heaven," etc., but when I came to that sentence "Thy will be done in earth as it is in heaven," suddenly my mind cleared; the preacher had said "There is no pain or sickness or death in heaven," I was of the earth earthy, if His will could be done in this body of mine, a lump of clay, an atom in His universe, as His will was done in Heaven, there would be no pain or sickness or death in my body. As this revelation came to me, I cried out to our Lord "Oh God, I know that some day soon, Thy will shall be done in all the earth, the human race shall be lifted to a sinless and sickless plane, but as Thou sayest in Thy Word, that we are NOW to know the power of the age to come, I claim my heritage NOW. Oh, Lord, if Thy will is done in the whirlwind and storm, if Thou dost ride upon the clouds and walk upon the waves, if lightning awaits Thee and thunders attend Thee, if Thou didst set the stars as lanterns of night in the sky, if the sun in his chariot of flame ever follows his well-beaten orbit, or the moon in its silver ship ever keeps her course in the trackless sea of the sky; if Thou didst embattle the mountains with hills, spread forth the valleys with the palms of Thy Hand and trace the rivers with Thy fingers; if Thou didst prepare the beds for the oceans, and say to them when encrouching upon the land, "Thus far shalt thou come and here shall thy proud waves be stayed," if Thou didst carpet Thy footstool with all this magnificent vegetation, then, if Thy will is done in me, I shall be whole." With this and similar prayers upon my lips, every joint in my body loosened and every organ in my body was healed. And yet, after having the use of all my body my ankles remained helpless, the sinews and bindings had become so stretched by months of rheumatism that they were as useless as though tin cans were tied to my ankles. Doctors and scientists said, I never would use them again. After some time through great necessity I learned to walk upon the sides of my feet, or rather upon my ankles with my feet thrown out to the side. In this manner I went back to college, though unable to walk except on smooth surfaces. I wondered all those monthy why, if God has healed the rest of my body, why not the ankles? Now readers, this may help you. Perhaps some of your afflictions remain with you for the same reason. If you have made a vow or promise to God, and have not kept that vow, we will have to perform such a vow unto God before we get complete healing. I had promised God my life in the ministry and woefully failed Him. But when at Christmas time I was asked to hold an evangel-istic service, I renewed my vow to God, and made a consecra-tion that I would quit college, if He wanted me to, and go into the ministry, if He would heal my ankles.

"Then one night, while praying, under a tree, to which I had crawled on the old College Campus, God instantly sent the virtue of healing like a mighty electric current through my body and my ankles were made whole, like the man at the beautiful Gate in the Temple. He is a wonderful Savior for soul and body.

"In the secret of His presence, how my soul delights to hide!
Oh, how precious are the lessons which I learn at Jesus' side!
Earthly cares can never vex me, neither trials lay me low,
If when satan comes to tempt me, to the 'secret place,' I go.

When my soul is faint and thirsty, 'neath the shadow of His
    wing,
There is cool and pleasant shelter and a fresh and crystal
    spring;
And my Savior rests beside me as we hold communion sweet;
If I tried, I could not utter what He says when thus we meet.

Only this I know: I tell Him all my doubts and griefs and
    fears;
Oh, how patiently He listens, and my drooping soul He
    cheers.
Do your think He ne'er reproves me? What a false friend He
    would be,
If He never, never told me of the sins which He must see!

Do you think that I could love Him half so well, or as I
    ought,
If He did not tell me plainly of each sinful word and thought?
No! He is so very faithful, and that makes me trust Him
    more,
For I know that He does love me, though He wounds me very
    sore.

Would you like to know the sweetness of the secret of the
    Lord?
Go and hide beneath His shadow; this shall then be your re-
    ward;
And whene'er you leave the silence of that happy meeting
    place,
You must mind and bear the image of your Master in your
    face.

You will surely lose the blessing and the fulness of your joy,
If you let dark clouds distress you and your inward peace de-
    stroy.
You may always be abiding, if you will at Jesus' side;
In the secret of His presence you may every moment hide."

                                    —Ellen L. Gorch.

Chapter II

SEARCH THE SCRIPTURES

 HILE attending school at Kansas City, Missouri the folks at my home near Tonganoxie, Kansas, wrote me of a wonderful revival being held in the "Pleasant-Valley School House". This was where I had gone to school before going to school at Kansas City, Missouri.

Charles F. Parham had come to this country district, a stranger, and had obtained permission to use the school house for revival services. He went upon a hill near the school-house, and there with hands stretched out over the valley, prayed that the entire community might be taken for God.

Believing that his prayer would be answered, the first night of the meeting, he arranged an old fashioned "mourner's bench." A revival meeting was something new in this neighborhood, and good crowds attended, though I believe my folks were about the only Christians at the time. They were all birthright members of the Friend's Church, and not used to taking much active part in public services, so when he called for testimonies and prayer, he had very little response. But real revivals are prayed down not worked up, and God answered prayer in a mighty way, and nearly all who came were wonderfully converted. Mr. Parham often stayed at Mr. Gowell's home, which was a real home, one of the old fashioned country homes where all were welcome. But. Mr. Gowell said he didn't see the need of a revival or of being converted. He and his family had always lived up to a high moral standard, and he believed that was all that was necessary. He hoped he was saved, and believed he was, but didn't think we could really know it, or have the assurance we were saved until we reached heaven. "You see it is like this," he said, "I drive to town, do my trading, and then start home, but it often begins to get dark before I get back. I believe, I hope I will reach there safely, but don't know so until I enter the gate at home and drive the old team up to the door."

Mr. Parham told him that his illustration did not rightly picture the Christian life as he believed it. That our way should not get darker as we neared our Heavenly Home, but "the path of the just is as a shining light, that shineth more and more unto the perfect day." Proverbs 4:18.

That God didn't want us to have a "hope so", "guess so" religion, but a real "Know so" experience and assurance of sins forgiven.   If we had something, we are not sure whether we had or not, we might lose it, and not know any difference. One night they "searched the Scriptures", and talked of God's plan of salvation.

"But we are all as an unclean thing, and all our right-eousness as filthy rags; and we all do fade as a leaf; and our in-iquities, like the wind, have taken us away." Isiah 64:6.

"What is man, that he should be clean? and he which is born of a woman, that he should be righteous?

"Behold, He putteth no trust in His saints: Yea, the heavens are not clean in His sight.

How much more abominable and filthy is man which drink-eth iniquity like water?" Job. 15:14-16.

"Is it any pleasure to the Almighty, that thou art righteous? or is it gain to Him, that thou makest thy way perfect?" Job 22:3.

'For I say unto you, that except your righteousness shall exceed the righteousness of the Scribes and Pharisees, ye shall in no case enter the kingdom of heaven." Matt. 5:20.

"As it is written, There is none righteous, no, not one. Therefore by the deeds of the law shall no flesh be justified in His sight; for by the law is the knowledge of sin. But now

the righteousness of God without the law is manifested, being witnessed by the law and the prophets. Even the righteousness of God, which is by faith of Jesus Christ unto all
and upon all them that believe; for there is no difference.
For we have all sinned and come short of the glory of God.
Being justified freely by His grace, through the redemption
that is in Christ Jesus. Whom God hath set forth to be a
propitiation through faith in His blood, to declare His righteousness for the remission of sins that are past, through the
forbearance of God.

To declare, I say, at this time, His righteousness; that
He might be just, and the Justifier or him which believeth in
Jesus. Where is boasting then? It is excluded. By what law?
of works? Nay: but by the law of faith." Romans 3:10,20-27

As they studied the Scriptures, conviction touched his
heart, but the next morning he went to the field to plow as
usual. Noon came, but he did not return. They pulled the
rope of the big old fashioned dinner bell and as the sound of
the bell was heard over the distant field, they saw him returning over the hill. He had plowed just one row across the field
but he had found the "Pearl of the great price," the "Lily of
the valley," a real personal Savior. I have heard of thee by
the hearing of the ear; but now mine eye seeth thee. Wherefore I abhor myself, and repent in dust and ashes. Job. 42:5-6.

Mr. Gowell knew Christ now, no more as one we read
about in history, who had lived and died, and fulfilled His mission, but as an ever present, living Christ; and he had a
"know-so" experience with God. This experience Mr. Parham taught all through his ministry, insisting that souls should
"pray-through" with a godly sorrow for sin, till they really
knew that they had the witness in themselves that they had
passed from death unto life. What rejoicing there was in that
home and in the entire neighborhood! This was the crowning victory of the revival.

How different our lives appear to us when God turns the searchlight of heaven upon us, and lets us see our lives as He sees them! Then we do not want to meet God in the filthy rags of our own righteousness, but we want to come before the King of Kings and Lord of Lords, in the beauty of holiness, standing in His strength, and clothed in His righteousness.

The oldest son, Ralph Gowell, was a great student being especially interested in stuffing birds and animals. He afterward graduated from the state University at Lawrence, Kans., and became a professor of biology in the University. .e was about the same age as Mr. Parham and they were reat friends. Mr. Parham was also a welcome guest in the of my grandfather, David Baker, who was a great Bible student. They spent many hours together studying the Scriptures, searching through a number of translations. My grandfather was a birthright member of the Friends church in England before coming to America, and believed in eternal torment for the wicked. As he searched the Scriptures he became convicted this doctrine was not Biblical, and thereafter he taught the destruction of the wicked. The church disfellowshipped him, but afterward accepted him, saying they were sorry they had treated him thus, as this was not considered an essential point of doctrine in the Friend's Church. Up to this time, Mr. Parham had also believed and preached eternal torment, but as he carefully studied the Bible with my grandfather, he too became convinced that he had been teaching the traditions and doctrines of men instead of the Word of God on this subject.

Through the following years of his ministry, he preached the destruction of the wicked, though this teaching was rejected by many, and brought much opposition and bitter persecution.

Chapter III

EARLY MINISTRY

MY school days in Kansas City, Mo. being over, I left my uncle's home there, and returned to my grandfather's home at Tonganoxie, Kansas. The revival meeting had closed, but they told me that I would have an opportunity to hear the evangelist preach, as the next Sunday, June 4, was his nineteeenth birthday and he was going to have an all day meeting at our school house. I was glad of this, as I was curious to see the one who had held such a gracious revival which had wrought such a change in the neighborhood. There was a good crowd at the meeting, and I never shall forget that day.

I am sure all young people feel a sadness and gladness in realizing our school days are past and the unknown future lies before us. As I sat in the old school house that morning my mind wandered back over the past. I looked at the little desk at the front, where I had sat when I first went to school; then at the larger seats which I had occupied later as I grew older. I saw, too, where we had scratched or cut our names on the desks in absent-minded moments, when we should have been studying, and it brought many pleasant memories of the past which can never be lived again. One of my teachers kept a motto on the blackboard which I have often thought of since: "I expect to pass through this world but once. Any good therefore that I can do, or any kindness I can show to any fellow being, let me do it now. Let me not defer nor neglect it, for I shall not pass this way again."

I then recalled the time, when I was about thirteen years of age that my grandfather had taken me to a Camp Meeting near Lawrence, Kansas. As they sang, "Where He Leads Me, I Will Follow," I knew for the first time, what conviction was and raised my hand for prayer. I had been raised in a Christian home, attended Sunday School and taught to believe in the Bible. I knew very little of actual sin, but that afternoon I realized I was a sinner, lost without God, and needed salvation. When I got home my heart was still heavy, but under an old tree on the lawn, I "prayed through," till the burden was lifted and I could say, I know MY Redeemer liveth, My personal Savior. "Thou art the Christ the Son of the living God."— Matt. 16:16. Flesh and blood has not revealed it unto me, but "My Father which is in heaven." Though today many argue about the divinity of Christ, and many books are written on the subject, the moment the Spirit revealed the Savior to me, I had a glimpse of Jesus, and knew for myself that truly He was the Son of God. Let us not discourage children when they are seeking salvation, for some children hear the call of God while very young. I could never doubt my experience, when Christ first became real to me.

While going to school in the city I still loved the Lord, but as I had gone with my young friends to first one and then another of the most fashionable churches, I had let worldliness come in. I had gone more to be with the crowd and have a good time than to serve God.

The songs and prayers were over, and as the people began to testify so earnestly, I realized that a great change had taken place in their lives since I had seen them last. But my thoughts were brought back from the past, and the wanderings of my mind ceased, as Mr. Parham began to preach. How different he looked, in his brown business suit and dark shirt, from the fashionable preachers I had been used to seeing! I listened with intense interest as he read 1 Cor. 2., "And I brethren, when I came to you, came not with excellency of speech or of wisdom, declaring unto you the testimony of God. For I determined not to know anything among you, save Jesus Christ, and Him crucified. I was with you in weakness and in fear, and in much trembling. And my speech and my preaching

was not with enticing words of man's wisdom, but in demonstration of the Spirit and of power. That your faith should
not stand in the wisdom of men, but in the power of God."

I felt a power in the meeting that I had not known in the
services I had been attending. How true were these verses
and how much there was in them for me! Though I had
heard many sermons of enticing words of man's wisdom, they
had failed to satisfy my soul. If our faith should stand in the
wisdom of men, or we just had a head knowledge of religion,
some one with greater wisdom might argue it from us. Surely the early Christians would have been persuaded to give up
their faith rather than endure the cruel torture that they did.
But if our faith stands in "the power of God," this power being wrought out in our lives, how sure is our foundation. The
gates of hell shall not prevail against it.

The sermon was surely all directed to me as Mr. Parham
continued to preach. "You can go to the fashionable churches
and belong to the Young People's Christian Endeavor Society,
reconsecrate your lives once a month, but know nothing of real
consecration, and the sanctifying power of the blood of Christ.
God wants us to present our bodies a living sacrifice; once for
all, yielding to Him all we know and all we don't know. If
you give me something, then every month come and tell me
you would give it to me again, I would begin to think you did
not want me to have it, and did not mean it in the first place."

What! Was he talking just to me? How did he know that
I had joined the Christian Endeavor Society especially to
please my chums, and to go with the crowd? Once a month
we were pledged to go and reconsecrate, or read a verse on
consecration. It was still fresh in my mind how I had got up
and read my verse, then sat down and cried, not having the
real experience and being naturally timid I was afraid to speak
before the public. His words had struck me as a thunder-bolt,
and sank deep in my heart.

I did not then understand that he was preaching without notes or writing out his sermon, as I had been used to preach-ers doing. Sometimes he did not know when he went in the pulpit what the message would be, but he trusted God to bring the Scriptures to his remembrance and inspire him to give out the meat in due season that would meet the needs of the people and feed hungry souls. The early Friends also believed in inspiration, and trusting God to give them the message by the Holy Spirit. "For the Word of God is quick and powerful and sharper than any two edged sword, piercing even to the dividing asunder of soul and spirit, and of the joints and marrow, and is a discerner of the thoughts and in-tents of the heart." Heb. 4:12.

As he preached "Jesus Christ, and Him crucified," I real-ized that I had been following Him afar off, and I longed to really consecrate my life wholly to Him who had suffered with-out the gates, that we might be sanctified. Truly I had re-ceived a message from the Word, backed up by the power of God.

The nurse is very anxious about the patient who has no ap-petite, knowing he is in a critical condition, but when the ap-petite returns there is hope. So the soul that is dead in tres-passes and sins does not care for spiritual food and it is useless to try to force them to take it, until the Spirit puts a hunger in the heart and a healthy appetite for the Bread of Life.

We are created for His glory, and the human heart is never really satisfied until we open our heart's door, and enthrone Him first in our lives. Let us give Him possession of that which is His. "What! Know ye not that your body is the temple of the Holy Ghost which is in you, which ye have of God, and ye are not your own. For ye are bought with a price therefore glorify God in your body, and in your spirit, which are God's. 1 Cor. 6:16-20. As the hart panteth after the water brooks, so panteth my soul after thee, O God.

"My soul thirsteth for God, for the living God; when shall
I come and appear before God?" Psalms 42:12. "Why art
thou cast down, O my soul? and why art thou disquieted
within me? Hope thou in God; for I shall yet praise Him,
who is the health of my countenance, and my God." Psalms
42:11. "Blessed are they which do hunger and thirst after
righeousness, for they shall be filled." Matt. 5:6. My plate
was full, I was hungry and had feasted on the Word of God.

We had enjoyed our spiritual feast, and now we were to
have our temporal one. But before the service was dismissed
for the basket dinner, a letter was read, then presented to Mr.
Parham. The community had chosen this opportunity to express their gratitude for the meeting he had just held. Since
I have been writing this book, I have found this letter. Mr.
Parham had it carefully put away in a leather bill-folder,
which my folks had given him two years later on his twenty-
first birthday (June 4, 1894).

Though both the letter and bill folder are much worn with
age, he had kept them in remembrance of his friends in his
early ministry, as he always appreciated so much every act of
kindness and word of encouragement. Some times I feel that
we fail to give words of cheer to the young preachers, as much
as we should. Let us not neglect to do this, for they may value it, and it may be more help to them than we realize.

The letter reads as follows:

"Charles F. Parham has held nineteen revival services in the
Pleasant Valley School House, district 68. The Christians in
the district thus unaminously express their thanks to our
Heavenly Father for sending him amongst us and for the clear
forcible manner in which the gospel has been preached. Many
have been brought into the fold. It has been a time of refreshing from the presence of the Lord, like rain upon the
mown grass. At the closing meeting it was unaminously

agreed to thus acknowledge our brother's labors among us. The following named persons are authorized to sign this expression of unity on behalf of the meeting."—Chas W. Hemphill, Lewis H. Peters, Benj. Penfold, T. H. Baker, David Baker, P W. Goswell, Geo. Mosser, B. F. Haas, Alfred Thistlethwaite.

This was not his last service at the Pleasant Valley School House, but he often held services here, and the people also were faithful in helping him in other meetings whenever it was possible. Some times they would have to "do their chores" in the middle of the afternoon, in order to go to the night service. Some walked, while others went in wagons and buggies. Mr. Parham would say they milked the cows twice in the morning, that they might come to the services, and no doubt to the cows the milkings did seem to come rather close together.

During Mr. Parham's nineteenth year he was called to fill the pulpit of Dr. Davis, after his death, who was the founder of Baker University. He had charge of this church at Eudora, Kansas for about two years and also the M. E. Church at Linwood, Kansas, where he preached every Sunday after noon.

He was faithful to his appointments through all kinds of weather. One Sunday the roads between Eudora and Linwood were so drifted with snow that they were impassable. The people of Linwood said, "Well, our preacher can't get here today." But when it was time for the service, here he came. He had walked down the edge of the frozen river. They rang the bell and a good crowd came thinking if he could walk that far, they ought to be able to come; so they had a good meeting that day, in spite of the weather.

One time when he had an appointment at our school house, it was very cold and a deep snow on the ground. We all thought it would be impossible for him to drive so far through the snow, but before night he drove up to our place, his faithful horse plowing through the snow. My brothers took care of the horse, and as he got out of the buggy we asked him if he was nearly frozen. He laughingly produced a brick which he had at his feet, and a hot water bottle from inside his coat which, he said, had kept him from suffering. My folks told him that he should not have tried to come, but he said he never intended to fail to keep his appointments on account of the weather, for if the people knew that he would not disappoint them, they would come too. He always carried out this principle though it often caused him untold suffering and hardships.

He often told the following story. "It was a bad night and the preacher walked the floor trying to decide whether he would try to fill his appointment. He looked out the windows, then out the door, thinking some one would tell him not to go. At last he said, "Even a dog would not go out a night like this." A half-wit then said, "Yes, he would, if he knew his master was there." Dogs will give their lives for their masters, or follow them until they starve to death. If dogs will do this, how much more ought we to be willing to die for our Master who gave His life for us."

He taught his workers to always keep their word and fill their appointments, pay their debts, and owe no man anything but to love one another. (Romans 13:8) He practiced what he preached, and counted this life as nothing that he might win Christ.

He preached sanctification as a second definite work of grace, as taught by John Wesley and the early Methodists, and, as I attended Mr. Parham's meetings at different times, I realized he was teaching and had an experience I did not possess. When I came to God for salvation, I had come repenting. "Therefore being justified by faith I had peace with

God through our Lord Jesus Christ." (Rom. 5:6) Now I longed to know God in a deeper experience, and I felt the Spirit leading me on to consecrate my life to Him. "I beseech you therefore, brethern, by the mercies of God, that ye present your bodies a living sacrifice, holy acceptable, unto God which is your reasonable service." (Romans 12:1) When Paul said, "brethern," he was pleading with those who had repented and knew the mercies of God, to consecrate their lives to Him.

In Eph. 2:1 Paul spoke of their condition before they were converted. And you hath He quickened who were dead in trespasses and sins. The soul that is "dead in trespasses and sins," has nothing to consecrate. We must come repenting and receive pardon, then we can consecrate our lives, and know His sanctifying grace. Now, as I consecrated all I was, and all that might come to my life in the future, all I knew and all I did not know, the joy of the Lord filled my soul. I had the assurance I was accepted, set apart in sanctification. I was not my own, but bought with a price and made a new creature in Christ Jesus. The love for worldly pleasures had gone out of my life. My hands, now consecrated to God, could never touch cards, that I had taken pleasure in playing. I hated even the sight of them, thinking of the lives they had ruined. "If we walk in the light, as He is in the light, we have fellowship one with another, and the blood of Jesus Christ, His Son, cleanseth us from all sin." (1 John 1:7) After we are sanctified, we can only keep sanctified by walking in the light, putting Him first in our lives, and wholly yielding to Him.

Sanctification destroys the sinful desires of the flesh, but the natural, human desires of the flesh we must die daily to, until we can say with Paul, "I am crucified with Christ, nevertheless, I live; yet not I but Chirst liveth in me." (Gal. 2:20.)

Chapter IV

EVANGELISTIC WORK

 QUOTE the following from the chapter entitled, "Life Sketch" contained in Mr. Parham's book, "A Voice Crying in the Wilderness," written in 1901.

"Finding the confines of a pastorate, and feeling the narrowness of sectarian churchism, I was often in conflict with the higher authorities, which eventually resulted in open rupture; and I left denominationalism forever, though suffering bitter persecution at the hands of the church, who seemed determined if possible my soul should never find rest in this world or the world to come. Oh, the narrowness of many who call themselves the Lord's own!

"Five years were spent in evangelistic work; hundreds were converted, scores sanctified, and a few healed. This latter part of the work, —praying for the sick—I drew back from and many were the severe punishments received from the Father for this rebellion; how many times He withdrew His presence because I refused to declare the matchless power of Him who bare our sicknesses. Not then knowing that it meant no more to pray for the sick to be healed, than to pray for a sinner to be saved. God finally conquered, I yielded my life, not only to preach salvation from sin, but healing as well.

"Looking back over theses years, I see how from the healing of a few individuals, I was lead to the establishing of a Healing Home in Topeka, Kansas; then followed the opening of the Bible School, where the presence of God was more wonderfully manifested than among any other people since the days of the apostles..

"I can truly say that from the inception of the divine life received at conversion to the land I hold today, whatever has been wrought through this instrument of clay, which is of righteousness, benefit or worth, 'twas none of self, but all of Christ."

Linwood, Kansas, being only about five miles from my home, we often attended services there during the time that Mr. Parham had charge of the M. E. Church. A great many others also attended there, who were members of other churches, as such a spirit of unity prevailed in his meetings that all felt welcome.

The church grew in grace and the attendance increased until a nice new church was built as the result of his labor. The higher officials in the church recognized his ability as a preacher, and though young, saw a great future before him in the ministry. They would have given him almost any work or position in the church that he wanted, if he would have yielded to their authority. But he had consecrated his life to God, to be guided by the Holy Spirit, and "must obey God rather than man."

The church did not accept his teachings regarding the future of the wicked, but he must teach what he believed to be the Word of God. They would have been glad for the great revival meetings which he held in tents and school houses, if he had insisted on the converts joining their church. But he told the people if they wanted to join the church, they could join any one they desired but that it was not essential to salvation to belong to any denomination. That what he was striving for was that they might really be saved, and have their names written on the Lamb's book of life. Salvation was purchased for us, by the atonement of Christ, and in the day of judgment, we would not be asked what church we belonged to.

This non-sectarian spirit did not please the church. The churches to-day seem to require their preachers to spend as much time, if not more, in preaching their particular church, and working for it, than in preaching Jesus Christ and Him

crucified, and the glorious Church without spot or wrinkle, of which He is the Head. I like the following Motto:
"In essentials, Unity,
In non-essentials, Liberty—
In all things, Charity."

If we Christians could live up to this, we would help to answer the prayer of Christ, when He prayed we might be one, even as He and the Father were One. But instead of this the preachers often emphasize and enlarge upon the non-essentials teachings to strengthen the sectarian bars about their denomination and widen the gulf between them and their neighbor churches. Mr. Parham felt too, that he could not accept the salary they gave him, which was raised by suppers and worldly entertainments. Surely the workman is worthy of his hire, and should be supported by the tithes and free-will offerings of the people, given as unto the Lord. His parents, being faithful members in the church, were very much disappointed when he withdrew from the church. They had hoped that he might do a great work in the church and now their hopes were crushed. Sometimes Mr. Parham would laughingly say, that they had tried to cut him out for a Methodist preacher, but found there was not sufficient goods, so they threw him in the "scrap pile" and he had been a "scrap" on their hands ever since. When finally he left the church, all manner of evil was spoken against him falsely. He was also persecuted by the drinking class, as he had taken an active part in temperance work, helping to put prohibition in Kansas.

He sought comfort at the home of his friends, Mr. & Mrs. Tuttle of Lawrence, Kansas, who welcomed him as their own son, and gave him a room where he could wait on God without being disturbed. He felt the need of prayer that the Lord might guide him, and give him the needed grace and strength to go on in His service. Though he had lived a life above reproach, and been zealous for God, his good name had been cast out as evil, and he feared that his work was ruined and he could not continue on in the ministry.

Long he prayed without considering time and his surroundings, until the Lord manifested Himself to him, as He does not to the world. As he felt the glorious presence of Christ, the Word came to him, "I made Myself of no reputation." God had answered prayer! Thanks be to God, which giveth us the victory through our Lord Jesus Christ. 1 Cor. 15:57.

He now saw that if Christ, the Son of God, could accomplish His Father's will without reputation and honor from men, he too, must continue in the work of God, walk even as He walked, not backed up by men but by the power of God. Christ said, I receive not honor from me. John 5:41.

He also received this Scripture, to encourage and strengthen him for his future work. "Behold, I have made thy face strong against their faces, and thy forehead against their foreheads." "As an adamant, harder than flint, have I made thy forehead; fear them not, neither be dismayed at their looks, though they be a rebellious house." Ezekiel 13:8-9. How wonderfully God fulfilled His Word to him through his ministry which followed, and made him strong to face persecution, slander, imprisonment, many times threatened with death in different ways, with a calmness that only God can give!

As he entered the undenominational evangelistic field, he held meetings in halls, school houses, tabernacles, churches, and a real revival spirit was manifest in his services everywhere. Great crowds attended the Camp-meetings which he held in the summer months, and he worked a great deal with the Holiness people until they began to organize.

Mr. & Mrs. Tuttle and a number of other spiritual workers, labored with him, in the gospel work. Mrs. M. J. Tuttle is now over eighty years old and I will quote a little from a letter which I received from her recently: "I know what it means to look for the last time on the dear loved one, who has for so long shared our joys and sorrows.   It brings tears to my eyes, as I read your paper and look at the dear face I have looked on so often when he was so young and full of life and ambition, hardly ever still unless he was sitting in the pulpit.

"No one was ever nearer or dearer to our hearts than he, out-side of our own family, and he seemed to belong to us. Oh, if we shall know each other as we did here, how grand and glorious it will be to talk our lives over.   No matter how it will be, we shall be satisfied when we awake in His likeness and see our Redeemer face to face who died for our sins, and has gone to prepare a place for us.   Oh, what will it be to be there!

"We always enjoyed being with Bro. Parham in meetings. I think of him so much; though ever busy, we were never afraid to go anywhere with him, for he was always considerate and kind, and so attentive to the needs of "Father and Mother Tut-tle." I thank you from my heart for the last paper (February number).   I mean to keep it loving remembrance of him."

During these years of Mr. Parham's evangelistic work, he was convicted that he should be baptized.   He wrote, "One day while meditating alone in the woods, the Spirit said, "Have you obeyed every command you believe to be in the Word?   I answered 'Yes'.   The question was repeated, the same answer given.   The third time the question was asked, I answered 'No,' for like a flood the convincing evidence of the necessity of obedience rushed in upon us, how Peter said, "Repent and be baptized every one of you in the name of Jesus Christ."   Was not this one baptism?

Then came the second: "And ye shall receive the gift of the Holy Ghost."   Again, Peter proceeded at once to baptize Cor-nelius, and all his house, who had received the baptism of the Holy Spirit, with the Bible evidence of speaking in tongues. These and other scriptures were so convincing that the next day I was baptized by single immersion."

Another Scripture which he always sought to carefully practice was, James 2:1-4. High and low, rich and poor, young and old, all found a hearty welcome at his meetings, and he treated them with equal consideration as much as possible. He was then a young man, and with his social nature and pleasing personality, of course there were many young ladies who would have appreciated his special attention, but he felt that if he showed any personal friendship of this kind it would be a detriment to the meetings, and he always put the cause of Christ first in his life.

In later years, when he often took a company of young workers with him, he always tried to show them the necessity of being very careful along these lines, warning them that it might afford an opportunity for criticism, and kill the spiritual power of the meeting.

It was not considered proper then, (at least with our circle of friends) for young couples to go any distance together without a chaperon. Though I had known Mr. Parham about four years, I only remember taking one buggy ride with him alone, before we were engaged. One Sunday morning we drove about five miles home from church together, and I believe this was planned by our friends, who hoped that our friendship might develop into a closer relationship.

While holding a meeting in western Kansas, he wrote and proposed to me, also writing to my mother at the same time. He told me his life was wholly given up to God and His service; that he did not know whether he would ever have a home or anything of this world's comforts, but if I cared to share his lot, we would both trust the Lord together.

We were married about six months later. Truly the promise, Seek ye first the kingdom of God and His righteousness and all these things shall be added unto you (Matt. 6:33) has been wonderfully fulfilled to us, and made real in our lives.

Chapter V

THE GREAT PHYSICIAN

E were married, December 31, 1896; the Friend's Ministers, Jonathan Ballard and his wife had charge of the service at my grandfather's home. Just a few friends, besides relatives, were present.

It was the custom then in the Friend's Church, instead of the preacher performing the ceremony the couple themselves, in the presence of God, pledged their lives one to the other. As we concluded by saying we would love, honor, and cherish each other, in sickness and health, for weal or for woe, till death do us part, we said it from our hearts, and meant it every word. I am glad we kept our marriage vows, and were true to each other. I have realized many times that it was the deep love and respect I had for my husband, that kept me true to God in the trials and hard places that followed.

It was to me a very solemn and sacred service. I remember ed the consecration that I had made to God, and asked Him to help me to be a real helpmate to my husband, and never be a hindrance to him in his life's work.

Young people marry now on a short acquaintance, without giving it much serious thought. They often do not consider it is for a life time, but think they will try married life, "take a chance," and if they do not get along well, can easily get a divorce. But this was not so at that time, at least not with us. What God hath joined together, let no man put asunder.

After dinner we were taken in a surry to Linwood, Kansas, then went by train to Kansas City, Mo., where we spent a few days. We stopped at Wellington, Kansas, for a short visit, on our way to Strong City, Kansas, and Cottonwood Falls, Kansas, where we held evangelistic services. Mr. Parham had conducted a number of successful meetings near here, and had many friends.

We stayed for a while at a home where an old lady lived, then about eighty years of age. Her eye-sight was failing so she drew me to the window as she was interested in seeing Mr. Parham's wife. As she looked into my face, she gave me her blessing, and said; "My dear, this world is like a great theater. We step upon the stage of life, as the curtains are lifted, the dawn of our lives is witnessed by the people. Some of us fill our places in the great plan of God, play our parts successfully and glorify God. Others utterly fail in the great privileges and opportunities of life and dishonor the great Creator. "The End" is written upon our lives, which have been viewed by a cloud of witnesses."

What a good illustration this dear old mother gave of life! We in youth and strength, were looking hopefully into the future, trusting to conquer by His grace, while the part she had played in this life was nearly over and she was soon to receive her reward. It is not all of life to live, nor all of death to die. If we have faithfully filled our place in this life, learned of the Great Teacher, and been guided by the Holy Spirit, had His will wrought out in our lives, we shall hear Him say, "Well done, good and faithful servant, enter thou into the joy of thy Lord." Surely, "Just one glimpse of Him in glory will the toils of life repay." There is no second chance. If we fail, we shall not have the opportunity to return to the stage and live our lives over again, all is lost. "Depart from me, I never knew you."

We had many meetings near here, also going out into the country where we held services in the school-houses, which were well attended in spite of the severe winter.

I well remember one stormy night we remained with seekers at the altar till nearly all were gone, except one family who asked us to go home with them. We gladly accepted the invitation. In the back of a lumber wagon we rode through the snow over hills and valleys and the blizzard continued. I do not know how far we went but at last we arrived at their home. They were very kind to us and made us as comfortable as possible but we were chilled through and the house being very open, during the night snow drifted in on our bed. You may think this was rather a hard life, yet we were happy in His service. The Christian's happiness does not depend on our surrounding circumstances and conditions, but comes by having God's love and peace in our hearts and the knowledge we are doing His will.

After we closed the meetings here we made a visit to my folks near Tonganoxie, then located for a short time near Baldwin, Kansas. Our furniture was either "second-hand" or "home-made," yet we enjoyed our first home and were contented. Our happiness seemed complete when on September 22, 1897, we welcomed our first born, Claude Wallace, a tiny baby, yet how precious.

But a shadow had risen, a cloud hung low which seemed determined to steal away our joy. Mr. Parham had not been well for some time, the doctor was giving him two or three different medicines for his heart which contained poison, yet he was growing worse, and had heart disease in the worst form. He had fallen as dead while preaching and the doctor told him that he must not ride his wheel, or walk up a hill as it might overtax his heart, and he must give up preaching entirely. The latter he said he would never do. If he died, he must preach the gospel. Though he had been so wonderfully healed before, up to this time, he had failed to preach healing as a part of the atonement, for "who-so ever will."

Our baby was not well either, and instead of growing and getting stronger, he was gradually slipping away from us. Only parents can know the joy that the first-born brings to a home, and understand the sadness we felt, as day and night we held the feverish little body in our arms, fearing he would not long remain with us. The doctor frankly told us that he did not know what was the cause of his sickness and could do nothing for him.

One day Mr. Parham was called to pray for a sick man, but as he began to pray the Scripture came to him, "Physician, heal thyself." Instead of praying for the sick man, the burden of his prayer was for his own healing. The power of God touched his body and he was made every whit whole. He came home with new life and hope, and told me how he had taken the Great Physician and was healed. Now, we would throw away all medicines, give up doctors and wholly trust Him as our Healer, and our baby too would be well. He was soon healed and began to grow and from that time, we have not trusted in the arm of flesh in sickness, but in the power of God.

Mr. Parham belonged to a lodge and carried an insurance on his life. He felt now that he should give this up also as it would seem inconsistent with his faith in healing. As he was trusting God for life and health, why make provision for death? I had been taught in the Friend's church not to believe in secret organizations, and was very glad for his decision. He did not condemn the lodge, but often said, if the churches would obey the command to feed the hungry, clothe the naked, and care for the sick, there would be no need of the lodge. If instead of spending so much money in fine buildings, how much more pleasing it would be to God to care for the widows and orphans in their afflictions, and keep unspotted from the world.

About this time Mr. Parham· received word that his friend, Ralph Gowell, was dead. He went at once. Indeed a death· blow had struck that home, for the ambition of the family seemed centered on the oldest son. He had finished his education, which he had obtained by hard work and sacrifice, had become a professor in the State University, and he was all his loved ones had hoped for him to be. The grief was more than the loving mother could bear, and about a week later she died with a broken heart.

Mr. Parham wrote, "As I knelt between the graves of my two loved friends, who might have lived if I had but told them of the power of Christ to heal, I made a vow that "Live or Die" I would preach this gospel of healing. If our dear baby was a hindrance to us, and it was God's will to take him, I would be willing to lay him in the grave, and still preach healing. But if He would fully restore the little one I would carry him if I had to walk from city to city, and proclaim His marvelous healing power."

How much suffering it takes sometimes to bring the human heart to a depth of consecration, that our wills may be wholly yielded to God, and His will can be wrought out in our lives!

Soon after this we moved to Ottawa, Kansas, where Mr. Parham began his first ministry in public on divine healing, though many had been healed here and there in answer to prayer before this time. Though he did not personally know any one else who was preaching divine healing then, he boldly preached Christ, the Healer, that "by His stripes we were healed." God confirmed the Word, by stretching forth His hand to heal, and signs and wonders were done in the name of the Holy Child Jesus. High and low, rich and poor came to our home, and all manner of diseases were healed. Mr. Parham never claimed the gift of healing, but I always believed that God bestowed this gift upon him, for a time at least, so great was the manifestation of the power of God to heal, through him.

I will give a few of the testimonies to healing that took place during our meeting at Ottawa, Kansas.

Mrs. Ella Cook, of Ottawa, Kansas, was healed of dropsy. She had been given up by the physicians with only a possibility of living three days. She was carried upstairs into our meetings, in the old Salvation Army Hall. When prayer was offered the disease was instantly killed so that she fell to the floor as one dead, or like one from whom the fever had just left. The audience arose as a mob to punish us for her seeming death. Mr. Parham stepped beside her body and ordered the people to stand in their places as she was not dead, as a few minutes would prove. In a few moments she opened her eyes, smiled and we assisted her to her feet. She not only walked down the stairs alone, but walked for over a mile to her home, shouting and praising the Lord; people along the way followed to see what would take place. Neighbors came running in and until three o'clock in the morning people were getting to God and others were wonderfully healed. Her recovery was complete.

A couple of doors from the case above mentioned, lived a young lady who was getting a pension from the government. She was a soldier's invalid daughter and was very low with consumption. Physicians, six in number, said she would not live two weeks. She was carried into the above named hall; when prayed for, a tearing away sensation passed through her chest and she was completely healed. Her eyesight had been so poor that, without glasses, she could not recognize anyone across a small room. This was also healed. So complete was her healing that in three days she put out a family washing, scrubbed the kitchen floor, and came to three o'clock meeting. She began to sew for a living, and gave up her invalid's pension. This proved her eyesight was made perfect. She soon married and is the mother of several children.

Miss Bessie Grove, a high school student of Ottawa, Kansas, was troubled with heart disease. The doctors gave certain symptoms that would precede the end. When these developed early in the morning, they sent for Mr. Parham at five o'clock. He went in the room to pray but was unable to get results. Then he said, "Bessie, have you anything in your heart against anyone that is unforgiven?" Very weakly she nodded, yes. He said, "Will you go to them if God heals you and ask their forgiveness?" She answered in the affirmative. After a few moments of prayer, she threw the covers back and arose from the bed, pacing back and forth across the floor shouting the praises of God. She attended school that day and had no further return of the disease.

As the power of God was manifest the opposition was great. People could not deny the sick ones were healed, and demon forces cast out, but some of them declared it to be by the power of Beelzebub, as they did in Christs' time. Matt. 12:24-28.

It is an old saying that "seeing is believing," yet the natural man can not understand the things of the Spirit for they are spiritually discerned. The eye of faith must first grasp the spiritual truths before they can become real to us. One day, I took my Bible and asked God to establish my faith in healing through His Word, that I might be able to quell all the fiery darts of the enemy.

Everywhere I opened the Bible, I read of healing, and I realized as never before, that healing for the body, as well as the soul, was purchased in the atonement. It is the "Children's Bread," and for us today, just the same as in the time of the disciples.

How blessed it is to believe, because it is God's Word, whether we see or do not see His power manifest. Jesus said to Thomas, "Because thou hast seen me thou hast believed; blessed are they that have not seen, and yet have believed." John 20:29. When a truth is revealed to us through His Word, it becomes a part of our lives; and we can not give it up, even though we do not always see the results our hearts desire, and it means suffering for Jesus' sake.

I had been raised a Friend and taught that the Scriptures referring to baptism should all be taken spiritually and that it was not intended for us to observe water baptism. Mr. Parham always gave liberty and never forced his belief on me. But I became convinced that water baptism was taught in the Bible and I wanted to go to the river, as Christ was baptized that way. So one peaceful Sabbath afternoon Mr. Parham baptized me in the beautiful river that flowed by our place. As I came up out of the water, what a peace filled my soul! A joy the soul can know only, when we have the assurance we are obeying God. A colored woman on the bank laughed heartily saying: "Look at that there fat woman, hugging the preacher." I suppose it would not have been so amusing to her if she had known I was his wife.

Mr. Parham was called to Topeka, Kansas to pray for the sick, and during his absence, it began to rain and continued till the water stood in the streets. One evening, about supper time, some of our friends, living in the other part of town, became anxious about the baby and me and waded through water during a heavy rain, to see how we were and bring us some provisions.

The next morning as I went out on the front porch, what a terrible scene lay before me. The dam had given away, and the field in front of our house in which we had planted potatoes was a raging torrent of muddy water. Trees, lumber, old houses and all manner of rubbish were being rapidly carried away by the swift current. I looked toward the beautiful place where I was baptized, but only the tops of the trees appeared, which were catching drift-wood in their wide spreading branches. We were now, as it were, on an island as our house and a bakery, which were on higher ground, were surrounded with water. I watched the water rise till it came over our well, and was glad when at last it began to lower and we could see land again.

Mr. Parham sent for us to come to Topeka, Kansas, and we were taken to the depot in the bakery wagon. The water, which was standing in the streets, came up to the hubs, and was still in a number of the stores.

With mingled feelings of gladness and sadness we left our Ottawa home, and fine early garden near the house, which was not hurt by the flood. Owing to Mr. Parham's faithful labor, rich soil, and abundant rain, it had grown rapidly, and was nearly ready to use. It seemed a shame to leave it, yet I knew someone would reap what we had sown.

We see this true in spiritual things; one soweth, and another reapeth. John 4:37. May the love of God so fill our hearts that we can "in honour preferring one another" (Rom. 12:10) toil and dig, sow in tears, and willingly let others reap the fruit of our labors. That both he that soweth and he that reap-eth may rejoice together. John 4:36. Let us, as sowers and reapers today, not be envious one of another but in love and unity render all the glory and honor to God, who "giveth the increase," and thank Him for the privilege of working in His vineyard.

We never returned to Ottawa, Kansas. Mr. Parham had already established a good work in Topeka, Kansas. Large homes, in different parts of the city, had opened their doors, to accommodate the people to hear the gospel. Soon a hall up town was secured, with an office where he prayed for the sick.

November 29, 1898 was Thanksgiving Day and also my twenty-first birthday. What a wonderful birthday present was mine this year, a fine baby girl, well and strong, who we nam-ed Esther Marie. I can never tell, how much it has meant to us to have the Great Physician in our home, and to trust in Him while raising our family.

"God knoweth well our every need
  He has promised to supply;
Then don't forget His Word to heed,
  And on Him to rely.

He says, On Me cast all thy cares,
  I'll bear them all for thee;
I'll take away thy every fear,
  And leave thee light and free.

Lean not thou on the arm of flesh,
  Lean on My strength, I say;
My promises are tried and sure,
  They never fade away.

I'll heal and bless you here below,
  All needs I will supply;
I'll give you power to reign o'er sin,
  Then you shall dwell on high.

Our friends on earth can often help,
  And oft they're kind and brave,
But from all dangers near and far
  God's hand alone can save.

You'll tempted be, I know you will,
  For Satan says, God won't fulfill
His Word, but brother, you assured can rest,
  God ne'er will fail you in the test.

So trust Him, cast away all fear,
  Walk by His side, keep very near;
Then 'mid the trials manifold
  He'll not one needed thing withhold."

Chapter VI

BETHEL HEALING HOME

N 1898, we established a Divine Healing Home on the corner of Fourth and Jackson Streets, Topeka, Kansas, which we called, "Bethel". It was a nice brick building centrally located and had all modern conveniences. From the outside, the building looks very much the same now, but it may have been remodeled inside. The ground floor furnished a large chapel, public reading room and printing office. The second floor had fourteen rooms, and we kept the large windows in the parlors filled with flowers, as Mr. Parham was a great lover of flowers and we wanted to make the rooms look cheerful to the sick. The third floor was simply an attic, but we used it for sleeping purposes when our bed rooms were all occupied.

The purpose of the Bethel Home was to provide home-like comforts for those who were seeking healing, while we prayed for their spiritual needs as well as their bodies. We also found Christian homes for orphan children, and work for the unemployed.

Our paper, "The Apostolic Faith," was published twice a month. At first we had a subscription price, later we announced for subscription price see, Isiah 55:1 and the Lord wonderfully provided. Each number of the paper was filled with wonderful testimonies to healing and sermons containing the teachings of the Home.

Special studies were given to ministers and evangelists, and many workers were instructed in Bible truths, and trained for Gospel work. We taught Salvation, Healing , Sanctification, the Second Coming of Christ, and the Baptism of the Holy Spirit, although we had not then received the evidence of speaking in other tongues, as we did later in the "College of Bethel."

We practiced water baptism by immersion, and partook of

the Lord's supper. Being raised in the Friend's Church, I had not been taught the importance of this ordinance, but God so wonderfully blessed us as we partook of the bread and the wine that I found it a sacred privilege to "do this in remembrance of Him." These services were a great blessing to the guests in the Home, and one of them gave the following report.

"A feast of fat things was enjoyed by the brothers and sisters Sunday night in the parlors of the Home when they partook of the Lord's supper, followed by the Sacrament. The praise and thanksgiving of many pure hearts ascended to God as they let their thoughts run back through the ages to the time when Jesus sat down thus with His disciples, and many felt His Presence. Earnest thought was given by each one as to whether, since we last met, any had played the part of Judas in betraying our Lord. It was an inspiration to see the happy expectant faces and eyes filled with tears of joy as the word was passed down the table that it wouldn't be very long until we would sit thus with Him in His Kingdom.

"Before passing the bread and wine, Brother Parham, gave some convincing thoughts, showing definitely that healing was in the atonement. Taking up the thought of the passover Lamb, both the body and the blood had their designed purpose; in taking in the sacrifices that typified Christ, the body as well as the blood had some definite purpose of atonement. While the blood was for the cleansing of the sin, His perfect body was broken for our imperfect bodies; that is, to bring us to perfect health. With His stripes we are healed. "Himself took our infirmities and bare our sicknesses." Summing up the whole matter are Paul's words in the eleventh chapter of 1 Cor., where he so definitely sets forth the doctrine of healing being in the body of Jesus Christ. For after repeating in several verses, body and blood he says, "Whosoever eateth this body and drinketh this blood unworthily, shall be guilty of the body and blood of Jesus Christ," again saying, "Whoso eateth and drinketh unworthily, eateth and drinketh damnation to himself, not discerning the Lord's body. "Why does Paul thus so definitely call our attention to the body? For this cause, that is, because they didn't discern the Lord's body, many were weak and sickly, and many slept. The bread and wine was then passed, and many received the bread with more joy when they knew the power of it in regard to the health."

I will quote from others that have written about the Home which will give you some idea of the work that Mr. Parham was doing at that time.

"This blessed Sabbath morning, this morning of all mornings, I am carried away in thought and in spirit from earth to higher thoughts. While sitting in the private office of the "Apostolic Faith" these beautiful lines come to me: 'By their fruits ye shall know them;' What are the fruits of Bethel? I was a stranger and they took me in; I was an hungered and they gave me to eat; was athirst, and they gave me to drink; was weary and they gave me a bed, without price, and more precious than all, gave me spiritual food that is digestible, that though a person be ever so unlearned, he can understand. I know that God is going to answer my prayer, I know I am going to be healed.

"Bethel is all that name implies, and more, and to be appreciated must be seen. It is certainly a fulfillment of the Scriptures, where we can come together though we be strangers, yet feel the assurance that we are welcome; where everyone is a brother and sister in deed and in truth. God will surely bless Brother and Sister Parham in their endeavor to build up His Kingdom upon earth. They are not waiting until we are placed beneath the earth that we may enjoy some of the foretaste of heaven upon earth, but that God's kingdom can be established here in man's heart, where all can dwell together in peace and love, for perfect love casteth out fear.

John 15:12 "This is my commandment, that ye love one another as I have loved you." May God bless Beth-el and its
pastors in charge is my prayer."

*   *   *   *   *

"As I have been a guest at Bethel, I feel impressed to write
something concerning the Home and its work. Who could
think of a sweeter name than "Bethel"? Surely it is none
other than the House of God. Everything moves in love and
harmony. On entering the rooms one is impressed with the
divine influence shed abroad there. Here is a place where the
sin-sick soul may come and be taught the way of salvation
and a higher life; also where those who are sick may be
taught that it is "God who healeth all our diseases and re-
deemeth our life from destruction." Psalm 103:3-4.

"It is a faith Home all the way through. Brother Parham
and his co-workers are heart and soul consecrated to the work
of God. They live by faith believing that "My God shall supply all your needs according to His riches in glory by Christ
Jesus," and truly God does verify His promise to them. I
have been afflicted for years with various diseases, today I
am rejoicing in a Savior that keeps me, soul and body. I also
received such an uplift spiritually, and the Bible is a new book
to me. Praise God for such a Home."

*   *   *   *   *

Eva Baker wrote—"To some of us who are looking to the
dawn of that bright day when the Son of Righteousness shall
rise with "healing in His wings" and usher in His reign of
peace and love, there seems a foretaste of the spirit of it, in
this "House of God." A stranger coming among the little
company of believers assembled here, cannot but feel here is
a Christian home in the highest sense of the word.

"To the comforts and informality of home life, is added
that spirit of cheerfulness and consideration for others which
reveals the Christ life within seeking earnestly to realize that

ideal life, being a bond of union to draw together a little community who see the necessity of living for the highest ends.

"God has wonderfully answered the prayers of His faithful followers; prayers that rise continually from all hearts.
Here the sick are healed, souls are saved, and rich and poor
have the gospel preached to them.   May God bless this noble
work, dedicated to suffering humanity; and deeply bless also
the devoted pastor, C. F. Parham, and his co-workers."

* * * * *

An elderly lady, Mrs. Ellen Tanner, was wonderfully healed in the Home and remained with us for some time.   Her
sweet Christian life was a benediction, and she was like a real
mother to us all.   In her testimony, she often praised God that
"He was not dead or gone on a journey," and how wonderfully we felt His living presence and power with us as she
testified.   She wrote the following account May 3, 1899, of
Easter Sunday at Bethel—

"The first sound heard on this sacred Sabbath, was the
singing of "Sweet Hour of Prayer" by Brother Parham.   This
as usual assembled the household in one of the front parlors
for worship, which is always a season of refreshing.   A chapter of the Word was read and explained by Brother Parham in
the most helpful manner, applying the Scriptures to our daily
needs and lives.   Our prayers were supplemented by two
brothers one having come to bring his invalid daughter whose
life was despaired of, that she might be taught how to receive divine healing; the other for a little physical and much
spiritual help.

"After we had partaken of an excellent breakfast with joyful thanksgiving, one of the sisters visited an invalid in her
room, and fervent prayer was offered that the Holy Spirit
might come in and abide with her.

"The morning service was a suitable memorial of the day
on which Christ arose from the dead; and the story as told

by the beloved disciple was read and accepted as the ground of our hope of a resurrection and immortal life. The pastor's subject was the earnest desire of Paul to KNOW Christ and the power of His resurrection. He set forth the blessed truth, that we were not to stop at knowing Christ on the cross, but were to follow on and know the Lord in His resurrection. To know Him as our chosen One, as Christ within us, with love, joy, peace and righteousness, health and strength, sufficient for all believers who will reach up with the arm of faith to bring down His riches in glory.

"The invalid and her father, not knowing that divine strength had been asked for, were astonished that she was able to sit through the services of the day without fatigue.

"The gospel of Healing is usually taught after the 2 P. M. Sunday School, but this Easter Sunday we listened to the gosple of love that casteth out fear—fear of death; fear of the assaults of our enemies; fear that God's divine power will not be sufficient for us under all circumstances. The love that Christ felt for all mankind, His enemies included; love that would mold all of God's dear people into His own image, and cement them together as one body in Christ Jesus, so that His last prayer might be fulfilled — that we might be one even as He and the Father were one. The preacher insisted that God would work mightily in answer to prayer, where so many agreed "as touching one thing" — either as regards the salvation of the sinner or the healing of the sick body.

"An altar service was held at the close of the service. Several sisters claimed healing, which is 'the children's bread'. God's presence was manifested in great power and the healing work was done. The cordial greetings always extended to the strangers and friends being over, the hall was deserted, except for a few who remained for the evening meeting.

"There had been a desire on the part of some of the best supporters of the Mission to organize, elect a board for the

Claude and Esther, "the babes of Bethel"
taken with their faithful dog.

supervision of the finances, etc., and pay the pastor a stated
salary. But the pastor having accepted Apostolic faith, peti-
tioned God most earnestly that He would set the divine seal
of approval upon the work by providing the means to pay the
month's rent on the building. The prayer was answered—the
rent was forth coming and thirteen dollars beside. Then
Miriam asked that thanks be offered to God at the crossing
of that Red Sea, and a few tender words of prayer were offered.

"The night service was a blessed meeting, "Jesus Himself
being in the midst and confirming the Word by signs following'. Two sisters testified to having been healed at Bethel that
afternoon. One lady went forward, confessed her sins and
was accepted of God. Three others sought the healing touch.
This was one typical Sabbath in this home of prayer.

"The family life was an earnest of heaven. Mrs. Parham
and her sister are of English Quaker origin. They are gentle,
peaceful, unselfish, thinking only of the comfort and welfare
of their guests. The babies of Bethel are truly "things of
beauty and joys forever."

"The doctrine is that of Holiness with the "I am holier than
thou" left out; of healing in answer to prayer after a complete
consecration of our lives and our all to God; peace with God
and all mankind. It is often necessary to explain that he who
lays hands on you and prays for your healing is no more a
divine healer than he who prays for your salvation from sin,
is a Savior. It is God who does the work in both instances in
answer to prayer.

"The mighty power of God as revealed in answered prayer,
made the world to recede and a light as from heaven shone
about me and led me to inquire "what kind of a world is this
you have here, with God taking such active part in all your
affairs?" One night while listening to the testimonies of God's
miraculous healing, I was for an instant carried back to the

days of the first diciples. I was in Samaria attending
Philip's revival. Peter and John had been sent down from
Jerusalem, and the power of the Holy Ghost had fallen upon
the people. Going back to the Apostolic faith, we find ourselves in a new world. The days of miracles are repeated.
'The prayer of faith shall save the sick and the Lord shall raise
him up;' and best of all, 'if he hath committed sins they shall
be forgiven him.' "

* * * * *

"The work that is being done here cannot be estimated. It
is a house of prayer, and the influence is felt on coming in the
rooms. Hardly a day passes that some one does not come for
prayer for their healing, and some days there are many. Con-
sumptives, dyspeptics, cripples, and people with almost every
known disease come for healing, and the best part of it all is
that those that come for healing always get a spiritual uplift,
such as they never knew before. It would be a miserable mortal indeed who would not praise the Lord after being healed by
His wonderful power.

"We have been boarding in the Home about six weeks, and
we have failed to discover anything that is not of God in the
life of the occupants. Everything moves in peace and harmony; and love prevails everywhere. I consider myself greatly privileged to be here. The power of God is here, the
peace that passeth understanding, and the perfect love that
casteth out fear pervades the very atmosphere of the place.
Praise the Lord, there is such a place in Kansas, or on earth,
in the midst of these dreadful times of doubt and skepticism.
My boy has been healed twice since coming here—once of a
very bad cold and once of a very bad attack of tonsilitis."

* * * * *

Mr. Parham wrote, "Once after returning from a hard day's
labor among the sick from the death bed of the President of
the Santa Fe Railroad, it being a few minutes past 11 o'clock,
the fact was suddenly flashed into my mind that the next day

the rent was due, with not a cent to meet it. Tired and weary, I looked into the star-lit sky, saying, "Father, this is Thy part of the work, I must have rest and sleep tonight, Thou hast never failed us, Thou wilt not now."

"Next morning before we had risen, there came knock at the door. Quickly throwing on a dressing robe, I answered the call. An Eastern gentleman, who was visiting in the city, and knew something of our work among the poor and needy in the city, greeted me with a cheery, "Good-morning" then saying, "Last night, between eleven and twelve o'clock (being the hour that I had prayed) I was suddenly awaken with the thought of you and your work; no sleep came to me until I had promised to bring you this." Handing me a slip of paper he said, "I bring you St. Patrick's Greetings," he lifted his hat and was gone. On entering the parlor, I examined the paper at the window and found it to be a check for forty dollars, the exact sum of our rent.

"At another time when a bill of seventy-five dollars was due, I arose in the morning with but twenty-five to meet it with. Asking God's blessing upon this sum that He would increase it, I passed on to the bank, which was situated in the center of the block. I was crossing the street, when a gentleman hailed me, saying, "I am so very glad to see you. We sold one of our farms yesterday, and as we always give a tenth, reserved this sum for you." He handed me a slip of paper. Not looking at its sum, (a practice I always follow) I thanked him for it, and entered the bank, where with pleasure and gratitude I discovered it to be a check for fifty dollars. With the twenty-five already in my possession, it made up the seventy-five due that morning.

"It made no difference whether our monthly expense amounted to a few or hundreds of dollars, just that sum was at hand to meet the demands, never having anything extra with which to become proud or puffed up and forget the origin of our help. 'He is faithful who has promised.' "

March 1, 1900, a new guest entered our Home, a fine brown-eyed baby boy, our second son. We named him Charles for his father. Soon after this a parsonage was provided for us ,which was more convenient, and we were glad the children could have a lawn for a play ground.

Some evangelists from the east held a few days meeting for us, as our work was undenominational and our Mission doors ever open to all who preached the Gospel. Our hearts were stirred to deepen our consecration, and to "search the Word.

Mr. Parham wrote: "Deciding to know more fully the latest truths restored by later day movements, I left my work in charge of two Holiness preachers and visited various movements, such as Dowis's work who was then in Chicago. the Eye-Opener work of the same city; Malone's work in Cleveland, Dr. Simpson's work in Nyack, New York, Sanford's "Holy Ghost and Us" work at Shiloah, Maine, and many others.

"I returned home fully convinced that while many had obtained real experience in sanctification and the anointing that abideth, there still remained a great outpouring of power for the Christians who were to close this age.

"Through underhanded scheming and falsehoods, the ministers I left in charge of my work had not only taken my building but most of my congregation. My friends urged me to claim my own, but the Word says, "We have heard that it hath been said, An eye for an eye, and a tooth for a tooth: "But I say unto you, That ye resist not evil; but whosoever shall smite thee on thy right cheek, turn to him the other also, and if any man will sue thee at the law, and take away thy coat, let him have thy cloak also." To practice His Word was our highest aim.

"God in a marvelous way had provided for my family during my absence. Though friends may fail, God is ever faithful and had put it in the hearts of His children in different towns and states, to supply their needs. One day, when there was nothing to eat in the house, the table was set for suuper looking for God to supply. Then came a knock at the door, and there stood a lady with a big basket in her hand. Though she had never been to the house before, she explained that she felt that she should fix supper for them, as my wife had done a big washing, and hoped it would be accepted. The big washing was not an unusual thing, as beside her own she did the washing for the poor sick ones at the Healing Home, desiring to help them all she could. Our neighbor didn't realize it was God who had put it in her heart to supply the need at the right time. Here was supper all cooked, ready to set on the table.

"Then came a stranger who had gone to the Post-Office to mail his tithes to foreign fields, but felt led to bring it to my wife instead. It is more blessed to give than to receive and he received a great blessing as he ralized how wonderfully God had led him.

"I went to my room to fast and pray, to be alone with God that I might know His will for my future work. Many of my friends desired me to open a Bible School. By a series of wonderful miracles we were enabled to secure what was then known as "Stone's Folly," a great mansion patterned after an English castle, one mile west of Washburn College in Topeka, Kansas."

How marvelously God made all things work together for good when we wholly committed our ways unto Him and left our case in His hands. Instead of taking up the work that we had, God had a greater, and grander work for us to do, as the following chapter will reveal. If we had not fully obeyed the Scriptures to "resist not-evil," and showed a Christian spirit, I am afraid we would not have received the baptism of the Holy Spirit. God had taught us that we were not only to preach the Word, but to practice it, and have it wrought out in our lives if we were to have His best.

"REMEMBERED"

By L. C. Hasler.

"Not forgotten, but remembered!
  Child of God, trust on with cheer!
Thy great Father's help is promised
  Every day throughout the year.
Not forsaken—but most precious
  Thou wilt ever to Him be;
Tenderly He whispers, "Fear not!"
  "I, the Lord, REMEMBER THEE!"

Not forgotten, but remembered,
  Is the pledge   Love Divine!
He who loves and understands us,
  Best can plan thy path and mine.
His own Word cannot be broken,
  "As thy days thy strength shall be;"
He, Himself, the word hath spoken—
  "I, the Lord, REMEMBER THEE!"

Not forgotten, but remembered—
  In His love for thee He planned,
Chosen, sealed, thy name engraven,
  On His pierced and peerless hand.
When He calls thee, "Come up higher,"
  Thou shalt then His wonders see—
Wonders of His mighty promise—
  "I, the Lord, REMEMBERE THEE!"

Chapter VII

THE LATTER RAIN

The Story of The Origin of The Original Apostolic Or Pentecostal Movements.

By CHARLES. F. PARHAM

E opened the Bible School at Topeka, Kansas in October, 1900. To which we invited all ministers and Christians who were willing to forsake all, sell what they had, give it away, and enter the school for study and prayer, where all of us to-gether might trust God for food, fuel, rent and clothing. The purpose of this school was to fit men and women to go to the ends of the earth to preach, "This Gospel of the Kingdom." Matt. 24. as a witness to all the world before the end of the age.

Our purpose in this Bible School was not to learn these things in our heads only but have each thing in the Scriptures wrought out in our hearts. And that every command that Jesus Christ gave should be literally obeyed.

No one paid board or tuition, the poor were fed, the sick were entertained and healed, and from day to day, week to week and month to month, with no sect or mission or known source of income back of us, God supplied our every need, and He was our all sufficiency in all things.

In December of 1900 we had had our examination upon the subject of repentance, conversion, consecration, sanctification healing and the soon coming of the Lord. We had reached in our studies a problem. What about the 2nd Chapter of Acts? I had felt for years that any missionary going to the foreign field should preach in the language of the natives. That if God had ever equipped His ministers in that way He could do it today. That if Balaam's mule could stop in the middle of the road and give the first preacher that went out for money a "bawling out" in Arabic that anybody today ought to be able to preach in any language of the world if they had horse sense enough to let God use their tongue and throat. But still I believed our experience should tally exactly with the Bible, and neither sanctification nor the anointing that abideth taught by Stephen Merritt and others tallied with the 2nd Chaper of Acts. Having heard so many different religious bodies claim different proofs as the evidence of their having the Pentecostal baptism, I set the students at work studying out diligently what was the Bible evidence of the baptism of the Holy Ghost, that we might go before the world with something that was indisputable because it tallied absolutely with the Word.

Leaving the school for three days at this task, I went to Kansas City for three days services. I returned to the school on the morning preceding Watch Night services in the year 1900.

At about 10 o'clock in the morning I rang the bell calling all the students into the Chapel to get their report on the matter in hand. To my astonishment they all had the same story, that while there were different things occured when the Pentecastal blessing fell, that the indisputable proof on each occasion was, that they spake with other tongues. About 75 people beside the school which consisted of 40 students, had gathered for the watch night service. A mighty spiritual power filled the entire school.

Sister Agnes N. Ozman, (now LaBerge) asked that hands might be laid upon her to receive the Holy Spirit as she hoped to go to foreign fields. At first I refused not having the experience myself. Then being further pressed to do it humbly in the name of Jesus, I laid my hand upon her head and prayed. I had scarcely repeated three dozen sentences when a glory fell upon her, a halo seemed to surround her head and face, and she began speaking in the Chinese language, and was unable to speak English for three days. When she tried to write in English to tell us of her experience she wrote the Chinese, copies of which we still have in newspapers printed at that time.

Seeing this marvelous manifestation of the restoration of Pentecostal power, we removed the beds from a dormitory on the upper floor, and there for two nights and three days we continued as a school to wait upon God. We felt that God was no respecter of persons and what He had so graciously poured out upon one, He would upon all.

Those three days of tarrying were wonderful days of blessings. We all got past any begging or pleading, we knew the blessing was ours with ever swelling tides of praise and thanksgiving and worship, interspersed with singing we waited for the coming of the Holy Spirit.

On the night of January 3rd, I preached at the Free Methodist Church in the City of Topeka telling them what had already happened, and that I expected upon returning the entire school to be baptized in the Holy Spirit. On returning to the school with one of the students, we ascended to the second flood, and passing down along the corridor in the upper room, heard most wonderful sounds. The door was slightly ajar, the room was lit with only coal oil lamps. As I pushed open the door I found the room was filled with a sheen of white light above the brightness of the lamps.

Twelve ministers, who were in the school of different denominations, were filled with the Holy Spirit and spoke with other tongues. Some were sitting, some still kneeling, others standing with hands upraised. There was no violent physical manifestation, though some trembled under the power of the glory that filled them.

Sister Stanley, an elderly lady, came across the room as I entered, telling me that just before I entered tongues of fire were sitting above their heads.

When I beheld the evidence of the restoration of Pentecostal power, my heart was melted in gratitude to God for what my eyes had seen. For years I had suffered terrible persecutions for preaching holiness and healing and the soon coming of the Lord. I fell to my knees behind a table unnoticed by those upon whom the power of Pentecost had fallen to pour out my heart to God in thanksgiving. All at once they began to sing, "Jesus Lover of my soul" in at least six different languages, carrying the different parts but with a more angelic voice than I had ever listened to in all my life.

After praising God for some time, I asked Him for the same blessing. He distincly made it clear to me that He raised me up and trained me to declare this mighty truth to the world, and if I was willing to stand for it, with all the persecutions, hardships, trials, slander, scandal that it would entail, He would give me the blessing. And I said "Lord I will, if You will just give me this blessing." Right then there came a slight twist in my throat, a glory fell over me and I began to worship God in the Sweedish tongue, which later changed to other languages and continued so until the morning.

Just a word: After preaching this for all these years with all the persecutions I have been permitted to go through with, misunderstanding and the treatment of false brethren , yet knowing all that, this blessing would bring to me, if I had the time and was back there again I'd take the same way.

No sooner was this miraculous restoration of Pentecostal power noised abroad, than we were beseiged with reporters from Topeka papers, Kansas City, St. Louis and many other cities sent reporters who brought with them professors of languages, foreigners, Government interperters, and they gave the work the most crucial test. One Government interpreter claimed to have heard twenty Chinese dialects distinctly spoken in one night. All agree that the students of the college were speaking in the languages of the world, and that with

proper accent and intonation. There was no chattering, jabbering, or stuttering. Each one spoke clearly and distinctly
in a foreign tongue, with earnestness, intensity and God given
unction. The propriety and decency of the conduct of each
member of the Bible School won the warmest comment from
many visitors.

Our first public appearance after others had received the
baptism of the Holy Spirit was in Kansas City, in the Academy of Music, about January 21st. The Kansas City papers
loudly announced our coming. Two columns appeared in the
Kansas City Journal, with large headlines on the front page.
These headlines, being the largest on the front page, attracted
the attention of the newsboys, and they not knowing a Pentecost from a holocaust ran wildly up and down the street
crying their papers, Pentecost, Pentecost, Pentecost, read all
about the Pentecost.

I have on record the sermon preached on this occasion. The
first upon the baptism of the Holy Ghost in all modern Pentecostal Apostolic Full Gospel movements. Also on file all
that the papers had to say about these things in those days.
Through great trials and persecutions we conducted the Bible
school in the city of Topeka itself, then one in Kansas City.

"That the trial of your faith, being much more precious
than of gold that perisheth, though it be tried with fire, might
be found unto praise and honor and glory at the appearance
of Jesus Christ".—1 Peter 1:7.

"Hedged about from every evil
Sheltered from all fear of ill,
Thru Jehovah's power protected
Even "The accuser's" voice is still.

But thy heart must feel the furnace
He thy Maker knoweth best.
And in love the hedge must vanish
That thy gold may stand the test.

"Tho He slay me I will trust Him"
Thus the King his promise gave,
And the Christ who prayed for Peter
Will thee thru temptation save.

For that prayer in heaven recorded
Thru the power of His Name,
Makes the trusting heart a victor
Sets the soul with love aflame.

Doubt no more but trust His promise.
He will not forsake His own,
Only sight is known to mortal
Faith proceeds from God alone.

He the Alpha and Omega,
The beginning and the end—
He who notes the falling sparrow,
Is to thee thy truest Friend!

In the center of His will,
There is Rest and Joy and Peace.
Care and doubt and slavish fear,
In His presence cease.

Just to hear His gentle whisper—
I will guide thy steps aright,
Stills the voices of confusion,
Fills the path with radiant light.

He sees the secret spring within,
That thou hast never known;
In patience and in tenderness
He teaches thee alone.

It doth not yet appear
What He would have thee be,
But blessed thought, to be like Him,
When thou His face shalt see."
                    —Lilian Thistlethwaite

Chapter VIII

THE WONDERFUL HISTORY OF THE LATTER RAIN
By Miss Lilian Thistlethwaite
The First Shower of the Latter Rain—Bethel Bible School

N the year 1900, Charles F. Parham, and his wife and family and a number of Bible students, gathered in the Bethel Bible School to study the Word of God, using no text book excepting the Bible.

The building procured for this school was known by the people of Topeka, Kansas, as the "Stone Mansion" or "Stone's Folly" because it had been patterned after an English castle, and he, having failed to "count the cost," was unable to finish in the style planned. The beautiful carved staircases and finished woodwork of cedar of Lebanon, spotted pine, cherry wood and bird's eye maple, ended on the third floor with plain wood and common paint.

The outside was finished in red brick and white stone with winding stairs that went up to an observatory on the front of the highest part of the building. There was also a cupola at the back of the building and two domes built on either side. Into one of these a door was cut, making a room large enough for a small stove, a table and a chair. This was known as the "Prayer Tower." Volunteers from among the students took their turn of three hours watch; so day and night prayer ascended unto God. Sometimes a student would desire to spend the night in waiting before the Lord and this privilege was allowed.

When the building was dedicated for the school, while in prayer, on the top of the building, Captain Tuttle, a godly man, who was with Mr. Parham said he saw (in a vision) just above the building a "vast lake of fresh water about to overflow, containing enough to satisfy every thirsty soul." This we believe was the promise of the Pentecostal baptism which followed later.

There were about forty persons gathered here including the children. The method of study was to take a subject, learn the references on that subject, also where each quotation was found, and present to the class in recitation as though they were seekers, praying for the anointing of the Holy Spirit to be upon the message in such a way as to bring conviction.

Mr. Parham also taught through lectures. I shall never forget the one he gave on the Songs of Solomon. How we were all lifted into the heavenlies and the room seemed filled with the glory of God's presence!

It was just before the Christmas holidays that we took up the study of the Holy Ghost. Mr. Parham was going to Kansas City to conduct meetings there and to bring some friends back with him to spend Christmas and be present for the watch night meeting. Before leaving the following is the substance of what he said:

"Students, as I have studied the teachings in the various Bible Schools and full gospel movements, conviction, conversion, healing and sanctification are taught virtually the same, but on the baptism there is a difference among them. Some accept Steven Merrit's teaching of baptism at sanctification, while others say this is only the anointing and there is a baptism received through the "laying on of hands" or the gift of the Holy Ghost, yet they agree on no definite evidence. Some claim this fulfillment of promise "by faith" without any special witness, while others, because of wonderful blessings or demonstrations, such as shouting or jumping. Though I honor the Holy Ghost in anointing power both in conversion and in sanctification, yet I believe there is a greater revelation of His power. The gifts are in the Holy Spirit and with the baptism of the Holy Spirit the gifts, as well as the graces, should be manifested. Now, students, while I am gone, see if there is not some evidence given of the baptism so there may be no doubt on the subject.

"We see the signs already being fulfilled that mark the soon coming of the Lord and I believe with John Wesley that at Christ's second coming the Church will be found with the same power that the Apostles and the early Church possess-ed."

Thus closed the regular Bible lessons, for a time, but there was individual and collective prayer and study of the Bibile continuously.

On Mr. Parham's return to the school with his friends, he asked the students whether they had found any Bible evidence of the baptism of the Holy Spirit. The answer was, unani-mous, "speaking in other tongues."

Services were held daily and each night. There was a hal-lowed hush over the entire building. All felt the influence of a mighty presence in our midst. Without any special direc-tion, all moved in harmony. I remember Mrs. Parham saying, "Such a spirit of unity prevails that even the children are at peace, while the very air is filled with expectancy. Truly He is with us, and has something more wonderful for us than we have known before."

The service on New Year's night was especially spiritual and each heart was filled with the hunger for the will of God to be done in them. One of the students, a lady who had been in several other Bible Schools, asked Mr. Parham, to lay hands upon her that she might receive the Holy Spirit. As he prayed, her face lighted up with the glory of God and she began to speak with "other tongues." She afterward told us she had received a few words while in the Prayer Tower, but now her English was taken from her and with floods of joy and laughter she praised God in other languages.

There was very little sleeping among any of us that night. The next day still being unable to speak English, she wrote on a piece of paper, "Pray that I may interpret."

The following day was Thursday. This day Mr. Parham observed as a day of special prayer and waiting upon the Lord. From 9 A. M. to 3 P. M., he believes to be the six hours Christ spent on the cross, so these hours were observed in special waiting on the Lord that all that was purchased upon Calvary should be wrought out in our individual lives. The "broken body" or the atonement for healing was especially honored in these meetings.

On this particular day the baptism of the Holy Ghost was sought earnestly, but no one received the gift. Having other duties in the home I had not searched the Scriptures to know the Bible evidence, nor heard the decision of those who had, but in my own mind concluded as the gifts are in the Holy Ghost any of the nine gifts would prove the baptism; and as Paul said "desire earnestly the best gifts," I feeling "faith" was the most to be desired was looking for this gift in some way to be manifested.

An upper room was set apart for tarrying before the Lord, and here we spent every spare moment in audible or silent prayer, in song or in just waiting upon Him. There was no confusion as only one prayed audibly at a time, and when more than one sang it was the same hymn. It was truly a time of precious waiting. His presence was very real and the heart-searchings definite.

Mr. Parham was holding night services in Topeka and before leaving he said, "I don't suppose I shall be able to understand any of you when I return."

Still I was not looking for "tongues", but some evidence from God, I didn't know of what nature that would convince me I had the baptism. We prayed for ourselves, we prayed for one another. I never felt so little and utterly nothing before. A scrap of paper charred by a fire is the best description I can give of my feelings. Then through the Spirit this message came to my soul, "Praise Him for the baptism for He does come in by faith through the laying on of hands." Then a great joy came into my soul and I began to say, "I praise Thee," and my tongue began to get thick and great floods of laughter came into my heart. I could no longer think words of praise, for my mind was sealed, but my mouth was filled with a rush of words I didn't understand. I tried not to laugh for I feared to grieve the Spirit. I tried to praise Him in English but could not, so I just let the praise come as it would in the new language given, with floodgates of glory wide open. He had come to me, even to me to speak not of Himself but to magnify the Christ,—and oh, what a wonderful, wonderful Christ was revealed. Then I realized I was not alone for all around me I heard great rejoicing while others spoke in tongues and magnified God. I think Mrs. Parham's language was the most perfect. Immediately following came the interpretation, a beautiful poem of praise and worship to Christ, proving the words of the Savior—"When the Comforter is come" —"he shall testify of me"—"shall not speak of himself"— "Shall teach you all things and bring to your remembrance whatsoever I have said unto you." Then as with a simultaneous move we began to sing together each one singing in his own new language in perfect harmony. As we sang, "All Hail the Power of Jesus' Name," and other familiar tunes, it would be impossible to describe the hallowed glory of His presence in our midst. The cloven tongues of fire had been seen by some when the evidence had been received. Mr. Parham came into the room while we were standing singing —kneeling he thanked God for the scene he was allowed to witness, then asking God if it was His will that he should stand for the baptism of the Holy Spirit as he had for healing, to give him the Bible evidence. His prayer was answered, the gift bestowed, and the persecution came also.

Never had such a hallowed joy, such a refined glor or such an abundance of peace, ever come into my life. The Comfort-

er had come and the words of Jesus being brought continually to my remembrance as Scripture after Scripture was un-
folded by day and by night filled me with a settled rest and
quietness my soul had never know before, I lived in the
heavenlies.

As we went into meetings it seemed impossible that any
could resist the messages given. Some understanding the languages were convinced but others fulfilled the prophecy,
"With men of other tongues and other lips will I speak unto
this people; and yet for all that they will not hear me, saith
the Lord." 1 Cor. 14:21.

On one occasion a Hebrew Rabbi was present as one of the
students, a young married man, read the lesson from the Bible. After services he asked for the Bible from which the lesson was read. The Bible was handed him, and he said, "No
not that one, I want to see the Hebrew Bible. That man read
in the Hebrew tongue."

At another time while Mr. Parham was preaching he used
another language for some time during the sermon. At the
close a man arose and said, "I am healed of my infidelity; I
have heard in my own tongue the 23rd Psalm that I learned
at my mother's knee."

The Bible School building was sold. We moved to a building in Topeka where we stayed for a short time, then went
to Kansas City. While living in Kansas City we heard that
the building where Pentecost first fell was burned. This was
not a surprise to us, as it had been turned into a road house
and the rooms that once had heard only the voice of supplica-
tion and praise to God, had been desecrated by worldly revel-
ry. Warning was given that such actions would not go un-
punished for the house was dedicated to the Lord from its
highest place of observation to the cellar.

In Kansas City, Mo., Mr. Parham held a Bible School, also

meetings. During this time souls were saved, some received their baptism and others were healed. The persecutions were great and we were learning many lessons.

In the third year of the work God mightily vindicated the cause and many souls were 'saved, wonderfully healings took place, and the falling of the Pentecostal Baptism was very con-vincing.

I do not know to what denomination all belonged who re-ceived the baptism at Bethel Bible School, but some were Methodists, others Friends, and some Holiness, while many belonged to no denomination.

There were only white persons present at the first Pente-costal shower. No colored people were ever in the school.

As Mrs. Parham's sister, it has been my privilege to be in their home or in touch with their work continually. To wit-ness Mr. Parham's zeal and untiring energy you would not believe it possible he had been a sufferer for years until heal-ed by the power of God. The work of his ministry was con-ducted entirely on faith lines. He looked to the Lord to open the field of labor and was obedient to that which he felt to be His will, then left the results with God, who hath said "His Word shall not return unto Him void." His family was dear to him. He enjoyed doing the little things about the home, car-ing for the children and giving the love service, which makes life worth living. Soon after they were married he was giv-en some land in the country, and I remember him saying to my sister, "If the Lord would only let me, we would have a little home and raise chickens." But choosing the "better part", to-gather they continued the life of service for others.

He taught as the discipline of the Movement he represent-ed and for his own life and practice, the keeping of the com-mandments of Jesus. He rejoiced in the opportunity to "over-come evil with good." He also practiced the command to "Give to every man that asketh of thee, and to him that

would borrow of thee, turn not away," and God rewarded
an hundred fold. Many times he gave the last cent he had,
or clothes and food that would be needed the following day;
but the Scripture obeyed brought the fulfillment of the promised "good measure" returned, even to the running over. A
marked characteristic of his work was his ability to reach all
classes, the rich and the cultured, the poor and the outcast of
society, with the same touch of understanding that makes of
one common brotherhood all God's creatures.

Having known the power of healing in his own life, and
believing God's promises are the same today for those who
could believe, he prayed for the sick who were healed, even
as sinners were delivered from the power of sin thru faith in
the atonement. When Mrs. Parham first wrote me about the
wonderful healings they were having among the people, I
could hardly believe it possible. I knew Christ and the disciples healed the people and I also believed that Mr. Parham
was healed, but I thought these were special cases. I had a
physical disorder that had troubled me for years, I would try
the Lord and see if He would heal now as when here in person. God, searching the heart, knoweth all things. How
great His patience and tender mercies toward us! He graciously healed me. Later I contracted a cold resulting in a
cough which instead of getting better grew worse till I was
confined to bed. My mother and the others were anxious
about me, feeling I should have a doctor. To this I could not
consent for I had not only been healed myself but had seen
many others healed thru prayer. I remembered I had come
for healing to prove God's promises, now I felt God was
proving me. They were praying for me at Bethel Bible
School where Mr. and Mrs. Parham were in charge, yet I still
remained sick. Later, Mr. Parham came into my mother's
home and prayed for me. I felt the healing virtue go thru my
body and was entirely delivered. I thank God for His great

love for His children; that He has purchased not only salvation for the soul but also healing for the body, which is the
temple of the Holy Ghost.   I also thank God for His faithful messenger, who has been an inspiration and blessing to so
many and truly given his life as a living sacrifice in service
for others, though his faith was often tried, as by fire.

*   *   *   *   *

We will let one of the students, Mrs. N. O. La-Berge, formerly Miss Agnes N. Osman, who was the first to receive the
baptism of the Holy Ghost in the school, give her testimony:

"I had been a Bible student for some years and had attended T. C. Horton's Bible School at St. Paul, Minn., and A. B.
Simpson's Bible School at New York City.   For some time I
had been doing mission work. In the fall of 1900 I was in Kansas City and heard that a Bible School was to be opened at
Topeka, Kans.   I had a desire to go to this school, and asked
the Lord that if it was His plan for me to go, to provide the
fare.   A sister gave me more than enough to pay for my fare
and so I felt assured it was God's will for me to go.   I was
living by simple faith in the Lord, trusting Him to supply all
my needs according to Phil. 4:19.

It was in October 1900, that I went to this school which
was known as Bethel Colllege.   We studied the Bible every
day and did much work down town at night.   Prayer was offered night and day continually in a special upper room set
apart as a prayer tower.   I had many blessed hours of prayer
in this upper room during the night watches.   As we spent
much time in the presence of God, He caused our hearts to be
opened to all that is written.

"I had some experience with the Lord, and tasted the joy of
leading some souls to Christ, and had some marvelous answers to prayer for guidance and in having my needs supplied.
I was blessed with the presence of the Lord, who, in response to my prayer, healed some who were sick.   Like some others, I thought that I had received the baptism of the Holy

Ghost at the time of consecration, but when I learned that the Holy Ghost was yet to be poured out in greater fullness, my heart became hungry for the promised Comforter and I began to cry out for an enduement with power from on high. At times I longed more for the Holy Spirit to come in than for my necessary food. At night I had a greater desire for Him than for sleep.

"We were admonished to honor the blood of Jesus Christ to do its work in our hearts, and this brought great peace and victory. A text often used was this, 'Now the God of peace has brought again from the dead our Lord Jesus, that great Shepherd of the sheep, thru the blood of the everlasting cov-enant, make you perfect in every good work to do His will, working in you that which is well pleasing in His sight, thru Jesus Christ, to whom be glory forever and ever. Amen' (He-brews 13:20-21)

"As the end of the year drew near some friends came from Kansas City to spend the holidays with us. On watch night we had a blessed service, praying that God's blessing might rest upon us as the New Year came in. During the first day of 1901 the presence of the Lord was with us in a marked way stilling our hearts to wait upon Him for greater things. The spirit of prayer was upon us in the evening. It was nearly seven o'clock on this first of January that it came into my heart to ask Bro. Parham to lay his hands upon me that I might receive the gift of the Holy Spirit. It was as his hands were laid upon my head that the Holy Spirit fell upon me and I began to speak in tongues, glorifying God. I talked sev-eral languages, and it was clearly manifest when a new dialect was spoken. I had the added joy and glory my heart longed for and a depth of the presence of the Lord within that I had never known before. It was as if rivers of living waters were proceeding from my innermost being.

"The following morning I was accosted with questions about my experience of the night before. As I tried to answer I was so full of glory that I pointed out to them the Bible references, showing that I had received the baptism according to Acts 2:4 and 19:1-6. I was the first one to speak in tongues in the Bible school and it seemed to me that the rest were wanting to speak in tongues too. But I told them not to seek for tongues but to seek for the Holy Ghost. I did not know at that time that anyone else would speak in tongues. I did not expect the Holy Spirit to manifest Himself to others as He did to me.

"On January 2, some of us went down to Topeka to a mission. As we worshipped the Lord I offered prayer in English and then prayed in another language in tongues. A Bohemian who was present said that he understood what I said. Some months later at a school house with others, in a meeting, I spoke in tongues in the power of the spirit and another Bohemian understood me. Since then others have understood other languages I have spoken.

"The hearts of other students were made hungry for the Holy Spirit and they continued to tarry before the Lord. On the 3rd of January some of the students went to the mission and others gathered in prayer at the Bible School praying for the Holy Spirit. God answered their prayers by pouring out His Spirit and one after another began speaking in tongues and some were given interpretation. It was some months later I was persuaded in my own heart about the evidence of the baptism of the Holy Spirit and I proved the Lord nine times concerning it. At that time the Holy Ghost was being poured out and God was working in many ways with saints and sinners. I saw a number of hungry hearts who were seeking. I watched nine different ones receive the Holy Spirit, saying to myself and before God, 'I will see if everyone talks in tongues.' One by one everyone who received the Holy Spirit began to speak in other tongues and as the Spirit gave them utterance. I felt satisfied that God was giving His own evidence to every one of us."

"O spread the tidings 'round, wherever man is found,
Wherever human hearts and human woes abound;
Let ev'ry Christian tongue proclaim the joyful sound:
The Comforter has come!

Chorus
The Comforter has come, The Comforter has come!
The Holy Ghost from Heav'en, The Father's promise giv'n;
O, spread the tidings 'round, wherever man is found—
The Comforter has come!

The long, long night is past, the morning breaks at last,
And hushed the dreadful wail and fury of the blast,
As o'er the golden hills the day advances fast!
The Comforter has come!

Lo, the great King of kings, with healing in His wings,
To ev'ry captive soul a full deliv'rance brings;
And thro' the vacant cells the song of triumph rings;
The Comforter has come!

O boundless love divine! how shall this tongue of mine
To wand'ring mortals tell the matchless grace divine—
That I, a child of hell, should in His image shine!
The Comforter has come!"

Night and day this song rang in triumph through the beautiful building! I have heard it sung many times since, but it has never sounded quite the same to me as it did then. We sang it with grateful hearts, in praise and thanksgiving to our Father who had fulfilled His promise and given us the Comforter, the Holy Spirit.

Chapter IX

JOY AND SORROW AT BETHEL

I do not want to repeat, but I wish to say that I was an eye-witness to what has already been told, and thank God for the blessed experience He gave us at Bethel, the baptism of the Holy Spirit. As we were gathered together in an upper room, in one accord, truly "God came down our souls to greet, while glory crowned the mercy seat." It is better felt than told, for only those who have had the same experience can know the joy we felt at that time. If you would like to know what we received, read Acts 2, which tells you of the outpouring of the Holy Spirit just as He came to us, manifesting His presence by speaking in other tongues.

While two or three were speaking in other tongues, as the Spirit gave utterance, I thought perhaps they were going as missionaries to foreign fields, and did not know whether this wonderful experience could be for me, I felt so empty and unworthy. I knelt down and prayed, "Lord if this is for me, I want it." My desire was to have all that had been purchased for me at so great a cost on Calvary. Jesus said, It is expedient for you that I go away, if I go not away the Comforter will not come, but if I depart I will send Him unto you. John 16:7. Though so unworthy, my heart longed for God's best, the fullness of His love, manifest in my life, and I prayed, "Lord, I want all there is for me." The glory of God filled my soul, I found myself repeating this prayer, and then began speaking in tongues. How glad we were when Mr. Parham returned from his meeting in Topeka and received the baptism of the Holy Spirit also. When at last we retired for the night, he said I talked in tongues in my sleep, still praising God.

The following days were mostly spent in prayer and thanksgiving. Our favorite songs, which we never tired of singing were "All Hail the Power of Jesus Name," and "The Comforter Has Come." Concerning these first days of the outpouring at Topeka, it was soon noised abroad that Pentecost was being repeated and shortly afterwards an article appeared in the Topeka paper ridiculing the speaking in tongues. Other newspapers began to hear it and send reporters, and articles appeared in the Kansas City and St. Louis papers concerning the outpouring. This advertised the work and letters came pouring into the school asking for explanations, and some came to see what the Lord had done.

One day my dear aunt came, who had always been like a mother to me. How glad we were to see her, also surprised as she always had told us when she was coming. After we had talked awhile she said, with a sigh of relief, "Well, you seem to be like you always were." We then understood, she had seen the newspaper reports, and fearing we might be losing our minds, had come to look after the children. You may be interested in reading a few extracts from some of the papers:

Topeka Capitol, January 14th, 1901.

"A Queer Faith, Strange Acts of the Apostolic Believers are Inspired from God, the Believers Speak in Strange Languages.

"The school at present numbers about thirty-five members and they certainly form a strange religious body, most of the thirty five come from Kansas City, some from Topeka. It seems that under the Apostolic Faith its adherents are prevented from asking for money contributions except through God Himself. They believe the Lord answers prayers and they pray for what they want giving little heed to the present practical need of making a living. The whole day is spent in prayer for be it known these adherents hold to an exacting creed that prayer and faith bring inspiration direct from God Himself, and when they arrive at a certain stage of perfection they have all the qualifications and attributes of the apostles of old. But the really strange feature of the faith is the speaking in tongues."

State Journal, January 15th, 1901:

PRAYER TOWER.

"Bethel College has a prayer tower in which some one stays all the time. The prayer tower is reached by climbing the spiral stairs of the tower to the house top and walking out over the roof to the door in one of the turrets of the building. The room is about six foot square and has a little stove inside to keep it warm and it is quite warm in the room even in the coldest weather. On the floor is a rug and a chair which has been provided for those who watch and pray at night. The women are assigned to the tower during the day time and the men during the night. Each one who goes to the tower remains there until relieved. The time each one stays is usually about three hours."

After some time of blessing in the school our hearts were burdened for other cities and Mr. Parham took a company of seven of us to Kansas City and a good meeting was held there. Some were saved and healed and a number received the Holy Spirit and spoke in tongues. From the beginning was proclaimed the importance of a clean, holy life of victory and power for every believer. We honored the Father, Son and Holy Ghost. We believed and taught all the words and commands of our Lord Jesus Christ, repentance, the forgiveness of sin, a sanctified life, separation unto the Lord and power over sin through the indwelling Christ.

Kansas City Journal, January 22, 1901:

Was a Pentecost "Apostolic Faith Believers Claim Speaking in Tongues, Strange Testimonials at a Strange Meeting Last Night.

"Rev Chas. F. Parham, Leader of the "Apostolic Faith" sect, which has recently attracted much attention in Topeka, Kansas, came to Kansas City yesterday accompanied by his wife and seven students who claimed to be endowed with the Apostolic "Gift of Tongues," to conduct a meeting here.

"The first meeting was held last night. In many respects it recalled an old-fashioned Methodist prayer meeting. Mr. Parham preached, expounded the tenets of their faith and then called on students and other members of the congregation to prophesy. "For two years," spoke a tall angular man, "I have been as much of an infidel as Robert G. Ingersoll, but tonight the Lord has healed me of my disbelief," as the tall man sat down, cries of "Amen" and "Praise the Lord" broke from all parts of the house."

Kansas City papers, February 1901:

At the Academy of Music, Rev. Chas. F. Parham of the College of Bethel, to Conduct Revivals in an Up-town Hall.

"Mr. Parham is the leader of the Topeka sect which has started out to induce the world to return to what its exponents call, the early Apostolic Faith. Mr. Parham and several of his followers claimed to have conferred upon them the speaking in tongues, and other powers the early disciples were said to have had, among them the power of healing.

Six Hours of Prayer. Parham and Students Hold Service at Shelly Park. C. F. Parham, with seven students from Bethel College Bible School at Topeka, Kans., held a session of prayer yesterday in a tent at Shelly Park. The session lasted six hours. From 9 A. M. to 3 P. M. during which time over 100 persons offered prayer, including many of the students, who prayed in foreign tongues by means of the Spirit. Last evening the Evangelist held a regular prayer meeting and several different languages were used by the people. The Bethel Bible School, according to its founder and present head, is the only religious institution in the world to the students of which the speaking in tongues been given from God. "We are not working for money," said a student last night. "We do not ask for money from anyone. The Lord will provide. If we are worthy, we will have plenty to eat and plenty to wear. If we are not worthy, we will starve. The workman is worthy of his hire. We are well fed and received considerable sums of money from those whom the Lord moves to give. When asked to explain the gift of tongues, a student said, 'It came to the students Jan. 1st last, direct from God. We could none of us speak any other language beside English. When the gift came from God, we could speak different languages, and by the grace of God we teach nothing that is not proven by the Bible. Our religion is the religion of truth, not the religion of fashion, as practiced by the churches. We do not preach come-outism or come-ism, but recognize all good Christians anywhere we meet them.'

Rev. C. F. Parham tells of his followers hardships. He spoke of the persecutions that have always attended every great reform, which he and his followers were experiencing in some degree. Our work is set for the restoration of faith and power and unity among believers. Mr. Parham claims that he and his followers thru their faith are able to preach in different languages. The sect has a school. The College of Bethel, Topeka, Kansas."

Later article from K. C. World:

They Believe in a Personal God. The Apostolic Faith as Taught by Chas. F. Parham of Topeka. Speaking in Tongues.

1. "And when the day of Pentecost was fully come, they were all with one accord in one place. 2. And suddenly there came a sound from heaven as of a rushing mighty wind, and it filled all the house where they were sitting. 3. And there appeared unto them cloven tongues like as of fire, and it sat upon each of them. 4. And they were all filled with the Holy Ghost, and began to speak with other tongues, as the Spirit gave them utterance." These verses give foundation for a new —'The Apostolic Faith,' it was founded by Rev. Chas. F. Par-

ham at Topeka, Kansas. This faith takes the Bible literally, and it is taught in a Bible school called 'Bethel College' near Topeka. These people have a faith almost incomprehensible at this day. Prevailing prayer, that's the sole tenet of their faith. They have exercised this faith so patiently in unusual ardor and continued prayer that they now claim to have received the "Speaking in Tongues" which means that they believe they can speak in many tongues. Following is a portion of Apostle Parham's sermon:

"The mighty power of God is just as capable in our lives today of performing His divine will as it was 1900 years ago. It is our privilege to put our selves in the hands of God and let Him use us to give His light to the world. The power of Pentecost is manifest in us. It has not been manifested in men for 1900 years, because the church has left the power of God. The Christian religion must be demonstrated. The world wants to be shown. Then let God's power be manifest thru us.

BELIEVE IN A PERSONAL GOD

"Let your bodies be clean. You cannot receive the gift of the Holy Spirit unless you are clean. Catarrh, consumption, all diseases are offensive in the sight of God. We are not Chritian Scientist. We believe in disease. A creed that teaches there is no disease, no personal God, no personal devil is a fake. There is pain and there is disease. Rev. Parham asserted that the power of the apostles has come again into the world. Then followed testimonies of God's power in healing and other things."

After returning to the Bible School in Topeka, Mr. Parham took a company of twenty students to Lawrence, Kansas for a meeting. It was hard to decide who should stay at the school for all wanted to go and proclaim that God had fulfilled His promise in pouring out His Holy Spirit. One morning one of the number who was to remain at the school came in with a glad smile of victory saying, "Brother Parham, we are

ALL going with you." He looked at her in surprise, questioning what she meant. "We are all going to be there in spirit
and so unitedly pray for you that you will feel that the whole
school is with you." We who did not go, truly felt the responsibility of prayer, and standing by those who went forth
to battle, believing as Mr. Parham often told us; "As his part
is that goeth down to the battle, so shall his part be that tar-
rieth by the stuff; they shall part alike. 1 Sam 30:24.

An old theatre was rented at Lawrence and the workers
made house to house visits during the day, going two by two,
praying for the sick in homes where they could get admit-
tance. Large numbers came to the meetings and many were
saved. The sick were healed and a good number of believers
received the baptism of the Holy Spirit, just as we did, speaking in tongues and glorifying God. The Lawrence Jefferson-
ian Gazette, had this to say of the meetings of the Full Gospel believers:

" 'Rev. Chas. F. Parham of the College of Bethel, Topeka,
Kansas with about twenty students will conduct a meeting in
Lawrence, Kansas, the meeting is for the restoration of the
Apostolic Faith and Power. The unity of believers the "Witness" evangelization of all nations in this coming century. No
churchism nor come-outism will be preached, the meeting will
be attended with the gifts of 1 Cor. 12th Chapter."

The Lawrence World:

A Great Worker Chas. F. Parham Will Hold a Series of
Meetings in Lawrence.

"Charles F. Parham, who has won an international reputation since leaving Lawrence five years ago will return and hold
a series of meetings. Mr. Parham is not the founder of any
new church or creed. He insists that his mission is to have
people return to the Apostolic Faith. His views are referred
to as strange and yet he claims that the country ought not to
regard the first principles of the Christian religion as strange.

He will bring about 20 of his students to this city and will take no collections, will not ask any man for a cent but will be well fed and supplied with all the necessities and many of the luxuries of life. Mr. Parham does not impress one as being a peculiar man. Indeed he is a right good fellow and is earnest in his life's work. Whatever may be said about him, he has attracted more attention to religion than any other religious worker in years. The most peculiar thing about him in his work is the speaking in tongues. His students can speak in languages they never heard before. It has been demonstrated that it is not gibberish but real languages and can be understood by foreigners.

"Mr. Parham believes that the world is ready to return to the Apostolic Faith and is going about preaching the Word and asking people to enlist under this banner. He is not representing any church and will not perfect any organization, but will preach the Word of God as he has the light. Two meetings will be held daily. Not only do his converts speak in many languages, but they cast out devils and heal the sick. This speaking in tongues is something new. It came to them with the present century, falling 1901; since that time it has been extended far and wide. Mr. Parham claims that this is not remarkable. It is simply a witness of his relation to the true Faith.

"Mr. Parham has an interesting personality. He has for a number of years preached in this city and country about and had great power in revivals. He is essentially a revivalist. He left the regular ministry about five years ago and since that time has been doing evangelistic work. He will be in the city for about ten days and the meeting will give those interested in the man and his work a chance to see for themselves what manner of work he is doing to attract such world wide attention."

We had known great joy and now we were to know great

sorrow. Our beautiful baby boy now a year old, whose big brown eyes seemed always to be looking with a gentle longing into the future, was taken very sick. He had never been sick before and we hardly realized how sick he was till March 16, 1901, he was gone. His loving gentle nature, ever ready to confide in all, had won the love of the school. It seemed impossible for us to give him up. Some of the students said, "Come let us all pray, God can raise the dead. Surely He will bring him back to life." But as I looked at his little face so pure and innocent, I felt that it would be a selfish prayer to try to call him back to a world of sin and sorrow. As God had seen best to take him, we must learn to say, "Thy will be done."

Yet how hard it is sometimes to leave it all with God without questioning why? Had it been a lack of faith on our part, or was it to test our faith to see if we would go on and preach the gospel of healing? You who have had like experience know how many questions will fill our minds and we often, perhaps unjustly, condemn ourselves. If we could always see and understand our sorrows and trials there would be no test of faith. We should be walking by sight, instead of walking by faith.

As parents our little children often ask us "Why?" but we do not always explain things to them, as they could not understand. So when Peter questioned Christ. "What will this man do?" Christ only answered, "What is that to thee, Follow thou me."

The sun that hardens clay, will also melt the wax. Sorrow will either harden our hearts or melt them. If we rebel against God's will, our hearts will be hardened, but if we yield to His will, He will tenderly draw us closer to Himself. Oh may we yield our lives to Him and let sorrow soften our hearts as wax, that He can mould and fashion us according to His good pleasure, that we may be made all glorious within. That

we may shine as gold, tried in the fire, till we reflect His likeness.

I wandered away from the house to pray, out on the beautiful lawn so fresh and green in the beauty of spring. Lost in
my own sorrow, I did not at first notice that someone else had
come out there for the same purpose. He was a guest at the
school, highly respected by all, but so quiet and reserved that
we did not know his hidden sorrow. When he saw me, he
came to me and expressed his sympathy. " Yet," he said, "your
sorrow is not as hard to bear as mine, yours is a dead
sorrow, with no stain of sin, mine is a living sorrow." He then
told me his story. His wife had left him, his home was broken
up, his life ruined.

How sad, I could not think of a word of comfort, but oh,
how many broken hearts there are in this world, carrying a
"living sorrow," trying to hide it with a smile, or bury it with
worldly pleasures. A few unkind words may break the tender
cord of human affection and thoughtless deeds end in a trag-
edy. How careful we should be each day to say or do nothing that we might have cause to regret. Yet those too, who
bear the "living sorrows" may take them to the Living Christ,
the Man of sorrows, the Great High Priest who can be touched with the feeling of our infirmities for He knows "the flesh
is weak."

As I returned to the house, Mr. Parham met me with a bou-
quet of flowers in his hand. I knew he felt the loss as keenly
as I did, yet he tried to be brave for my sake. He gave me
the flowers saying, "These are not for little Charlie, they are
for you." How often I have thought of this. Kind words
and flowers can not help the dead, but how much comfort
they may sometimes bring to the living. Though the flowers
soon fade, how long sometimes, they will remain fresh in the
memory, and the loving thought of the one who gave them. I
think of the beautiful poem by L. M. Hodges.

"Closed eyes can't see the white roses,
Cold hands can't hold them, you know,
Breath that is stilled cannot gather
The odors that sweet from them blow.
Death, with a peace beyond dreaming,
Its children of earth doth endow;
Life is the time we can help them,
So give them the flowers now.

Here are the struggles and striving,
Here are the aches and the tears;
Now is the time to be smoothing
The frowns and the furrows and fears.
What to closed eyes are kind sayings?
What to hushed hearts is a deep vow?
Naught can avail after parting,
So give them the flowers now."

We went by train to Tonganoxie, Kansas where we were to
bury our baby. Mr. Parham was very patient with me, re-
minding me that I had yet much to live for as he pointed to
our two children, Claude and Esther, sitting side by side in the
seat before us, looking sad, though unable to understand it all.
Sometimes our minds are so centered on our sorrows and losses, that our eyes are blinded to the blessings and loved ones
who are still ours. Everyone was very kind to us, yet we
could feel that some of our friends, who did not believe in
healing, were hoping now that we would give up this belief.

Could we give it up? No. If our faith was in what we
could see in the natural, truly our faith might now be shatter-
ed, but our faith had been established in the Word of God.
As we had seen healing and salvation so closely connected. in
the atonement, we felt to give up our faith in healing, we
would also lose our hope in salvation and all was lost.

If part of the Bible is false, it is all untrue, or else it is all true. God's Word is true, even though seemingly we had failed and been defeated. Yet perhaps it was not defeat. God's infinite plan might have been carried out, though we could not understand it with our finite minds.

We returned to Topeka and continued the work at the Bible School, but before the summer was over the beautiful building was bought to be used as a pleasure resort. We had dreamed that the building had been bought and that it had burned to the ground. Mr. Parham told the men, and warned them that if they used the building (that God had honored with His Presence) for ungodly purposes, they would not prosper. They may have thought we told them this with a selfish motive but this was not so.

We believed nothing could come to us except as God permitted. If we had to give up the building, the purpose of the school must have been accomplished. We were willing to go elsewhere as He might direct. The building was bought and the students went to different places, some of them remaining with us in Topeka where we rented a building for a short time.

While there a lady from California visited us. She was hungry for the baptism of the Holy Spirit. We tried to explain it to her but she seemed unable to grasp the truth.

She wrote us, that after she got home her heart was still longing for more of God. She prayed, "Lord, even though I don't understand, give me what they received on the day of Pentecost," and she began to speak in other tongues. How glad and encouraged we were to get her testimony.

We then left Topeka, Kansas, and went to Kansas City, Mo.

Chapter X

"A VOICE CRYING IN THE WILDERNESS"

R. Parham wrote, "Through great trials and persecution in Kansas City, Mo., at which time I wrote the first book published by any Full Gospel people called, "A Voice Crying in the Wilderness" in which was set forth what is now being taught in different movements through out the world. I started to write the book, with no means on hand to meet expenses, but by the time I had it finished, the means for having it published were provided from a most unexpected source. The Lord knoweth what things we have need of before we ask Him. Praise the Lord.

"Both the pulpit and the press sought to utterly destroy our place and prestige, until my wife, her sister and myself seemed to stand alone. Hated, despised, counted as naught, for weeks and weeks never knowing where our next meal was coming from, yet feeling that we must maintain 'the faith once for all delivered to the saints.' When we had carfare we rode, when we did not we walked. We entered every open door but did not try to force doors open; when buildings were closed to us, we preached on the street."

We were not surprised, but sad, when we received the word from Topeka that the building that had been our Bible School was burned down. Our friends there sent us some of the carved wood work from the doors.

We were living in light-house keeping rooms, and Christmas of 1901 was drawing near. The Lord was providing our daily bread, and we learned to be content with such things as we had, like Paul we knew how to abound and knew how to suffer want, and tried to obey the command of Jesus to take no thought for the morrow.

Well, here came a Christmas box from my mother containing a big turkey. With questioning eyes we gazed at it.

What should we do with it! Here was a strange problem, we hardly knew whether to laugh or cry. A fine turkey for Christmas and nothing to eat with it, and as our light-house keeping accommodations were so very light, we did not even have a proper way to cook it. It was so large and beautifully dressed we could get a good price for it, yet we dare not sell it as we never let our relatives and friends know of our needs. But how often we worry "too soon" or when it is "not necessary to worry." A friend came and said they would like to have us spend Christmas day with them, but could not furnish as nice a dinner as they would like to. Of course we very kindly offered to furnish the turkey and all was lovely. One day after this, I was wondering what we would have to eat, it was about noon, our supply was gone, and no means. I answered a knock at the door and there stood a strange man. Though rather poorly dressed, he looked clean and respectable. He asked if this was where Mr. Parham lived. He said he had been saved by hearing him preach on the street, had now got work, and wanted to give Mr. Parham his first tithes, and handed me thirteen cents.

You may think it strange that he would walk so far across the city to hunt us up and give so small an amount but it was much to me at that time, as it came when we needed it. I found that I had two cents, which added to the thirteen, was sufficient (at that time) to buy bread and milk, which made our dinner. I felt God had led him to give it, and had helped him to find us, and blessed him for it as He commended the woman who gave her mite. A tenth is the Lord's and as we render it unto Him, He will bless and prosper us. We have found it so in our experience.

"Nine parts for thee, and one for Me,
Nine for Earth, and one for Heaven;
The nine are thine, the one is Mine,
But oh, how slowly given!"

June 2, 1902, another son was born to us. We wanted him to have a Bible name and called him Philip Arlington. Tom Alley, an old gentleman who had lived in Jerusalem for ten years, was often a welcome guest in our home. He gave Mr Parham a bottle of water he had brought from the Jordan River. We did not believe in sprinkling babies, as a special ordinance, but used it simply as a consecration service. Our friends came in for prayer, and we dedicated him to God.

Our friends, the Wades, have contributed the following:—

"We well remember the first time we met Bro. Parham. It was prior to his moving to Kansas City, Mo. He came here and held a few meetings in a mission at 16th and Main Sts. We were greatly impressed with his teachings, for he taught the Full Gospel. We were already believers in divine healing and several members of our family had been healed. Then a little later he moved his family to Kansas City and from that time on for twenty-nine years we were very close friends of him and his family. We knew him when he wrote his book "A Voice Crying in the Wilderness" which is still a cherished possession in our home. Then he opened a Bible School at 11th and Oak Sts., which we had the privilege of attending every afternoon and night for four months. We learned more of the teachings of God than we had ever learned before.

"We also know of some of the things he had to endure while living in Kansas City. A good many persecutions that he suffered at the hands of so called ministers of the gospel. Do not think for a minute that Mr. Parham told us a word for he never did. We do not think we ever heard him say a harmful word of a living soul or ever utter a word of complaint. We remember at one time he took a minister and his family (and his family consisted of six members and he also brought a deaconess with him) into his home and kept them for nearly three months as he was down and out and had no where to go. Bro. Parham gave them the best room in the house, and treated them as royal guests. Then when they fell heir to a small amount of money just before Bro. Parham closed the Bible school, they did not give Bro. Parham one cent and even left his personal bills for Bro. Parham to pay, which Bro. Parham did without a murmur, for which God honored and prospered him.

"While Bro. Parham was walking to church with a preacher, he saw that his friend had no overcoat and that the night was cold. Bro. Parham took off his coat and gave it to him saying he felt that the Lord wanted him to do this. For some time no one noticed that Bro. Parham was going without a coat, as he concealed it by being the first one at the night meeting and the last to leave. When it was discovered what he had done, means were given for a coat, and one of the leading tailors of Kansas City offered to do the work free of charge if the material was furnished. Thus the Lord rewarded his sacrifice with a better coat than he had given away, although we felt sorry that he went without one as long as he did.

"A short time before Bro. Parham moved to Kansas, he told us of a young minister who seemed to be branching out on the Full Gospel Lines, and was at this time holding meetings. Bro. Parham asked us to attend his meetings and help him in every way we could. This we did but had not attended there long until this young minister, through some friends of his, tried to turn us against Bro. Parham, and not only us but a number of others, some of which (I am sorry to say) listened to the false accusations and did turn against him. We watched very closely the lives of these persecutors and saw them one by one come to naught, while Bro. Parham went on to higher and deeper things in God, never saying one word in his own defense. He was like the Master, "too busy about his Father's business" to bother himself with the things the devil was trying to stir up.

"We recall another time when a minster told Bro. Parham that he could preach a certain night in his mission and he sent cards to all his friends stating that fact, and we went and found the mission packed (friends expecting to hear Bro. Parham) and to our great disappointment this minister took charge of the service, and never even asked Bro. Parham to the platform, after promising him he could preach that night. A few weeks later we saw Bro. Parham hand this minister's wife one dollar, and heard her say, "The Lord knew I just lacked that one dollar of having enough money to go to my husband." (he having left the city a week or so before). So you see, he was always returning good for evil. I have often thought that there would have been very few that would have been willing to stand the persecutions and hardships that he and his faithful wife endured as they were being "tried as gold in the fire." Bro. Parham was often wounded in the house of his friends, and mistreated by those who he did the most for, which we know sometimes he felt very keenly, even though he did not retaliate or resent it.

"We read the following piece in a paper and as it made us think so much of Bro. Parham, we will quote it here. "Many wear scars, deep soul scars, made by friends who rudely, crudely thrust their clumsy fingers among their heart-strings. We say cruel words, they may even be ill-timed words of truth, and we do not stop to consider how brutally they pierce and sting.

"I read a beautiful story the other day in the American magazine about a man who lived every day in eternity. He had many heart piercing trials, as we count trials, and he bore them all with such beautiful serenity that people wondered. He was known to carry in his pocket and to consult frequently a much-worn little leather folder. After his death it was discovered that it contained a card which his wife had written him just before she was killed in an accident. On this card she had written this motto: "God won't look you over for medals, degrees, or diplomas — but for scars!"

"Not many of us are ever going up out of life like conquering heroes. Not with floating banners and gleaming armor. Not with glad shouts of triumph. I think God will look upon as much as men looked upon soldiers returning from the Civil War— dusty, ragged, limping scarred veterans of a long conflict. If God finds scars, He will know we didn't shirk, nor hunt easy places nor run from our duties."

"If there could be one thing more than another that proved to me the wonderful Christian life Bro. Parham lived, it is his family of four sons and a daughter, who, with their families, are every one of them honest, honorable, upright Christians, proving that through his faithful Christian life they too have accepted their father's God.

"He always made our home his whenever he was in the locality where we lived; staying with us from a few days to as much as three weeks at a time, which we felt an honor and a privilege to have him do. His being in our home so much and always the same cheerful Bro. Parham he was the first time we met him, made him very endeared to us. While we sadly miss him, his memory will ever be cherished in our home."

Before winter we moved to Lawrence, Kansas, and Mr. Parham held meetings in different places, but the people seemed slow to accept the truth, some declaring it was not the power of God, which enabled us to speak in other tongues.

One day, sorely tried, I went to the Lord in prayer for some word of encouragement, This Scripture came to me, "For if this counsel or this work be of men, it will come to naught, But if it be of God ye cannot overthrow it. Acts. 5:39. These words meant much to me at that time.

Many years have passed since then, but I thank God today that the Holy Spirit is still real in my life. How wonderfully the vision that our brother had on the roof of the Bible School has been fulfilled in the multitudes who now enjoy the baptism of the Holy Spirit which went out from that place to refresh hungry hearts. Though there has been persecution, trials, fanaticism and counterfeits, the real truth of God stands. "The gates of Hell cannot prevail aginst it."

We continued the fight here until the spring of 1903 when a lady minister, who was brought into the faith when we had held a meeting in Lawrence in 1901, invited Mr. Parham to hold a meeting in a mission she had established in Nevada, Mo. Here the Lord blessed us and we learned some needful lessons, as we saw some fleshly manifestations, and giving out of messages we had not witnessed before. Here Mr. Parham carefully and prayerfully tested these things. The word tells us to "try the spirits" and "prove all things". If we had not done so, he would not afterwards have known how to rebuke fanaticism, when it was manifest in such force and power.

One day, when in prayer, a power seized my lower jaw, which began to tremble, then shake with increased violence. Mr. Parham came to the door. He did not condemn or criticize but I knew he was praying silently. The power, over which I had not control, left me and I realized it was not of God.

During the summer months we felt lead to El Dorado Springs, Mo., where people came from all over the United States to try the virtue of spring water for the healing of their bodies. Mr. Parham with his workers, stood at the corner of the park where steps led down to the spring. People came by the hundreds to hear the message and many were healed, witnessing to the truth, in many different states.

Our home was continually filled with the sick and suffering seeking healing, and God manifested His mighty power.

Among the many who came to our home and were healed was Mrs. M. A. Arthur from Galena, Kansas. We will let her tell the story in her own words.

"I was afflicted with dyspepsia for fourteen years also with prolapsis, hemorrhoids and paralysis of the bowels, but my greatest distress was in my eyes. The optical nerves were afflicted in a way which might culminate at any time in sudden blindness. My right eye was virtually blind from birth. I could only see bright colors with it for a few moments at a time and then all would turn dark. All my seeing depended upon my left eye. I sought help of many prominent oculists and tried allopathy, homeopathy, hygiene, osteopathy, and Christian Science. In the summer of 1898 a Kansas City doctor operated for a second time upon my eyes, after which they grew much worse. To reduce the inflamation and nerve strain, he prescribed the blistering of my temples, back of my ears and back of my neck constantly for six months. This was done, I spent two summers in a dark room and could neither read or write for pain and fear of sudden blindness. Five years passed in which I knew no moment apart from pain, and every thing I tried for relief only ended in a new dissapointment.

"The story of blind Bar-timaeus was ever on my heart. I often asked, 'Will not Jesus heal to-day as when He was here upon earth?' The only reply was, 'No, He has given us doctors to do this work now.' I had not heard of anyone being healed by faith and prayer but I kept earnestly seeking God every day until one morning in February 1903 He gave me a promise in James 5:14-15. 'Is there any sick among you? let him call the elders of the church; and let them pray over him, anointing him with oil in the name of the Lord; and the prayer of faith shall save the sick, and the Lord shall raise him up; and if he have committed sins they shall be forgiven him.'

"My husband told me to go to Eldorado Springs, Mo., but I reasoned with him that I had been there for three summers without benefit and that it was no use to go again and that I would rather stay at home. The enemy was secretly tempt-ing me with thoughts of suicide if I suddenly went blind. My husband insisted on my going to Eldorado Springs so I went in August. A few days after my arrival I was in the park and heard a small number of people singing. I heard the preacher announce, 'If there be any here seekng God for salvation or healing in their bodies, come to my house to-morrow morning at nine o'clock.' The next morning I went to the meeting and God's gracious Word was opened to me and I saw the truth that Christ Himself took our infirmities and bore sickness in His own body on the tree, and that His atonement provided a full and complete redemption for my spirit, soul and body. My heart was glad and hope again sprang up as I heard these wonderful words. The minister and helpers then prayed for the sick.

"A day or two later I was again in this cottage meeting and told them how the Lord had led me to believe that He would heal my eyes, and I asked them to pray for me according to James 5: 14-15. They did so and I asked them what I should do with my glasses. I was wearing two pair, one over the other. The minister said, 'Sister, if you take the Lord for your Healer you will get along faster without the glasses.' I thanked him and stepped outside the door, wondering how I could get to my room. I folded my handkerchief and held it over my eyes, and took the hand of my four years old daughter. She led me on to the main street where she asked me for some tomatoes and cookies. She went two blocks to get them and returned. She let go my hand to eat the cookies. I spoke to her but got no answer. Then, alarmed for her, I lifted the handkerchief off of one eye and saw her half a block behind me.

"I could open my eyes in the light and had no pain, and oh, it was so wonderful to me. I looked on a new white awning, then up at a white cloud, then at the noonday sun, and it was so beautiful. I cried 'Praise God the work is done.' And He answered me, 'You are every whit whole.' Then His mighty healing power surged thru my body from head to foot, and I was made to feel like a new person. It was like being lifted from a dark pit of despair and suffering, to the mount of Transfiguration. I gained twenty-nine pounds in a short time and could eat four meals a day. No more starving dyspepsia. The glasses and all remedies were all cast away. I could read day or night and have never had another burning ulcer since. I hastened home to tell my husband. The family and friends joined in our rejoicing. There was someone in the house almost continually to hear that wonderful story. One husband and wife came at eleven o'clock one night to hear my story. Men came to my husband's office to hear it, until the whole town heard of my healing. I was healed on August 17, 1903, and joy and gladness filled my soul continually."

Space will not permit me to tell of all the wonderful healings, but I especially wanted to tell of Mrs. Arthur's experience, as it was because of her healing that the way was opened for us to go to Galena, Kansas, and the wonderful revival which followed was begun in their home.

"Prayer changes things, beloved, prayer, earnest prayer.
It moves the hand of God, to do, to dare;
God loves to see His children come to intercede;
That He might grant, and satisfy their every need.

Prayer changes things, beloved, prayer, just prayer;
Bring everything to God, and leave it there;
Believe His word, trust HIM, watch and wait;
Lest He should come and say, too late, too late."
                                        —A. A. Wilson.

Chapter XI

THE FAME OF JESUS WENT ABROAD

S Mr. Parham had been shown, this gospel of the baptism of the Holy Spirit should go through a testing time for about three years, before this wonderful power should again be manifest in any remarkable way. We had experienced our years of trials and testings and now the time had come when God was going to visit His people in mercy and the Holy Spirit again be poured out.

We came to Galena, Kansas, in the fall of 1903, and began meetings in the Arthur home, which (though large and commodious) soon proved to be too small to accommodate the crowds of hungry people who came to hear the message of the full gospel, which Mr. Parham had brought to them.

A large tent was pitched on a vacant lot nearby and the revival continued until after Thanksgiving. Here the blind, lame, deaf and all manner of diseases were marvelously healed and great numbers saved. I remember the joy and thanksgiving that filled the tent one day when a lame man was prayed for and walked off and left his crutches! How we worshipped the Lord as we realized that "with God all things are possible." We can not now see Jesus, the "Son of Man" in His natural body, as they did when He walked the shores of Galilee, healed the sick and went everywhere doing good, but I am glad that His power to heal is just the same. We can to-day, with the eye of faith, see the risen Christ, the Son of the living God, and as we touch the throne of grace, His power is the same to make us every whit whole! "God sent His own Son in the likeness of sinful flesh, and for sin, condemned sin in the flesh". (Romans 8:3)

Jesus suffered for us that He might "be touched with the feeling of our infirmities." (Heb. 4:15). yet His power to heal was not through the natural (the Son of Man) but through the spiritual (the Son of God.)

When He laid down His human body, did that lessen His power to heal? No. Jesus Christ the same yesterday, and to-day and forever. (Heb. 13:8.)

"Wherefore He is able also to save them to the uttermost that come unto God by Him, seeing He ever liveth to make intercession for them." (Heb. 7:25).

As cold weather was approaching, the "Grand Leader Build-ing", an immense double store room was secured and seated to continue the meeting. Though the building would accom-modate a large crowd, the doors were many times thrown wide open as the crowds overflowed into the street. Two meetings were held each day and all the city was moved. Large num-bers came from the surrounding towns and God stretched forth His hand to heal by the hundreds and many signs and wonders were wrought. Hundreds were saved, sanctified and filled with the Holy Spirit.

There was deep conviction, heart-searching, great humilia-tion and wrongs were righted as the believers sought the bap-tism of the Holy Spirit. Some would receive the Spirit while Mr. Parham was preaching, and others in their homes while at work. No sacrifice was considered too great when souls be-came hungry for God. The Lord had done exceeding, abun-dantly above all that we had asked and thought. We stood amazed in His Presence as we witnessed the mighty miracles of God and another wonderful out-pouring of the Holy Spirit.

As the people came from far and near, and the influence of the meeting was so far-reaching, it would be impossible to real-ly tell what was accomplished. Mr. Parham did not make a practice of "counting the converts," as he said God only knew the results of a meeting. We might count one converted, who

had not really experienced the change of heart, and others
might be truly converted by hearing the Word, that we might
know nothing about.

A great crowd atended the watch-night meeting, and about
four hundred remained in service till morning. It was a
meeting long to be remembered by all who attended.

＊ ＊ ＊ ＊ ＊

Mrs. Fred Campbell (then Libby Preston), lived in Galena,
Kansas, at that time, and gives her testimony regarding the
meeting.

"Many years ago, in the little mining town of Galena, Kansas, came the wonderful story of Jesus and the fulness of the
old-time gospel. Altho I was then but a little child, how well I
remember how God swept that town with a mighty revival
and how He anointed our beloved friend and brother,
Charles F. Parham, with the Spirit of the living God, for indeed 'His minister was a flaming fire.'

"Hundreds of hungry souls flocked to hear the wonderful
messages of salvation for the soul: sanctification for the
church: healing for the body: the baptism of the Holy Spirit
with speaking in other tongues or the Latter Day Rain of the
Holy Spirit which had at that time recently fallen in the city
of Topeka, Kansas; then the message of the Second Coming of
Christ and the unfolding of many other wonderful truths.
Many scores of people were saved, sanctified and received the
wonderful infilling of the Holy Spirit. Numbers received
healing, blind eyes were opened, the lame walked and can-
cers and other incurable diseases were absolutely cured.

"The wonderful work continued until millions of people
now believe in the light of the original Apostolic Faith as first
brought to us in these latter days by our Brother Parham,
who God had so wonderfully healed when crippled, diseased
and dying."

Mrs. Lou Love of Galena, Kansas, has given us the following report of the meeting. Since that time she has given most of her time to evangelistic work.

"It was early in the fall of 1903 that we heard of an unusual meeting being conducted in our town, Galena, Kansas. We (my sister and I) had been converted only a few months. There was a carnival going on that week and our husbands being unsaved said to us, 'If you will go to the carnival with us this week we will go with you to the meeting next week.' We were sure anxious for the week to pass by. When we did get started we saw the supernatural power of God through the message in a way we had never heard before.

"One sister, a woman unsaved at the time, had the arrangements made for a very serious operation. She came to the meeting, was prayed for and immediately healed. She said, 'If the Lord heals my body it is very selfish for me to withhold my life from Him.' She made a complete surrender to the Lord and was graciously saved. Her bodily temple being cleansed, she was also baptized with the Holy Spirit.

"My! how the days flitted by, meeting day and night. The Holy Spirit brooding over the place until we, (the multitudes) could not stay away. Soon the winter weather set in and Brother Parham was compelled to close the tent meeting and find a larger and more comfortable place for the services. The largest store building in the heart of town was secured and throngs packed the place day and night.

"Some evenings Brother Parham would look so tired and worn he would scarcely look able for the night services. He was certainly pouring out his life for the people, not praying for those who had cards in their turn, but for all who came. When he could no longer stand before the long lines of people who came he sat down and prayed until the last one had passed by. Then a few moments alone with God and he came into the night meeting with his body sur-charged with the power of God, as tho it was his first sermon. Oh! for the rapture of those days gone by. But our God is just the same yesterday, today and forever. The people may change but.He remains the same.

"The meetings continued with great power resulting in untold numbers being the recipient of salvation, sanctification, and healing, also the baptism of the Holy Ghost, and the blessed message of the coming of our Lord. How well I remember the watchnight meeting, we stayed all night and went home next morning after the sun was up. The night was not long for our Heavenly Guest tarried all night to own and bless.

"It was at the close of this meeting that those who had consecrated to the hundred-fold service went out as the disciples, armed with the message of power and blessing, that brought deliverance to the untold thousands.

"Brother Parham stayed at the battle's front until the Lord called him to lay down earth's cross and take heaven's crown."

*   *   *   *   *

The Joplin Herald and the Cincinnati Inquirer, in writing up this meeting declare it to be the greatest in power and miracles ever held since the time of the Apostles. I will quote a few extracts from some of the daily papers which will give a description of the meeting as viewed by the press.

BLINDNESS AND CANCER CURED BY RELIGION

Special dispatch to the St. Louis Globe Democrat

Galena, Kansas, Jan. 1, 1904.—"The Evangelistic meetings which have been held at this place by the Rev. Parham for the past six weeks celebrated the New Year by baptizing the converts in Spring River this afternoon.

"These meetings have been a success from the beginning and fully 500 have been converted. Some have already been immersed, but today's list counts 250. Many of the most prominent people in town have professed to having been healed of blindness, cancer, rheumatism and other diseases, and it has been such a spiritual revival as Galena has not experienced in years, if ever.

"The services were to have been closed last night with the all-night watch meeting, but the business men rallied and made good the expenses for another month's service."

WONDERFUL CURES IN KANSAS.

From Cincinnati Enquirer and Joplin News Herald

Galena, Kan., January 27, 1904. "It is doubtful whether in recent years anything has occured that has awakened the interest, excited the comment or mystified the people of this region as have the religious meetings being held here by Rev. C. F. Parham, familiarly termed "The Divine Healer."

"Over three months have elapsed since this man came to Galena and during that time he has healed over a thousand people and converted over 800. When Rev. Parham first began to attract attention he was holding services in a large tent and soon the streets in that vicinity were crowded nightly with people who were anxious to see and hear the wonderful man who was healing the sick, the maimed and the blind without money and without price. When it was found that the tent was utterly inadequate to accommodate the crowd who assembled, a large double storeroom that would shelter 2,000 people was procured, a platform was built at one end, stoves were set up, rough pine boards were installed to be used as seats. Here the past six weeks Parham has preached to a crowded house and the interest shows no sign of abatement. In this rude temple cures that are looked upon almost in the light of miracles have been performed. During the services there have been as many as 50 people at the altar at one time seeking to be restored in soul and body. Here people who have not walked for years without the aid of crutches have risen from the altar with their limbs so straightened that they were enabled to lay aside their crutches, to the astonishment of the audience.

CURED BY FAITH

"These cures, they claim, are affected solely through prayer and faith. Nothing else is done, though Rev. Parham often lays his hands upon the afflicted one while the devotions are going on, with the result that some say it is due to his own magnetism that so much is accomplished.

"Parham and his followers do not advocate Christian Science or Spiritualism, but their belief condensed is that God is able to overcome all, cure diseases of both body and soul, and will do so if they live a consecrated Christian life and depend on Him for all.

"The Healer" makes no charges and takes no credit upon himself, saying that he is only teaching the people the "true way." He takes no collections during the meetings, but, notwithstanding, has had the needs of himself and family well provided for by donations from a grateful public.

"Mr. Parham is a slight, spare man extremely delicate looking, and, in fact, he has said that he was an invalid and badly crippled until he was healed through prayer. His face is pale and earnest looking, while masses of brown hair cover his remarkably shaped head. Mr. Parham is the possessor of such a wonderful personality that some have accused him of hypnotizing his followers.

"Others go as far as to term him a fanatic, but one and all regardless of sect or prejudices, agree that he has brought about conditions that were never before witnessed in this section. Evening after evening the large room is packed with people, many of whom 'have gone to scoff but remained to pray.'

"Here the man of prominence and position clasps hands with the uneducated son of toil or oft times of those who have had a prison record back of them. Here women who have formerly lived for society and gayety kneel beside some fallen sister and endeavor to point her heavenward and here the

'followers' receive what they term 'the Pentecost' and are
enabled to speak in foreign tongues, languages which they are,
when free from this power, utterly unfamiliar with.

"Last week a woman rose during the meeting and spoke
for ten minutes, no one probably knowing what she said, but
an Indian who had come from the Pawnee reservation that
day to attend the services stated that she was speaking in the
the languarge of his tribe and that he could understand every
word of the testimony. Others have spoken in Latin, in Hebrew, in Chinese and various other tongues and while such
manifestations have filled the public with wonder some are of
the opinion that the religious demonstrations of this band are
carried to extremes.

"One evening recently (watch night meeting) over 400 remained at the meeting the entire night singing, praying and
speaking in different languages. Not until daylight did they
disperse and a strange sight they presented, wending their way
homeward in the gray light of the morning.

"On another occasion hundreds congregated on the banks
of Spring River during one of the coldest days in winter and
witnessed Mr. Parham immerse almost one hundred converts
in its icy waters, not one of whom, however, contracted even
a cold.

"But of all the wonderful things which have transpired in
connection with these meetings, nothing has attracted the attention of the public as has the "healings" which have not
been confined to an ignorant, uneducated class of people. On
the contrary, some of the most conservative, intelligent persons, not only here, but within a radius of over a hundred
miles, have visited 'the healer' with wonderful results.

"The list of those who have been benefited by Rev. Parham's visit to this section is indeed a large one and has done
much to regard the man with almost superstitious awe, but
when one meets him in his every day life he is so quiet, so un-

ostentatious, so sympathetic that he invariably wins confidence. His wife, Mrs. Parham, is in every sense of the word a
home woman and heartily in sympathy with her husband's
work, although on account of the three little ones is neces-
sarily not able to take a very active part in it. However, her
sister, Miss Thistlethwaite, is a close attendant at the meetings
and an earnest worker. The Parham home, or "stopping
place," as they call it, is always full of visitors, some of whom
have come many miles to consult 'the healer,' others are ob-
jects of charity, whom the couple are befriending. In the last
two weeks branches of the Parham meetings have sprung up
in almost a dozen of the different mining camps of this district
all of which are attracting large crowds and it is difficult to
enter a company where the wonderful results of these meetings are not the chief topic of conversation."

         *   *   *   *   *

Mr. Parham and a number of workers then held a meeting
in Baxter Springs, Kansas, and the same spirit and power was
manifest, and scores were brought to the light and accepted
the blessings of the full gospel.

On March 16, 1904, another brown-eyed boy came to our
home, whom we named Wilfred Charles. When he was very
young he began to show an interest in spiritual things, and it
often perplexed me to answer his questions about God and the
future life. He also had a sense of humor, and on one occasion used the Scriptures to defend himself. He had been giv-
en some pennies and wanted to go to town and spend them. I
tried to show him the importance of saving his money till he
could get something worth while, but he laughingly said, "Oh
Mama, what's the use to heap up treasures for the last days?"

When Wilfred was about a month old, we moved to Baxter
Springs, Kansas. For some time our furniture had been stored, and we had lived in furnished rooms, but the Baxter
friends had rented a large, comfortable house, and when I got
there with the children, Mr. Parham had got our furniture

placed in the house, and it seemed so homelike. A number of friends were there to greet us, and supper was ready, and an extra supply in the kitchen. How much we appreciated the home the Lord had provided for us, through His children.

Meetings were held in Melrose, Kansas, a small village twelve miles west of Baxter Springs, Kansas. As a result of this meeting, the first Apostolic, Pentecostal or Full Gospel Chapel of all modern movements was erected at the crossroads at Keelville, Kansas, ten miles west of Baxter Springs, Kansas.

*　*　*　*　*

Mr. Ed C. Aultman, (an elderly man then) is now deceased, but we still treasure his memory, and the report he gave of the Melrose meeting.

"Brother C. F. Parham came preaching the way of salvation and life, to all those who would believe and receive the full Gospel as recorded in Holy Writ. But he found us a stiff necked people. We were so bound up in creed and tradition of men, that we just 'sot back' in the harness and our long deaf ears refused to hear the Bible. My! yes, dignified we were; not ready to endure sound doctrine. (II Timothy, 4:3, 4.) But praise be to Christ our Lord, who gives victory; Bro. Parham was determined to preach nothing (no creeds or tradition) but Jesus and Him crucified. (I Corinthians, 2:2) Preaching Jesus, His teaching, His salvation and life and power to heal. Brother Parham surely preached God's Holy Word straight from the shoulder; in chunks, big, pure and hard enough to knock the scales from our eyes. Tradition, formalism, sectarianism and all other isms began to peel off and we became hungry to hear God's truths. People began to pray in earnest for full salvation; and God came in mighty power to save, to cleanse, to heal; and all praised God for the 'Old Time Religion' once more returned to bless and fill us with joy unspeakable and full of glory. (1 Peter, 1:8).

Chapter XII

THE LORD CONFIRMED THE WORD

 O many were so marvelously healed in Mr. Par-ham's meetings that some would speak of him as a "healer." He always corrected them by say-ing that he was not a "healer" and had no power or virtue in himself to heal any more than he could save. That God had called him to "Preach the Word," and as he went from city to city, telling what God could do, the Lord confirmed the Word with signs following. (Mark 16:20).

As Mr. Parham preached the living Christ, whose power had not changed, many heard the full gospel, and were made new creatures in Christ Jesus.

* * * * *

His next meeting was at Joplin, Mo., and Mrs. (Walken-shaw) Parham who lived there then, has given us the follow-ing report of the meeting held there.

"In the fall of 1904, Bro. C. F. Parham came to Joplin and held a tent meeting on 15th and Joplin St. From the very first meeting a great interest was manifest. Deep conviction came upon the people and many were saved, sanctified and healed. 'The power of God came down our souls to greet and glory crowned the mercy-seat.' Blind eyes were opened, the sick healed and 'God confirmed His Word with signs follow-ing.'

"Mrs. Belle Deorge was brought to the tent in a wheel chair having been unable to walk for years. After Brother Parham prayed for her, she was wonderfully healed.

"The revival continued in the tent for about four weeks, then the meeting was moved to the Roosevelt Flats, at 9th and Main St. Here the good work went on several weeks longer.

"Mrs. Rosana Trapp was the first one in Joplin to receive the baptism of the Holy Spirit with the evidence recorded in Acts 2:4. After that in quick succession many received and enjoyed that great blessing, God working with mighty signs and wonders and gifts of the Holy Spirit.

"Mr. Parham was taken very sick, his physical strength giving away under the stress of constant labors. Unable to eat for some time he lingered between life and death. His life would have been despaired of, had it not been for our trust in God, who answered the prayer of faith, and in love and mercy reached down and touched him by power divine, and restored him to health. God gave him a new lease on life, and he continued on in the service of God, working for lost humanity."

*   *   *   *   *

Though the battle had been hard and the work strenuous, a great victory had been won for God and souls, for during the year of 1904 many hundreds of people from Carthage, Mo. through southeastern Kansas to Miami, Okla., were now believers in the power of the faith once delivered to the saints.

We have found in our experience, and perhaps you have too, that if we expect to enjoy the blessings of God, we must endure the suffering and go through the testings. The devil contests every inch of ground gained for God and His Kingdom established in our hearts and will try to defeat us, in every possible way.

While the meeting at Joplin, Mo., was going on to victory, our oldest child, Claude, was taken very sick with what seemed to be a severe case of rheumatism. When any serious affliction attacked the family, the thought of the children always was that if their father would come home, all would be well. Claude was suffering intensely, and wanted me to send for his father. I did not want to do this for I knew that it would be hard for him to leave the meeting when so much was depending on him being there. I always tried not to burden him with family cares and troubles when he was in meetings if it was not necessary, as I did not want to hinder his work for God and souls.

So I sent for some friends who were near to come and pray for him. We prayed, but he got no relief. At last Claude cried out desperately, "It's no use, your prayers are not doing me any good. You will have to send for papa."

Though Joplin, Mo. is just about sixteen miles from Baxter Springs, we did not have the convenient automobiles in those days. It was then midnight, but when we got the word to his father, he came as soon as possible on the early morning train. As he prayed, God touched the suffering little body, he was healed and continued to go to school. It did not develop until sometime afterwards, that his limb which he had suffered so much with became a little shorter than the other.

The following year, (1905), while we were in Texas, a doctor who attended the meeting, inquired why our boy walked a little lame, and Mr. Parham told him all about his sickness. The doctor said we were mistaken in thinking that it was rheumatism, but that it was a very severe case of hip disease, which was very hard to treat successfully in a medical way. He recognized that the Lord had done a wonderful work in his body, and said he was glad we had put his case in the hands of the Great Physician, and that we should be very thankful that he was not an invalid, for life, and that he could run and play without pain as he did.

As has been stated, at the close of the Joplin meeting, Mr. Parham's health gave way and he went down even to the valley of the shadow of death, but God was with him, and restored him to many more years of life in His service.

He always gave God the glory for his health and strength, saying that he "was a poor, sickly wretch," when God raised him up and gave him more than natural strength, which enabled him to go, night and day in all kinds of weather. But it seems sometimes God withdraws His strength, that we may appreciate it more, and that we may continually realize the weakness of the flesh and our entire dependence on Him.

After the Lord touched Mr. Parham's body in Joplin, he returned to his home at Baxter Springs, to rest and regain his strength, although it was not till spring when he obeyed the call to go to Texas, that he was fully restored. But God supplied our needs through our kind friends at Baxter Springs, and Keelville. Many loads of coal and wood were hauled in from the country to keep us comfortable through that very severe winter. Then Chas. Wall called for "a wood chopping bee," and many willing hands responded to the call. The commandment to "love thy neighbor as thyself," was practiced as they cared for our needs as well as their own.

It was about this time that Mr. Parham's old friend, Tom Alley, who had lived in Jerusalem about ten years, again came to visit us. He especially loved the children, and he was a great favorite with them. He said that in Palestine, instead of calling children "little dears," as we do, they called them "little hogs." When he went to town, the children watched eagerly for his return, as he would often open the front door and empty a sack of candy over the floor, calling "hogs, hogs, hogs". Altho really it was not necessary to call, as the "little hogs," were right there waiting for the "hog feed" as he called it.

Mr. Alley gave lectures and showed pictures of the Holy Land. He also had fifteen costumes which he had brought with him from that country. Mr. Alley felt that he was getting too old to manage the showing of the costumes with his lectures, and wanted some money to go to the Old Soldiers Home in California, so Mr. Parham bought the costumes from him.

Mr. Parham had always been deeply interested in the Holy Land and they spent much time together talking about the land where our Savior lived, and he would say that when he did get to go "over there", he would know something about it.

He often gave lectures on the return of the Jews to Palestine, not only in the north, but also in the south, and had the workers wear the beautiful costumes. I will give a report from the paper of one of these meetings, which will give our readers an idea of many similiar meetings that he held, not only in Kansas and Missouri, but also in Texas.

THE ZIONIST RALLY

Over 2,000 Persons at Rev. Parham's Services Last Night. Gorgeous Costumes Worn.

"A crowded house that rivaled the audience at Governor Folk's meeting in the same hall was present at the Zionist rally last night. Over 2,000 persons were present and every available space was occupied at 7 p. m. Fifteen persons dressed in gorgeous Oriental costumes took their places on the stage, led by the minister, Chas. F. Parham, clad in the robes of a bishop. Though having a very busy day of it, he appeared fresh and ready for the night services.

"At 9:30 a. m. he conducted a funeral, at 11 a. m. and 3 p. m. preached at the hall and at 4 p. m. again talked to a crowded house at the Y. M. C. A.

"For one hour he held the audience in rapt attention while he plead the cause (so near his heart) of 'The Restoration of Religion's Birthplace to It's Rightful Heirs.' Then followed a separate description of each costume. This collection of costumes is the finest and largest private collection in America and they were all purchased in the Bible lands.

"A host of people have been clamoring today for a repetition next Sunday evening. The audience was one of Joplin's greatest religious gatherings, composed of Jew and Gentile, rich and poor."

THE LITTLE CHAPS' FAITH

"It's a comfort to me in life's battle,
When the conflict seems all going wrong,
When I seem to lose every ambition,
And the current of life grows too strong,
To think that the dusk ends the warfare,
That worry is done for the night,
And the little chaps there at the window
Believe their daddy's all right.

In the heat of the day and the hurry,
I'm prompted so often to pause,
While my mind strays away from the striving,
Away from the noise and applause,
The cheers may be meant for some other;
Perhaps I have lost in the fight,
But the little chaps wait in the window,
Believing their daddy's all right.

I can laugh at the downfalls and failure;
I can smile in the trials and pain;
I can feel that in spite of the errors
The struggle has not been in vain.
If fortune will only retain me,
That comfort and solace at night,
When the little chaps wait at the window
 Believing their daddy's all right."

Selected from Mr. Parham's Scrap Book.

Mr. Parham With His Son, Philip.

Chapter XIII

THE WORK BEGUN IN TEXAS

R. and Mrs. Walter Oyler, of Orchard, Texas, attended the meeting in Galena, Kansas, and both of
them received the baptism of the Holy Spirit.
They also attended his meeting held in Joplin, Mo.
in the fall of 1904, where they met Mrs. Hall, who
accompanied them back to Orchard, Texas, March 21, 1905.
Here they told the people of the "full gospel" which had
meant so much to them for both soul and body.

They prayed that the Lord would send Mr. Parham there
for a meeting, and God answered prayer. We know that
when God works, He deals with lives at both places. As Cor-
nelius and his house were ready for the gospel, God showed
Peter to go and preach to them. While God was preparing
the hearts of the people at Orchard to receive the Gospel, God
also laid it on Mr. Parham's heart, and definitely showed him
to go to the south-land.

He was still weak from his complete breakdown, but when
he arrived at Orchard kind friends welcomed him, and he was
taken to the home of H. H. Aylor, which became a real home
to him, and later to a host of workers. He was soon restored
to perfect health and strength and preached his first sermon
on Easter Sunday, 1905, at Orchard, the birthplace of the
Apostolic Faith Movement in Texas!

A glorious wave of salvation swept over Orchard, and whole
families were swept into the blessings of full salvation. Even
to the A. T. S. F. Railroad Section crew No. 13, every man got
saved that was not already saved. At an all-day meeting at
Mrs. Hall's home, nine received the baptism of the Holy
Spirit and many others received it at other times.

So many were healed, saved and baptized with the Holy Spirit, that there seemed to be scarcely one left to plead the cause of the evil one. The whole community had been transformed, restitution had been made, lives had been changed and led into the deeper things of God. The vicinity of Orchard was awakened out of their dead forms and were now alive with the mighty power of the Holy Spirit.

*   *   *   *   *

During the Orchard meeting, Mr. Parham wrote the following letter which was read in the Galena Mission, May 15, 1905.

To the dear ones at home:—

I came to Texas on an excursion of twenty-one days, and stopped at Orchard where the people all begged for meetings.

There were only five or six Christians here but in two weeks, there were only about that many sinners. In the whole section, from far and near, they come and are converted.

The second Sunday of the meeting, more than two-thirds of the audience took the sacrament at 11 a. m. Services at 3 p. m. followed by a grand baptizing at the lake. At night I ordained five to the ministry, closing one of the grandest day's services I ever conducted. On Tuesday and Wednesday, we had a time with the devil; a fearful bondage came over the meeting. On Thursday, fast day, we had a meeting and there was some confessing up. Sister Hall and I gave them a rousing talk on victory, and we were just coming up to a shout of victory when the postman came in and brought your letter from Galena. I opened it and found a letter of "Greetings to the new church of the Apostolic Faith in the Southland," and word that some in Galena were praying for us; enclosed were testimonies from Sisters Preston, Hinkley and Anderson.

When I read, I could not refrain from weeping for joy to be thus remembered in our battle in the South, and many in the audience praised God and wept.

Then came two or three exhortations that this Gospel might go to all the world and a young man fell on his face and prayed aloud for power to go and tell the story.

Oh, what shouting! Then seeking sinners came down through the audience, shouting victory for the witness of sins forgiven, until for over an hour we wept and shouted; strong men with hands uplifted gave glory to our God and high and low were melted together in the furnace of His love.

It was the grandest scene I have witnessed since the outpouring of the Holy Spirit in the Bible School in Topeka, Kansas. At the same hour a scene occured on the railroad among the section men. They were all men of good families and were all converted in the meeting except the Boss. He was a fine specimen of young manhood but proud and wicked and had made fun of our meetings, baptizing, etc. God convicted him of his sins and for two nights he wrestled at the altar with no results.

On Thursday, at the hour of our victory, he was pacing back and forth near the men. He sat down and with his face to the ground, he cried aloud to God for pardon. All the men came to him and on Section 13 of the Santa Fe Rail Road they spent over an hour praying the Boss through;— the best hour's work of their lives—and he came through one of the brightest converts in all our meetings. Glory to God for one set of section men who were really all converted.

They are bringing the sick twenty miles in wagons for healing and I am as well and strong as ever. Pray for us and may God bless you all is my prayer. Charles F. Parham.

*   *   *   *   *

About May 20, Mr. Parham returned to Baxter Springs, to fill some appointments he had planned and went rapidly from city to city, proclaiming the gospel, encouraging the believers by having "rally days" in different cities, and making arrangements to take a company of workers with him to Texas. I will give an extract from a report of the meeting at Melrose, Kansas, June 4, 1905.

"God's little ones in Melrose, Kansas, offer our notes of gladness to swell the anthem of praise to our God. The darkness of formality was so dense upon us, except among a few who were praying to God to break it's power that when the great wave of "refreshing from the presence of the Lord" struck us something more than a year ago through the preaching of the true gospel of the Kingdom by the Spirit of the Lord through Brother Chas. F. Parham, and later in the year by Sister Lillian Thistlethwaite, our people sat and listened in a sort of dead indifference, night after night for about three weeks. But then what a miracle the Spirit of God wrought among us! There was a mighty shaking of "dead bones." Sinners in large numbers were converted, luke-warm Christians awoke from their deadly stupor and were roused into a zeal for God, according to knowledge, and multitudes who had scarcely thought of Him before, suddenly found themselves hungry for God. Besides, there were many cases of healing, and people who had 'hooted' at these truths now opened their hearts to receive them.

"So, when on June 4, 1905, and a few days preceding, we held a grand rally meeting in the hall, as we reviewed the past year we gave heart-felt glory to God as we marked the wonderful contrast between that day and the beginning of the work among us. Men and women, who then were stolid as rocks, now gave free and joyous testimonies to their God for the blessings He had wrought in their individual hearts and in their homes. Several from Melrose, Kans., and Keelville, Kans., consecrated their lives to God, and were among Mr. Parham's company who went to Texas."

*　　*　　*　　*　　*

Mr. Parham also held a "rally" in Joplin, Mo., which we have a report of, given by Mrs. D. M. Preston, and printed in the paper at that time.

"The Lord has done great things for us; whereof we are glad. Bro. C. F. Parham's sermon Sunday night in Joplin was a brief outline of his work up to the present time, God having through him established these wonderful truths, founded on the Rock upon which Christ is building His church. Experimental salvation, true holiness of heart and life, healing, and the baptism of the Holy Spirit, with the Bible witness of speaking in tongues; this not only brings a crown of rejoicing to us who have received, but gives us power to witness for our Master even unto the ends of the earth. As John baptized the whole body of Jesus in the waters of the Jordan, so must His body, the Church, be baptized in The Living Water, 'He that believeth on me as, the Scripture hath said, out of him shall flow rivers of Living water,' but this spake He of the Spirit which they that believeth on Him should receive, for the Holy Ghost was not yet given.

"Through terrible persecutions, God has upheld His servant proving except the Lord build the house they labor in vain who build. For over two years truth seemed crushed to earth, and if it had not been the Lord was on our side, then the proud water had gone over our soul. The third year God set His seal upon the work, and from the watch night meeting in Galena, Kansas, Jan. 1, 1904, to that in Joplin, Mo., Jan. 1, 1905, the work has grown and been established in many places. A few months ago God called Bro. Parham to Texas, where hungry souls drank in these truths until almost every one within miles of Orchard had drank deep from the wells of salvation.

"Infidels fell under the power of God's love, miracles were wrought in healing, and they that sowed in tears now reaped in joy. He that goeth forth and weepeth, bearing precious seed, shall doubtless come again, with rejoicing, bringing his sheaves with him.

"We of the North now send greetings to the South, uniting our hearts in brotherly love, establishing the spirit of unity for which our brother was called and ordained of God. And we received him now as our teacher, our friend and brother, and praise God daily, that through the faithfulness of one man has been made known to the sons of men , His mighty acts, and the glorious majesty of His Kingdom and they shall speak of the kingdom and talk of the Power."

*   *   *   *   *

A company of consecrated men and women were now ready to accompany Mr. Parham to Texas and begin the fight for souls. A large tabernacle was erected in Galena, Kansas, where the fare-well meeting was held, July 2.

Here were gathered together the various missions of Kansas and Missouri, to bid God-speed to our loved ones, who were leaving us, called of God to so great a work. Amidst the waving of handkerchiefs and the heart-felt, "God be with you till we meet again," from a host of sympathizing friends and relations, Mr. Parham, with a company of fifteen faithful soldiers of the cross, returned once more to the south-land, having a final farewell, as they passed through Baxter Springs.

They arrived at Orchard, Texas, July 4, where an all-day meeting was planned with a big barbecue, but a heavy rain made it necessary for other arrangements to be made for the noon-day meal.

With a Christian love and fellowship, born of God, the Kansas and Missouri volunteers clasped hands with their Texas comrades and other workers joined the company. Mr. Parham, now with twenty-five workers, went on to Houston to begin the revival meeting, to lay seige to the city of Houston in the name of the Lord, July 10, 1905.

Bryan Hall had been secured for the meeting which cost fifty dollars a week, and a company of twenty-five were provided with board and lodging without any known source of income. Without soliciting and begging they trusted God to supply all their needs. Henry Aylor sold a mule and donated the money to help in the opening expenses of the meeting, and so they laughingly said, "they were riding into Houston on a mule." In many different ways from various places, the means was provided to carry this meeting on to a glorious victory.

They preached on the streets, visited from house to house, until a mighty revival swept the city and surrounding towns, such as had never been known before. Many scores were converted, sanctified and baptized with the Holy Spirit. Many were healed in answer to the prayer of faith, and others possessed with evil spirits were delivered.

*   *   *   *   *

Mrs. J. M. Dulaney, who was injured in a street car collision over two years before, was completely restored to health and strength, which stirred the city, as her condition was well known far and wide. I will give her experience as she wrote it for the paper.

"I am truly glad I am a living witness to God's great healing, saving and sanctifying power. I praise my Heavenly Father for His healing power. I received an electric shock in a street car collision on the 18th day of November, 1902, and was afflicted for two years, eight months and 18 days. I was completely paralyzed on my left side; could not raise my left hand to my head, and my left foot was turned under and toes clamped together under my foot. I had a knot on my back larger than a goose egg, caused from drawing in the spinal cord. I lost my mind for five months; did not know any of my family. I would have spasms until my head and heels would almost meet. They would have to pour chloroform down my spine. They used three hundred dollars worth of chloroform. Whenever the weather would be damp and cloudy, I would have those spells oftener. The doctors had given me up and said nothing more could be done for me; said I would have to sit in my invalid's chair until death, which was likely to come any moment, but praise God, it did not come.

"I had prayed to God to take me, or send someone to heal me, and that night God sent a vision. In that vision I saw Brother Parham. He was not then in this city, but came to this city some time in July, but I did not get to see him until the 4th of August, though it was a joyful meeting when I did meet him, for I knew God had answered my prayer and sent those dear workers and messengers from the Lord to pray that I might be healed and removed from my invalid's chair and bed of affliction. I had to sit in my invalid's chair from morning to night and had to be cared for the same as a baby.

"When I first saw Bro. Parham, he was preaching on the Market Square, on the 4th day of August. When I saw him I said to the lady who was with me, 'There is the man that I saw made me walk!' I had a high fever and headache, and he prayed for me and my fever and headache immediately left me, and the next evening, the 5th of August, they drove me down to the Market and 'Sister Effy' prayed for my foot and hand, and after she got through praying, we drove away. We had not gone but four blocks when my hand flew up and my foot turned straight.

"Next evening, the 6th, my husband took me to Bryan Hall, where Bro. Parham was holding meetings at that time. Four or five of the young workers carried me up in the hall where the service was going on. After the sermon was finished, they began praying for me. They had prayed for ten or fifteen minutes when a voice said, 'Arise and go, my child,' and I said to 'Sister Effy,' 'Some one says, I can get up,' and I said, 'Do you think I can?' and she says, 'Let's try.' She took my arm and I raised and praised God.

"I have been walking ever since that time, going every-where telling everybody of God's healing power, and the great power there is in the Apostolic Movement. I was rais-ed a Catholic, never had read a Bible until I met those dear messengers. They have taught me and put me on the right road and the right faith, and I do praise God for sanctification and the baptism of the Holy Ghost. And I praise God that He has turned my home from darkness to sunshine. Praise the holy name of Jesus, who healeth all my diseases."

* * * * *

The following was written for the paper by Mrs. Roth-rock: "I have had brought forcibly to my mind some vivid recollections of the time Bro. Parham introduced this great Apostolic Faith Movement in Texas, in a series of meetings in Bryan Hall in Houston, in 1905. The meetings continued for five consecutive weeks with unabated interest, and daily dem-onstrations of the same Apostolic power witnessed in Jerusa-lem in fulfillment of the promise of Christ, were witnessed there.

"Bro. Parham came to Houston with a band of about twen-ty-five workers, and from their arrival until their departure no collections were taken, no subscriptions solicited, and yet all their living expenses were met.

"There is always emitted to me, from the memory of those meetings a fragrance of divinity which inspires to holier living. The meetings from first to last were characterized with such freedom to follow the Holy Spirit, such a separation from the bondage born of creeds and churchanity, set rules and regula-tions, and yet all in such sweet harmony with the direct com-mand to 'let all things be done decently and in order,' that one's finest sense of propriety never received even a tremor. This commanded and received the utmost respect from the best and most highly intelligent people in the city.

"Those who came to see and denounce, remained to investigate, to wonder and admire. At the evening meetings the large auditorium was well filled, and after the preliminary praise service by the consecrated workers who graced the stage, (their faces fairly shining with the glory and power of the indwelling Christ) Bro. Parham gave the usual sermon of the evening, which both instructed and amused his audience and created in many of them an intense hunger to know for themselves something of the complete salvation he proclaimed.

"But the most intense interest of the audience was centered in the altar services which followed, where some were seeking pardon from sin, others were renouncing all for a sanctified life, and many were receiving the baptism of the Holy Ghost, attended by the gift of tongues as described in Acts 2.

"During the wonderful altar service, the audience, having been previously dismissed, moved quietly and informally about, hearing and witnessing the marvelous demonstrations of the power promised to believers. Sometimes as many as twenty various languages were spoken in one evening, not an unintelligent utterance of mere vocal sounds, but a clear language spoken with the intonations and accents only given by natives, who repeatedly gave testimony to that effect.

"It was my privilege to be frequently in concourse with some professors from the city schools and colleges, all of whom spoke some foreign language and one of them spoke five languages. He said that to him the most marvelous thing about the use of these languages was the original accent they (the workers) gave. They demonstrated that under instruction, it was impossible for an American to learn. They gave the REAL FOREIGN ACCENT SO PERFECTLY, that when he closed his eyes, it seemed to him as though he were listening to utterances from his native masters in the Old World.

"To me, this was very convincing, coming from those unbiased and competent judges. They oftimes interpreted for

me when languages they knew were spoken. Many foreigners
came to the meetings and were frequently spoken to in their
native tongue, with the original accent that could not be perfectly acquired. This, more than anything else, convinced
them that it was wrought by some power above the human.
Their hearts were always touched and they frequently went to
the altar for prayer, convinced that it was the real power of
God.

"But the singing! O, the heavenly singing in the various
languages, under divine inspiration, was something one could
never forget. One evening Sister Oyler arose and began to
sing in tongues. Three others immediately joined her, each
singing the same melody, the same words, and the four parts,
soprano, alto, tenor and bass were beautifully carried through,
and such music as that quartet rendered would do credit to an
angelic choir. The entire audience was instantly hushed, aw-
ed and enraptured. I have listened to a number of the finest
singers of the world, but that quartet, improvised and prepared by the Holy Ghost, not even knowing what language they
used, so far excelled them all comparison would be irreverent.

"Each night the audience would usually remain until the
janitor began to turn out the lights, five minutes of twelve
o'clock.

"Thus began the great Apostolic Movement in Texas; with
power and purity, it held it's sway, winning respect and turning mutitudes from sin to a life of purity and gospel power.
Marvelous demonstrations of healing were also witnessed,
which were very convincing to the people and proved the
completeness of the great salvation they proclaimed.

"God hasten the day when this great movement, separated
from fanaticism and falsity, which, through the unholy ambition of self-appointed shepherds over the flock, have accru-
ed to it, shall arise and shine forth in it's purity and power as
presented by it's founder, Bro. Chas. F. Parham."

Miss Rilda Cole, a Bible teacher who had been in Christian work for several years, was one of the company who with others, went with Mr. Parham from Keelville, Kansas, and she wrote this letter regarding the meeting.

Bryan Hall, Houston, Texas
August 1, 1905.

Dear Ones:—

There is in our midst this morning a great shout of victory of "Glory to God in the highest," from our hearts and lips and inmost beings which, in one great harmony, like a glorious anthem too deep and marvelous to find expression in human voice, delights the heart of God and causes joy among the angels. Each week is better and still better, but the events of the last few days simply beggar description, though I will try to lift at least a little corner of the curtain, so you may have enough of a glimpse to unite your voices with us in thanksgiving to our God for answer to your prayers and ours.

Sunday—July 30, ended a three days fast for victory and power. All day we had great liberty in song and in the sermon. In the evening we had one big street meeting, and a big crowd to hear at the court-house.

At night at the hall we had the largest crowd that has yet assembled and so many Christians of the city gave free testimony to the great blessings which God had brought to them through our coming to the city and how henceforth they are one with us in our work. We had a glorious sermon by Bro. Parham and he showed the people how God will hold them responsible if they do not join in this great crusade with our Captain, Jesus Christ, against sin and satan.

This was followed by the Lord's Supper and then a great altar service at which one sweet young lady of the city received the baptism of the Holy Spirit.

But Monday was one great day. Brother Parham said it was the greatest Monday meeting he had ever witnessed. During the morning service there were three converted, one or two sanctified and one received the baptism of the Holy Spirit.

At our street meetings on the different corners, we had glorious meetings and large crowds of attentive hearers. In front of the large saloon where our crowd was, you have no idea how hungry the sin-stained, dissipated faces looked.

Then the crown of the whole day came at the night service, when a man of about fifty arose and gave a soul-stirring testimony as to how God had that morning powerfully converted him.

Heedless of his mother's prayers, he went on in sin until about two weeks ago, when without apparent reason he lost a fine position in another town, so came back to Houston. He heard us talking on the street, then was led to come to the hall, and realized God had brought him back to Houston to be in this meeting.

For five days and nights he had no rest but just as the sun rose Monday morning, God spoke peace to his soul. He praised God for about half an hour, then a fine appearing woman, wife of the Secretary of the Governor of Texas, arose and sang a sweet hymn.

Brother Parham asked that everyone who would like to offer the right hand of fellowship to the newly converted brother would wave their handkerchiefs and fans while we sang, "I am so glad that Jesus loves me".

O, the happy faces was a sight to gladden any Christian's heart! Then for a final climax, Auntie—the colored cook— came rushing down the dining hall stairs saying, "I just can't stand it any longer — Praise the Lord" While she grasped his hand in a hearty hand-shake.

As I sat drinking in the joy, I remembered at what cost of time, strength and money each of the sixteen northern workers had stood; then there was added to it the Orchard reinforcements, then remembered the fatigue of the actual Houston seige and the great responsibility that had rested on Brother Parham; then the cost to the homes we had left and your continual prayers for us and the work here. Now with a great thanksgiving in my heart, I realized that this man's salvation was worth infinitely more than it all.

One colored woman who came here a cripple left her crutches and walked off. Today as I looked over the hall and saw this woman and the other one I told you of before, walking as straight and firm as the rest of us, my heart was glad with an unutterable joy.

There are so many things I long to tell you of homes and hearts made glad and whole; truly only eternity can tell what this invasion into Texas in the name of the Lord is worth.

Praise ye the Lord; be Thou exalted, O God, above the heavens; Let Thy glory be above all the earth. Rilda Cole.

* * * * *

I will quote a few extracts from newspaper reports:

THE APOSTOLIC FAITH
Representatives of the New Religion in Town—July 10 at Bryan Hall — Will Begin Business

"Rev. Chas F . Parham and about 25 co-laborers are in the city and commencing Monday night, July 10, will begin a series of religious services at Bryan Hall. Mr. Parham is from Melrose, Kansas, where he publishes a religious paper called "The Apostolic Faith."

"A gentleman from Lawrence, Kansas, states that Rev. Parham has been a preacher living near that city for a number of years and has had remarkable success as a revivalist. He left the ministry five years ago and since then has been doing evangelical work exclusively.

"One of the interesting things about Mr. Parham's meetings is that no collections are taken up and no one need stay away for fear of being asked to donate. Though not calling himself a divine healer, he claims that Christ is the only divine healer and no one can be cured of mental or bodily infirmities without faith in the real Christ. There is no doubt his meetings will attract a great deal of attention and call out large congregations. The News will watch and notice their progress with much interest."

APOSTOLIC FAITH MEETINGS.

"Charles F. Parham, projector of the Apostolic Faith Movement, is holding forth daily at Bryan Hall. The meetings are not denominational, says Mr. Parham, but are intended for the benefit of members of all churches who desire to get more power with God.

"It is explained that no effort has been made to get a church in which to hold the meetings for the reason that persons of every faith and order are invited and the selection of a church of any denomination might keep people of other denominations away."

APOSTOLIC CLAIMS

The Houston Chronicle, August 13, 1905. Houstonians Witness the Performance of Miracles. Mysticism Surrounds Work of Apostles of Faith — Speak in All Tongues Known to Man.

"Among the languages spoken by the professors of the Apostolic Faith the government intrepreters have made investigation and authoritively report that all known languages have been demonstrated, including 20 Chinese dialects.

"And so is exemplified the doctrine of the band of followers of the Apostolic Faith, who aver that with the gaining of the faith, as in the days of old, it was given to the apostles not only according to the teachings of a given school, but to speak all the languages of the world as spoken by the most lowly in their corruption of the vernacular or as used by the most classic scholar in the retreat of his library. He may command the classics of a Homer or talk the jargon of the lowest savage of the African jungle.

"But this power of language comes only when in the service of the Master. A sermon to move the multitudes may be delivered from the pulpit, but the merest platitude may not be interchanged upon a subject frivolous or personal. The disciples may preach the gospel to every living creature, but he speaks the words put into his mouth and knows not what he says. So when asked what they said in their prayers they announced that they did not know nor could tell what language they spoke."

THE LEADER OF THE FAITH

"Charles F. Parham and a brigade of some twenty-five followers, young men and women whom he styles 'student workers,' came to Houston a month ago from Kansas. Since that time they have held meetings at Bryan Hall, have preached their peculiar gospel, that of reclaiming Zion to the Jews, and the leader has received the lame and halt and the afflicted, and stories of marvelous cures have gone abroad.

"The brigade has wandered far and it's members have preached as they have gone. Dr. Parham, himself, once pastor of an orthodox church near Lawrence, Kansas, has preached in languages of the native wherever he has gone and brought about marvelous results.

"He says he knows not the language he speaks while he is addressing his audience, but he is as if he were not and knew not, being merely an instrument in other hands, and his body and vocal organs working under the dictation of an inspiration. Often, he states, he is inspired to speak in a language he knows not, and often have sayings of wisdom been translated back to him by foreigners. His converts are blessed with the gift of language in various degrees. With some the power is absolute and without limit, while with others it is barely perceptible."

AGE OF MIRACLES

"And yet more marvelous than the story of many languages are the rumors that are being shed abroad of the marvelous healings that are being performed at the instance of Dr. Parham.

(Here follows an account of several healings, among them Mrs. Dulany's, which I have already given.)

"The members of the faith declare the "age of miracles" never passed away, but that the power was lost through waning faith. There are many who profess to having been present when these 'works of faith were wrought'. One reputable resident of Houston who claims to have seen a woman restored to health, declares it to have been a fact but does not pretend to solve the mystery."

SCENE AT THE ALTAR

"The scene about the altar of the healer at the close of the nightly service is one of pathetic interest. The weak in body but strong in faith surround 'the healer' and with his hands on their forehead are blessed and supposedly rejuvenated in the matter of health. The blessings are received in abject faith, and the reports of marvelous healings increase as the time passes.

"In brief, the members of the Apostolic Faith hold that, as the power of the languages was given to the disciples of old, so that power is given to the devout followers today and as miracles of healing were performed in days of old, so are they performed today, and the modern apostles stand ready to prove their allegations."

＊　＊　＊　＊　＊

Mr. Parham being forced to return to Kansas to fill other engagements, the meeting in Houston was closed, although still in the height of victory and power. Some of the workers accompanied him while the rest remained in different parts of Texas to continue the work.

The town of Brunner had been one continuous flame of re-vival power. Meetings were also held in Richmond, Katy, Alvin, Angelton, Needleville, Crosby and many other places and the power of God was present to save, sanctify, heal and baptize with the Holy Spirit.

"THE INVITATIONS THREE"

"I am a God of Reasons—
The Father speaks with me—
Come, let us talk to-gether,
Tho sins like scarlet be,
White as snow, I'll wash them.
Tho they be crimson red.
Reason with Me, Child of Mine,
With Me. The great God Head.

Not only from the Father
Do I hear the still small voice;
In accents mild, my Jesus too
Says, "Child, make Me thy choice."
Come unto Me, ye weary.
And be ye yoked with Me,
I bore the cross, I paid the price.
Remember Calvary!

The Spirit and the Bride say, "Come"
Let who-so-ever will!
And him that is athirst—
"Come," freely drink his fill!
The "Invitations Three" I claim,
From, Father, Spirit, Son.
I'll reason, drink, I'll bear the Cross
For these, the Three in One."
                    —Ernest Hilliard.

Chapter XIV

BACK TO THE "SUNFLOWER STATE"

E were now living at Melrose, Kansas, but the Camp meeting was to be held at Baxter Springs, Kansas. At that time the old soldiers had a reunion every year at Baxter Springs, and a beautiful shady camp ground was provided for the soldiers and their families and friends to camp, and seemingly every kind of amusement was furnished from different sources for their pleasure and entertainment.

It was in the valley which joined the "Reunion Grounds" that Mr. Parham had secured grounds to hold the Camp-meeting during the time of this celebration, trusting that we might reach some who had come for pleasure, with the gospel of salvation.

August 28th, the Apostolic Faith Camp was set up in the valley of "Camp Logan", and the managers of the grounds did everything in their power to make the meeting a success. Notwithstanding the noise, meetings were held from six o'clock in the morning, until about twelve o'clock at night, and the songs of praise could be easily heard by those camped on the grounds on the hill. Many came down from the hill-top with tears in their eyes, saying, "I heard the singing and I could not stay away."

They had a "Shoot-the-Shoot" down the hill, and sometimes as the passengers "shot" down into our grounds they would be attracted by our meeting and remain for the service.

The workers were also busy on the hill-top, giving out papers, telling the old gospel story of full salvation and praying for the sick. A sister here could be seen kneeling by the side of some unfortunate woman, trying to point her to "the Lamb of God who taketh away the sins of the world," while over yonder two of the men talked to a gambler, whose face showed the same hunger for the same Jesus. They cast "bread upon the waters," sowed seed and left the result with God.

Friday was a great day in Camp from half past eight in the morning until after the noon hour, with only a few minutes intermission, about four hundred people were held in the tent in praise and worship and listening to the Word of God, while the Indian barbecue was in full blast about one hundred yards away from the tabernacle. The Governor of Kansas, who was visiting the Old Soldiers Encampment, highly complimented Mr. Parham on his ability to hold such a large audience while there was so much excitement and attraction so near by, but Mr. Parham gave all the honor to the power of the Holy Spirit. It was a good meeting, for during the week many were saved, sanctified and baptized with the Holy Spirit.

A number were baptized in Spring River on Sunday, and Monday morning there were still others to be baptized. Bro. Hilliard from Galena, had received the baptism of the Holy Spirit during the meeting and as Mr. Parham lead him out into the water the Spirit so rested upon him that when asked his given name, he could only answer in a foreign tongue. His wife, who was standing on the bank, had to tell his name. It was a time long to be remembered by those present for a holy joy rested on the service. The Camp was then broken up and we went to Columbus, Kansas, for our next meeting.

September 6th, we pitched our tents on Pennsylvania, Ave., three blocks east of the square and from the very beginning of the meeting great interest was manifest in the preaching. Never before had such deep interest been aroused in so short a time, but as Mr. Parham preached fearlessly against sin and ungodliness the opposing forces were also aroused and he was advised to leave town, as a mob was threatening to cow-hide him. This, however, was not carried out, neither did he leave town, but the following night during the 8 o'clock service the

mob came back and mingling among the crowd on the out-
skirts of the big tent occasioned some little disturbance.

After the altar call, while Mr. Parham and some of the
workers were praying for the sick, they proceeded to cut several of the ropes. They did not see the ropes which were tied
up in the trees, which I believe was what saved the tent from
falling down. Mr. Parham calmly counseled non-resistance,
saying that the Lord would take care of His own, which He
did. Finding they could not provoke a combat or even a combative spirit, they finally left in disgust.

"God moves in a mysterious way, His wonders to perform."
For it seemed no better way could have been taken to arouse
public interest and call attention to the message of the gospel.
"What shall we then say to these things? If God be for us,
who can be against us?" (Romans 8:31). We truly knew
that God was with us, as He manifested His presence and
power in our midst. Many were saved, sanctified, healed and
baptized with the Holy Spirit.

One young lady of the city received the baptism of the
Holy Spirit Sunday afternoon, about five o'clock and came to
the street meeting that evening and under the inspiration of
the Holy Spirit, delivered a message in the unknown tongue.
A real Pentecostal shower followed later where several received the baptism of the Holy Spirit, while men and women,
with tear-stained faces praised God for His wonderful manifestations of power. Interest was aroused for miles around
and large numbers came from the surrounding country.

Sunday afternoon hundreds partook of the Lord's supper
and it was estimated that three thousand witnessed the bap-
tising that followed. At night the crowd was so large that two
workers went out on the street and held an over-flow meeting.

Mr. Parham had announced that the meeting would continue
until October 1. He had arranged for the use of the grounds,
until that date, but the interest manifested was so great that it

was impossible to close the meeting then. A committee was appointed to ask for the use of the grounds for one more week, which was granted. So the meeting continued for another week, and closed in victory Sunday night with a large crowd and the altar full of earnest seekers.

Thus ended Mr. Parham's work in Columbus except for the farewell meeting, which was called for the following Sunday, October 15th. During this week, he with some of the workers visited the Missions at Galena, Baxter Springs, and Melrose, Kansas, and Joplin, Mo.

During the progress of the meeting a call for help had come from Texas one Saturday, and without enough funds on hand to pay a day-rate telegram, Mr. Parham waited until after 6 o'clock and sent the workers in Texas a night message to "hold the fort" that help would come to them the following Tuesday. By the appointed time, the Lord supplied the means for their car fare, and my sister Lillian Thistlethwaite and Sarah Bradbury went to help with the work in Texas.

On Monday, October 9th, Mr. Parham again asked the workers to pray for the sum of five-hundred dollars to be furnished that the band of twenty workers might leave for the south by the 15th of Oct., and God supplied according to His riches in glory. The Lord had provided and made it possible for the children and me also to accompany Mr. Parham and the workers to Texas.

Great crowds attended the farewell meetings held Sunday and Monday, Oct. 15 and 16. As Mr. Parham and the company of about twenty workers gathered on the platform to say good-bye, souls continued to come to the altar, under deep conviction, seeking God in the pardon of their sins, and were still praying as we left for the depot. We bid good-bye to a host of friends and left for the south about 1 A. M. with the assurance in our hearts that the prayers of our loved ones would go with us.

Wednesday morning, about 8:30 o'clock, we arrived at Orchard, Texas, and were warmly welcomed by God's children. We remained here till October 21, holding services day and night, and showers of blessings refreshed hungry souls.

Saturday 6:30 A. M., we left Orchard en route for Houston, Texas. We had to lay over at Alvin, Texas, for about five hours, and two street meetings were held, one in the morning and one after lunch. The people were so pleased that as we were getting ready to leave, several citizens came to Mr. Parham and requested him to return and hold some meetings there.

At about 4 o'clock we arrived at Houston and were met at the depot by several of the first-band workers, who had accompanied Mr. Parham to the south.

That night, while a street-meeting was being held in the slums, a crazy man broke into the midst of the band, and proclaimed himself Jesus Christ, offering to forgive all the sins of any one who would touch him. Mr. Parham quietly lead him out, explaining to the audience that he did not belong to our band.

Sunday all day services were held in Bryan Hall, and a large crowd of people engaged in worship and praise to God.

The workers loved to sing the following song. With their hearts filled with joy and love, it rang forth with real consecration and devotion to the service of the Master.

BATTLE HYMN

I am going to live for Jesus,
No more I'm going to wander,
My heart cries out for Jesus,
I will not live thus longer.
My soul is filled with sadness,
I long for holy gladness,
My heart cries out for Jesus
And I must go.

CHORUS:
I'm going forth with Jesus,
I'm going forth with Jesus,
I'm going where the joy of service flows;
For I hear my Savior calling,
"Go save a lost world falling,"
My heart is one with Jesus,
    And I must go.

With a little work for Jesus
    I tried to live a Christian,
But all in vain, 'twill never do,
    For a Christian's life's a mission;
And as I'm growing older,
I prove a faithless soldier,
Unless I live for Jesus,
    And onward go.

Thus mounting up on eagle's wing
    Above all worldly pleasure,
The Holy Ghost anoints my eyes
    To see eternal treasure.
Henceforth the world shall see us,
    In partnership with Jesus,
Gathering precious jewels
    As on we go.

And when life's work is over,
    The jewels all been gathered,
I'll place the diamonds in His crown,
    To sparkle there forever,
And on the streets of glory
    We will tell redemption's story,
Of how our Savior blessed us,
    When down below.

                    —Mrs. J. W. Hutchins.

Chapter XV

A BIBLE SCHOOL AT HOUSTON, TEXAS

N October 1905, a meeting was held in Galveston, Texas. As they held meetings on the streets, men came and listened in amazement to the wonderful truths of the gospel of the kingdom and saw the signs follow. One night, Bessie Tuthill prayed in an African dialect, and a man in the congregation told what she was saying and was so convinced of the baptism of the Holy Ghost, that two nights later he came to the altar and was reclaimed. A German sailor boy came to one of the street meetings, and heard the gospel preached, then came to the hall and was converted. His life was so changed that the rest of the sailors noticed it, and were astounded not to hear him swear when things went wrong. He sailed for Germany and took the full gospel with him, also one of Mr. Parham's books, "A voice crying in the Wilderness."

At another street meeting, a young lady of Galveston spoke in several languages, and interpreted it. While she was talking a man came up and asked one of the men where the girl came from. The man asked "Why?" And he said, "she was speaking in the Hindoo language." Then the man whom he addressed, told him that was his daughter, for it happened to be her father.

* * * * *

I have copied some reports from papers, printed during the meeting.

"All available space in the building was taken up last night by the crowds that assembled to hear Charles F. Parham, the leader and founder of the Apostolic Faith Movement.

"Beside those that filled every seat in the hall, quite a number of people congregated on the side-walk about the doors, eager to hear what the founder of the new faith might have to say.

"From newspaper reports and from the mouths of the workers themselves, it is believed that by the virtue of 'the faith once delivered to the saints' great miracles in healing the lame and sick are enacted. There are wonderful manifestations of the Spirit in the bestowal of languages; a gift to the faithful which enables them to pray and preach in all known tongues.

"As stated by themselves, the Apostolic Faith workers compose a religious band whose creed is the teachings of the Savior, Jesus Christ, in all their benign simplicity, and whose tenets are those of the Bible. In their worship they are unhampered by ritualistic dogma and give heed to no sectarian dictum. The basic principles of their teachings is faith in the Bible and the teachings of the Master. All denominations are privileged to worship with and become a part of them and assist in making divine worship as simple and pure as the life and sayings of our Savior.

"As stated by Mr. Parham in the introductory to his lecture last night, the Apostolic Faith Movement has been uplifted by God for the purpose of restoring primitive Christianity and the work has been up-held by mighty deeds and wonderful manifestations.

"The work in Galveston is being done by Mr. Parham and about twenty-four 'student workers.' A feature that distinguishes the Apostolic Faith workers from other religious bodies, is that a collection is never made, or money solicited for any purpose. The defrayment of the expenses is entirely dependent on voluntary contributions.

"Last night Mr. Parham delivered a lecture entitled, 'The Restoration of Palestine to the Jews.' He announced that the subject of the restoration of Palestine to the Jews is one that was very dear to his heart and has been of no little concern to him.

"In delivering the lecture, he wore a white linen robe, while arranged on the platform about him were fourteen of his 'student workers' dressed in costumes purchased in the Holy Land.

"'These costumes,' Mr. Parham said, 'are the costumes worn in the Holy Land today as they were worn in Biblical times for the fashion never changes.'

"In describing each costume, he told quite an interesting bit concerning the habits of the people and the customs of the country of which the costumes were representative. The costumes worn by the workers last night were as follows: The 'roustabout' or menial; Arab Sheik, village caste, high caste lady (white costumes), high caste lady (purple and gold costumes); two styles of beautiful Jewish shawls; Jerusalem dude, official class, garment of Ruth, Greek Catholic robe, girl of Bethlehem and the Turk."

THE APOSTOLIC FAITH
Workers of This Sect Attracting Attention in the City— Believe in Faith Healing

"Considerable interest has been created by the appearance on the streets the last few days of a small band of workers of the Apostolic Faith. The Apostolic Successionists claim to be of no church and no creed; but to have for their sole purpose the 'restoration of the faith once delivered to the saints.' They teach experimental salvation, healing by faith, lives of holiness, and the baptism of the Holy Ghost. Considerable stress is laid on this last tenet, it being held that as the praying believer receives the gift of the Holy Ghost he is given unusual powers of speech, just as the apostles did in the time of Christ.

"One of the principle passages of the Bible quoted by those who hold to this belief is the injunction as set forth in Mark 16:15-18; 'Go ye into all the world and preach the Gospel to every creature. He that believeth and is baptized shall be saved, but he that believeth not shall be damned. And these signs shall follow them that believe: In my name shall they cast out devils; they shall speak with new tongues; they shall take up serpents, and if they drink any deadly thing it shall not hurt them; they shall lay hands on the sick and they shall recover."—Galveston News.

* * * * *

We have found in our Christian experience that all new territory possessed in the land of Canaan, is contested by the enemy of our souls and every promise which we claim as ours from the Word of God will be tested to see whether we will stand upon it until it becomes a reality in our lives. Perhaps this was why after quoting the Scripture—"if you drink any deadly thing it will not hurt you" (which the public press made note of) that we must go through some testings along that line.

Several of the workers were taken very sick. We felt sure they had been poisoned in some way. In answer to prayer they were all healed and delivered from pain and suffering.

At another time, Mr. Parham took a drink of water from a glass back of the pulpit, as he had been in the habit of doing after preaching. He had only taken a swallow when he was struck with an awful pain. He began to pray, saying, "Oh Lord, Thou hast said"— and the pain instantly left him. The glass with the water that remained was taken to a chemist who said that there was enough poison in it to kill a dozen men. If we wilfully take up serpents and knowingly drink poison, I believe we are tempting God and will have to suffer the consequences for our presumptious sin. But if we accidently or ignorantly do these things (enemies or unbelievers putting the promises to the test for us) we can with confidence claim these promises as ours and find deliverance in Jesus' name. This was only one of the ways the enemy tried to take Mr. Parham's life but he always said that God was protecting him and that nothing could kill him until his work was done.

Under the leading of the Holy Spirit, Mr. Parham decided to go to Houston, Texas, for our headquarters and conduct a Bible School. Scores of persons, married and single, were consecrating their lives to God, and volunteering for His service without money and without price to preach this gospel, but. felt the need of Bible teaching. So Mr. Parham consented to go to Houston to spend the winter, not only to engage in training students but to firmly establish this great growing work in Texas. In a few days $100.00 was given for the rent of a large residence, completely furnished, and we secured the building in December 1905. The following announcement was made in the daily paper.

Apostolic Faith Leader Will Spend the Winter Here.

"A reception will be tendered Mr. and Mrs. Chas. F. Parham at their home, 503 Rusk, tonight. Mr. Parham conducted a revival at Bryan Hall last summer and has decided to make Houston the headquarters for the Apostolic work in Texas and will personally superintend the work for a time until it can be left in other hands. During the winter and spring months a Bible Training School will be located here under his instruction."—Houston Chronicle.

*   *   *   *   *

Mr. Parham wrote the following article regarding the school in the December number of "The Apostolic Faith".

"In looking upon nature, we behold the wisdom and power of God revealed through the seed time and the harvest. All things come in order. 'First the blade, then the ear, then the full corn in the ear.' Christ Himself used this to illustrate a spiritual truth.

"So we find God has divine order in the spiritual world. There is the seed time and the harvest. But to produce life and proper development certain conditions are necessary. Here is where we have failed in Christian growth, in not working in harmony with God's laws, for human effort is fruitless, and it is the Holy Spirit who was given to be the leader and guide into all truth.

"So in our work for God, we have sought each new step taken to know what is the mind of the Spirit, that His cause might be advanced and prosper.

"In the southern part of Texas the cry had come from many consecrated hearts, for a more perfect knowledge of the Word of God. We are told to be 'workmen that needeth not to be ashamed, rightly dividing the Word of truth.' (2 Tim. 2:15.)

"Realizing the time to act is when the need confronts us, a Bible School will be opened at the beginning of the new year in Houston, Texas. Here a thorough finishing course of successful evangelistic work will be given.

"Not only are the students expected to receive a knowledge of the written Word, but a practical realization of it in their lives. It is not enough to admire the perfect life of Christ and the disciples, but the command is 'to walk, even as He walked.' (I John 2:6) As He gave His life for us, so ought we to give our lives for the brethern.

"Many are coming to attend the school from different parts of the country. The sick are also invited to come that they may learn God's way of healing. Owing to limited accommodations it is requested that all those desiring to attend, either students or invalids, will send in their names several days prior to their arrival, that proper arrangements may be made. No tuition is charged, and the students who can not be accommodated in the school may find rooms for light-housekeeping and board themselves."

*   *   *   *   *

This school was supported, as was the rest of the work of the movement, by free-will offerings. It was understood that military rule was exacted of the school, and each one saw the necessity of working together in harmony.

Those who came to the school, earnestly seeking to know more of God, were greatly helped and went out from the school better prepared to preach and teach the Word of God.

This was not a "Theological Seminary" but a place where the great essential truths of God were taught in the most practical manner to reach the sinner, the careless Christian, the backslider and all in need of the gospel message.

From this school went out many flaming evangelists who held meetings far and near and God blessed them in a wonderful way. Some of them are still standing true to the cause and preaching the gospel.

One colored man, W. J. Seymour, became a regular attendant each day for the Bible lessons. In Texas, you know, the colored people are not allowed to mix with the white people as they do in some of the other states; but he was so humble and so deeply interested in the study of the Word that Mr. Parham could not refuse him. So he was given a place in the class and eagerly drank in the truths which were so new to him and food for his hungry soul.

While the students were studying the Bible, they also had certain times to hold street meetings, fill appointments where there were calls for meetings, visit the sick and other practical Christian work.

Though the expenses of the school were very heavy, God laid it on the hearts of different ones, far and near, in a marvelous way to supply our needs. For an example J. Ed. Cabaniss of Katy, Texas, will tell you how he was lead to the school to help us in a time of need.

* * * * *

"While Brother Parham was teaching a Bible School in Houston, I was living at Katy, Texas, and while not at that time saved, (having church membership only), I had heard Brother Parham preach and had fallen in love with 'the Way,' and a great desire came into my heart to do something for the

Lord myself. At that time I was secretary of the Katy Rice Milling Association and was in charge of the "Clean Rice Department", and the disposition of the clean product. Clean rice at that time was hard to dispose of, there being a huge crop grown that year, and the mills all over the rice belt were full of it, and no demand. So it was decided by the secretary of the Rice Millers Association to call all the 'Clean Rice men' to Houston on Monday for a consultation, to devise ways and means of getting rid of the stores of clean rice at a price that would prove profitable.

"I had arranged with the treasurer of the mill to go to Houston in my place and meet with the other members, on the Monday night in question, and so gave the subject no further thought.

"Monday morning at about 4 o'clock, I waked up and was told 'to go to Houston' by a voice almost, if not perfectly audible. I got up and told my wife that I had to go to Houston this morning. She replied, 'No, you remember, Mr. Weller is going to attend the meeting in your place.' This satisfied me, and I laid down again to rest until morning light. Again the voice said, 'You get up and go to Houston, and in a HURRY.' Immediately I obeyed the command, caught the early train arriving in Houston before good day.

"After getting my breakfast, I tried to think why I had come on the early train, and not waited until a train several hours later, as the meeting was not to be called until that evening at the Rice Hotel at 8 o'clock. While pondering over this, something seemed to say, 'Why not visit Brother Parham and his Bible School?' 'Sure,' I said, 'that is what I will do,' as I had never visited such a place and one supported by free will offerings. Then something seemed to say, 'what do you want to go there for, your experience won't do them any good.' 'No,' said I, 'but I want to go anyway,' then the thought came, 'and you have no money to give him.' No, that's right, but anyway, I want to go, and go I did.

"As I came to the gate of the yard, Brother Parham was sitting on the front porch, and as he rose to meet me, he said, 'Come in, Brother Cabaniss, I was looking for you.' 'Well,' I said, 'I did not know I was coming myself, how did you know I was coming, and what can I do for you?' 'Oh nothing,' he said, 'go in and listen to Brother Benson, as he is talking to the students.' I went into the lecture room, but I can't remember a word that Brother Benson was saying to the students, for I was wondering in my mind HOW DID BROTHER PARHAM KNOW I WAS COMING TO HOUSTON?

"After the meeting was over, I said to Brother Parham, 'There must be something I can do for you.' To this he replied, 'Yes, you can loan us $50.00 if you will.' 'Well,' I said, 'let's go down town, and we will see if I have this much money in the bank;' for wife kept the bank account, and I did not know for sure the money was in the bank. When I made out the check and got the money out of the bank, and handed it to him, something seemed to say 'Now you've played the wild, how do you know this man who has nothing behind him, will ever pay this money back, and when the money is due the state of Texas for the land you have homesteaded, what will you tell your wife?'

"No doubt Brother Parham saw my face, for at this time he said, 'Now, Brother Cabaniss, I will tell you why I said I knew you were coming down this morning. Last night, before we retired, we prayed and told the Father that we needed $50.00 as our rent was due, and some of the students wanted to go and hold a meeting, and we didn't have any money, and this was His part of the business to furnish the means, and if He could not send us the money, send someone to us who would loan the money to us, for before the end of the month, Brother Aylor of Missouri would send us $100.00, and you, Brother Cabaniss, stood before me as plain as I see you now. This morning I awoke about 4 o'clock and prayed about the matter again, and again you stood before me, so I knew you were coming down.'

"Before the month was out, and in plenty of time to meet my obligations to the state, Brother Parham handed the amount back to me. Such a joy seemingly, as I had never had before, came into my heart, for I felt that God had indeed used me, and had answered the longing of my heart, to do something for Him."

*   *   *   *   *

As the Bible School was to be held but a short time, the students did not have time for any study but the Bible. They took the subjects of conviction, repentance, conversion, consecration, sanctification, healing, the Holy Spirit in His different operations, prophecies, the book of Revelation and other practical subjects coming in for careful study in their due order. Everything that could be found in the Bible by the school on these subjects, was searched out, written down and discussed, and Mr. Parham gave a lesson each day in connection with these studies

The workers took it in turns to do the cooking, which was usually done cheerfully as unto the Lord. Ed. Cabaniss now kept us supplied with rice, which became our usual bill of fare for breakfast. You know it is hard for an inexperienced cook to prepare a large quantity of rice without letting it scorch, and occasionally we shall have to admit, the results were pitiful! I remember especially, one morning our young cook was greatly distressed over her work, and was afraid the rice could not be eaten. I announced that the first one who complained about the cooking should be appointed cook for the next day. Then followed a good-natured laugh and it is needless to say the rice was eaten, there were no complaints made and our cook was comforted. The majority of the workers, at least, felt that they were there as soldiers of the cross and put the spiritual things before the temporal comforts.

One day the "cooking crew" announced that dinner was ready "except the bread" and there was no money in the treasury. The meal was begun with about one-third enough bread, but when the last company of workers returned from the "shop meeting" they brought a "big round dollar" and we returned thanks and sent out and bought the bread.

This was only one of a multitude of incidents that made our pathway glow from day to day and we thanked our heavenly Father for His love and care. We did not pray so very much about the temporal needs but simply trusted Him to supply, for we remembered Jesus said, "your Father knoweth what things ye have need of before ye ask Him." (Matt. 6:8)

Perhaps there was a touch of envy in the remark made by a Salvation Army officer when he said, "Oh, any preacher could come to Houston with as strong a company of workers as Mr. Parham did and have a good meeting. If I had as many fire-baptized soldiers in my corps, I could shake Houston for God."

•But Mr. Parham had the workers, and it was because he had not shunned to declare all the counsel of God and had given them such a full gospel which had sank down into their hearts and caused them to make the consecration and yield their lives for the service of God that make them soul-winners for the Master.

As it drew near time for the school to close, companies of workers were making arrangements to go out into the evangelistic field. Mr. Parham did not dictate to the workers where they should go, but asked each one to pray that they might be led by the Holy Spirit.

W. J. Seymour, the colored man who had attended the school so faithfully, had received all the truths and teachings that we had held from the beginning, though he had not yet received the baptism of the Holy Spirit. It was expected that he would take this teaching to his own people in Texas as he had formerly had charge of a small church in the suburbs, and we were rather surprised when he said he felt led to go to California. So early in the spring of 1906, Mr. Parham made up his car fare and we bid him God's-speed to the western coast.

The workers all went forth to different places, or fields of labor. Thus our wonderful company of workers was broken up, never to be assembled together in this life. They went forth, to give to others the teachings and tell the experience they had received, sowing precious seeds. According to the talent God had given them, and their faithfulness in keeping their consecration to God, they have brought forth fruit, some an hundred fold, some sixty-fold, some thirty-fold. Matt. 13:8. Many are still in His service to-day in different ways and places and I am sure that all who entered the Bible School to unselfishly serve God, have never regretted the time spent there.

The first anniversary of the entrance of the Apostolic Faith Movement into Texas, was celebrated with a convention at Orchard, Texas, April 14th and 15th, 1906. Several hundred people gathered with Mr. Parham and the workers, who were nearly all present.

The meeting began Saturday with an informal convention of the workers; personal testimonies and praises to God occupying the forenoon and reports and discussions of the work in the afternoon. Saturday night a general praise service of great and increasing power occupied the time.

Sunday morning the crowds assembled for a great praise service and after dinner another praise service which was followed by a baptizing at half past four, about two miles away. Twenty-four were immersed, with songs and shouts of joy and then hungry hearts gathered around the altar.

The altar service began about six o'clock and lasted until midnight with power and victory. No sermons were preached and none were needed. About midnight the altar service was converted into one of praise. This lasted for an hour or two and resulted in another altar service.

About fifteen received the baptism of the Holy Spirit that night and about twenty-seven workers were ordained. At three o'clock (Monday morning) the work of assigning the workers to the different fields of labor was undertaken, and eight companies were made up. Every one was eager for the coming battles, and consecrated to go anywhere as the Lord lead.

The Houston company hoped to catch the train at five o'clock, but it failed to stop. Standing there in the gray dawn of early morning, Mr. Parham started an open air meeting, and first one and then another spoke. Mr. and Mrs. Quinton sang and Mable Smith preached under the inspiration of the Holy Spirit.

As the next train stopped at the depot, with joy and sadness the workers and friends bid Mr. Parham good-bye as about sixty filled a car by themselves. Many sad hearts were settling down (as best they could) to the disappointment of not receiving the baptism of the Holy Spirit, which had been so wonderfully poured out on others, when to their surprise, Mr. Parham came smiling through the train to give them a word of cheer. He caught the train at the last minute to go with them to the next station and return. Truly the Holy Spirit lead him to do this. As he took the hand of one of the disappointed shop boys from Houston, the Spirit fell on the boy, his face lit up with heavenly joy and he began to speak in other tongues. Before Mr. Parham left the train, another Pentecostal shower fell and by the time they arrived at Alvin to change for Houston, ten had received the baptism of the Holy Spirit in that car!

The experience they received was very different to what many today consider Pentecostal power. There was no yelling and screaming with violent physical exertion and consequent exhaustion. There was no nervous strain in connection with any of the demonstrations.

The power was truly Pentecostal. It is not tiresome to pray in tongues; the power to do so coming from the Holy Spirit. The speaking in tongues and the shouts of joy and victory can best be described as given in Acts 2:2. "And suddenly there came a sound from heaven, as of a mighty rushing wind, and it filled all the house (train) where they were sitting."

Mr. Parham returned to Orchard thanking God for so wonderfully pouring out the Holy Spirit, even on the train, as the workers were going forth in His name. The God who is no respector of persons, is no respector of places also. God is a Spirit; and they that worship Him must worship Him in Spirit and in truth. (John 4:24).

It was indeed wonderful how such a large gathering of people were cared for by the little community of Orchard. There were no "train committees" no "entertainment committees," neither was there any big cafes and hotels to help to entertain the crowds. The home people of the vicinity filled up their wagons and other vehicles with visitors, took us home with them and fed us bountifully while the overflow had good basket dinners on the ground. "He that gathered much had nothing over, and he that gathered little had no lack."

While they provided us with the temporal things, God rewarded them with the spiritual food, and we all feasted on the "Bread of Life."

We returned to Kansas after the fare-well meeting which was announced in the Houston daily paper.

PARHAM'S FAREWELL SERVICES

"Rev Chas. F. Parham, the Projector of the Apostolic Faith Movement, who has been laboring in Texas during the past winter, is preparing to leave on a tour of the north in the interest of his movement. He will preach a farewell sermon to the Texas people of his faith in the Brunner Holiness Tabernacle on Sunday night, April 22, to which the public is cordially invited. The apostolic faith has been accepted by hundreds of people in this section within the brief period of one year, and Mr. Parham leaves half a hundred workers including a number of evangelists."—Houston Post.

TEXAS GIVES GOD GLORY

"There is joy among the angels,
For the work in Texas done,
Since the Apostolic Movement
Its blest labors have begun.

Joy, indeed, in courts of glory,
Joy in homes and hearts below,
Love for God and for each other
Makes our hearts to overflow.

Praise the Lord, that to our borders
His true messengers were sent,
Faithful, earnest and true-hearted,
On their Master's errand bent.

Happy day they came among us!
Blest the message they have brought;
'Whosoever cometh to me
I in no wise will cast out'

Praises to our God forever,
For salvation full and free,
For the Gospel as Christ taught it
By the shores of Galilee.

In the highways and the byways,
In the lowest haunts of sin,
Following their Master's footsteps,
These true workers enter in.

'Heal the sick and cleanse the lepers,
Cast out devils in My name.'
These commands He gave His workers,
He today is just the same.

Not ashamed to own their Master,
Not ashamed His cross to bear.
Well we know that when He cometh,
They shall palms of victory wear.

Then press on, ye dauntless workers,
Till your task on earth is o'er,
And you still shall follow Jesus,
To where He has gone before."

                                    —E. G. F.

Chapter XVI

THE CALL TO ZION CITY

e had given up our home at Melrose, Kansas, when we went to Texas, and our furniture was stored, but soon after we returned to Kansas we were comfortably located in a little home at Keelville, between Melrose and Baxter Springs, and during the month of May, Mr. Parham held a meeting at Galena.

June 1, 1906, another brown-eyed baby boy came to our home. Of course one of the first important questions to be answered is, "What are we going to name the baby?" Robert was quite a family name on the Parham side of the family, so I said, "Lets call him 'Robert,' that is a good name and won't be nicknamed." I immediately saw my mistake as some one called out, "Why, hello Bob!" Though to me, he has always been "Robert" he has been better known as "Bob", especially among his young friends.

Mr. Parham held an all day meeting for Keelville and Melrose, which was a time of praise and thanksgiving to God for His many blessings. After the praise service he preached from the text "Expecting" in which he urged and exhorted the whole church to rise to the expecting of Jesus as He is "expecting till His enemies be made His foot-stool." That we should arise and thank God for and use all the power He promises to us through Jesus' name, and be heavenly patriots.

After the basket dinner, short talks were made by five of the workers. Twenty-one were then baptized, thus making a public confession of their faith in the divinity of Jesus Christ. Many of these were heads of families. The day was fine and there was a great crowd, a large number being there from Baxter Springs.

After holding some other meetings in this vicinity, Mr. Parham again returned to Texas and held a camp-meeting at Brunner, which was then a beautiful little suburb of Houston. The meeting began August 3, and lasted three weeks.

After the first night or two, the altars were filled with seekers and the visitors began coming in. It was a wonderful camp-meeting, still remembered, I am sure, by those present. A large company of workers and preachers were boarded at a camp restaurant, and their needs were wonderfully provided.

It was estimated that for two weeks from fifty to one hundred seekers filled the altar each night, and as the Christians gathered around them to pray, the whole front half of the tabernacle was one great altar service and God gave wonderful victory.

As the young workers, who had been in the Bible School the preceding winter, preached under the anointing of the Holy Spirit the wonderful truths of God, their parents and friends marveled at the wisdom and power of God, which was manifest through them.

Street meetings were held in Houston and one Saturday afternoon, fifty workers accompanied Mr. Parham to preach on the street. The workers were divided into four companies and the meeting excelled anything that had ever been witnessed in street work.

It was during that camp-meeting that Mrs. Hall said she felt lead to go to California and she soon got a definite call to come, Mr. Parham also receiving letters telling of the need of help in W. J. Seymour's meetings. The car-fare was soon supplied for her to go, and she was followed by Mr. and Mrs. Oyler and their son Mahlon.

A great deal of prejudice was broken down by this meeting at Brunner and the newspapers gave quite favorable reports of which I will quote some extracts.

APOSTOLIC RALLY

From the Houston Chronicle

Brunner Tabernacle held Big Crowds Yesterday. Parham Speaks on Movement and what it Stands For. Baptismal Service Postponed Because of Rain.

"Yesterday was a great day with the Apostolic Faith people at Brunner. The big tabernacle on Patterson avenue was crowded with hundreds of the faithful, and the services from morning to night were attended by enthusiastic audiences. Rev. Charles F. Parham, Projector of the movement, addressed the various assemblages of the day. The baptismal services, which had been announced for yesterday afternoon, could not take place on account of the heavy rains of the morning and the preceding night which muddied the stream and made the banks slippery.

"At 3 o'clock in the afternoon the great crowd of workers and others identified with the movement lined up in front of the tabernacle and had their picture taken.

"When the camera snapped and the photographer motioned that it was all over there was a rush for seats in the interior of the audience shed. Projector Parham struck up a hymn and the crowd joined in with lusty voices as they moved into the seats on the platform and other seats in the body of the building. Another hymn was sung and then another, 'just give them time to tune up,' said the leader, 'and you'll hears some music.' Then he announced a new hymn. 'You old Methodists, and Baptists, and Presbyterians and the rest of you can sing this, was the comment. The hymn was 'Onward Christian Soldiers,' and they sang.

PARHAM SPEAKS

"In his address, Charles F. Parham told something of the history of the movement. He laughed and related humorous incidents in the course of his address, about the 'hireling preachers' who 'have a fine flow of language,' and a theological education.' Mr. Parham himself, as he remarked yesterday was licensed 'an exhorter' by the Methodist church when he was 14 years of age.

"He told something of the history of the movement during the course of his address yesterday afternoon. He referred to the prophecy in the Bible in which it was said that before Christ should come again this gospel must be preached to every people. 'Bible religion declined when formalism took root and drove true religion out,' he said. 'Luther rejuvenated the gospel with his resurrection of the doctrine of justification by faith. Wesley reclaimed another truth, the truth of sanctification and so others have found bits of lost truth and restored them. The Apostolic Faith Movement has gathered the fundemental faith from every church and from every sect and from every age.

HEALING BY FAITH

"He remarked on the doctrine of healing held by the adherents of his faith. 'Over 100,000 people in the United States today are trusting God for healing, and they are not Christian Scientists or Spiritualistic healers, either. I may be crazy and a monomaniac on religion, but I know what I am talking about. I was sick, the doctors nearly ruined me and stunted my growth by their medicines. Ossification was setting in and nothing, it seemed, could save me from that. You know an ossified man lives forever. That's what's the matter with these church members. They are ossified.' 'I thought you preached to sinners?' somebody asks. 'I do.' ' But you are preaching to church members.' 'Well, two-thirds of the church members are not saved. It is a hard fact, but it is the truth.'

" 'I was healed from all my ailments, and today my health is perfect. And then God has manifested other powers. Six years ago God actually fulfilled the second chapter of Acts at the Bible School in Topeka, Kansas, and the students went out speaking in tongues.'

A REVOLUTION

" 'Now, we do not come to establish another church. We are not a new sect. We haven't anything for you to join. We proclaim a revolution. A revolution against sin, sin in the church and out of the church, sin in high places and low places.'

"An altar service followed the general service. Calls were made, the service being under the leadership of Miss Mable Smith, and dozens of men and women came forward and knelt at the rude wooden benches. Some of the workers came forward and with them prayed in their native tongue loudly and persistently; others were quiet and self possessed in their praying."

THOUSANDS AT BAPTIZING

Apostolic Faith Ceremony in White Oak Bayou Draws Big Crowds.

Houston Post, August 27, 1906

"Forty-four converts of the Apostolic Faith Movement, the visible fruits of the State encampment just closed, were baptized by immersion in White Oak bayou, north of Brunner, yesterday afternoon and fully two thousand people witnessed the ceremony. The spectators crowded both banks of the stream, small boys occupied vantage points in trees overhanging the water, and during the hour in which the religious rite was being administered the woods in the vicinity were literally alive with tip-toeing and curious humanity.

"The baptizing came as the formal ending of the State Encampment of the movement that has been at Brunner for three weeks. The forty-four persons who went under the water yesterday as a token of their renunciation of a life of sin are those who have been converted to the faith during the preaching at the encampment, and they represent all ages of life. One was an aged gray-haired mother, and there were wives clinging to their husbands as both went out into the muddy stream together; young men and young women and a few boys yet in their teens. Some came from other sects and some were forming their connections with a religious organization for the first time. All were uniting in a movement which they believe and preach to be "Bible-time Christianity brought up to date."

"All of them believe that they are the subjects of divine providence and that they have within their power manifestations so strange and uncommon as to be classed miraculous. All have not received "Pentecost" yet. But they have heard others speak in strange tongues and they confidently expect ultimately to have the same gift.

PREACHING PRECEDES BAPTIZING

"The announcement that the baptizing service would be held yesterday drew immense crowds from the city and the preaching service in the tabernacle, which preceded the baptizing, was attended by many other than Apostolic Faith people. The minister preached on "The baptism of the Holy Spirit," and declared, that while the water baptism was necessary as a seal of membership in the Christian church, the great and absolute necessary thing is the baptism of the Holy Spirit. 'The baptism such as the disciples received on the day of Pentecost in Jerusalem,' the preacher said, 'the baptism of the Spirit is manifested in this twentieth century in the identical manner in which it was made known in the first century, by the gift of tongues. That marvelous gift came as the evidence of the Holy Spirit's absolute possession at the beginning of the Christian dispensation, and the gift comes today as the crowning feature of experimental religion.

"It is not necessary that people speaking in tongues understand the language spoken. When a man who speaks German finds himself using words of that language intelligibly and finds it a part of his religious experience, he knows that the gift of speech is the gift of God. And that is enough for him.'

" 'Now we as a movement do not stand for any foolishness any fanticism or any absurdity. We stand simply and plainly for the gospel of Jesus Christ, and if anything not a part of this has crept in it is the work of the devil and not our honest desire. The devil is in every work they say, and it is true. He is here in this tabernacle today in some form, trying to baffle the will of God's people, trying to mar the work they are doing. We stand for the simple gospel. Bible-time Christianity up to date and working in the twentieth century in obedience to Christ's commission. If that great commission is carried out, if the evangelization of the world is to be accomplished, it must be through this movement, I believe. Beginning both in Judea and Jerusalem, and in Samaria and unto the uttermost parts of the earth, it must be preached, and this movement is the agency that, in the providence of God, is to fully accomplish the world wide work.' "

"It was after four o'clock when the preacher finished his sermon and announcement was made that time for the baptizing had arrived. There was a rush from the tabernacle, candidates for baptism jostling with the others in the effort to get on the grounds first and get a convenient location, but scores of people from the city, knowing where the baptism would take place were already there. Buggies were hitched to trees all around, and from the tabernacle there was an added activity and an increased stir.

"Hymns were sung, several of them, and then one of the workers in the Texas forces waded out into the stream, waded further and further, until the water level stood just above his belt. He stood there, looking about him and apparently sounding the bottom in his vicinity, until an assistant waded out from the shore bringing a woman candidate with him. She was taken in hand, by the officiating minister the usual words were said and the candidate was immersed in the water. Forty-

three others followed in quick succession, the baptized meeting the unbaptized as the one left the water and the other entered."

*   *   *   *   *

Mr. Parham told rather an amusing incident which happened at a baptizing in Texas, which perhaps might have been at
this time.

As such a large crowd were going to the baptizing, they
had chartered a street car to accommodate the crowd. As the
conductor came through to one man to collect the fare, the
man said in broken English, "We don't pay fare on this car,
this is Apostolic, this is free." The conductor failed to make
the man understand the circumstances, and Mr. Parham over-
heard the conversation and motioned to the conductor to come
to him and he would pay it. We have often since, (in fun),
used this for a quotation, "This is Apostolic, this is free."

W. J. Seymour had written before of the work on the
coast and after Mrs. Hall arrived, he wrote Mr. Parham the
following letter which I have in my possession. It is yellow
with age, but I will copy it, as it may be of interest to those
who were acquainted with W. J. Seymour and his work in
Los Angeles, California.

312 Azusa Street, Los Angeles, Cal.,
August 27th, 1906

Dear Bro. Parham:—

Sister Hall has arrived, and is planning out a great revival
in this city, that shall take place when you come. The revival is still going on here that has been going on since we
came to this city. But we are expecting a general one to start
again when you come, that these little revivals will all come
together and make one great union revival.

"Now please let us know about the date that you will be
here, so we can advertise your coming and the date. I shall
look for a large place, by God's help, that will accommodate

the people. Hallelujah to God! Victory through the all cleansing blood of Jesus Christ! I expect an earthquake to happen
in Los Angeles when you come with other workers filled with
the Holy Ghost; that God will shake this city once more.

"Satan is working but God is mightier than satan for he is
a conquered foe and a defeated creature. Glory be to God in
the highest! God has been breathing on the dry bones with
the Holy Ghost and the Word,, until dry bones are coming together and flesh is coming upon them, life is put into them,
until God has got a mighty host in this city standing for the
faith that was once delivered unto the saints. Please answer
soon, Yours in Christ and in the faith that was once delivered unto the saints. W. J. Seymour.

*   *   *   *   *

The beginning of September, Mr. Parham returned to Kansas to hold a Camp Meeting at Baxter Springs, and a number
of the Texas workers and preachers came to help in this meeting. The Camp Meeting was held on a block of ground, centrally located in the town and shaded with beautiful forest
trees and called "Springs Park." There were two good springs
on the grounds at that time, from which Baxter Springs got
its name.

The meeting was a very successful one, and for several years
after this, a Camp Meeting was held here nearly every summer, and a wooden tabernacle was erected for this purpose.
Many still remember with thankful hearts the blessings received on these grounds before it was sold and used for building
purposes.

It was during this Camp Meeting of 1906 that Mr. Parham
received his call to go to Zion City, Ill. He was expecting to
go to Los Angeles, Cal., as W. J. Seymour was still writing
urgent letters appealing for help, as spiritualistic manifestations, hypnotic forces and fleshly contortions as known in the
colored Camp Meetings in the south, had broken loose in the

meeting. He wanted Mr. Parham to come quickly to help him discern between that which was real and that which was false and weed out that which was not of God. However it must have been the plan of God to let the wheat and the tares grow together, as Mr. Parham was definitely lead to go to Zion City first.

Dr. Dowie had been discredited and displaced and the people were in a terrible state of confusion and unrest. Hatred and malice, envy and strife reigned in this place which had been planned for a city of righteousness and peace.

From a natural standpoint, it looked like a very unfavorable time to go to Zion City with any hopes of having a meeting, but "all things are possible with God" and He can make a way, where seemingly there is no way.

Zion City was largely made up of fine, intelligent people from far and near, coming from many different countries of the world. Many sweet consecrated Christians had come, because they loved the truths Dr. Dowie had taught them, especially on divine healing.

God saw many honest hearts there who needed help, and deliverance at this terrible crisis, and sent Mr. Parham to them with the message of the baptism of the Holy Spirit, which brought love, joy and peace to as many as would believe and receive the truth.

When Mr. Parham entered the city, it was impossible to obtain a building to hold a meeting in as all doors were closed against him. His first meeting was held in a private room at Elijah Hospice (hotel) at the invitation of the manager. The next night two rooms and the hall way were crowded out and from that time onward the meetings increased in number, attendance and power.

He then began cottage meetings and many of the best homes in the city were opened for meetings. Fred F. Bosworth's home was literally converted into a meeting house.

On some Sundays, morning and evening, four rooms have been closely packed with people at one time, generally uniting in one meeting, but sometimes for a few minutes being divided into three separate testimony meetings until a hymn begun in one room would be taken up in the others until the whole assembly was welded into one body of praise. I am sure those who participated in the divine enthusiasm of these meetings will never forget their sweetness and power. I was permitted to be in the cottage meetings the following winter, and know how the dear people of Zion City did worship God in spirit and in truth as their hungry hearts were filled with the Holy Spirit.

Every night they had five meetings running which lasted from 7:00 P. M. until about midnight, and the large residences were crowded upstairs and down. While other ministers and workers came and helped in these services, Mr. Parham visited all these meetings preaching at each place as long as time would permit, driving rapidly from place to place.

One night some young men despitefully removed the burrs off the wheels on two buggies outside the meeting place. Had it not been for God's goodness, in warning them of the danger Mr. Parham, Mr. Lang, and also the horse, might have been killed. The horse, being spirited, on one occasion had maimed itself when the harness was cut. How wonderful it is to trust in God and to have His protecting care over our lives.

Even though bitterly persecuted, as a result of these meetings and others that followed, hundreds were reclaimed from a backsliden state, marvelous healings took place and Pentecost fell profusely.

Hundreds of ministers, evangelists and workers went out from Zion City after these meetings, with deeper truth and a fuller gospel than they had previously known and some of them are still among the leading preachers of the world today. No doubt, as the psychologists would say, Mr. Parham came to Zion City at the "psychical" moment but there is a time-liness about all God's movements. The infinite God makes no blunders. When the need is fully ripe, God will lay His hand on some one to do the work.

The religious life of Zion City judged by the best spiritual standard known here, was at an exceedingly low ebb. One ecclesiastical officer was so deeply impressed with this well-nigh universal condition of spiritual decline and depression that he predicted that when relief came, it must come from the out side, and his assertion proved true. Here was a community of several thousand intelligent, deeply religious people, hundreds of whom had literally come from 'the ends of the earth' with the millstone of a broken-down commercialism hanging about their necks.

Disappointed hopes, the wrecking of cherished ideals, the strife and passion attending legal contests and in hundreds of instances the difficulty of securing the necessaries of life, were among the many painful causes of prevailing spiritual disorder.

But God never leads His people into the wilderness and for-sakes them, and His faithfulness did not fail this patient and long-suffering people. Truly nothing less than the real baptism of love and the oil of the Holy Spirit, could have calmed the troubled waters.

Mr. Parham has kept a number of news-paper clippings, some are rather amusing, some bring back to our memory the bitter fight which was waged against Mr. Parham that I do not care to recall, but I will just quote a few extracts from some of them which may give a better understanding of the circumstances at that time.

DECLARE PARHAM IS GAINING

Reports from Zion are that the new Prophet is making Big Inroads upon other Prophet's Following.

Zion City, Ill.; Sept. 28. (*Special to the Gazette*)

"Prophet Parham is said by many to be gaining fast in his

inroads on the former overseer's followers as well as Voliva's people. In fact, in some sections it is said he is making tre-mendous strides for the short time he has been here. People with means and considered among the most influential peo-ple of the city have invited Parham into their fine homes, and seem to be showing him every possible attention.

"In a circular, Parham says: "We stand for the restoration of the faith once delivered unto the saints, unity of Zion, the old-time religion, camp-meetings, revivals, missions, street and prison work and Christian unity everywhere.

"We are not fighting men or churches, but seeking to dis-place dead forms and creeds, or wild fanaticisms with living practical Christianity. 'Love, Faith, Unity,' are our watch words; and 'Victory through the atoning Blood,' our battle cry. God's promises are true. He said, 'Be thou faithful over a few things and I will make thee ruler over many.'

'From the little handful of Christians who stood by the cross when the testings and discouragements came, God raised a mighty host.'

Chas. F. Parham, Projector,

Elijah Hospice.

"When Overseer Voliva sent a message to Mr. Parham to know how long he was going to stay in Zion City, he answer-ed that he was going to stay 'till Kingdom come.' He added, "I suppose there may something come of this, but I am going to stay, as long as the Lord wants me here?"

* * * * *

Another newspaper clipping:

DOWIE HAS HIS SAY

"While Voliva was in Chicago, Dowie and Parham were holding the stage in the three-cornered fight in Zion. Dowie in addressing a number of his followers, paid his respects to Parham, criticising him for his utterances and actions in Zion.

"Parham, however, in an address before a large crowd, denied that he was attempting to seek the downfall of Dowie
or Voliva. He spoke kindly of Dowie and praised him for
what he had done. He told his hearers that Dowie was
not right in his mind but if placed under his care would soon
be restored to his former self."

* * * * *

It was about the last of October, 1906 that Mr. Parham felt
free to leave the work in Zion City in the care of others and
hurried to Los Angeles, Cal. to answer the call from W. J.
Seymour.

QUIT YOU LIKE MEN, BE STRONG

Too noble for resentment,
Too strong to know defeat,
Too true to stoop to falsehood,
Too upright for deceit.

Though hard may be the death to self,
That Christ alone may reign,
It is only he who gives his life,
Eternal life shall gain.

It is not the sword of vengeance
Bringing pain and woe,
But Truth and Holy living,
That routs the vily foe.
                    —Lillian Thistlethwaite.

Chapter XVII

"TRY THE SPIRITS"

E will now leave Mr. Parham, as he takes the train from Zion City, Ill., to the golden west, and go before him to Los Angeles, Cal., and get a glimpse of the conditions which he will have to face when he arrives there.

A number have testified that when W. J. Seymour first came to Los Angeles, he came with a humble spirit, giving forth the teaching he had received in the Bible School at Houston, Texas. Those who had come from Texas and had heard Mr. Parham's lessons were surprised at his wonderful memory, as sometimes he would give forth word for word the lessons and the teachings which he had received from Mr. Parham.

Mrs. Walter Oyler wrote a report of this meeting which was printed in "The Gospel of the Kingdom," a paper published in Texas by J. G. Campbell.

"It was at the Bible School in Houston, Texas, that W. J. Seymour and Lucy Farrar (colorer) received the light of the full gospel, and they seldom missed a service. They were hungry for all of God's blessings.

"After the school closed, the Lord called W. J. Seymour to Los Angeles, Cal. Lucy Farrar came later, who had received the baptism of the Holp Spirit in Kansas. They found many hungry hearts here and they received with joy the glad tidings that God was indeed pouring out His Spirit in these days. Many that were waiting on God, prayed through to the Pentecostal blessing. Sinners were saved and believers sanctified. The sick were healed and the people were awakened to the fact that God was walking in their midst.

"The enemy of our souls could not stand this, so he came in and caused many to get what they thought was the baptism of the Holy Ghost, but sad to say, their lives proved that they did not have the real experience. The more of the Holy Spirit one gets the more natural we will act and can very easily prove that we have been with Christ and learned of Him.

"When we came here from Texas, we went to the Azusa Street Mission, and it was very plain to me that God was doing a wonderful work and satan was trying to tear it to pieces. Many things were done that were far from being the work of the Holy Spirit. Soon there was bitterness, strife, division and lack of brotherly love. We leave it all with the Lord."

*   *   *   *   *

K. Brower, a godly Christian man, who was a resident of Los Angeles, also wrote an article concerning this meeting for the same paper.

"The teaching here came by a colored man, (Seymour), and a mulatto woman, (Lucy Farrar.) Both came to bring the blessed teachings they had received in Houston, Texas, of Brother Chas. F. Parham, to the "black race" here, but found no open doors among the colored people; but a door was opened among the Holiness people, where both black and white held cottage prayer meetings in a house of one of the members on number 214 Bony Bray; and Mr. Seymour received the baptism of the Holy Spirit here. Men and women sought more of God and their labor was blest. They sought wider fields, and rented an old building down town on Azusa St. All were true to God and men, for Mr. Seymour stated how God had wonderfully healed a little man, who taught him that blessed truth he was preaching here in Los Angeles.

"The writer was very anxious to see the real man called of God to this wonderful work. I wrote to Chas. F. Parham in Zion City that I longed to see him. When he came to Azusa Mission, Seymour introduced Chas. F. Parham to the Azusa

people as his 'Father in this gospel of the Kingdom'; and all
wanted to see the 'father' of the black son. This stirred up
the devil in a great shape; satan's servants who had been at
work in the mission in great power, saw their destruction.
The next day he closed the door against his 'father'."

* * * * *

Those who have had experience with fanaticism know that
there goes with it an unteachable spirit and spiritual pride,
which makes those under the influences of these false spirits
feel exalted and think that they have a greater experience than
any one else and do not need instruction or advice. This
seems to be as a protection of the enemy to hold his power,
yet how sad it looks to us, for it puts them out of the reach of
those who see their error and would willingly help them if
possible. Mr. Parham wrote:

"I hurried to Los Angeles, and to my utter surprise and astonishment I found conditions even worse than I had antici-
pated. Brother Seymour came to me helpless, he said he could
not stem the tide that had arisen. I sat on the platform in
Azusa Street Mission, and saw the manifestations of the flesh,
spiritualistic controls, saw people practicing hypnotism at the
altar over candidates seeking the baptism; though many were
receiving the real baptism of the Holy Ghost.

"After preaching two or three times, I was informed by
two of the elders, one who was a hypnotist (I had seen him
lay his hands on many who came through chattering, jabbering and sputtering, speaking in no language at all) that I was
not wanted in that place.

With workers from the Texas field we opened a great revival in the W. C. T. U. Building on Broadway and Temple
Streets in Los Angeles. Great numbers were saved, marvelous healings took place and between two and three hundred

who had been possessed of awful fits and spasms and controls in the Azusa Street work were delivered, and received the real Pentecost teachings and many spake with other tongues."

*   *   *   *   *

W. J. Seymour, in his first paper gave a true account of the origin of the work, but after he failed to receive the message Mr. Parham brought, he was possessed with a spirit of leadership artd sought to prove that Azusa St. Mission was where the baptism of the Holy Spirit first fell. Mr. Parham went to him and plead with him to repent to God and man for trying to deceive the people, and reject leadership and exalting of self or God would humble him. We may deceive men, but we cannot deceive God.

*   *   *   *   *

Mr. Parham wrote the following in his paper later: "As we look backward, we see that the saddest and most awful experience of our whole Christian life was the months we spent under similar control, from which we only escaped by the mercy of God. There were moments of joy in believing we were obeying the voice of God, but oh, the hours of torture we endured when we unwittingly disobeyed, and the spirit-control would threaten us with dire vengeance in the death of one of the children or some great calamity. As in this letter business and many other cases in the world, it came as a seducing, flattering spirit, but when it gained the supremacy of our lives it used the lash.

"How grateful Sister Lillian, wife and I are for deliverance from this stuff. Yet it has been a school to us and we come to you, one and all, and beg you to be careful, for when your confidence is betrayed by one of these false seducing spirits, you feel like the poor betrayed girl in a strange city; you have not the courage to return and face your father and you just throw away your life.

"To those who have had their spiritual power prostituted in this or similar manner, we ask you to come home to Father's house. God bless you! To those nibbling at the tit-bits of the devil's seductive artifices and bouquets of flattering poppy flowers, beware! The devil as an angel of light is imitating every phase of Christianity today."

* * * * *

As Mr. Parham used to say, even a crow could tell the difference between a real man and a scare-crow in the corn field, and a goose could pick out the grains of corn from among the little stones. So we as God's children should be able to tell the real from the counterfeit, and be able take the wheat and leave the chaff, if we will "try the spirits". As Mr. Parham had tried the spirits, and discerned between the two; he condemned fanaticism in no uncertain way and warned the people of this danger. This brought him bitter persecution from those who were under the influence of this power, but he loved the truth, and blessed experience we had received of the baptism of the Holy Spirit, and was willing to give his life, if need be, to defend it.

Some time after this, I stepped into a fanatical meeting in another city where I was a stranger to all present. During the prayer service, some one simply mentioned Mr. Parham's name in prayer, and the meeting exploded as though a bomb had been thrown in the midst. The audience began to hiss and rebuked her, chattering and jabbering, and shaking their fists in her face until she left the meeting. It is needless to say that I "took the hint" and left also, realizing that I was "in the wrong pew." and where I had no business.

Unless we have witnessed something of this kind, it is impossible to realize the bitter hatred and prejudice which exists, without any apparent cause, among some who call themselves Christians. These people did not know Mr. Parham, nor was this a "natural human hatred," but "a devilish hat-red," born of hell, because he had denounced fanaticism, and exposed the wolf in sheep's clothing.

There is bitterness in religious prejudice and fights which some times even rival that which is manifest in the business and political world over the natural and temporal things. Why? Because this war-fare of division and strife is created and backed up by the very forces and power of darkness and hell itself.

"Beloved, believe not every spirit, but try the spirits wheth-er they are of God." (1 John, 4:1.)

Mr. Parham wrote the following letter from Los Angeles, California, December 1, 1906, which was printed in the Jan-uary number of the Apostolic Faith, then published in Zion City, Ill.

A NOTE OF WARNING

"Throughout the history of all religious reformations and movements which have brought to light new spiritual life and power, the truth always has been veiled by the shadows, mists and clouds of wild-fire, fanaticism, and everything else that the devil through his agents could invent to conceal the real and the good, and to mystify those who were seeking for more light and power. Everything that could be brought to bear has been thrown about it to hide it from the world.

"As it has been in the past, so it will ever be. Only those who are willing to go down beneath the veil, tearing it away that they may view the real in all it's beauty and splendor, and expose the counterfeit that seems so like the real, facing the fanaticisms, in a self-forgetful spirit—only such will be able to bring to the surface the pure truth of God, that the world may view His great wonders which are revealed so myster-iously.

"Never were God's servants surrounded with more decep-tive counterfeits of real divine experience than in this day and age; and never was it more imperative that all should stand firm and steadfast for the truth.

"So many different agencies are employed to imitate the real and the 'magician's' work is so well nigh perfect, that it often is indeed hard to distinguish the true and false.

"It is for his reason that I am writing this. And I earnestly urge all to search their own hearts, that they may learn for a certainty that they are in no way deceived or mislead, or in any way coming short of the truth and the light, for which we are looking; and that they may know for a certainty that they are really on the Lord's side and led by no influences save that of the Holy Spirit.

"I have witnessed great dangers in the work here in Los Angeles, and in pointing them out I shall not refer to indi-duals, but to the work itself as a whole, that we all may see the error of our way and get back to God.

"Throughout the summer I was greatly encouraged, and truly rejoiced at the reports of the work that was sweeping the California field. Every breeze across the continent wafted tidings of victories achieved until it seemed as if the whole Pacific Coast would be taken for God. Through this glorious onward march, although absent in body I was present in spirit beholding the wonderful victories and triumphs, as well as some defeats, and waiting patiently for our God to free me from many hindrances and allow me to come here that I might be used of Him in every helpful way.

"After much hard labor in Missouri, Kansas and Texas and the conduction of the great state rally in the city of Houston, and the visiting of many missions throughout Texas, I went north to conduct the encampment for the States of Missouri and Kansas, held in Baxter, Kansas. When this meeting was well under way God told me to go to Zion City, and the work accomplished there is now known far and near.

"For some time I had been in touch with many friends who knew the extremes that had crept into the meeting in California, and also with others who were anxious to know if the work there truly represented the teachings of the Apostolic Faith Movement; meanwhile workers which had been sent there and who were well acquainted with the work wrote me repeatedly to come quickly to the rescue.

"At last, the work in Zion City being thoroughly established, God said to me, "Go to California." So, leaving the work there in the hands of thoroughly competent persons, I came to Los Angeles.

"I feel that it was in God's order for me not to reach here sooner than I did, and I may say here that, although many forms of fanaticism have crept in, I believe every true child of God will come out of this mist and shadow stronger and better equipped against all extremes that are liable to present themselves at any time in meetings of this kind.

"Let me say, in speaking of different phases of fanaticism that have been obtained here, that I do so with all lovingkindness and at the same time with all fairness and firmness. I have no desire to assert my authority (for I have none to assert over the people of God), but to help and strengthen, and forever make plain to all people that extremes, wild-fire, fanaicism, and everything that is beyond the bounds of common sense and reason, do not now and never have had any part or lot in Apostolic Faith work and teachings.

"Let me speak plainly with regard to the work as I have found it here. I found hypnotic influences, familiar-spirit influences, spiritualistic influences, mesmeric influences, and all kinds of spells, spasms, falling in trances, etc. All of these things are foreign to and unknown in this movement outside of Los Angeles, except in the places visited by the workers sent out from this city.

"A word about the baptism of the Holy Ghost. The speaking in tongues is never brought about by any of the above influences. In all our work the laying on of hands is practised only occasionally, and then for the space of only a minute or two. No such thing is known among our workers as the suggestion of certain words and sounds, the working of the chin, or the massage of the throat.

"Nonsense! The Holy Ghost needs no help! When the recipient of the Holy Ghost comes into proper relations with God the speaking in tongues comes as naturally as any other gift from Him. There is always the real and the false, and anything outside of the operation of the Holy Ghost is counterfeit.

"There are many in Los Angeles who sing, pray and talk wonderfully in other tongues, as the Spirit gives utterance, and there is jabbering here that is not tongues at all. I know that people sometimes fall under the power of God, and that there are times that God thus deals with his creatures that resist Him; but these cases are exceptional and are not general. The falling under the power in Los Angeles has, to a large degree, been produced through a hypnotic, mesmeric, magnetic current.

"The Holy Ghost does nothing that is unnatural or unseemingly, and any strained exertion of body, mind, or voice is not the work of the Holy Spirit, but of some familiar spirit, or other influence brought to bear upon the subject. The Holy Spirit is always strengthening, uplifting, vitalizing, and invigorating; while that of any other spirit is always devitalizing and degenerating, with the tendency to drag down.

"How vastly important it is that we try the spirits; and not yield to every influence brought to bear upon us! Let us guard carefully against every form of fanticism, and stand firm and true, helping one another and reasoning together.

"Having guarded this Pentecostal blessing from it's earliest infancy, I feel that it is still my duty to stand against anything and everything that will in any way prove a hindrance to others, or to the advancement of the work. The corrections which I seek to make are for the good of all, and the condemnation of none, that we may rise to all the heights of power and strength possible, and go on together in His name for the evanglization of the world. The Holy Ghost never leads us beyond the point of self-control or the control of others, while familiar spirits or fanticism lead us both **beyond** self-control and the power to help others."

THE POWER OF PRAYER

Lord, what a change within us one short hour
  Spent in Thy presence will avail to make!
  What heavy burdens from our bosoms take;
What parched grounds refresh, as with a shower!
We kneel and all around us seems to lower;
  We rise, and all the distant and the near
  Stands forth in sunny outline, brave and clear!
We kneel, how weak! we rise, how full of power!
Why, therefore, should we do ourselves this wrong
Or others, that we are not always strong;
That we are ever overborne with care;
  That we should ever weak or heartless be,
Anxious or troubled, when with us in prayer;
  And joy and strength and courage are with Thee?

—R. C. Trench.

Chapter XVIII

BACK TO ZION CITY

R. Parham returned to Zion City in December and as still no building was obtained for a meeting a large tabernacle was pitched on a vacant lot in a central part of the city.

The children and I joined him here and we received a royal welcome from his many new friends.

It seemed almost incredible to me that it would be possible to hold a tent meeting where it was so cold with snow and ice on the ground. But with several stoves up and the tent made warm by being banked around with straw, it was a very comfortable meeting place, and well filled with an enthusiastic congregation.

It was a great pleasure to Mr. Parham to preach by the hour to the appreciative audience which filled the tent day and night. They were a hungry people and were mentally and spiritually able to digest the deep and rich truths which he was giving them under the mighty anointing of the Holy Spirit.

I listened with astonishment to the testimonies as the people told of the good they had received and were receiving from the meetings. They told how they had to make confessions, restitutions, write letters and in many ways make wrongs right before they could receive the many blessings that God was bestowing upon their lives. I especially remember the testimony of a sweet-faced lady of refinement and culture. As she testified her face fairly shown with the glory and love of God. She told how hatred had so filled her heart that she believed she would have killed Dr. Dowie if she had had the opportunity to do so; but the meeting had wrought such a marvelovs change in her life. She had repented, and God had taken away all bitterness and sweetened her life with His love and filled her with the Holy Spirit. There were scores of similar testimonies. Instead of grieving over their financial losses, they were now rejoicing over their spiritual gains.

Mr. Parham told them that perhaps it was necessary for them to lose their temporal things, that they might get their hearts and minds on the spiritual things which were eternal. That they were "stripped for the race" and it would not be hard now for them to make a "hundred-fold consecration," and go forth to preach the full gospel to the ends of the earth.

He told them about his experience in Los Angeles, and that it would not be long before fanaticism would come to Zion City also, which proved to be only too true! He plead with the people to establish their lives in God and His Word, that when wild-fire, fanaticism and every wind of doctrine did come, they would be able to stand.

The meeting continued in the tent till after the first of January, and the following is a clipping from the newspaper:

HELD A BIG MEETING

"At the Parham meeting in Zion City, New Year's night, it is reported that there were 2000 persons in attendance. Parham preached two hours on the baptism of the Holy Ghost.

"The leaders declare the revival is on in earnest, and many visitors were present to take part in it. It is said many are there from adjoining states and there were a number of states. represented.

"Several preachers to carry on their work in Canada, were chosen and they are to start out in evangelistic work soon."

*   *   *   *   *

While Mr. Parham had been getting the people together in the bonds of love and the unity of the spirit, a spirit of organization and leadership had taken possession of some of the preachers. They saw this wonderful congregation of people, "as sheep without a shepherd." As Mr. Parham had brought them the message of deliverance of course they were looking to him for help. They recognized how easy it would be for Mr. Parham to declare himself their leader, organize the Movement, and appoint them for different offices. But this plan did not appeal to Mr. Parham as being of God, and he would not organize in any way.

He had told the leaders of the city, and repeatedly announced both publicly and privately, that he was not there for any personal gain, or for a following and to make himself a leader, and he meant it. That God had lead him to Zion City to bring peace and love to hearts that had been torn by envy and strife through leadership.

He had given them the message of the baptism of the Holy Spirit and many had received the Comforter; and he had rejoiced in preaching a full gospel, free to who-so-ever-will. He now urged the preachers to go forth in the name of Jesus, and give the message to others as God lead them. "Freely ye have received, freely give." (Matt. 10:8). He told them there were enough churches, that we didn't need any more churches but more spirituality in the churches. That the preachers should be called of God, not man, and if they had a message of value the people would support them without a financial board, or organization back of them.

Mr. Parham was lead to leave the Methodist Church for the evangelistic field, thus having the opportunity to preach to the people of every name, sect and order, the gospel of Christ. His experience with the Methodist Church lay before him.

John Wesley had brought to the world the teaching of sanctification and holy living, preaching it in purity and power. Now his work is organized and expensive churches built.

Truly the message God gave John Wesley is as true and as much needed today as it was then but if he should return now and preach it in the church, would they receive the message and accept him as their leader? I leave this question with you.

It was not without sacrifice that Mr. Parham had left the church. Beside the offers of position, honor and salary which were before him, he felt very keenly the disapproval of his dear parents, and "going home" did not seem the same now, as in his boyhood days.

He had made the consecration and conscientiously left denominationalism forever, but still held firmly to the teaching of sanctification, and the truths taught by John Wesley. As he had gone on sacrificing all to have these truths made real in his life, God blessed him with the baptism of the Holy Spirit and trusted him to give this teaching to the world.

Could he now take this blessed truth and organzie a new church and make himself the leader of a new organization? Mr. Parham emphatically said, "No." God did not lead him to organize, but to preach a gospel full and free to every creature. Have not all the organized churches organized under the revival of some new light and blessed truth? In their infancy they were pure, as a little child is pure but as they grew older, they flirted and compromised with the world for popularity and power, and became corrupt, instead of being true and paying their consecration vows to their Beloved, their Lord and Master. If a new church was organized, now, founded upon the teaching of the baptism of the Holy Spirit, would there not be the same danger of it becoming as worldly as the rest?

Dr. Dowie's experience in leadership also was a lesson to others. Had he not proclamed to the world in no uncertain way, the gospel of healing? While we were there, people told us how they had been healed and brought back to life when given up as dead, by Dr. Dowie's prayers. Those who knew him in his early work, when he lived humbly, said he had power with God, and wonderful answers to prayer.

He then built Zion City, was the leader and head of the church with the tithes of the city at his command.

Do we not often see, as religious leaders gain in popularity with the world, and wealth is at their command, they lose their power with God?

Jesus said, "My Kingdom is not of this world." (John 18: 36).

"I receive not honor from men." (John 5:41). "How can ye believe, which receive honor one of another, and seek not the honor that cometh from God only?" (John 5:44).

I fear there are many religious leaders today seeking honor from men, wealth and fame, and using the gospel to reflect the glory unto themselves instead of humbly seeking to hide behind the cross, and giving all the honor and glory to the Father, Son and Holy Ghost.

Mr. Parham refused any thought of leadership, or to organize the movement in any way, prefering to go on in the despised way, free to follow the Lord as He lead, rather than be a leader, appointed by men, which might end in wealth and honor from men but crowd out the spiritual, divine appointed leadership and power with God.

At the close of the tent meeting, Mr. Parham felt that his work was finished in Zion City for that time, and answered a call to New York and other eastern states.

Other preachers took charge of the tent and continued the meeting. But alas, it did not last very long. Our house was not very far from the tent, and as I looked from my window one morning, there was our faithful tent, that had stood the winter so bravely, laid flat on the ground!

I will quote a piece concerning organization and leadership which Mr. Parham printed in "The Apostolic Faith" published in Zion City, 1907.

* * * * *

"In resigning my position as Projector of the Apostolic Faith Movement, I simply followed a well-considered plan of mine, made years ago, never to receive honor of men, or to establish a new Church. I was called a pope, a Dowie, etc., and everywhere looked upon as a leader or a would-be leader and proselyter.

"These designations have always been an abomination to me and since God has given almost universal light to the world on Pentecost there is no further need of my holding the official leadership of the Apostolic Faith Movement. Now that they are generally accepted, I simply take my place among my brethern to push this gospel of the Kingdom as a witness to all nations.

"I shall still remain the same to my brethren in assistance, advice, and in donating to them my extra cash, as when I bore the meaningless title of 'Projector.'

"The Lord used the Apostolic Faith Movement as an apple-cart to push the truth of Pentecost along in, until it became a world-wide blessing. It 'had fulfilled its mission, and now fades in the light of recognition of a general world-wide fellowship in extending the hand of love to all Full Gospel Movements and Churches. The heritage of this truth is the divine right of all the children of God, and the result cannot be harvested by one man or one movement.

"Brethren, let us not become sectarian and seek to have everybody come our way, because others have as much right to demand that we should join them, as that they should join us. Let us hold to our first principles: to reveal an unsectarian, untrammeled fellowship for all true children of God, thus proving that we are Apostolic Christians. We have no head but Christ, but are seeking to be fitly joined together and compacted by that which every joint supplies, (the oil is the Holy Ghost) until we all unitedly come into the unity of the Faith, (all together) to the fullness of the statue of a man in Christ Jesus.

"Unity by organization never can be realized; for all churches, movements, and leaders want the supervision of that unity. Therefore all present movements, churches, and leaders will have to be shaken to pieces; then the truth held by real Christians will prevail, and the unifiying be accomplished by the Holy Spirit.

"Brethren, let us cease wasting time at this juncture in systemetizing or organizing the work of God. Let each minister go forward doing his work, and leaving local Assemblies under local elders; and as often as God premits revisit to strengthen the missions, and let the bond of love and unity of the Spirit prevail. Thus, as the truth soaks in, God will unify His people, bringing harmony among us all; then no set of ruling ecclesiastical directors will live off the toil and labor of others. Each one will subsist on the merits of his own work"

*   *   *   *   *

In spite of Mr. Parham's protest, we all know what followed. The Pentecostal work has been organized not only into one church, but many different organizations. Many small churches have been built, and many beautiful and expensive churches and temples, which have equalled or excelled (in some places) those which have been built by the old line organizations.

But the sad fact that faces the Pentecostal work today, is the strife and bitterness that exists between the different churches of the faith, in many places.

How do you imagine it appears to the eyes of our God of love as He sees two or three churches in the same town, practically of the same belief, at variance with each other? Each church magnifying the others faults and failures, that they may keep their own bunch in their own particular church.

Let us set our house in order, for the coming of the Lord draweth nigh. "When the Sun of Righteousness shall arise" the organizations shall dissolve, the glory and honor given unto them and to human leaders will fade away as the mist in the morning before the brightness of the sun, every knee shall bow, and every tongue shall give all praise and honor to God.

*   *   *   *   *

Several years later, Mr. Parham printed the following in his paper:

"My experience has been that people always turn a preacher down, slander and persecute him when they can no longer live up to the truth he preaches. It is the same old story of Jesus and the chief priests and elders. They either had to accept the truth He taught and live it or crucify Him. They chose the later. In olden times religous differences were settled by men killing their opponents. The law prevents that now. They can only kill the character, which is far more dastardly. Religious leaders and sectarians now use but one weapon, scandal.

"Brethren: I feel perfectly satisfied in my attitude from the beginning of this movement to the present time regarding non-organization, doctrine and labor.

"I have maintained the original teachings of this movement in strength, labor and sorrow; took the shame, persecution, loneliness and poverty of the way of the cross without complaint, while others were applauded and harvested the results of my labors in golden shekels. Trials and troubles well-nigh overwhelmed me until I found my heirship in Jesus, the Christ; then in times of storm I can take a rapture and rest in the sunshine of heavenly places till the clouds have flown.

Through it all, I have had the divine approval in my heart and the conversion and healing of many thousands. Amen. Blessed be God!

"The people who are to compose the glorious church without spot or wrinkle will be the truly spiritual who will be drawn out of all these babylon churches and movements into a free and independent Christian living, thus permiting the Christ of God to assemble this material into the glorious Church.

"In spite of all our prejudices, divisions, sisms, creeds, doctrines and teachings that now separate the true people of God, that day is soon coming when purged from sectarianism, self exaltation, etc, all the true people of God are going to be brought into blessed unity, fellowship and love, (see eye to eye, have the same mind and same judgment) and then, and not until then will the mighty work of Christ and the apostles again be seen on earth.

"When fair as the sun, clear as the moon, terrible as an army with banners, the Christed Church will go to the ends of the earth in the last evangelistic war of the age raising the dead, casting out devils cleansing the lepers, healing the sick and causing multitudes to flow into the hill of the Lord."

*   *   *   *   *

Some day Christ's prayer will be answered;

"Neither pray I for these alone, but for them which shall believe on me through their word; that they all may be one, as thou, Father art in me, and I in thee, that they also may be one in us: that the world may believe that thou hast sent me. And the glory which thou gavest me, I have given them: that they may be one, even as we are one." (John 17: 20-22.)

THE CHURCH

1. "No man-made church, but God's alone,
    Is built on Christ, the Corner Stone.
    Though wicked men this church assail,
    The gates of hell can not prevail.

Chorus

    With Jesus alone, with Jesus alone,
    For the only foundation and Chief Corner Stone,
    Through faith in Christ, through Jesus' blood,
    We're members of the church of God.

2. This holy temple in the Lord,
    If fitly framed, without discord;
    Of polished stones her walls are laid,
    Complete in one, as Jesus prayed.

3. God joins the members, every one,
    Unto this body of His Son,
    Their names are in the book of life,
    This holy church is Jesus' wife.

4. Built up in Christ, their living Head,
    Together quickened from the dead;
    This church of God is from above,
    Its only bond, the bond of love.

5. I dare not trust in human aid,
    Nor join a church that man has made;
    Built on the sand, a Babel tall,
    When storms arise her walls will fall."

Chapter XIX

RESIST NOT EVIL.

A STATEMENT BY CHARLES F. PARHAM RELATING TO HIS WORK IN ZION CITY.

N view of the fact that the circumstances under which I began my work in Zion City, and my object in continuing it, are misunderstood by many, it has seemed wise to make a brief statement in the interest of truth and justice.

"In the first place, it should be understood by all that I did not come to Zion City from personal choice, but because God sent me. My inclinations lay in other directions, in the following of which partial arrangements had already been made.

"When I understood and promised to obey God's will to turn from my original purpose and carry a message to Zion City, I was instantly healed of a severe sick headache which was a source of concern to me in view of the fact that I almost always enjoyed perfect health.

"I came with a message of peace to a divided, suffering people, in the hearts of many of whom factional strife and disappointment had engendered discouragement and bitterness. The wisdom of God in sending this message of love and hope is manifest in the daily testimony, both by word and deed, of the hundreds of people in this city whose spiritual life has been divinely quickened. Some have been saved, some healed, and many have been sanctified and baptized with the Holy Spirit.

"Substituting discouragement and bitterness in the hearts of hundreds of people with divine love and hope, ought never to be an occasion for complaint or critcism in any community.

"In the second place, it ought to be perfectly understood that I brought no 'new gospel' to Zion City. I have always preached the fundamental truths of the Full Gospel—Salvation, Sanctification, Healing, the Coming of the Lord to reign in person on the earth, and the restoration to the Church of the nine gifts of the Holy Spirit. If I differ at all from Zion with respect to any of these truths it is only as individuals in Zion differ among themselves.

"Moreover, I always have stood for what might be called a proportionate presentation of these very practical doctrines—that is to say, I do not believe in exalting one truth, or even a few truths, out of all proportion to the other doctrines of the Bible. I believe, and I preach, the whole Word of God, to my utmost knowledge and ability.

"Some attempt seems to have been made to make it appear that we unduly exalt speaking in tongues. We do not! We exalt the Gift of the Holy Spirit, and honor speaking in tongues only as the Bible evidence of that Gift, as it seems to us after long and diligent study of the Word of God."

*   *   *   *   *

If I were writing a novel, I would omit part of this chapter and just mention the pleasant things that people enjoy reading. However, as I am giving you a real life sketch, it would leave a false impression if I failed to give you a glimpse of the persecutions and suffering which Mr. Parham endured. In going through an art gallery, we have seen many beautiful pictures, but we may turn away from a bright colored one unsatisfied, some way it didn't look natural. We behold another picture, and we stand entranced. It is not as bright as the other, what makes the difference? Ah! Now I see! It is the soft shadows in the valley that has made the picture so complete. We are the handiwork of God, His workmanship; so the sadness, hardships and bitter persecutions which come to us, God uses, as the shadows to soften our lives, and make us more kind and sympathetic. "This life is not all sunshine, nor is it yet all showers."Our blessings and troubles will all draw us closer to God, if we will let them. We must take the bitter with the sweet and not complain, when we eagerly grasp for the beautiful roses, if we are sometimes scratched by the thorns. So when we consecrate our lives to God, "earnestly contending for the faith once delivered to the saints," seeking by faith to reach into the treasure house of God and obtain God's best, for ourselves and others, should we be surprised if we are bitterly attacked by the enemy of our souls, who is ever seeking to hinder us and des' troy our service for God?

Mr. Parham seldom spoke about his persecutions, saying what he had endured for the gospel looked so small besides what Christ had suffered for him, and what the apostles had gone through, that he did not feel like calling it persecution. That the Lord paid him every day for all he had done for Him, so when he comes to the courts of glory he said the Lord would not owe him anything. "It pays to serve Jesus. It pays every step of the way." But Jesus said, "If they persecute me they will also persecute you." He was betray' ed by His friends, and if we follow in His footsteps, we will be also, and often by those we have done the most for and loved the most.

As you know Zion City was a religious town; the whole city was interested more or less in religious subjects, so they took sides for or against us.

We had many true friends and also bitter enemies and sometimes, as you may know, it is hard to discern between the two. Though Mr. Parham was now in New York, the results of his work still remained, and the fight still raged bit' had turned against him because he refused to organize.
terly against him, which was also joined by our friends who

We were aware that many scandalous reports were being scattered and published, but this did not surprise us, for we knew the ear-marks of the Christians in Apostolic times, were good and evil reports and we now saw Mr. Parham well marked on both sides and rejoiced in the fact that he was going on for God and his work was being blessed.

As he refused to enter denominationalism again, he faced the same bitterness—that had been thrown at him when he had left it.

However, he did not let this bitterness enter his heart, neither did he seek to retaliate. He not only preached non-resistance but practiced it, and would sometimes welcome those, who had betrayed his confidence, back to his meetings in such a cordial way, his true friends would feel a little jealous.

A ship may sail safely across the great waters, but if it leaks and the water enters the ship, the ship will sink. So may we sail on safely for God, surrounded by hatred and strife, if our lives are so kept by the power and love of God that bitterness cannot enter.

I am glad Mr. Parham did not let bitterness come in, neither did I, and as I write this, it is not to condemn anyone, but to explain the principles which he stood for, in the face of every opposing force.

I have often thought that even his enemies must have had great confidence in his religion, knowing that he would not resist or resort to the law. They would not have dared to make such a scandalous attack on a worldly person, knowing they might have to pay the penalty at the courts of justice.

*   *   *   *   *

His friends often urged him to make some self-defense, which he answered as follows.

"When asked why we do not answer criticism, false and unfriendly attacks made upon the work or workers in the paper, we want to say: This is entirely unnecessary and it would be out of place to use the columns of a Christian paper—one devoted to the sacred work of the restoration of the apostolic faith—for is it not to bear the stamp of forgiveness and long suffering; not entering Satan's arena with low, scurrilous critcisms and strife but to lift up Jesus, and when He is lifted up He will draw all men unto Him; not in man's wisdom, lest we should boast but in the demonstration and power of the Holy Ghost, until the children of men shall say, 'The thing proceedeth from the Lord.'

"Let no one be disquieted by the vile rumors, persecutions and slanders heaped upon us.

"If any one should feel concerned enough to know the truth a personal letter will be answered gladly; we cannot take valuable space in this paper devoted to present truth, to discuss the work of our enemies.

"With our eyes on Him, we are marching steadily on, despised and rejected of men, but owned of God, to water His drooping lilies; with altars full, and the power, gifts, and graces of God attending. Hallelujah!"

*   *   *   *   *

Those who wilfully and maliciously fought Mr. Parham did not prosper. This has been true all through his ministry, and many have noticed it and mentioned it. He explained it in this way. "They are not fighting me, it is the truth that I bring. As I am faithful in giving out the message God gives me, He defends His truth."

"But we have this treasure in earthen vessels, that the excellency of the power may be of God, and not of us.

"We are troubled on every side, yet not distressed; we are perplexed but not in despair.

"Persecuted, but not forsaken; cast down, but not destroyed," (2 Cor. 4: 7-9).

Merton Wade, who had come from Kansas City, Missouri, to help in the meetings, was staying with me, and several of the other workers made our home their headquarters.

One day, two preachers came to make a "pastoral call," but for some reason, Merton and I both mistrusted their purpose and determined we would say nothing that could be misconstrued and "add fuel to the flame."

We heard afterwards they reported that they were sure we knew nothing of the evil reports, as they found us happy in the Lord, and gave them no opportunity to bring up the subject.

Later, I received a letter with all manner of evil spoken falsely against Mr. Parham, ending by saying they would provide for me and the children, as they didn't want us to suffer.

For a moment, it seemed that my heart stood still. What did it mean? I could not understand it, as I did later. I read the letter again. They misjudged me if they thought I wished to be left out of any deprivations or suffering which Mr. Parham might have to endure, for I was not afraid of these things. We had together endured many trials and expected to stand as one for this gospel, as long as life remained, whatever the cost.

I took my pen and paper to answer the letter but only had written the date when the Lord spoke peace to my troubled heart, and the words came to me, "resist not evil."

Would it not be only right for me to deny the charges and let them know at least how I stood?

But I had got a glimpse of Jesus. And when He was accused of the chief priests and elders, **he answered nothing. (Matt. 27: 12.)**

If he were not so near to me, it might have been different but he was my husband. It would be the same as answering in my own defense.

Then the Scripture came to me "Vengeance is mine, I will repay," saith the Lord. (Romans 12:19) and His Word was fulfilled.

The letter was never answered. I put my writing material away and read for my evening lesson Romans 12, that wonderful chapter on Christian living.

I trust that I shall never forget the sweet lesson the Lord gave me alone that night and that I may ever have the grace and love of God so shed abroad in my heart that I shall be able to live up to it. "He had given peace, perfect peace to me."

"These things I have spoken unto you, that in me ye might have peace. In the world ye shall have tribulation, but be of good cheer, I have overcome the world." (John 16:33) The Christ that calmed the boisterous waves of Galilee, can also say, "Peace be still" to our troubled hearts.

Another problem confronted me. Claude and Esther were being jeered at and ridiculed at school on account of our faith, which seemed hard for me to bear. One day Claude came home in great distress. Pork was not allowed in Zion City and the children took pleasure in calling our children "Part-ham."

"Papa is so kind to everyone, why do they call him a dangerous man?" "Why do they tell people not to go to hear him preach?" and many like questions they asked equally hard for me to explain to their young minds. I felt that some change must be made for the children's sake.

Much as I had tried and desired to be with Mr. Parham in meetings, at least part of the time, this now seemed impossible, as his work was rapidly growing and his ministry now reached from coast to coast. I knew his calling was from God and I was determined not to hinder him in his work. He had often said to me when leaving the home, "I know it is lonely for you, wife, but you have the children, and I have no one."

As the children must now go to school, it seemed necessary for me to settle down where things would be pleasant for them. I thought of my country home on the farm. My brother David, had a six-roomed house, just across the road from the old home-stead where my mother and aunts still lived and where I had been raised. David offered us the house to live in, saying he expected he would be an old batchelor and not need it. I told Merton I was afraid it would seem rather lonely in the country after being with so many friends, but she promised that she would come to visit me after we got located.

Of all our many dear friends in Zion City who were so good to us and we loved so dearly, we are still in correspondence with some of them.-

*   *   *   *   *

Mrs. Emma Lang is still in the work of the ministry and has written her testimony regarding the meeting.

"As for me, I shall never forget the time when our hearts were so sad and torn in Zion City, that we did not know just which way was best.

"One night when I was praying for guidance, I had a vision. I seemed to be standing in the middle of a street that led down to Lake Michigan. While I stood there, darkness, oh, such darkness came over the city! I said 'Lord, what does all this mean?' A voice said to me, 'The darkest time has not come to Zion City yet.'

"Then I looked at the lake and saw two boats. One wood-colored boat and the other one a white boat with a man in it, all dressed in white, handing out great nuggets of gold, (all tied in white bundles) to men that had rowed out in small white boats to the big white boat where the man in white was standing. As the men received the nuggets of gold, they were bringing them to shore. The wooden-colored boat stood off a way from the other, and I saw the man in that boat was just the opposite to the man in the white boat.

"This was before Brother Parham came to Zion City and I had never seen or heard of him at that time. The times grew worse in Zion City, till we could hardly stand it any longer. All this time, we were praying for God to send some one to come and bring deliverance to the people.

"One day a lady came to my house and told me that there was a man that was holding meetings in the city and I went to hear him. I was early, so I went in and took a seat in the front. In a few moments Brother Parham came in, dressed in a white suit and I saw the man of my vision.

"He labored under great persecution. The leaders of the city would not let him hold meetings in any of their buildings, but the people opened their homes to him and cottage meetings were held until the crowds, filled eight large houses and people came from many other cities to hear the wonderful message of the full gospel.

"Hunderds were saved, others sanctified and many were baptized with the Holy Spirit and spoke in other tongues. (Acts 2-4). Also many wonderful healings took place. The good that was accomplished through Brother Parham's ministry in Zion City, eternity alone will fully reveal."

*   *   *   *   *

As Mr. Parham taught that we should try the spirits, he also taught that we should be careful about visions and dreams and test them by the Word of God, saying, "We know many dreams are caused by something that we have eaten or an over-loaded stomach." Yet he also believed, that sometimes visions and dreams were from God to definitely direct or encourage our faith in a time of need, as Peter was shown a vision that he should go and preach the baptism of the Holy Spirit to the house of Cornelius. (Acts 10.)

As Mrs. Lang was shown Mr. Parham in a vision, how wonderfully it encouraged her to receive the truth when he brought it, and how much her influence helped and strengthened the faith of her friends. Truly the precious truths that Mr. Parham handed out to those who would receive them were as great nuggets of gold, which were passed on to other messengers, not only in this country but around the world.

When Mr. Parham was sick in Jerusalem in 1928, he sent to the Christian Missionary Alliance Church for some one to come and pray for him. Two brethren came and as they prayed, God wonderfully touched his body. One of these ministers was a convert of F. F. Bosworth of Zion City. When he found out who Mr. Parham was he said that he was not only the fruitage of Bro. Bosworth's labor but of his also. In the darkest part of Syria, north of there, he had forty converts. So he said, "The Bread you cast on the waters has drifted to many shores and found its way to darkest Syria," and that he was Mr. Parham's grandson in the gospel.

Mr. Parham was greatly encouraged by this, and he said it made him feel that it had paid to consecrate his life to the service of God, and that his labors had not been in vain.

While the children and I were having our trials—"our light afflictions" as St. Paul calls them—Mr. Parham was carrying the truth to new fields in the East. One time, when he was in a large city, a man stopped him on the street and asked him for money to buy a bowl of soup. Mr. Parham told him that was all the money he had and that he was on the way to the soup kitchen to get a bowl of soup for himself. As he looked at the man, he thought how much better off he was than he, as he had faith in God and this poor man had nothing, so he gave him the money and as there was now no need for him to go on to the soup kitchen, he turned and went down another street. As he walked seemingly aimlessly along, he met a friend who said, "Why, I have been looking for you, where have you been?" and handed him ten dollars. Had Mr. Parham gone on to the soup kitchen, perhaps the man might not of found him to give him the money. How wonderfully God rewards us, one hundred fold for every sacrifice we make for Him. Praise the Lord.

Mr. Parham not only preached but always practised the commandment of Jesus, "Give to him that asketh thee, and from him that would borrow of thee, turn not thou away." (Matt. 5:42).

*　*　*　*　*

Mr. Parham wrote the following letter regarding his eastern trip, published in the Apostolic Faith, April 1907.

"In January 1907 at the close of a fortnight's meeting of great power and victory in Zion City, I felt led of God to begin a campaign of truth to the eastward.

"My first halt after leaving the 'City of Laces' was in beautiful Cleveland , wherein I visited the Quaker Church and Bible School, tarrying a day and a night.

"These people have reached an elevated plane in Christian experience. I was warmly welcomed, and was greeted at night by a large truth-searching audience. I was thankful for a special anointing that enabled me to show clearly the difference between the true manifestations of the Holy Spirit and those of other forces.

"This was a most profitable meeting. For the rubbish and disgust that had lodged in the minds of many from the reports of certain meetings in California were completely swept away.

"My next move was to drop back to Toledo, to address a congregation composed of honest people of all denominations, who were anxious to learn more of the enriching blessing of Pentecost.

"God walked in the midst of the people that night, and blessings were added to the lives of many.

"Leaving the extension of this work in the hands of Sister Lillian Thistlethwaite, I followed divine guidance to Toronto, Canada.

"The Canadians had been praying the Lord to send me there. They had sent a wireless message straight through to the throne of God. No wonder I was obliged to invade the British Dominion!

"Upon my arrival at Ontario's frozen Capital, I soon found the Zion gathering.

"Immediately after entering their hall, the liberal, broad-minded Elder, invited me to the pulpit. By way of introduction the Elder addressed his people thus:

'I suppose you all have your ideas concerning the man before you, I don't believe in hanging a man before trial; and I haven't such a narrow, contracted brain as to prevent his speaking to you today. I shall invite him to preach, as I wish to hear him, and know that you do too. I intend to listen, but don't propose to believe his doctrine until I know its right.'

"I count that a very fair introduction.

"While I preached that afternoon I felt the flow of congenial fellowship, and in the evening service, together we were sprinkled with the showers of God's mercy and love.

"At the close of the evening sermon the Elder rose and said 'Every one in this assembly who desires to invite Bro. Parham to conduct our meetings down-town, and who wishes to turn them over to him for a season, rise to your feet.'

"They arose en masse.

"The next day these good, consecrated people rented a hall and placed it at my disposal.

"As the days slipped by, persons from other meetings, ministers and Christians from over the province came to hear of the glorious tidings of a restored Pentecost.

"I had a glorious time among these people, although there was no revival to speak of, except among God's children. Ministers and Christians were unified, and prejudice melted away.

"May the Lord deliver us from tagging with movements and churches. I haven't a single church or movement to build up. My mission is to preach Jesus Christ and the doctrine he brought into the world and thus I am enabled to get into churches and missions that I could in no wise enter in the name of any church or movement.

"To head out into a church or a movement is to get sec-tarian and to lose the sweetness of the spirit of universal brotherhood. Unity can only be obtained by the truth, and the truth shall make us free.

"We must get the truth of God, preach it, practice it, carry its force in our lives, and get others leavened with the same leaven. By this process, the true children shall be leavened into one body in answer to the prayer of Jesus.

"When three weeks were told, we felt that the time had arrived for us to separate from these blessed Christian friends.

"I next touched at Lisbon Falls, Maine.

"After pleasant association with old friends, I went by boat to Boston.

"'Tis true you can easily tell a man from Boston, but you can't tell him very much. They bit on the wooden nutmeg joke so long that they became wise, and you cannot induce them to invest before showing them the inside of the package.

"But at the expiration of a few weeks' meetings, held by our workers, the inhabitants of the hub of the universe began to use a phrase common in that great manufacturing section: 'If this is a sample, please send the whole bolt.' Yet they are so doubtful there that they will add after you complete a straightforward story: 'I want to know!'

"When old, sensible Boston awakes and gets a glimpse of the real, then will come such a sweeping revival as will turn Unitarian, Christian scientific New England upside down, or rather rightside up, heaving them out of their anti-divinity, demonized theories into the faith of the Son of God.

"Our meetings were crowded. A precious work was done. Nearly all the missions were represented and most of the mission leaders were present. The whole city is now ripe for an old-time Pentecostal revival.

"I hope to be able in the near future to arrive on the scene with at least twenty-five live evangelists and conduct a revival on an immense scale.

"There are multitudes of substantial people in the metropolis of New England who are craving the best in God's storehouse.

"The last Sunday I spent in Boston I preached five times, occupying in all seven hours. Great is the power of this Holy Ghost oil to run the machinery built for His use.

"I had a delightful journey from Boston to New York; first by rail to Fall River, Mass., thence by boat to New York.

"Here the work is difficult, but gratifying. The town is infested with cranks, and they often disrupt the meetings.

"A friend rented the Volunteer Hall on forty-second street for two weeks. Here many people came to listen and to learn the deep things of God. Truly these were days of feasting on the 'Bread of Heaven,' 'the hidden manna'—'the honey in the rock.'

"This meeting was a great success, and God touched the lives of many whose whole aim, now is to know and to do the Master's will.

"My last Sunday in New York was one of power.   In the morning I preached for Bro. Merritt.   The presence of the Holy Spirit was so evident that a great glory rested on the service and all enjoyed a feast at Father's table.   God bless Bro. Merritt, 'the Holy Ghost man.'

"This portly and humorous old gentleman presented me to his audience with the following statement:—'I introduce to you a man who knows all things.'   He also spiced this by the use of a few other cutting remarks.

"In return I could but say, 'If what Bro. Merritt has been teaching you for years be true I can meet your expectations, for He, the Holy Ghost, knows all things; and if I be yielded to Him, He will teach you today all things He desires you to know.'

"Bro. Merritt was pleased with the services.   When the truth is presented void of error or fanaticism it will cling tenaciously to the minds of the intelligent.

"Returning from New York I stopped at Syracuse, and we had two excellent services in that city.

"Many excellent persons in that section are enlisted for God's service and we hope to soon return to labor awhile in this field.

"I was again permitted to spend a refreshing season with the Christians of Cleveland.   First, we visited the former Zion gathering.   The pastor and many others are on their faces for Pentecost.   They also conduct a mission where the revival power is present each night and many precious souls are daily merging into the Kingdom.

"This gathering is one of the most spiritual I have ever ministered to, and the prospects are that many gleaners will step from here into the harvest fields of God.

"When I left these dear ones my heart was full to overflowing.   How I rejoice in what God permitted me to see, to hear and to do!   How I rejoice in anticipation of results!

"What does this prevalent spiritual hunger and activity mean? Ah, 'tis but a partial answer to the prayer of all saints: 'Thy Kingdom Come.' Let every one who reads this, pray it over and over again.

"Upon nearing Zion City, I began to realize that three months had slipped away since I had seen my precious wife and babes. I can't be with them much, but I found that the Lord had provided for them in the severity of Zion's climate as He did under the Italian skies of Texas. When they run a little short no one knows it but God; and knowing that nothing can happen to her and her little fledgelings but what God permits, wife reasons that either some one has refused to carry out divine impressions or that others need it worse than we.

"It's no trouble to get joy and comfort out of God's invitation, 'Come.' But to get the same blessings from the command, 'Go' one must have a burning desire to serve Him and he must be attached by sympathy to every human creature. There's hardly time in the Master's work to 'Keep the bright reward in view.'

"When I depart from home wife does not follow me to the door begging me not to go, but with her shoulder to the gospel wheel and her hand to my back, her parting remark is, 'God speed you and bring you back safely some time.' Pardon this disgression, please.

"My reception in Zion City was a gracious ovation. We had four days of glorious, powerful services, and our heart turned again toward our children in sunny climes.

"We soon landed in Texas, the land of cotton and roses. What a joyous welcome we received at Orchard, where our first gospel children of the South were born!

"Oh, it pays to serve Jesus—I speak from my heart;
He will ever be with us if we do our part.
There's naught in this old world can true pleasure afford.
But there's peace and contentment in serving the Lord."

"The workers in the East greet you all in other States. They have lacked no good thing, and are bravely facing the foe, triumphant in God.

"Thus closes one of the most fruitful winters of my ministry; and now spring buds are swelling with wondrous prospects!"

* * * * *

Before Mr. Parham went on to Orchard, Texas, he got the children and I comfortably located in our country home near Tonganoxie, Kansas.

Regarding the Orchard meeting, W. M. Gray wrote:

"A few weeks previous to this occurrence, Bro. Parham hinted by mail that if God would release him from the work in the East, he would make a desperate attempt to arrive in time to open our second anniversary of the entrance of the Apostolic Faith doctrine into the Empire State of the South.

"A hint at refreshing times from our 'Gospel Daddy' was sufficient; so words of solicitation were soon speeding towards New York, prayers towards Heaven, and money towards Zion.

"'Tis futile to attempt a description of the welcome extended him by our citizens. If there is a man, woman, or child here who does not love Bro. Parham, I have not found it out.

"Easter dawned bright and fair at Orchard. God's children came teeming in from all directions, and we had a glorious day. As I listened to testimonies, and tongues, and praises the first telegraph message flashed through my mind: 'Behold, what God hath wrought!' It doesn't seem possible that such a marvelous work could have been accomplished in two year's time.

"Hundreds revel in the light Bro. Parham brought us, and he has the love and esteem of his Texas children in the Gospel of Jesus:

"We missed many faces which were seen at our last year's reunion; but God leads, and we know there comes a grander reunion, where the elect of God will separate no more.

"Bro. Parham has begun a week's meeting with us, then we'll lose him again."

*   *   *   *   *

After his wonderful Easter meeting in Orchard, he went to other places in Texas for meetings. One day I received word that he had been arrested while preaching but some of his true friends had immediately came to his release and he continued the meeting. The city attorney told him that he would not have to appear, because he (the attorney) would not even call the case for trial for he "was satisfied it was all spite work."

I was with him in Texas, at the date set in the indictment, but the case was never called, the prosecuting attorney declaring that there was absolutely no evidence which merited any legal recognition. In the eyes of the world such testimony is sufficient, but alas, how merciless are some of God's professing children! Oh! that we might raise the standard of Christianity and brotherly love!

Perhaps you may be shocked at the thought, but is it not a fact that many professed full gospel people today even fail to keep the ten commandments? Do we not often see the ninth commandment, "Thou shalt not bear false witness against thy neighbor," broken? How sad that professed Christians and even preachers seem to justify themselves in casting a shadow over a brother's reputation by spreading false reports, if by so doing, they think they can further their own selfish purposes.

*   *   *   *   *

Mrs. M. E. Parham (then Mrs. Walkenshaw) wrote the following:

"Few men have suffered persecution as Mr. Parham did.
'It must be that offences come; but woe to that man by whom
the offence cometh.' (Matt. 18-7.)

"Christians are not burned at the stake these days, but it
would be far more merciful to do so, than to drag one's reputation through the mire and filth, concocted from slander,
hatched in the very pits of hell!

"Many listened to the devil's lies, and through this brought
the gospel that he preached into disrepute. Everywhere he
went he met this vile slander. The devil saw to it that it
was well circulated but God gave him a 'face of adamant'
and he went on preaching the unsearchable riches of Christ
and thousands were won to the standard of the full gospel.

"When I first heard this vile stuff, I was astounded. It
was carried to me by two preachers. When they were gone,
I fell on my knees before God and cried out in agony of
soul, 'Oh God, I never knew what purity of heart and life
was until this man taught me, through Thy Word. We
expected persecution, but nothing like this. Thou hast said in
Thy Word, the witness of man was great but the witness of
God was greater. Show me what to do in this case. Make
it very plain, for I fear Thy Name.

"Sweetly the words came. 'Read I Thess. 1-5 and chap. 2-
10.' I arose from my knees, took my Bible, held it in my
hand for a moment, almost afraid what I should read. The
Spirit said, 'If the son asks bread, will the father give him a
stone?' I said, 'No, Lord, what ever this is, I take it from
Thee.' This was what I read. 'For our gospel came not unto you in word only, but also in power, and in the Holy
Ghost and in assurance; as ye know what manner of men we
were among you, for your sake' Glancing to the next Scrip-

ture I read, 'Ye are my witnesses, and God also, how holily, and justly and unblamebly we behaved ourselves among you that believe.'

" 'Thank you, Lord,' I said, 'You have given me a greater witness than men's witness. I shall not be moved.' I am sure Mr. Parham was a man chosen of God, sanctified and meet for the Master's use.

"How my heart ached for him as this vile stuff was thrown at him wherever he went. A constant dripping on a stone will in time wear it away. I am confident that his great, tender, loving heart was in time broken. So that the under-taker wrote on his burial certificate 'Died of an over-taxed heart.'

"In my last conversation I had with him the day before his death, he said, 'I can not boast of any good works I have done when I meet my Master face to face, but I can say, I have been faithful to the message He gave me, and lived a pure, clean life.'

"Truly more precious than the approval of men, is to have this testimony that we have pleased God."

*　*　*　*　*

A rather amusing incident occurred one time when Mr. Parham was holding a great revival meeting in Missouri. He had preached a wonderful sermon under the anointing of the Holy Spirit, and at the close of the meeting a lady said to me, "That was a wonderful sermon, surely Mr. Parham must have got back to God." I said, "Do you think so? I did not know that he had ever been back-slidden." "O yes," she said, "had not you heard ......" and she proceeded to tell me a long, sad story of how he had left his wife and family etc. When she finished speaking I said, "I am glad I can tell you that all this is untrue." "But how do you know?" she asked.

I smiled and said, "I am his wife." The expression on her face was pitiful, to say the least, she left without saying good-by and I never saw her again.

Perhaps it was meanness and mischief in me, which caused me to keep still and let her "expose her ignorance," but I trust she got a lesson out of it, and I was really glad she told it to me, instead of some one else who might not have been so able to correct her.

Utterly failing to prove anything against his character, they called him a "no-hellite".

This he emphatically denied, saying that he believed in a hotter hell than they did. While they might believe in a hell that would torment, he believed in a hell that would completely destroy.

I believe, however, that the main secret of the fight against him, was that he did not believe in organizations. Not giving any of his time to build up any demonination, he preached a free gospel everywhere to all who would receive it, giving God all the honor and glory and without soliciting or begging, salary or a financial board, trusted God who supplied all his needs.

* * * * *

On Mr. Parham's fortieth birthday he wrote the following:

"For my enemies I have only an abiding sympathy; no words of condemnation, but only sorrow for the souls, who, through their fight on me, have been wrecked and ruined. I think the greatest sorrow of my life is the thought that my enemies, in seeking my destruction, have ruined and destroyed so many precious souls.

"The introduction of new—old truths has been freighted with many hardships and sorrows, yet the toils of the road have been nothing compared to the glory. Glory to His Name.

"The dews of night, and the sun by day, have drawn and burned my feet till they bled, but dashing the tears from my eyes, I shouted on, refusing to even shed a tear 'when the footsteps of Jesus made the pathway glow.'

"Though in trials, persecutions, mobs, oft slanders and scandals, though many times in great straits among false bre-thren and followed by hired assassins for years, yet, through it all, He has always caused me to triumph.

"I am more than grateful to the many thousands of my faithful friends for their sustaining prayers and financial help through all these years. Brought by the grace of God from a life of sin and sickness, you have been my helpers and sup-port. God bless you all."

BE TRUE TO THE CAUSE

"Here's to the cause, how we love it,
The cause, our glory, our pride,
Awake! be up and reaping,
In God's harvest fields so wide.

Jesus is coming, soon coming,
Our song of triumph shall be,
Hark! I hear the low rumbling,
Of his chariots, from sea to sea.

Soon in all earth will be sounding
That joyful trumpets' loud blast,
Telling our King is coming
And His cause will triumph at last."

Chapter XX

RETURNED TO BAXTER SPRINGS, KANSAS.

R. Parham held a meeting in California during the winter of 1907. He had many friends in California now, and preached to many hungry souls on the western coast. On January 12, 1908 he began a meeting at Los Angeles, Cal., in the W. C. T. U. Temple on the corner of Temple and Broadway.

This was his second trip to Los Angeles and in the years that followed, he spent a great deal of time and labor on the western coast; going there many times. Space would not permit me to give a detailed account of his work in the west, even if it was possible for me to do so, but in the following pages I will make mention of some of his meetings held there.

After closing his meetings in California, he went to Orchard, Texas, for the third annual Easter meeting to be held there. I will copy a part of a general letter that he wrote to the Kansas and Missouri Missions regarding this meeting.

Houston, Texas
May 9, 1908

To my friends and brethern:

I will write you a letter concerning the great meeting we have just closed at Orchard, Texas, which was one of the greatest meetings we have ever held in the state. I can scarcely frame words to tell you how the power of God was manifested there.

Lives of individuals were read out like an open book in the light of the Holy Spirit: such deep truths brought to light that men and women stood in awe in the presence of the mighty power of God.

The nine gifts of the Spirit were made manifest; one day on the camp grounds, they were all used in a wonderful way. Not that they were permanently bestowed, but God gave them for the time they were needed and how we worship Him for the power He bestowed.

Nor was that all, but in the saving, sanctifying and healing power, He was with us in a wonderful way. In the deliverance of those fettered and bound by demoniac forces, there was power in the name of the Christ to liberate and to free.

As the great Apostle said, "When ye come together, every one hath a psalm, hath a doctrine, hath a tongue, hath a revelation, hath an interpretation. Let all things be done unto edifying." (I Cor. 14:26). So it was here. There was no confusion: when everything is in the hands of the Holy Spirit, all is harmony and love.

The multitudes who attended the meeting were fed free. The renting of the tabernacle and the living tents were also a great expense, but God gave us the means to pay every dollar of the indebtedness, though we had less than five dollars when we went on the grounds.

We believe this meeting has not been surpassed by any other assembly since the days when that little "Apostolic lad" was asked to spread forth the "loaves and fishes" which the Lord blessed and fed the multitudes. So likewise was the circumstances with us; there was sufficient and to spare.

There were people there from Missouri, Kansas, Virginia, California and from all over the state of Texas, who came especially to attend this meeting. At the close of the ten days session (the time advertised for the meeting), it was impossible to close, so it was continued a week longer, closing with power, light, life and truth to all. Thus ended the third annual Easter meeting at Orchard, Texas.

After the conclusion of the battle here in Houston, I am going to Alabama and Mississippi for a little season, then to Kansas and Missouri for meetings there.

In these days of "spiritual wickedness in high places;" of such awful forces that are binding the children of God: such demoniac spirits abroad in the land, with sin abounding; with powers and forces at work to mislead, to deceive and to draw away: with the devil as "the accuser of the brethern", how close to God we must live.

How we should live true to one another: how we should pray mightily for one another: how we should trust and honor God to bring our erring brethren out of the pit falls they may have fallen into, and how we ought to practice the real gospel of the Christ and reach out loving, helping hands, to bring the wanderer, fallen and wayward one back to the fold.

In conclusion let me say, as the beloved disciple of the Master said, "Little children, love one another."May our eyes be fixed on Jesus, and our watchword be, "Onward and Up-ward." Let us live true to God and hold to Him and He will give us the desires of our hearts. Praying the Lord to keep each of you until we meet again and until He shall say, "Come up higher."

I am your father in the gospel, Chas. F. Parham.

*   *   *   *   *

A newspaper clipping makes the following announcement regarding the meeting;

"The Apostolic meeting at Orchard 'holds the boards' in that city for another week. All the people are fed from a public kitchen and dining room without cost to those who dine, and the city restaurants excel not the menu. Twenty nine converts were baptized Sunday by Charles F. Parham, who never tires, but preaches day and night and jokes during intervals.

"People from many other places were there. The members of the Apostolic Faith are having a hallelujah time at Orchard and greet all comers with the hand of fellowship and good cheer."

After closing a convention at Houston, Mr. Parham left (May 17) for a general visitation among the missions in Alabama and Mississippi, which was followed by a general convention for both states which was held at Crichton Ala., and continued for ten days.

Meanwhile our children were enjoying the privileges and freedom of country life at Tonganoxie, Kansas and our friend, Merton Wade, had not failed to pay us the promised visit to keep me from being lonesome, and her visit not only helped in that way, but also changed the course of several lives.

My brother, David, decided that after all, he did not want to be an "old batchelor," as he had expected to be, but that he had now found the girl of his choice.

But the possibility of leaving the country home was not good news to the children, especially the older ones. Claude said, "We have no more home than a jack-rabbit. It just gets a nest in the grass patted down and here comes some one and scares it, and away it goes! It's the same way with us, isn't it?"

It was some time, however, before the new family was established and after that we remained for sometime; dividing the house, we found room for all.

After Mr. Parham had finished his work in the south, he returned home to Tonganoxie and the two younger children and I went with him to his next meeting which was to be held at Tulsa, Okla.

* * * * *

Mrs. C. O. Frye, who still lives at Tulsa, has given us a short account of this meeting.

"In August, 1908, we invited Brother Charles F. Parham to come and conduct a revival in Tulsa. He came in response to the call and was accompanied by his wife and a small band of workers. Our family were the only ones of this faith living there at the time. We had lived in Joplin, Mo., during the time that Brother Parham had held his meeting there, and had accepted the light of the full gospel.

"A large tent was secured and the results of the meeting were very gratifying, as there were nearly one hundred con-verted to the faith, quite a good number received the baptism of the Holy Spirit and many were healed of various diseases. The meeting continued for three weeks, after which the work was left in the care of elders.

"Now after nearly twenty two years, there are many dear ones, who came into the light at that time, and are still stand-ing faithful and true, proving the work was genuine. From that meeting the truth has spread to many states and even to foreign fields. There are now thousands in and around Tulsa who believe in this gospel. I am now seventy years old, and I thank the Lord, I have lived to see this day."

* * * * *

I have many pleasant memories of this meeting, and the kindness shown us by our friends there, and we thought the fine melons they brought us were the best we had ever tasted.

Mr. Parham then held a camp-meeting at Carthage, Mo., and my sister brought our three oldest children and joined us here. Our oldest boy was converted and baptized with a number of others at the close of the meeting, which had been a blessed time of refreshing to many souls.

During September, Mr. Parham held a number of meet-ings in Kansas and Missouri, and in October, he returned to Texas and Alabama for meetings there.

For some time Mr. Parham had felt a desire to go to the Holy Land, so he returned home to bid us good-bye and make his final arrangements for the journey, starting for the east, Dec. 4, 1908.

He stopped at Zion City for a special campaign for unity

and God's blessing was realized in a marvelous way. Many were saved and sanctified and a real spirit of unity was brought about.

* * * * *

The Daily Sun. Waukegan, Ill., Monday, Dec. 7, 1908.

"Parham passed through Waukegan at nine yesterday morning. 'I am in Zion City merely on a visit,' he said, 'and am the guest of no leader or of no faction. I bring simply a message of peace and unity, and for the cessation of factional warfare, and my visit is not to be construed as having a mission.' In fact he modestly refused to admit himself the leader of any faction or class in Zion City despite the tremendous following he is credited with.

"Two years ago Parham turned Zion City upside down, inducing thousands to a belief in the speaking in tongues, in non-resistance, in the doctrine that 'the Lord will provide' and in a missionary spirit that has carried some of the Zion people to remote corners of the earth; to South Africa, China, Japan, Korea, Australia and various parts of this country."

* * * * *

After closing his meeting in Zion City he reached New York, and had expected to sail about the first of January, but before he had purchased his ticket, he was knocked down and robbed. We do not know how long he remained unconscious, but how grateful we were that his life was spared.

A friend loaned him some money and he returned home. We will not attempt to tell the pain and disappointment he suffered; yet we know that some times our disappointments are God's appointments, and decided perhaps this was not the time for him to make this trip, and we still felt His loving care over our lives.

We decided to move to Baxter Springs, so by March, 1909, we were comfortably located there and enjoyed being with our Baxter friends once more.

Chapter XXI

TESTIMONIES FROM SAN ANGELO.

INCE the entrance of this gospel into Texas, a meeting had been held in Orchard, Texas, each Easter, but this Easter arrangements were made to hold it at Brookshire, Texas, April 11, 1909; after this followed the meeting at San Angelo, Texas.

The meeting that Mr. Parham held there was perhaps not a greater or more successful meeting than many others that he conducted which are only recorded in heaven.

However this particular meeting is held sacred in the memory of many who received definite experiences and answers to prayer there and some are giving testimony to them through these pages.

* * * * *

Mrs. Maggie Pettit wrote, "I want to write my testimony in honor and gratitude to God for sending our dear Brother Parham to San Angelo, Texas. He surely was God-sent and came with a band of workers, preaching the full gospel and brought me the truth and light on the Word of God.

"I was sick in bed and could not raise up without fainting. The doctors had done all they could and given me up to die, saying there was no hope for me except through an operation and I was too weak for that. I had a complication of diseases and such misery as I suffered I can not describe. No medicine could reach my case.

"Brother Parham came on Friday and Mr. Pettit went to the meeting three nights and told me of the wonderful meeting. He said Brother Parham preached the whole truth and the power of God to heal. So on Monday night I sent for him to come and pray for me.

"As he prayed for me, I felt the power of God go through my whole being. As he left, he said, 'You get up, as the Lord gives you strength to do so.'

"I did not feel any better right away. Mr. Pettit took Brother Parham to town, which was about four blocks, and when he came home I was up and dressed. Praise the Lord.

"The meeting continued and the signs followed. There were all manner of diseases healed. Many were saved, sanctified and received the baptism of the Holy Spirit.

"Brother Parham surely came in the demonstration and power of the Holy Spirit and he brought light and truth such as we had never heard before.

"How I thank God that through His servant my blinded eyes were opened to His wonderful truth and the power of the gospel.

"May God bless this testimony to the good of others, is my prayer."

*   *   *   *   *

Evangelist S. W. Ditto has given his testimony. "In 1906 a party of workers came from Houston, Texas to Snyder, Texas. Sister M. McClendon, a young lady just out of Brother Parham's Bible School at Houston, preached (under the mighty anointing of the Holy Ghost) the power of God to save, heal, sanctify, cast out devils, and baptize with the Holy Ghost and fire with the same evidence the disciples had on the day of Pentecost. God gave many souls and a mighty meeting was held.

"They told us of the little man, Charles F. Parham, and about his work and the Bible School at Houston; also of the Bethel Bible School at Topeka, Kansas and the beginning of the Latter Rain there.

"Of course this put a great longing in our hearts to see the man so wonderfully used of God. Later I got in touch with him by letter, and received his promised to come and hold a meeting for us, but it was impossible for him to come at that time.

"We heard many evil reports about him, but as we prayed over it, it seemed to us that the religion of Paul and Peter was here. Surely he was suffering for righteousness' sake and a deeper love came into our hearts for him.

"A few more months rolled around and he came to Snyder, Texas, and God wonderfully blessed in a great revival. I received a wonderful hold on the deep truths of God's Word, I had never seen before. God began to call on me for my full time for the ministry. I tried to get by, doing pastoral work for I did not want to leave home and take the evange-listic field, but my health failed. With hemorrhage of the lungs and painful swollen feet, I went down in weight from 196 pounds to 130 pounds in ninety days.

"I was very weak with fever, but a man took me from Snyder, Texas to San Angelo, Texas where Brother Parham was holding a meeting and wonderful healings had taken place.

"Some invalids had been healed, one blind man received his sight and I believed I would be healed if I could only get there. We found where he was rooming and he came out on the porch to meet us.

"I began to tell him how I was suffering. He smiled and said to the young man with him, 'Wells, here is a man who has played off sick to get his wife to let him come to meeting.' So I hushed and shall never forget his prayer. 'Oh God, take the spirit of rebelliousness out of this man's heart, make him willing to do your will and heal him for Jesus' sake, Amen.'

"He then left me quickly. I wanted to see him and talk with him, but he would not give me an opportunity to do so. He told me afterwards that he could not without showing too much sympathy, and so he hid away and prayed for me. That night the meeting was rained out. The next night he invited me into the choir. I went though I knew I could not sing. But as they sung,

'He hath given peace, perfect peace to me.'
I heard myself singing, with all my might,
'It is mine, mine, blessed be His Name.'

"I felt no harm, so I knew of a certainty I was healed and it was so. Praise our God!

"Through all these years since, I have been in close touch with him and in many of his meetings. He has come to my help many times in the battle of life, and truly, I do esteem him very highly for his work's sake. To my way of thinking he was the greatest preacher of this age, and preached more of the gospel than any man since the days of the apostles. I trust many others may go on unselfishly doing their work as he did his. He never gave up under the shell fire of the devil's artillery. Even under the worst persecutions, he was faithful to Him that called him to so great a work. In the San Angelo meeting, after I was healed he spoke for forty minutes or more in another language at a prayer meeting. Four were wonderfully saved but he did not seem to notice them at all. He shouted and prayed in a new tongue, a language he had not used before.

"When he had closed his prayer, a fine looking Spainard came in and said he had heard the gospel in his own tongue.

"Brother Parham said, 'Praise the Lord, I had always wanted to speak in the Spanish tongue and know it.'

"I have been with him in lots of meetings and he has been in our home much, and I can say, he was a willing servant and true to his call and the power of God was with him in a wonderful way all through his ministry.

"His works will follow him and he will ever live in the hearts of multitudes that he has been a blessing to. As other great men have come, done their work and gone to rest, so has he. Let us also be faithful and do the work the Lord has for us to do."

* * * * *

A MILLINER'S EXPERIENCE IN A DEEPER LIFE.

In the year 1908, I realized, though my experience was founded on the solid rock, it was a very shallow one. Many times since my feet had been taken from the miry clay, I had longed to be in the place where my life would more fully harmonize with the Christ-life.

Sorrow, the loss of loved ones, had brought me to a place where the need of a personal Savior was realized in a greater measure than ever before.

Several times different ministers had preached on the life of Christ, a clean heart, and in my willingness to draw near the Lord, I sought Him with all my heart and was always blessed and encouraged. I consecrated all I knew, but an extremely high temper seemed to be my besetting sin.

For several days, and one time for nine months, I walked under the illumination of the Holy Spirit and lived a victorious life.

One day everything seemed to go wrong. As quick as a flash, I found myself so angry I could scarcely contain myself. Instead of going straight to my knees saying, "Lord I have failed, let Thy blood cleanse me, and take this out of my life, etc." I proceeded to look at my failures, mistakes and blunders. "Alas! alas!" said the tempter, "You can't live it. Where is your sanctification now?" "Well," I said, "it won't keep me, though I do believe it will some folks."

So I gave it all up, feeling it was really no use for me to try to be an overcomer, but I would try to be the best Christian I could. I went on with family prayer, Sunday School teaching, prayer meeting, paying the preacher, etc., but somehow the real joy had all leaked out. How dead, dry and formal it all was, for I was only doing these things from a sense of duty. Oh, how heavy the task became without the joy of the Lord to lift the load and illuminate the soul!

Often my heart's cry was, "Lord it this the best I can do? Is this the best you have for your children?" I was discouraged, sick in body as well as soul. For fifteen years, I had suffered from that horrible disease asthma.

Having been engaged in the milliner business for three years in Oklahoma, my sister and I decided to take a little vacation and go back to the old home in Texas, where about five years before we had laid to rest our parents. We looked upon the little mounds, that held almost all in life that was dear to us.

We enjoyed our visit at the old home and with our brothers and sisters but I was still sick in body, weary in soul, always longing for a closer walk with God .

Long ago physicians had said that a change of climate would be beneficial but after a few months the same extreme suffering would return, and the hypodermic and ether was all that could be done. Oh, I wonder how many bottles of ether I have used and my arms were all speckled with the prints of the needle.

Neither of us were anxious to return to our Oklahoma home and business, so we decided to stay for a year in that healthy western town of San Angelo, Texas and have a good rest. But I soon became tired of resting. Oh, dear reader, it was Jesus I needed.

I thought perhaps work would drown my lonely, dreary feeling, so I applied and got work at a milliner store. I had not been trimming hats long until a gospel tent was pitched where I had to go by it as I went to work.

The people there appealed to me, they were so neat and clean, always speaking so polite and kind. They seemed so different to the people I had been selling hats to.

I wanted to go but I was sure the lady of the store would not approve of any of her girls going there as they talked and made fun of the tent people all day long, saying they were "funny people." But really there was nothing strange about them after you knew them. These people were none else than Charles F. Parham and his evangelistic party.

One day as I passed by the tent, a very kind old man came out and invited me to the services and spoke of the blessing of the baptism of the Holy Spirit. This seemed very strange indeed to me for I had never heard anything about the Holy Spirit only as the ministers pronounced the benediction or baptized in the name of the Father, Son and Holy Spirit.

My father often prayed for a Pentecostal blessing, but surely that just meant he wanted to see three thousand added to the church, and I never remember reading the second chapter of Acts experience. I shall never forget the first time I heard Brother Parham preach. He spoke of how the Lord saved, healed, sanctified and baptized with the Holy Spirit. Jesus had never been presented to me in such a way before. I did not know He had the same power as when He walked the shores of Galilee. What! Still healing His people?

I went home to say, "I think he is a smart man, but he surely has too much on his program to ever have wrought out in this world." Nevertheless we began reading our Bibles to see if it was there. I had believed when Jesus went to heaven, He took His power with Him. I had over-looked the Scripture. "Verily, verily, I say unto you, He that believeth on me, the works that I do shall he do also; and greater works than these shall he do, because I go unto the Father. (John 14:12). As I continued to read these truths impressed me more and more.

Three weeks we searched the Scriptures and it sure was there, the Healer of His people. And I was so in need of Him, I began to seek Him. It was not long until I began to find more things the matter with soul than body. Though often before consecrating and failing, yet I still felt a deep concern to draw closer to Him.

One night I found myself making my way to the altar. I was so discouraged and disgusted with myself, all seemed so dark so far away from God; it really seemed almost useless to try, yet deep down in my heart, I resolved to know the will of God, if sanctification was for me, I wanted it.

If I had all there was, then I would throw the Bible over the fence, so to speak, would fall in with the class that would make my business in this world go.

The Bible was open before me, and I knew that it taught that Jesus came to cleanse and purify the Church that He might present Himself with a glorious Church without spot or wrinkle.

So one day during a testimony meeting, I arose and said I was convinced that the sanctifying grace of God was for me and I was determined to have it or starve to death in the attempt to get it. I had not thought of fasting when I said this. Then came the thought, what have I said or done? "Have it or starve?" Oh well, I'll go to the altar tonight and get sanctified, but I did not. I went to the altar and sought the Lord as earnestly as I could, but no blessing came. I went home and spent most of the night inquiring of the Lord what His will was concerning me. Next morning no break- fast, most of the day was spent in inquiring. "Lord, what would Thou have me to do?"

I must tell you I had been a bit critical about how people worshipped, especially about street meetings. That looked like a Pharisee, did it not? Well, that was alright for other folks, but not me, No, No. To my utter surprise about the first thing I seemed to have to do was to go on the street with that humble crowd to a street meeting. Oh, no Lord, anything else in the world but please don't have me go on the street. Now Lord, what else? There seemed not one other thing else to do. But I comforted myself with this thought, they never do ask any one to go and of course, I will not be expected to go without an invitation. So I dressed in my usual costume, wearing an expensive pattern hat that had been given to me by the lady I had been trimming for. After the afternoon meeting I thought I would go alone somewhere to pray as I had not yet been sanctified. But lo and behold, that particular afternoon three of the workers asked me to go to the street meeting with them. I did so, forgetting all about the unpleasant job of going on the street.

As I looked at those old drunkards, the bar-tender in a white suit came out and swept the street for us to stand on, assuring us no drinks would be sold while we were there.

My, how I did sing and testify, for there was such a splendid chance to work for my Lord and I was so happy to do so. But soon my attention was called to the passers-by as they peeked through the crowd. All seemed to be looking at the woman with the green hat on. What was she doing down there? Oh, but I did want to be at home when the traveling salesman showed up and as I stepped to the sidewalk, he looked at me as if to say, "What are you doing here?"

Ladies passed who had been looking at that hat, all seemed to think I was out of place. As I started home, the devil said, "Now have you not made a fool of yourself going on the street?"

I noticed I had lost my sister's cut-steel bead purse she thought a great deal of and the old tempter came up again. I was disgusted, half mad, the more the devil derided the worse I felt. I wanted to quarrel or fuss so if Sister would just scold me it would help some. So I stepped in the door and said, "Well, I sure have made a fool of myself." "Why, what have you done?" she asked, so calm and sweet. "Well, I went on the street corner this evening with that gang and lost your little purse with what money, milk and bread tickets there was." "Well," she said, "there was only $2:50, the little purse was getting old any way, and there were not many milk and bread tickets."

So there was nothing left for me to do but to go and pray some more for if sanctification would help my temper, as they said, I needed to be seeking the Lord all the time.

The first thing that night when we went to church, here came Brother Parham with the purse. Some one had found it and given it to the workers. Now I would have to go on the street again.

I was still fasting and seeking sanctification. Now the tempter said, "You are acting foolishly, you are going to starve to death, there is no such thing as sanctification for you, so you just as well quit starving yourself." Well I thought it over and decided since I had been convinced there was and I was going to have it or starve to death, and since I did not know just what questions would be asked me when I went to the pearly gates; if they asked, "Are you sanctified?" I would rather say, "No, but I starved to death seeking it," than to say, "I never tried." So there was no more trouble on that line and I went on seeking.

I had what I termed a "consecration bundle" so now I had brought it to the altar, cut the binding so I could assort it. The wheat to be put in one pile, the weeds in another. There really was not much wheat, but one by one, I went over all the things in my life whether good or bad, they were assorted.

As yet no satisfaction had come in my life, only I had received such a blessing from going on the street, almost feeling as though I could spend the rest of my days there.

What else Lord? Show me, lead me. The next hard thing was to send some money back that I had decided might not belong to me, but to my brothers and sisters. Some four years prior to this, my sister and myself had taken the care of our aged parents who were sick. My father did not carry a check book, preferring to have the cash. When he took sick, he had about one hundred dollars in his pocket, which we spent without bothering him, and other money that came in.

Father passed away two months before mother, so she said she wanted us to get some black dresses as it was the custom to wear mourning in those days. One day my sister brought me ten dollars and said, "Here is the money for your dress." I said, "I think there is enough in my trunk to get one." "Yes," she said, "but I am taking this, I think this is what father would like to have us do and mother said to get them." I took the money and really don't remember whether I used that for my dress or not. But now it seemed that it was not quite right so I must fix it for I had started in to have the old account settled. Never before in this long time had I felt it was wrong, but now I must have this fixed.

We had always prided ourselves on our honesty. We never had sold hats at an unusual price just because we had a good buyer. Now after all our careful lives, here was this thing. Now what was I to do? It was nothing, only to defeat the devil and kill my pride. I came in from prayer, quite decided to be called a thief or anything rather than lose the chance to be sanctified. Anxious to do the Lord's will, I seized the pen in such a determinate way, Sister said, "What are you going to do?" When I told her, she said, "Why I never thought of that not being right." I did not either till now, but I would settle the doubt and kill my pride.

"I am going to write to our brothers and sisters, send them the money and tell them here is the money I stole while mother was sick." "Oh, dear, are you going to say stole, I never felt we stole it." "Yes, I am going to say stole. If I did not steal it, no one will be hurt, if I did this will fix it." I was so blessed when those letters were mailed, I almost shouted , but yet I was not satisfied. Again and again I said, "Lord, if there is anything else, let me know and I will do it if it kills me."

I never thought any more about my letters until my brother returned his and the $2:50 saying, "My dear sisters, this is not mine but yours and much more should have been yours. What is the matter with you anyway?" Some of the others, did not return theirs. Perhaps they felt we had done wrong. Be that as it may, we beat the devil, killed our pride and settled the old account. Many other little things the Lord used to kill my pride, I seemed to be on the death route. Still I asked the Lord, "Is there anything more? I will do it, or die."

He spoke to me, no voice and yet so still and clear this thought came. If I want you to, will you be willing to pack your suit case, turn away from those you love best; go into the lowest hovels of the city and tell the story of Jesus as it came to you, whether you ever see any one accept it or not. Oh, Lord, if they would only accept it, but give my life to those who do not care? I hesitated for some time. After all my firm promises I staggered and said, "Lord, I will gladly go if I ever see any one accept it or some one to encourage me, just a-God bless you when I am weary and tired." But no, that was not it; go, give my life, time and strength whether I ever saw any one who believed it or not. After prayer I was willing, so willing I just wanted to go then, but no leadings at that time

The devil seemed to be wise enough to know I was almost
ready to receive the blessing of sanctification, so he had to
do something to delay me. Coming in like a flood, he said,
"Here you are seeking sanctification and you have never been
saved." "Oh, haven't I been saved?" "No." "Well," I
said, "what about that sweet little experience down at that
old Methodist altar at Moody, Texas when I was a little eight
year old child. There where gross darkness took its flight
and the sunshine of God's love and grace came into my soul,
like a hush that stilled the tempest tossed soul?" The devil
still argued that was not salvation. What was it? I know
something happened that I had not got over no "Think so"
either. That was a knowledge of sins forgiven. Now I was
in more gloom than ever, it seemed. I made my way down
to the afternoon meeting. The people were all so happy and
praising the Lord, but myself. I felt I did not have anything
to thank God for, but all eyes turned on me for my testimony. I slowly arose and said, "It is splendid to see you all so
happy and praising the Lord in such a wonderful way, but
I have not much to praise the Lord for. I started in to have
a clean cut experience and I want a witness to all I have. I
have been asking the Lord to sanctify me, but I am afraid I
am not saved. All of you pray that I may have a witness to
my conversion for I want to know it. I do thank the Lord
for a knowledge of sins forgiven, but I want a witness to my
salvation." About six of the workers said, "Amen, the knowledge of sins forgiven is a witness to your conversion." I
was quite relieved, the burden was going now. I went home,
but did not care to read or pray; the load was lifting. Three
days and nights had passed and still I was fasting. As I sat
there, my inner most being was flooded with innermost joy.
Then came the words of that dear old song; "Joys are flowing
like a river, since the Comforter has come."

Oh, how I wanted to shout for joy. For nineteen years, I had been a Methodist, free to shout, but nothing like this had ever come to me. Indeed, this was the most earnest seeking I had ever done. I did wish I was somewhere with a high brick wall built to heaven, where only God could hear me. My, wouldn't I praise Him to my heart's content.

I suppressed the feeling by holding my arms in a folding position, though feeling like I would almost have to give vent to my feeling or I would burst. There was a "Ha! Ha!" in my soul to the will of God. My whole being rejoicing in Him as I had never known before. The whole wide world seemed to be in harmony with Him.

I shall never forget that wonderful Saturday afternoon. The clouds looked different, the lightning flashing across the sky are still most beautiful pictures in my memory. The roaring thunder that had so often made me shudder, now soothed me as the voice of God Himself speaking in tenderness to me. Oh, how I loved Him! God was so near me now and wanted me to know He loved me too. The song of the birds, the rain pattering off the eaves, all added one more note in this harmonious orchestra that had begun its music in my soul.

My whole being was flooded with joy. Every organ of my body, lungs and heart all harmonizing in a "Ha! Ha!" to the will of God. "Not my will, but Thy will be done." About two o'clock the next morning I awoke my sister laughing and said, "I never wanted to say—Glory to God and Praise the Lord—as much in my life." She said, "The way is open, help yourself."

So I gave vent to my feeling and no one in the house seemed offended but all rejoiced with me. Next morning, the man of the house (though not a Christian) hastened down to tell Bro. Parham and the workers, saying "I wish you could see Miss Stockton, she is the happiest woman I ever saw." As I came down the street, they said I looked like I was walking in mid-air. It did seem to me with this heavenly blessing, like I was scarcely touching earth as I went to the meeting. They all had known something of the consecration I felt I should make. So after my testimony, which blessed all who had been so earnestly holding me up in prayer, Brother Parham came in with a small tomato can in a little paper bag. Presenting it to me, he said, "Here are your equipments for the high-way and hedge call, these are also your credentials." (Forsaking all).

I began telling the story of Jesus from house to house. Some came to me saying, "Now you have the Holy Spirit, don't seek Him any more." The asthma left me as this wonderful experience came in, and now my consecration was made to go or stay, yet I felt I needed the baptism of the Holy Spirit to give me power to witness.

We had heard a lot about fanaticism. I did not want any of that but I did want the real baptism that would give me power to witness. So with my sister and our chum, we would go to the woods to pray and tarry for the baptism. Again I began a fast, as I had accomplished more in fasting than other wise.

For ten days I did enjoy waiting on the Lord. Surely this was the same experience the disciples had on the day of Pentecost when they tarried in the upper room.

During the ten days, some strange words fell on my lips. I repeated them once and then said, "I will not say that again, I heard Bro. Parham say that". I had also heard him say words in English and had repeated them, but no, not this. I did not understand it anyway. I realize now, here I grieved the Holy Spirit. Though I continued to seek without food, I was not happy. I had fasted fourteen days, but the last four days were more confusion than blessing.

The Scriptures say, "And grieve not the Holy Spirit of God, where by ye are sealed unto the day of redemption." (Eph. 4: 30.)

In a few weeks we came to Oklahoma; instead of going into the ministry as I should, I went out in the country to nurse a sick sister. The work was hard, things inconvenient and sin on every hand. I overtaxed my strength, almost had a complete breakdown. It was only a few weeks, before, that I had been in this condition and with the effect of the drugs I had been taking for fifteen years going out of my system, I became violently insane. They pronounced me incurable and sent me to Supply, Okla. With no hopes of ever being sane again, satan was surely working hard to keep me from the Lord's work.

When my reason became dethroned, it appeared to me my sister was demon possessed. I beat her up terribly, trying (as the spirit that had me told me) to beat her until this evil spirit left her. Oh, the horror of it all! How it did hurt me to strike my dear sister, who had been my best and closest friend all these years. But this evil spirit insisted, if I would do her a kindness, I must beat her until she was delivered of this demon. The officers were called and I was so violent I must be locked up.

There were a few things in life I feared and often wondered if they would ever come to me; one was insanity. Would I be willing to be called insane? No, I would not. What glory or honor would that be to God? I feared it as Job said, "For the thing which I greatly feared is come upon me, and that which I was afraid of is come unto me." (Job 3:25)

Another dread was if some time, while on duty in the slums in the red-light district, I should be suddenly closed in behind bars.

God wants us to know, He is large and merciful enough to take us through, any of these places even though we are unable to see and pray for ourselves.

The horrors of my stay there in Supply, Okla., no one can know only those who have experienced it, which I trust no reader of this book ever will. Oh, those dark hours in those barred cells, with all kinds of evil spirits that ministered to me. For three long weeks never closing my eyes in sleep and being so tormented by the powers of darkness, I surely feel I have had a little taste of hell. Not being able to name the name of Jesus when we need Him so, is a horrible thing.

The head physician said to me one day, "This is the greatest school you were ever in." I did not know just what he meant, for to me it was indeed a prison and torment. The powers of hell seemed to get hold of me, and I was powerless to resist. When I did resist, it took about six to eight people to manage me, hence the lock and keys was turned on me. Though earthly doctors, with all their skill could only say, "hopelessly insane," yet in answer to prayer the Great Physicians undertook my case, and within four months I was out. Thank God. Only His power can loosen a bound captive, like I was.

You say it was the medicine. No, I had very little medicine; it is no small job to medicate a demon force.

I felt I must resist everything they tried to do, as they had not told me where I was going and where I was. The other insane patients looked so terrible to me, I thought surely this was the dreaded place in the slums, so I would fight until I died and be sure not to obey one thing they desired me to do. So under this impression, it took eight strong people and a good hard lick on the bais of the brain, to put me in the cell the first night.

I knew everything but was driven by evil spirits, so they thought no use to try to explain anything to me. They were indeed doing well to keep me any way, with the unnatural strength of demons which now controlled me.

Oh! dear reader, grieve not the Holy Spirit until He takes His flight and unholy spirits come in.

But praise the Lord, I am glad there was a bright side to it all. Through these tormenting things there was the loving Hand of the Savior reached out to me. If I only could reach it, He would take me through.

Among all the doctors and nurses, there was only a few of them that understood me. They were kind and were a real blessing and help to me. God bless them, especially if they are still trying to care for poor demon possessed beings. If only they could get them to trust in the Lord, He would take them through and bring them to their loved ones sane again.

Many were praying for me; old friends of my childhod days also my immediate family. Brother Parham was sent word and had special prayer for me. Thank God, some one prayed the prayer of faith, and He answered prayer.

God surely wants us to die out to what people say or think. But when I had become willing to remain there the rest of my days and help administer to those unfortunate ones by helping the night nurse (which I had arranged with her to do) one day all so unexpected to me, a great bell rang. The little nurse who had been so lovely, looked at me and said, "Some body's folks have come for them. Would you like to see yours?" Sure, but that would be impossible; yet in answer to prayer, it was true. My dear sister's husband had come for me. Oh, how happy I was to see him.

I went home with them and remained in their home about nine months. I continued getting stronger and my general health so improved that during the Christmas rush I helped in a Dry Goods and Millinery Store. I also became happy and thankful; my heart felt praise increased daily to God for His blessing.

Feb. 17, 1910, is another date that will always live in my memory. As I pillowed my head that night, my whole being was rejoicing and truly I never had been so grateful before, as only a few months before, I had been judged hopelessly insane. Now my health and strength had returned, no evil tormenting spirits annoyed me, for I was completely healed of all my afflictions.

Five months had passed since the tormenting evil forces had taken their leave. I was indeed thankful to be at myself again. Oh, it was so good to be able to sleep all night without being awakened.

I had slept like this, when I awakened on the morning of the 17th of February and felt as well as I did at San Angelo, Texas, when I had breathed in the fresh air of the plains. But this morning there was something unusual. The room was all filled with a white brightness, so bright that the clear morning sun, seemed like a shadow in that room.

My entire body was thanking and praising the Lord. Something, even down below my heart, was talking. I could not understand it all, but often I had longed for words to praise my Savior. Now this something came slowly up and slated itself in my heart. Oh, it was so wonderful. All I had to do was just to open my mouth. He, the Holy Spirit took my tongue and praised the Lord in His own language. I did not understand it, but I was satisfied with the praise. I wanted to fold and gently hold it, since it was so gentle and dove-like; I did not want to grieve or displace Him again, for now He had come to abide. Praise the Lord.

The Holy Spirit still abides within and often witnesses for Himself. Since then I have spent more than nine years in trimming, making, buying and selling hats. From a success-

ful career as a milliner, I began to study the Bible and preaching the Word. Woe is unto me, if I preach not the gospel.

I am happy in the service of the King, but unhappy outside
of duty. In December, 1925, I graduated from Mrs. Mc
Pherson's Bible School and then spent two years in evangelistic work. After this, I returned to Guymon, Okla., where
I have been pastor up to this time.

Dear reader, I hope you have enjoyed and been helped by
my testimony and that you will never grieve the Holy Spirit
of God, "whereby ye are sealed unto the day of redemption."
May God bless you all.

Yours in the glad service of the King.

Mrs. Della Bigger (nee Stockton)

*   *   *   *   *

Mr. Parham often asked Sister Della to give this testimony
before large audiences in his meetings and as she told her
experience, with tears of joy and sorrow flowing down her
cheeks, the people were held in wrapt attention as they listened to the story of her suffering and how God had so wonderfully delivered her.

Mr. Parham had made a special study of demonology and
often preached on the subject, telling the people that many
were possessed with devils now as they were in Bible times,
and devils could as then, be cast out in the name of Jesus.

Many were made to realize that they were controlled by a
demon force and as they sought God and asked Mr. Parham
to pray for them, were wonderfully delivered from these
powers, which had been tormenting their lives, driving them
to distraction and wickedness of various kinds.

Both of these sisters were dear friends of ours, and Sister
Etta spent the last few weeks of her life in our home.

She seemed to know several months before she passed away
that the end was nearing and said she would like to attend a
meeting that Mr. Parham was going to hold at Galena, Kan-

sas in November 1916; her desire being to spend her last days in service for the Lord.

She came to our home and I went with her to the meeting at Galena. She put her whole heart and strength in the meeting, was seemingly in perfect health, and dearly loved by all.

This was a good meeting and as the war clouds were then hanging low, we all especially felt the need of drawing close to God.

Mr. Parham then held a meeting at Prosperity, Missouri, and I accompanied her there also. Great numbers were saved in the meeting and it lasted until Christmas, when we returned to our home in Baxter to rest during the holidays.

Mr. Parham had planned a big watch-night meeting at Joplin, Missouri, but Sister Etta said she would stay at home and rest. The Lord wonderfully blessed us as we watched the dawning of 1917. Mr. Parham's watch-night services were always especially precious as we were reminded of the New Year when in Topeka, Kansas, God had so wonderfully poured out His Holy Spirit on our lives.

Sister Della came to the meeting and accompanied us home. We found Sister Etta quite sick and before the month was over she was at rest.

Mr. Parham conducted many funeral services, and always made them as sympathetic and informal as possible. His friends would often send for him to come long distances to conduct funeral services for their loved ones, feeling that they must have his ready sympathy and help in their time of trouble. But to me, this funeral service which he held in our home, ever remains in my memory, as the sweetest and most-blessed funeral service, I ever attended.

We gathered together as one big family of sympathizing friends, and after prayer, Mr. Parham called for a testimony meeting. The spirit of love and tender sympathy rested on each one, as they told what our sister's life had meant to them. All were melted to tears as Sister Della arose and standing before the open casket, reconsecrated her life to God, promising to fill up the broken ranks, and if possible do double duty for the Master.

All felt the inspiration of her sweet example of fortitude, and as soldiers of the cross, we should rally around the blood-stained banner of King Emmanuel and press forward in the battle, even though our ranks are broken, as our loved ones go on before us.

She was buried in the Baxter Springs cemetery, her loved ones erecting a beautiful monument, on which Mr. Parham had them put the following inscription.

> "Her life the music,
> Her deeds the sermons,
> Her memory a lasting benediction."

We sorrowed not as those who have no hope, for though the parting was sad, we knew she loved the Lord and had made her calling and election sure.

Christ said, "I am the Resurrection."

He paid the penalty for sin on the cross, when He made the supreme, sacrifice for you and me. The Father hid His face from Him, that Christ might really suffer as a sinner and take the sinner's place. He endured the anguish of separation from His Father, when He cried, "My God, my God, why hast Thou forsaken me!"

What a complete sacrifice He made when "He bore our sins in His own body on the tree."

What a grand and glorious victory was won when He arose triumphant over death, hell and the grave and became the first fruits of them that slept!

Blessed and holy is he that hath part in the first resurrection; on such the second death hath no power.   (Rev. 20:6.)

Chapter XXII

OUR NEW HOME.

ISTER Rilda Cole, a sweet Christian lady who lived at Keelville, Kansas, (and went as chaperon with the first company of young workers, who accompanied Mr. Parham to Texas), gives a report of a meeting held there, which was published in "The Gospel of the Kingdom."

"Through the fall and winter our people at Keelville were heavily weighted down by the spiritual status in which we found ourselves.

"Our young people, who attended our services, seemed to be drifting away further and further from salvation, while we Christians had no power to help, though our hearts really ached for them.

"So we agreed among ourselves to take the matter definitely to God, that He would send us help, and give a revival in our place that would shake things up from the foundation, and it is with praise to the Lord and joy in my own heart that I am writing you the story of how He answered prayer.

"We asked Bro. Chas. Parham to come out and hold a meeting. At first he gave us no satisfaction, but we kept on praying and finally the Lord sent him to us.

"The campaign began about the last week in January, 1910, and the first drop in the revival shower was when a man who was a sinner of about fifty years, arose and asked our prayers and before we left the house, God gave him the evidence of sins forgiven. Besides he was so marvelously healed, that it equaled the Bible stories of Christ's power to heal.

"Now the amen corner and front seats, were filled with young men and women, whose hearty hand shake, beaming eyes, smiling faces, glad songs of praise, heart felt testimonies and sincere prayers, all gave public witness to sins forgiven; new hearts, and lives consecrated to Jesus.

"A young man from Washington, who was visiting at the home of his parents in Melrose, Kansas, when attacked by those who fought our work, saying the speaking of tongues and healing of the sick was not of God, received this answer from him:

" 'Well, I know it is certainly not of the devil, for if it was, I would have had it long ago, for I have had everything else that belongs to him.'

"Many accepted divine healing and see with us the soon, and now to them, glad coming of our Savior, the Lord from heaven. And so today, while the angels strike their harps anew, God's listening ear hears our hallelujahs too."

＊　＊　＊　＊　＊

During this meeting, Mrs. Mary C. Bennett of Baxter Springs, Kansas was taken very sick. She had taken the Lord for her Healer during the first meeting in Baxter Springs and had been healed several times, but now was going through a very severe test, and she gives her testimony as follows.

"One Wednesday night one week from the day that I was taken so bad with pneumonia, satan came to me as real as any person and laughed and scoffed in my face and said, 'You have no God'. But I threw out my hand and said, 'You are a liar.'

"On Thursday morning I could not talk at all, my throat and lungs were so filled and so tight that I had got passed raising anything and for about half an hour before my deliverance, I could hear the death gurgle in my throat.

"But the Lord had laid it on the hearts of Brother Parham and Brother Wall to come and pray for me, so they drove ten miles, (with horses then) reaching here at one o'clock.

"The twenty-third Psalm is a part of what I went through that day: I passed down through the valley and shadow of death.

"But, oh, when those brothers poured out their hearts in earnest prayer to God, asking that I be delivered from the pangs of death, God just reached down and lifted me up into the very sunlight of heaven. Oh, how I praised Him who had loosed the bonds, that had bound me and set me free. Praise His dear Name."

* * * * *

After the meeting at Keelville closed, Mr. Parham held a very successful meeting at Galena, Kansas. Many who had grown cold, returned unto the Lord to serve Him. Several were wonderfully healed in this meeting who were given up by the doctors.

We were still living in Baxter Springs but in March had moved on a small farm at the edge of town near Spring River. It was in a grove by our place near the river that Mr. Parham held an all day rally—June 5, 1910. The meeting was held in remembrance of Mr. Parham's thirty-seventh birthday, and was largely attended by friends coming from far and near, enjoyed theirselves, in praise and worship, and listening to the Word of God.

At night Mr. Parham returned to Galena for the closing service of his revival there, and June 7th he left for Los Angeles, California, accompanied by Henry Aylor.

* * * * *

"The Gospel of the Kingdom," published two letters from Henry Aylor regarding this meeting of which I will quote a part.

July 22, 1910.

"The meeting started the first of the month, and it has been running nicely from the start. Brother Parham is doing some good preaching: giving us the truth, the whole truth.

"We have a good place for the meeting on 209 East Street. Good crowds most of the time and real good interest.

"We have street meetings every evening at six o'clock, and several came in from the street meetings and were converted. Many have received the truth and have been blessed and have a better understanding of the Apostolic teaching than ever before.

"We don't know just how long the meeting will continue. The house is full of people just hungry for the real truth, and here is the place to get it. There are lots of people coming from the other missions and they are so glad to find a place where there is a real Christian unity.

"The people are taking hold with much interest, and we have plenty of good help to run the meeting. Glory to our God."

Aug. 8, 1910.

"We are sure having a fine meeting, yes, a glorious meeting. Nine were converted one night last week and some converted most every night. They come in during the day to be prayed for and are converted and go out praising the Lord—Glory to God."

* * * * *

After closing his work in the west, Mr. Parham returned to Baxter Springs, where he held another camp meeting in Springs Park beginning in September.

These camp meetings still remain as bright spots in the memory of multitudes who received many blessings here.

At the close of the Camp meeting, Mr. Parham went to Texas, and was engaged in meetings there, during the winter.

For some time Mr. Parham as well as others, thought that we should begin to publish a paper again, and while holding a meeting at Brownwood, Texas, he had the opportunity of buying a complete job plant, from H. W. Schermer.

Francis Rolland Romack, who had been engaged in evangelistic work about a year, helped in this meeting. He consecrated his life to God to be used in His service, anyway for His glory, and decided he should now give his life for the publishing of the gospel, so came to Baxter Springs in February 1911, to take charge of this work.

We had rented the place in Baxter Springs where we were living for one year and our year had now expired.

Our friends in Texas were very anxious for us to move to Texas, promising to buy us a home there, and offering us every possible inducement. As Mr. Parham's work had kept him there so much of his time, it seemed perhaps that it would be best for us to do so.

However, when the possibility of our leaving became known to our Baxter friends, they were not willing for us to go, saying if we would stay, they would help us to buy a home here instead.

Property was cheap in Baxter Springs at that time, and we finally decided on a large brick building which had been built for a brewery before prohibition came into Kansas. This seemed to be the best place that we could get that would give us sufficient extra room for a printing office.

Not only was there plenty of house room, but also a block of ground and we saw a splendid opportunity to raise chickens, garden and keep a cow, and the children's other pets which had been such a nuisance on rented property.

The building was owned and occupied by old friends of ours, John Seibert and his wife, who wanted to sell and buy a small place and they sold it to us for a very reasonable price.

How thankful we were to the Lord and our friends, who had made it possible for us to have a home of our own, for it seemed like a haven of rest after moving so much.

We had started out to serve the Lord not expecting to have a home in this life, but God who knoweth what things we have need of before we ask Him, had done exceedingly, abundantly more for us than we had asked or thought.

Mr. Parham was always so busy in the Lord's work, he had very little time to spend in his home but he found it a blessing to have a place to stop for a little season where there was also room for his workers and friends, who we always tried to make feel that it was their home also.

The "Springs Park," where the camp meetings were being held each year, joined our place and we were always glad that we could accommodate so many friends during these meetings.

IF EVERY HOME WERE AN ALTAR

"If every home were an altar,
  Where holiness vows were paid,
And life's best gifts in sacrament
  Of purest love were laid;

If every home were an altar
  Where harsh and angry thought
Was cast aside for kindly one,
  And true forgiveness sought;

If every home were an altar
  Where hearts weighed down with care
Could find sustaining strength and grace
  In sweet uplift of prayer;

Then solved would be earth's problem
  Banished sin's curse and blight;
For God's own love would radiate
  From every altar light.'

Chapter XXIII

WHAT HATH GOD WROUGHT?

R. PARHAM was again called to California and of the meeting at Perris, Mrs. Helen Finley wrote: "December 10th., 1911, Bro. Chas. F. Parham came to Perris and began revival meetings in the Mission. Among those that were saved was Samuel K. Clark, better known to us as 'Ky.'

"My real knowledge of the meeting began on New Year's Day: in the afternoon we met at the Mission. The altar service lasted from afternoon till evening with an altar full of seekers. I never heard such praying: altar workers were lost sight of, and every one was praying through.

"The baptism of the Holy Spirit fell upon Bro. Clark and he began to rejoice in tongues and glorify God. If lightening had struck in front of us, we could not have been more surprised, for very few of us had ever witnessed 'Pentecost' before. A quick swath was cut through to belief in the mighty reality of God.

"Friends from Los Angeles were with us, among them Sister Lucy Brower (now Stanley) who inspired us by her sweet singing.

"The crowd continued to increase so a tent was secured to accommodate them. Opposition also had developed and it also increased as we went into the tent. We were made to realize with the New Testament saints, that everywhere this doctrine was spoken against.

"About fifty came to the altar and repented. Nearly all saved in this meeting were wives and mothers saved with their husbands.

"The teaching on healing was new to most of us; the thought of the broken body of Christ for our healing—so beautiful and true— captivated every one. It seemed so easy to grasp faith for healing when revealed to us in the atonement.

"Thursday, Jan. 18, was given to prayer and fasting. We met at Bro. Andy Noble's and prayed until we were lost in God. The effect of that day will not be lost to that little company. Bro. Noble was saved and healed that day.

"On Sunday, Jan. 21, eighteen were baptized in a small reservoir in the suburbs of the town. Words of mine fail to express the emotion felt on that occasion. There was no shouting: feelings were deep and subdued. The serious look and tearful eye were eloquent. Two were taken at a time and buried in the watery grave by Bro. Parham, assisted by Bro. Clark. Bro. Parham pronouncing the beautful words of the ceremony.

"The last week of the meeting was devoted to Bible lessons, and we were clearly shown the difference between the Word of God and the tradition of men.

"Monday, Jan. 29th., the ordinance of the Lord's supper was observed and followed by the consecration of children. The first to receive the beautiful and impressive ceremony were the baby girls of Brother and Sister Hunter. Then a score of other children were brought by anxious parents to be prayed for and consecrated to God.

"No water was used to sprinkle, but we were all reminded of the time when Jesus held the little children in His arms and said, 'Forbid them not, for of such is the kingdom of Heaven.'

"The earnest prayers and council of Brother Parham sunk deep into our hearts and placed a new light on the responsibility of parents. We sat again in the little hall (Jan. 31) and with tearful eyes yet joyful hearts, we listened to the farewell words of Bro. Parham, our real spiritual father. He bade us lift up our eyes for our redemption was nigh and not to look at the partings, but to the joy to be revealed in the redemption of our bodies. Our farewell was also extended to our young brother, Ky Clark, for from the time that he received the baptism of the Holy Spirit, it was evident that the hand of God was on him for service."

* * * * *

They left Perris on Wednesday, Jan. 31, 1912, and the next meeting was to be at Los Angeles, California.

In opening the meeting there, Mr. Parham asked how many would like to enter a ten days fast, for a personal victory on their lives, and for the success of the meeting. A number decided to fast among them, Mrs. S. Finney.

The Lord had healed her many times of other diseases, yet one terrible trouble remained: a tumor which the doctors had failed to cure or remove. The fast began on Friday and on Sunday night, while in the agony of death, she was wonderfully healed. As she rejoiced and thanked God for deliverance from all pain and suffering, she received the baptism of the Holy Spirit, and praised Him in other tongues. Mrs. Finney went to the meeting on Monday and as she told her experience Mr. Parham wept for joy and all rejoiced and thanked God for so marvelously answering their prayers.

The fast was broken before the ten days were over, as God had given such wonderful victory the purpose of the fast had been already accomplished.

Mrs. Finney is still living and when we were in Los Angeles last June, (1929), we visited her. She rejoiced as she told us of her wonderful healing and how God was still blessing her in her old age.

Mr. Parham returned from his work on the coast in time to hold the annual camp meeting in Baxter Springs, which began July 14, 1912.

Preachers, workers and friends gathered from different states and surrounding towns till many tents were pitched on the old camp meeting grounds. But one notable feature this year was the absence of lunching on the grounds, for the first ten days, as a fast had been announced for that time or as long as the individuals wished to continue it. Sinners were saved, and it was a mighty upheavel for the Christians as they went on into the deeper things of God.

*　*　*　*　*

I will quote letters regarding the meeting from two of our California visitors.

K. Brower: "For years I have had a desire to attend the Apostolic Faith Camp Meeting, at this place and I am glad that the Lord has permitted me to come.

"There are some present who accepted the teaching in 1901 and have stood all the testings that have come and have been true to God's chosen vessel, who gave the teaching of the baptism of the Holy Spirit to the world.

"We have the pleasure of having in our meeting, Mother Palmer, of Topeka, Kansas, who was in holiness work with Brother Parham eighteen years ago.

"Sunday, July 28, was indeed a real feast to God's people. Bro. Parham preached to a large audience on the fulfilling of the promises of God concerning the seed of Abraham. People in all walks of life and church members of many denominations, listened to Bible truths.

"As I have talked with people of all classes while here, I find that Brother Parham, by his real Christian life, has won the respect of the people of this town and vicinity, even from those who do not believe as he does.

"I had always been anxious to see Sister Dulaney of Houston, Texas, who was so wonderfully healed. She is here, and how she loves to minister to the suffering ones on the Camp grounds, and she has been a real blessing to many. We have seen many healed of dreadful diseases, and hundreds praising God for deliverance from all kinds of ailments and habits."

Mrs. E. R. Gray. "Thursday Aug. 15, will long be membered. A young lady, a school teacher from Tex   e-ceived the baptism of the Holy Spirit. There was no jerking of any kind, but while quietly kneeling at the altar, she burst forth into sweet singing; first in English, then in a foreign language, one song being, 'O, how I love Jesus.' She has since talked in an unknown language, giving the interpreta-tion to some of her sentences. Saturday evening, three others received the witness of Pentecost.

"The lessons on prophecy by Brother Parham have been very much appreciated and were very instructive."

*   *   *   *   *

Mother Palmer, though 84 years old, was in good health, spoke in a distinct voice, and still had a clear mind. She had spent over thirty years in the Lord's work, and was a great Bible student keeping in touch with Mr. Parham's teachings on prophecy. She was very much pleased when Mr. Parham asked her to take charge of the morning Bible study, and the people greatly enjoyed her lessons.

Ky Clark had been Mr. Parham's traveling companion ever since he had consecrated his life to God during the Perris meeting. He took charge of the music, and sometimes, while he was singing a solo, the Spirit would so anoint him, that after singing in English, he would also sing in another lan-guage.

The whole audience was touched and melted into a holy hush as they were convinced, and realized the presence and power of the Holy Spirit.

Since the camp meeting at Baxter Springs had become an annual event a wooden tabernacle was erected for this pur-pose, and it was an ideal camp grounds.

At that time, there were two good springs in the park and also one on our place joining it, and a clear stream of water flowed through our ground. About a block further down in the woods there was a nice little pool, used by the young people of the town for swimming, and Mr. Parham often baptized there.

One Sunday afternoon during the meeting, he took two candidates there who wished to be baptized. But after arriving at the pool, men and women were convicted that they had only been baptized into the church-into a head-knowledge of creeds and doctrines of men, but now being really converted, they should be baptized into Christ. So, one after another, handed their watches and pocket-books to their friends, and joyfully walked out into the water, dressed in their "Sunday best." Mr. Parham baptized them into Christ, in the name of the Father, Son and Holy Ghost.'

The holy joy and feeling of God's approval that rested on the services, I am sure is still remembered by some of the many that were present that day. While only two had planned to be baptized, fifteen had volunteered and declared afterwards that their best clothes were not too good for such a precious service.

The meeting closed Aug. 25, the battle over, the victory won! As the camp was broken up, and fond farewells were said, all agreed that it had been the best of all the Camp meetings.

Mr. Parham had received earnest calls to come to Texas as fanaticism, envy and strife were seeking to break the bonds of unity. So Mr. Parham's winter work was in holding meetings at different places in that state, having a convention at Houston in October, and the work was blessed and prospered.

When, in the beginning of 1913, Mr. Parham left Texas to take up the work in California, S. E. Waterbury went to Texas to continue the work there.

Chapter XXIV

THE PRESS ROOM DEDICATED.

R. PARHAM held a meeting in Perris, California, in February, 1913. I am giving part of a newspaper clipping regarding the meeting, which also gave a report of Mrs. Oyler's healing.

Chas. F. Parham, Preaches to a Large Audience.

"The Apostolic Faith Mission was crowded Sunday night to listen to a sermon by Chas. F. Parham, the founder of the mission.

"Mr. Parham preached a sermon on prophecy. The six thousand year period will close and be followed by the millenium. At present there are wars and rumors of wars, and much bloodshed.

"We live in an anarchistic age and the world is entering a period of awful trouble. The period of appalling destruction of life and property will close with the battle of Armageddon, to be followed by the millenium of a thousand years.

"Mr. Parham explained that when we read of the world being created in six days, that each day represented a thousand years, and that six thousand years were occupied in the work of creation. Then followed the sabbath of rest.

"Since the creation of Adam, the world has been passing through another six thousand year period which will soon close. Then will follow the millenium of a thousand years when Christ shall reign on the earth.

"Mr. Parham does not believe in infant damnation, nor in hell as a place of eternal torment. He says the wicked will be destroyed and that the wages of sin is death. He gets his belief from the Bible and declares he simply believes what the Bible plainly teaches.

"Owing to the great interest taken in the meetings, Mr. Parham has decided to remain another week.

"On next Sunday, he will preach at the usual hours." Perris Progress.

A MIRACLE

"Last week Mr. Parham was called to Los Angeles to pray for the healing of Mrs. T. W. Olyer, wife of a retired rancher, and he gives the following account of her healing: 'For years she had suffered with an alcerous tumor which finally resulted in congestion producing convulsions. She had suffered two days thus, when a phone message came here for the minister to come on the first train. As there was none till the morning the mission here all prayed with the result in relief of the convulsions till the next morning. They returned harder than ever, so that by the time Mr. Parham arrived her life was despaired of. The trained nurse said she could not live till noon, but after a few words in English, Mr. Parham began to pray in tongues, and at once the hemorrhage ceased and great strength came to her so that in a short time she was able to get up and go down stairs, to meeting for which they are praising the God of Heaven.' "

—   Perris (Cal.) Progress, 2-20-1913.

Besides Lewis L. Hunters, several other families of this faith had moved here from Missouri, which made it quite a center for the work, and from here the teachings of the Apostolic Faith spread to many other places.

In the spring of 1913 Mr. Parham held a revival meeting at Webb City, Missouri. The meeting lasted about eight weeks and from the first was attended with great power and victory. Scores of souls were blessed, whole families saved and delivered from the bondage of sin.

Mr. Parham preached the practical benefits of salvation. When sinners were made to see that God would not only save from sin but heal the body and deliver from the effects of sins and evil habits, they became hungry for salvation. Many were healed of all matter of diseases, and delivered from demon possessions, and God mightily confirmed the Word with signs following.

June 1, 1913. Mr. Parham celebrated his birthday by an all day meeting at Baxter Springs. The meeting was held in the tabernacle in Springs Park and was well attended.

The morning was spent in praise and testimony and after a bountiful dinner, Mr. Parham preached on the coming king- dom. Then followed a baptismal service at the river.

The subject for the night meeting was divine healing. There was a large delegation from Webb City, the scene of the recent revival.

All now were looking forward to the camp meeting which began July 25.

Friends came from far and near and at nights the seating capacity of the tabernacle was full and large crowds on the outside.

The power of God was present to heal during the meeting. One sister came from western Kansas for healing. The Lord so wonderfully touched her body that she could take care of herself and sent her attendant home the next day.

She returned home alone and wrote us of her continued good health, and how astonished her neighbors and friends were at the marvelous change that had taken place.

When I recall the love and unity manifest in those meet- ings, and how, as with one voice, praise ascended to God, it seems to me it was just a foretaste of the time to come, when before God's throne we shall worship the King of Kings, and Lord of Lords.

A. R. Haughawout wrote:

"As to the singing, I never witnessed such a chorus at a camp meeting. The special songs were certainly honored of

God, which were given by Sisters Casey, Caylor and Allen of Missouri, the four Morton sisters from Arkansas, Sister Lang from Michigan, (a music teacher, who directed the choir) Ky Clark and many others I can not recall. Of course wife and I had to sing, 'Naaman' and 'The Church' and some other songs, again and again.

"People of all creeds and colors were made to feel at home in the meeting and they certainly used their liberty in the Lord. (without fanaticism.)

"White people, colored people and Indians, all took part in the meeting and as Bro. Parham remarked, 'We had the Gospel in black and white and red all over.' The colored people kept their place and respected and appreciated the welcome given them.

"Let us not forget to pray for the one on whom, more than all others, rests the responsibility of this great work—Bro. Parham. God is certainly with him. Every year makes a change in this man and he is broader, and deeper now in the love of God than ever before.

"But he is a target for the enemy and we must not forget that all hell is on his track. God only knows the conflicts through which he is called to pass, the burdens he carries, the sufferings he endures.

"He never murmurs or complains; he never falters by the way. He will tell you that 'the yoke is easy and the burden is light' and he just acts like it, everywhere and all the time.

"But read 2 Cor. 4:8-13, and you will know his experience. God bless the man."

* * * * *

The baptism of the Holy Spirit was bestowed during the meeting, and when one brother was asked how he felt, he said. "I can't describe the sweetness of my experience. It seems as though tubs of honey were being poured into my soul."

J. C. Seibert from Los Angeles, California, listened to a man speak in German who had received the baptism of the Holy Spirit, and being of German decent, understood the language.

As he testified to this, others were convinced and said this was the religion they wanted.

I will quote some newspaper comments:

THE BIG CAMP MEETING.

"The four weeks' camp meeting at Springs Park closed last Sunday night, and to say it was a successful meeting is putting it light. While we can not swallow some of the doctrine preached by the eloquent Rev. Parham, we cannot help but say his meetings have been beneficial to the city and the means of saving many souls. Because a person does not believe a doctrine is no excuse for them attending the meeting and ridiculing their belief. If you do not like the talk you hear, there is plenty of room to make your get-a-way, and the best thing to do is to "23", and keep silent.

"There was a large gathering of people from all over the United States, and delegates were present from Michigan, Texas, California, Colorado, and all nearby states. Many car loads of people came in on Sunday from Joplin, Webb City, Galena and Miami. Large numbers were camped on the grounds and many took their meals at the hotels, while others brought their provisions and cooked at the tents.

"It was a meeting long to be remembered and the attendants feel thankful for the many courtesies shown by the good people of Baxter."—Baxter Springs paper.

* * * * *

"Several people from Chetopa have been in attendance at the Apostolic Faith camp meeting at Baxter Springs, and report a wonderful meeting. Sunday, Aug. 17, was a grand day and God was present in a wonderful power. There are people gathered there from the Pacific to the Atlantic, and from the Gulf to the Lakes, and a spirit of fellowship and unity is manifested that is seldom seen among the people of today."—Chetopa, Kansas Paper.

* * * * *

Sept. 3, about fifty of our friends surprised Mr. Parham with a fare-well party, bringing donations of different kinds.

After song and testimony we partook of the Lord's Supper.

During the camp meeting, a number of the men had devoted their spare time to putting a floor in a large room to be used for a printing office, as we had, up to this time, no suitable place for this purpose. They also made a large cement porch leading into the room.

After the simple but blessed ceremony of the bread and wine, we all entered the new press room and dedicated it to the work of printing the gospel.

Mr. Parham then made a few remarks, thanking Rolland Romack for his faithfulness and his consecrated life, so fully given up to the publishing of "The Apostolic Faith." We closed by forming a large circle, joining hands we sang, "Blest be the tie that binds."

With best wishes and prayers, our friends bid good-by to Mr. Parham and Ky Clark, who were to leave on the night train for Guymon, Oklahoma, which was a new field.

* * * * *

The following is a part of a report of that meeting given by Mr. & Mrs. Fred Daly, at that time.

"We are thanking God for the true gospel, which has been preached to us by Brother Parham and for the services rendered by Brother Ky Clark and Mrs. Preston, who have helped in the meeting.

"The old Opera House has been filled night after night, and all carried home a message which sunk deep in their hearts.

"The meeting was heartily indorsed by three-fourths of the town people and many have been saved and others re-claimed.

"The meeting closed in triumph, the hall crowded, and the street full. The altar was filled with penitents. The noon hour prayer meeting Saturday resulted in the conversion of six. Sister Lillian Thistlethwaite is coming to be with us for the regular meetings till we are made strong in the Lord."

* * * * *

Miss Della Stockton, (now Mrs. Bigger) who has given her testimony in this book, lived with her sister in Guymon and since they had accepted the full gospel while visiting in San Angelo, their efforts had been untiring to have Brother Parham hold a meeting in their home town. How grateful they were for the way the Lord had answered their prayers.

* * * * *

After this meeting, they went to Wichita for a meeting of which Mrs. M. E. Parham wrote:

"In the winter of 1913, a call came to Brother Parham to hold a meeting in Wichita, Kansas. The meeting was begun in an upstairs room but very soon the crowds were too large for the place and a much larger place was secured near the heart of the city—which was soon filled to its utmost cap-acity.

"Night after night, the altar was filled with earnest seekers weeping their way through to salvation, consecrating their lives to God and tarrying for the baptism of the Holy Spirit. Many were the shouts of praise as the seekers touched the throne of grace for the blessings sought.

"There were many marvelous healings, one being a young lady who had for years been subject to epileptic fits and her mind was so effected she had to be confined to her room. As Brother Parham laid his hands on her and commanded the demon forces to leave, she arose from the bed a well woman. She attended every service afterward, and testified to the perfect healing, her mind clear and her body well. She was converted, sanctified and received the baptism of the Holy Spirit during the meeting.

"One night a crowd of ruffians collected on the street corner with weapons of various kinds to waylay Brother Parham as he went home and do him an injury.

"A great big man came to Brother Parham and said, 'I am going home with you tonight.' 'What's the idea?' Brother Parham asked. 'Well, I am going to protect you from the mob,' he answered.

"Brother Parham smiled, looked him over from head to foot (he looked like a boy beside this big man) and said, 'I am trusting God to protect me.' 'But,' the big man persisted, 'How do you know but God sent me to protect you this time?'

"They proceeded to go, but as Brother Parham started home the usual way this man said, 'No, come this way?'

"After they had gone a few blocks, this man said, 'Don't show yourself, but peep around the corner of this building.' And there sure enough was a mob of men arrayed with clubs, pitch-forks, etc, waiting for him to come this way, but they had missed their victim. God wonderfully undertook in that meeting; some of the precious fruit gathered is still standing today."

*   *   *   *   *

Mrs. Preston, who had received the light of the full gospel in the Galena meeting in 1903, had now moved to Wichita and her daughter, Libby, was reclaimed and consecrated her life to God in this meeting.

The last Sunday afternoon many partook of the sacrament of bread and wine for the first time, discerning the Lord's broken body; Mr. Parham and Ky Clark left Wichita, Kansas, January 28th, 1914 for other fields of labor.

Chapter XXV

LO, I COME TO DO THY WILL, O GOD.

ten days convention began at Webb City, Mo., in the Aylor Hall, February 6, 1914, but when the time for the convention had expired, a real revival had begun.

Mr. Parham expected each week to close the meeting, but it continued for many weeks, with unabated interest and power.

Almost every night the altar was filled with from twenty to thirty seekers, high, low, rich, and poor bowed at one common altar and bodies were healed of all manner of diseases.

One Sunday afternoon four received the baptism of the Holy Spirit; such a manifestation of God's presence, as had never been witnessed before in Webb City!

The altar service continued from four o'clock in the afternoon until ten o'clock that night, several others received the baptism of the Holy Spirit, and the town was stirred.

The Texas State Convention was held at Temple, Texas, beginning Easter Sunday, April 12 to April 26, 1914.

Workers came in from other states, as well as from different parts of Texas, and the meeting continued with great success under the inspiration and power of God. The people were hungry for the truth and a great work was accomplished.

In spite of torrents of rain, which flooded the ground where the tent stood, the great crowds refused to stay away but nightly waded mud and water for the privilege of enjoying the testimonies, and the preaching of old time religion.

The tent was filled and often many who could not get in remained on the outside to listen.

Some who at the beginning of the meeting warned others to stay away, came themselves and were converted before the meeting closed.

One Saturday night, the "revival fire" broke out. The testimony service had scarcely begun, when people began to praise the Lord all over the audience. Sinners and backsliders, overpowered by conviction, arose to their feet and called upon the Christians present to pray that God would have mercy upon them.

A backslider came to the altar of his own accord, weeping over his lost condition. Immediately a great altar service was on and such a scene as followed! It was estimated by some present that between thirty-five and forty prayed through to real salvation that night.

*   *   *   *   *

I will give the testimony of W. W. Wilkerson, who was converted in this meeting and became a Baptist minister.

"Brother Charles F. Parham came to my home town and began a series of meetings. About the middle of the meeting I went out to hear him.

"The first night that I was there, a large crowd was in attendance and I was out in the extreme out-skirts of the meeting. Suddenly Brother Parham let out a tirade against some disturbance of which I was part. He read my whole history in about one minute. I wondered where he got his information about me, having never seen me.

"He said that some low-down, cigarette-smoking, sparking devil was disturbing the meeting. I felt certain that he meant me, and from that night on, he seemed to just pick me for a subject and never let up, but just hit harder and harder. In about four evenings, he had me skinned, salted, peppered, and hung up to dry.

"I could not stand it any longer. I ran to the little board altar, fell on my knees and there found the sweetest experi-

ence that man could ever know and was delivered from tobacco habit, gambling and every other devil possession."

* * * * *

When my son, Robert, his wife and I visited at the home
of Mr. & Mrs. Keet Reed at Temple in April 1929, Robert
showed Mr. Parham's pictures of Palestine, in the Baptist
Church there. We met W. W. Wilkerson's mother
who thanked God for sending Mr. Parham to hold that meeting which had been the means of changing their home from
darkness to light. I was told that he gave this experience
in Temple in June, 1929, saying that, "It is the Holy Spirit
that drives the truth home to hearts." How true this is.
Mr. Parham often said, "You can't kill bears with the same
shot you use for squirrels or use squirrel shot for bears. Some
times it takes dynamite to jar some people loose to see their
lost condition and dynamite must be directed by the Holy
Spirit to accomplish its purpose. If spoken of self, it will
fail to kill and make alive."

Instead of the meeting at Temple closing at the appointed
time it lasted six weeks; then Mr. Parham left the meeting for
other ministers to continue.

Mr. Parham and Ky Clark then came to Baxter Springs to
prepare for the convention to be held at Cave Springs, Arkansas, this year instead of at Baxter Springs, where the camp-
meeting had been for so many years. May 24th, Mr. Parham
held an all day meeting at Webb City, Mo., and in the
afternoon preached from the Scripture, "Come out of her my
people." He warned the people against fanaticism on one side
and sectarianism on the other, which seeks to erect little
fences between us and others who do not see as we do.

He said he would never permit himself to be tied to any
little band or bunch of people: that the world was his parish,
and if he expected to catch the ear of the Christian world,
he must fellowship the Christ in others.

Brother Cabaniss of Katy, Texas, gave in his experience as a business man, telling how the Lord not only delivered him from sickness and sin, but also from bankruptcy and despair; enabling him to pay off a mortgage that ran up into the thousands.

At night Mr. Parham preached on redemption. He placed no limit on the power of God to redeem man from sin and give him victory over the world, the flesh and the devil. As the Spirit anointed the message, waves of glory rolled over the service.

After Mr. Parham's birthday meeting at Baxter Springs, the first Sunday in June, the meeting was held at Cave Springs, Arkansas which assumed the proportions of a national convention, as many came from other states to camp and seek God in healing and the deeper blessings.

Mr. Parham and workers, then went to Chicago, and after a meeting there were urged to come to Zion City, "at least for a few days." In August, the meeting began there in a private home which soon became too small to hold the crowds and a gracious revival had begun. In spite of the opposition a good hall was opened up to them. Many came who were possessed with demon forces and were delivered by prayer.

Mr. Parham was assisted by a good company of about ten workers, and the meeting continued with marked success until small-pox started in the city, and the state quarantine temporarily closed the meeting.

Mr. Parham and part of the company then began a meeting at Adrain, Missouri, November 7, and a real revival lasted four weeks. The Lord added to the Church of the living God, daily, such as should be saved.

They then held a two weeks meeting in Wichita, Kansas, especially given to Bible study.

In the early spring, Mr. Parham returned to the battle in Zion City, and at the close of this meeting, came home.

It seemed hard for us to realize that our family were now nearly grown and that our only daughter was to be married, April 14, 1915.

They had a simple but pretty home wedding; only relatives invited as we could not accommodate our large circle of friends.

Mr. Parham performed the ceremony; praying earnestly for the young couple; he committed his only daughter to God and the care of her husband.

They were very practical and immediately got in their buggy, taking a setting of eggs with them to their country home that was waiting for them.

Only parents can know the mingled feelings, of pride and sorrow as their children leave home to face the responsibility of life for themselves. But the boys did not take the occasion so seriously, and assisted by Rolland Romack, mischieviously tied an old shoe to the back of their buggy, which (unknown to them) swung in the breeze as their beautiful black horse bore them swiftly away. In Mr. Parham's last days he said he was thankful his daughter was in the care of one who had proved so worthy.

From June 1, until June 8, Mr. Parham and workers, conducted meetings in Baxter Springs, securing the Opera House for the last four nights of the meeting.

He preached especially on prophecy setting forth clearly the condition and position of the world according to the Bible.

To those to whom these teachings were new, it seemed terrible to hear, but I had heard Mr. Parham preach about the wars, troubles and revolutions which were to come, ever since I had known him, and felt sure, sooner or later, these things must needs come to pass.

As the people began to see that the wars and rumors of wars, were fulfilling prophecy, many cities were begging him to come and give them teachings on these subjects.

They went to Wichita, Kansas for a week's meeting but soon after this Ky Clark had to leave the work, as he was called home on account of his brother's sickness.

In August 1915, Mr. Parham held a meeting in Oklahoma City, Okla., and it was in this meeting that Fred Campbell, and other members of the family, received the teachings of the full gospel. Soon after this Fred Campbell consecrated his life to God, and for many years travelled with Mr. Parham in evangelistic work.

About the holiday season of 1915, a special need of getting together for prayer seemed to impress the workers, and Mr. Parham called a two weeks convocation at the mission at Baxter Springs.

Many came from other towns and states to attend this meeting, and our Baxter Springs friends opened their doors to accommodate them.

It was a special time of waiting on God, and many hours each day were spent in prayer.

Under the overshadowing of the Almighty, amidst the throes of a great humility and a most wonderful spirit of consecration, a new and living message was given as the Word of God fell upon our ears. We were in His presence and message after message, under the mighty function of the Holy Spirit poured forth, showing most clearly that the "Highway and hedge call" was on.

Seventeen received the real baptism of the Holy Ghost.

We took for our watch word for 1916; "LO, I COME TO DO THY WILL, O GOD." (Hebrews 10-9).

The meeting out grew the mission and was continued in the Opera House, and closed with wonderful victory. One was raised as it were from the dead, after the breath had left her body twice, and in twenty minutes came shouting on the platform.

A few Convocation Echoes.

Mrs. W. E. Walkenshaw (Parham) Webb City, Missouri.

"I thank God, I was permitted to attend the Convocation where the oil of the Holy Ghost was poured out upon us. We felt anew His function and power, and were built up in Him.

"I believe if there was any one thing in the Convocation more beauiful than another it was the many eager, earnest, enthusiastic young men and women who took up the watch' word, 'LO, I COME TO DO THY WILL, O GOD' and consecrated their lives to go out and carry this gospel."

Fred C. Daley and wife, Wichita, Kansas.

"Servants, servants, did we hear the call of the most High to serve in the highway and hedge call?

"He is our Master who redeemed us from the world and self by His own precious blood, that we might be made ready to serve humanity in this dark hour, and make the consecra' tion that Christ made in the garden and be baptized with the suffering with which He was baptized for us.

"Father, in Jesus' name, help us who attended the Convoca' tion to realize what it means, and the responsibility that rests on us, in giving out the deeper truths we have learned."

Fred Campbell.

"The greatest thing I received in the Convocation was to let God have His way with me. I have learned one of the greatest lessons of my life, that when we get self out of the way, God will overflow His blessings on us. I am glad we can prove God's promises true, and that this Convocation was held, that our lives might be deepened in God.* We have learned more in these two weeks than we could have learned in a year out in meetings."

A WORKER'S PRAYER

Lord, speak to me, that I may speak
In living echoes of Thy tone;
As Thou hast sought, so let me seek
Thy erring children, lost and lone.

O, lead me, Lord that I may lead
The wandering and the wavering feet.
That I, Thy hungering ones may feed,
 Upon Thy manna sweet.

O, strengthen me, that while I stand
Firm on the Rock and strong in Thee,
I may stretch out a loving hand
To wrestle with a troubled sea.

O, teach me, Lord, that I may teach,
The precious things Thou dost impart;
And wing my words that they may reach,
The hidden depth of many a heart.

O give Thine own sweet rest to me,
That I may speak with soothing power,
A word in season, as from Thee,
To weary ones in needful hour.

O fill me with Thy fulness Lord,
Unitl my very heart o'erflow
In kindling thought and glowing word
Thy love to tell, Thy praise to show.

O use me Lord, use even me
Just as Thou wilt, and when and where,
Until Thy blessed face I see—
Thy rest, Thy joy, Thy glory share.

Frances R. Havergal.

Chapter XXVI

WARS AND RUMORS OF WARS.

N 1916, Mr. Parham and a company of workers held meetings in Michigan and the following is a newspaper report from "The Daily Commercial" Three Rivers, Michigan.

A. L. Branch States That The Meetings Will Be Free From Denominationalism.

"Chas. F. Parham of Baxter Springs, Kansas, the earliest leader in the present Pentecostal or Apostolic Faith movement, will be here for two weeks or more with a band of earnest workers to preach and teach the full gospel privileges that were purchased for every child of God by the atoning sacrifice of Christ on the cross of Calvary, including salvation from sin; sanctification for soul and body, and the baptism of the Holy Spirt.

"Mr. Parham follows none of the present day methods of evangelism; does not depend upon excitement, nor seek to create it. He will not tolerate fanaticism or wild-fire in any form in the meetings. He takes no collections neither do any of his workers for their support, but are wholly dependent on God to supply their every need according to His promise. He is not forming a new sect or denomination, but is absolutely free from demoninationalism. He preaches the Word of God in its fullness, and seeks only to bring people into a living union with a living Savior. He is one of the most loved, and at the same time one of the most hated, men in the United States.

"One of his helpers is J. E. Cabaniss from the vicinity of Houston, Texas. He is an extensive business man and is known as 'the rice man of Texas.' He is here out of gratitude to God for saving him from the judgement because of his sins, for saving him from death because of disease, and for saving him from bankruptcy because of thousands of dollars of indebtedness. His story thrills with interest and sparkles with humor and reveals the mighty love and power of God as a present reality in the lives of men today rather than a theological theory about which men dsagree.

"There are thousands of sin-sick souls who would come to Christ today if they knew there was a reality in the Christian religion to set them free from the captivity of sin."

* * * * *

Of his meeting at Port Huron, Michigan held February 10, 1916, Mrs. Lang wrote:

"During the meeting here, Brother Parham was at his best preaching the gospel. Truly it would be impossible to give expression to the wonderful way the gospel went forth under the power of the Holy Ghost.

"A large number of God's people went down in humility before the Lord and sought for the deeper works of grace. We too, received much blessing and learned some lessons that are a great help to us.

"A number of hardened sinners turned from sin to Christ; backsliders were reclaimed, others were sanctified, and baptized with the Holy Spirit and much good came to all who attended the meetings."

* * * * *

After closing the meeting in Port Huron, Mr. Parham held meetings in Zion City, and Chicago, Ill. The following report of the Zion City meetings was written for our paper.

"As we look back upon the past events it seems to us there could never have been a campaign begun under less favorable circumstances or with less promise of success than that begun under the leadership of Bro. Parham in Zion City in the fall of 1914. The 'Powers That Be' were aroused to a desperation that amounted almost to a frenzy when it became known that Parham was coming to town. Huge posters denouncing him as a desperately vile criminal were placed over town. Hand-bills of the same character were spread broadcast and were taken to every home in the city. People were warned publicly and privately against attending the meetings or having anything to do with any of those responsible for it. Not a place of worship in the city was opened and every church and assembly was bitterly opposed.

"But God had a people who were hungry for the deep things of God. Brother and Sister Campbell opened their home and for some time meetings were held there. The interest and attendance grew until it soon became evident that larger quarters were necessary, so a comfortable room capable of seating about two hundred and fifty people was secured in a basement under the drug store.

"God inspired His servant to preach and teach the kind of religion that reaches the hearts and lives of men and women and in spite of all opposition the interest increased, the people came and were convinced, sinners were saved, backsliders were reclaimed and the people of God made to rejoice with great victory in their lives and the glory of God shone on their faces. Before the meetings closed hundreds had been blessed, many healed, many brought out of fanaticism, many saved, sanctified and made happy in good old-time salvation.

"When Brother Parham came back in the winter of 1916 to hold a ten days Convocation conditons had considerably changed. The fierce and unholy prejudice had wonderfully subsided and people from every mission and meeting in town came together in the sweet spirit of love and unity and a glorious and inspiring time was had. The message was filled with the power of old-time religion and present day salvation. The message of the Everlasting Gospel was sounded forth with a new ring and power, and a new and deeper consecration seized the people as they realized that the Midnight Cry, 'Go ye out to meet Him,' is being sounded.

"On April 9, 1916 Bro. Parham again visited our meeting where Bro. Albert Miller was conducting services. At both the morning and night services the hall was overcrowded, with the aisles full of chairs and all the standing room was taken.

"A characteristic of all these meetings has been the absence of any fanaticism, or unusual or unseemly demonstrations, but they have been pervaded with an air of intense enthusiasm and interest and real spiritual power.

"God is wonderfully blessing. Victory is on our side. Many are responding to the call to the highways and hedges and are going out, giving freely of their time, talents and means to spread the wonderful message of the age and tell the wonderful story of real old-time salvation that saves, cleanses, heals and keeps.

"Brother Parham's work is the most spiritual and shows the healthiest growth of any in the city."

*   *   *   *   *

We have some testimonies concerning the Chicago meeting.

"About fourteen years ago I found a small dirty book which I suppose some one had thrown away. It was written by Bro. C. F. Parham and gave the teaching on the baptism of the Holy Ghost. The book was a great help to me, it made things so clear.

"Later I was in Los Angeles while Bro. Parham was holding meetings there, and knowing he was the first preacher in these last days that taught the baptism of the Holy Ghost evidenced by speaking in other tongues, I had a great desire to hear him, but was kept away by people telling me he was no good and crooked in doctrine. The devil cheated me the same way later when he was in Chicago, and when he was recently in Zion City I still held the same attitude toward him.

"Bros. Wm. Bacon and Thoro Harris spoke so well of him and his teachings and urged me to go and hear him, that I finally went and enjoyed the message very much. At the close of the meeting Bro. Bacon said to me that he would like for Bro. Parham to hold a ten days meeting in Chicago, so we arranged for him to come.

"The Lord wonderfully blessed Bro. Parham who brought us truths we had never heard before. Many saints testified to being wonderfully helped. Two things have been made very clear to me: that unreasonable manifestations and organizations are a hindrance to God's work.

"The Lord worked wonderfully in saving, sanctifying and reclaiming power and the mission was crowded with hearts hungry to hear the Word preached."

*　*　*　*　*

"The meetings conducted by Bro. Chas. F. Parham in our Lake Street Mission were eye openers. Surely such preaching was needed in Chicago. The message of the Everlasting Gospel was forcibly presented, fanaticism was fearlessly assailed, and the prophetic significance of the time of trouble into which the world is entering was clearly portrayed.

"This series of meetings has left a good impression upon our people. They love the message and the messenger, and look forward to his return. A goodly number of people from Zion City participated in this feast of good things."

Thoro Harris.

*　*　*　*　*

"I can truly say, it is wonderful what the Lord can do. The meeting conducted by our Brother Parham in Chicago, has been a blessing to many hungry souls.

"The gospel messages had a wonderful melting and drawing power that filled our souls with a hunger for reality. The yeast of unleaven truth has been planted, it has begun to raise the lid and the real 'Bread of Life,' is being revealed, Many sweet testimonies of renewal to the blessings and favor of God were given by rejoicing saints.

"Our coming together was for the better; with real heart searchings which resulted from the preaching of the Word being mixed with faith by those that heard it.

"While the Mission at large stood for truths diverse from Brother Parham's teachings before he came, no strife, no crossing, or disrupted service occurred; contrary our eyes and ears were opened to truth that will stand and be a part of our real preparation for the coming of our Lord and redemp-tion."   Wm. Bacon.

*   *   *   *   *

On March 2, 1916 our first grandchild was born, Charles Ernest Rardin. He was named Charles for his grandfather, and Ernest for his father and we were always very proud of our only grandson.

Mr. Parham had been laboring in the north during the cold winter weather, and now summer had come, he was going to the south to hold meetings in Texas.

People often told him, he should arrange his meetings more according to the seasons, going south for winter, and north for the summer months, and it would be more to his com-fort and pleasure in traveling. But he said that he could not consider his own comfort but must go as he felt lead, for the glory of God and the good of the people.

For four months, he and his workers labored in the state of Texas. The work there had been so defiled with fanati-cism that those who stood for the Apostolic Faith teachings were looked upon as cranks and the people had sent for Mr. Parham to come, believing that he could lift the shame from the work as no one else could, and place the work upon a high-er spiritual basis. The meeting at Alvin was reported the best which had been held there for several years and great crowds heard the gospel with intense interest as the messages went forth under the power of the Holy Spirit. All who attended were greatly blest; even the sinners appreciated and were loud in their praise of the sermons on prophecy.

After successful meetings were held in several other missions, a most beautiful auditorum was secured for a month's meeting in Houston, Texas. The Lord supplied the means, and the standard of Christianity was lifted up, for the glory of God.

The meeting at Temple, Texas came next, which began July 21; the services were held in the Skating Rink and a great work was accomplished.

Mr. Parham and the workers motored over to Belton each day for street meetings. Hundreds there heard the Word and rejoiced to know they could be Christians and enjoy all the gifts and graces of God without uniting with modern churchanity. The country was stirred for miles around and multitudes were made to believe in the truth of the gospel of Christ.

They then went to Killeen, Texas to hold street meetings for a few days. Mr. Parham found here a real work to do. He often expressed his preference for street work rather than in buildings, saying that he enjoyed being able to look up into the blue skies above, the great canopy of God, with nothing between.

The city marshal and different business men said this town and surrounding country became interested in real salvation as never before. The theater man did not make his expenses and on the last Sunday night the churches were emptied that they might be in this meeting. Hardened sinners, who had not been reached by the churches broke down, fell on Mr. Parham's neck and cried out as of old, "Almost thou persuadest me to be a Christian."

In October, Mr. Parham held a meeting in Joplin, Mo. A
vacant lot in the central part of town was seated for this
meeting, of which the paper wrote:

"Brother Chas. F. Parham is at present in this city holding a series of meetings in the open air on Main Street. He
has his big guns trained on the worldliness and falseness in modern churchanity and he is surely shooting them to a frazzle.

"Large crowds are attending his meetings and are surely
filled with wonder and admiration as they see and hear the
apostle of freedom pouring the broadsides of gospel truth
into the ranks of sectism."

Before the watch-night meeting which was held in Joplin,
Mo., this year, Mr. Parham conducted meetings in Galena,
Kansas, in November and then in Prosperity, Missouri. I
have referred to these meetings in a previous chapter, but will
now give you a further report.

*　*　*　*　*

"From start to finish the meeting held at Galena, Kansas,
revealed the evidence of divine appointment and a confirma-
tion of the Convocation held a year ago at Baxter Springs that
we were in the dawning of the "highway and hedge"call. Reports of gracious revivals by many tried and true warriors
from many fields, and the evident quickening into revival fire
everywhere, impressed us that this has been the best year in
the last twelve years. The altars were crowded with seekers.
Scores were saved. Many were sanctified, there were some
very wonderful healings, and ten received the baptism of
the Holy Spirit. The force of the meeting went out into all
the country round about.

"How we worship God for the last week devoted to
teachings on prophecy. The glorious spirit of prophecy was
upon Brother Parham. From every part of the Bible he
brought out the Scriptures to prove that we are in the last
days; while from history and current events he astonished

the audiences night after night, as he piled up the proof that it was time to set our houses in order for the coming of the King.

"These facts were ever before us: These wars, sooner or later, mean the end of the nations, the end of the Gentile age, the return of the Jews, the closing of the door of mercy, the redemption of the saints, the time of trouble (Anarchy), then the beginning of the last seven years of this age (three and one-half years ruled by the association ten-toed kingdom and three and one-half years ruled by the Antichrist), then the coming of the Lord, the battle of Armageddon, and the opening of the millenial reign of the seventh or sabbatic thousand years."

*   *   *   *   *

"The great revival in Prosperity, Mo., begun by Sister May Hinckley and continued by Brother Parham broke out afresh after the Inter-State Convention at Galena. Brother Parham was called to Prosperity to preach the funeral of a man who was saved during the revival and who died shouting happy and he found the revival flame still burning. Meetings were announced for one week. Large crowds filled the hall and yards. The entire community was under conviction. Scores were saved, many of them old church members, while Pentecost falls at every service. Some very wonderful miracles were wrought in healings. Many were saved in their homes. This meeting exceeded all bounds: the oldest citizens have never witnessed such scenes and the meeting continued until the holidays."

*   *   *   *   *

As we watched out the year of 1916 in Joplin, Missouri, we were grateful to God for all the blessings it had brought to us. But as we welcomed 1917, and prayed that His grace would be sufficient, it was not without some misgivings and question in our minds what would this new year bring?

"Wars and rumors of wars" now sounded sadly on our ears. Would this year bring us great trouble and evolve our beloved country in grief and suffering?

During the first month of the year, sickness occupied our time in the home, and as I have told you, we bid farewell for a short season to our dear sister in Christ, who had labored with us in His service for the last two months.

Some hearts are crushed and subdued by sorrow and seeming defeat and others are able to rise above all discouragements victorious.

Mr. Parham seemed to redouble his energies, renewed his strength in the Lord and continued the battle for God and souls.

Though we had no boys of our own who were old enough to be called to war now, our hearts were sad for other homes which might soon be broken up.

There were a great many homes over all the United States where Mr. Parham had made his home while holding meetings and had always been welcomed as one of the family.

Boys from these homes, who he had seen grow into manhood, would no doubt be called to war and perhaps give up their lives on the battlefield. He shared the sorrow of these homes, and received scores of letters for advice and comfort.

On the 10th of April, a meeting was begun at Nevada, Mo., Mr. Parham was assisted in this meeting by W. R. Norton and his wife, Fred Campbell and Clarence Heckendorn, the boy preacher, who seemed so called to the ministry that Mr. Parham took him with him for several years to train him in evangelistic work. The meeting was begun in a residence, which would accommodate from seventy-five to one hundred people.

At the end of the first week this home became too small for the crowds that attended so the meeting was continued in a large Baptist Church, within a block and a half of the public square.

Open air meetings were held in the court-house yard in the afternoon, where large crowds gathered to hear Mr. Parham's sermons on prophecy; also to hear Clarence, the boy preacher.

Numbers were saved, many received the blessing of sanctification and God's healing power was marvelously manifested; many testified to instant healing.

Mr. Parham labored here for about four weeks, then W. R. Norton and his wife continued the meeting.

* * * * *

During this summer, Mr. Parham and a company of workers went to Nebraska and other states for meetings, of which he wrote the following;

"We left Baxter Springs, Kansas on a tour of western Kansas, Nebraska and eastern Colorado in two autos. One consisted of Bro. Cabaniss and family of Katy, Texas and Lucy Romack, Rolland's sister, (now Mrs. Waterbury.) The other of special workers, Bro. Romack, Fred Campbell, Clarence Heckendorn, Bert McGuirk and myself. We arrived in Wichita and pitched our forces in front of the post office. Here nightly the multitudes came to hear the wonderful testimonies and the preaching of the Word. A general outline of the full gospel was given in great power, though most of the time was given to prophecies. The people there were so hungry and seemed to drink in every word.

"From Wichita we traveled as led to Bartley, Nebraska, and what good times the soldiers had enroute. We were welcomed there by the family of J. R. Wade, who for twenty years have been defenders of the faith. On their ranch, with all the modern conveniences, we fared grandly. They, in their big six, and we, in our smaller cars, invaded Cambridge every afternoon and Bartley at night. The work here exceeded all our expectations. The compelling power was literally on the great crowds and a wonderful work was done for God. Eternity alone will reveal the blessed results of these labors.

"Special help was rendered here by the Christian minister, a lady with a blessed sanctified experience, who opened her church to us and came to assist us in the open air services. Many of the best women of the community came and sat upon the curb stone to hear and were glad to get the place. Some brought their tatting and sat an hour before meeting to hold a place, while cars filled the center of the street for a block and came a long time before meeting time to get a place, so great was the press to hear the Word. The first day's service set the town afire, both with those interested and those bitterly opposed. We were threatened with arrest for declaring the truths on prophecy for these days, but through all this we were more than conquerors. Praise the Lord!

"Brother Cabaniss had to leave us before we closed the meeting in Bartley. After a great farewell meeting in which hundreds came in line to say good bye, some weeping, others shouting, while all were in a deep spirit of earnestness, we separated to go to our next place. Long will be the time ere we forget the good times and the good friends of Bartley.

"From here we went to Colby, Kansas. Here we found good and loyal friends with whom we had corresponded for years, especially Brother Barger and family.

"Although the Chautauqua was on the way, our crowds were fine and a great victory was in the air.

"Many who had not been in a church for years listened for two hours every night and the prophecies literally swept all opposition before them and compelled the people to believe in the second coming of Christ.

"While we were holding most interesting meetings in Colby, Kansas, a telegram was sent by some vicious enemies—

who were most terribly hit by the message in the last place, Bartley, Nebraska— to the effect that we were German spies, so as to enrage the people against us. It developed one night, when I was driving into the yard where I stayed in a shower of eggs, all fresh, however. None of them hit me, but there was enough unbroken ones to make noodles the next day for dinner. The officials did nothing in the way of examining us to see if the charges were true or not.

"The next night, as I had finished my sermon and about six hundred people were about me, including many women and children, a fifty pound lard can full of water was hurled from the building in front of me. My head was bowed in prayer for a sick man. The can hit the awning and swerved just about four inches and fell on the arm of the chair at my side, denting it into a mass. Within three feet of where it fell were gathered women and children.

"A great crowd of men rushed to my aid as the can fell and water surrounded me; but such a sweetness, like honey-dew, fell over me and I raised my hands and quieted them and found myself saying, 'Peace. This is just what we expect; our lives are in God's hands. Praise the Lord.' Then a great spirit of prayer welled up in my soul for all of them and the community, for I knew that God had sent us there and would judge the town that thus treated His little ones. We then closed the meeting with, 'God Be With You Till We Meet Again,' as it was our last night there. The next day we went to Denver for our next meetings."

* * * * *

One time, when Mr. Freeman, a man who lived in this vicinity, was working on a well drill, he was suddenly stopped and lead to pray. He knew at once that there was something that the Lord would have him do and it soon became clear to him that he should send Mr. Parham thirty dollars. He was willing to do this but thought at first that tomor-

row would be soon enough to send it but he was then impressed that it should be sent at once, so he stopped his work
and went to town. The post-office was closed so he telegraphed the money.

He soon received a letter from Mr. Parham thanking him
for it, and telling him how it came in direct answer to prayer.
He was holding a meeting where the people had been greatly blessed, but were unable to give much toward the support of the work and he had prayed that the Lord would supply their needs from some other sources. He and his workers were packed up, and ready to go some distance to their
next appointment—trusting God to supply the means—when
the money came which was just the amount needed.

Mr. Parham had scores of similar answers to prayer, which
made service sweeter to him than the salaried ministry and
made him feel the approval of God on his life and work. But
he often had his faith sorely tried, and like Paul, knew how
to abound and how to suffer want, and in whatever state he
was to be content.

As Mr. Parham preached on the streets of Denver, Colorado, hundreds heard the message nightly, and tourists were
there from all over the United States and owing to the intense
interest they stayed there longer than they had expected.

Fred Campbell, who for so long had been Mr. Parham's
traveling companion in evangelistic work, was called for
physical examination which he passed, and might be called
now at any time to enter the training camps.

On the 10th of October, F. R. (Rolland) Romack who for
so many years had been the able office editor and manager
of our paper, also passed the physical examination and was
accepted for the service of his country.

As our principles and belief forbid the shedding of blood,
papers were filed for his exemption from combative service
which however was not granted.

* * * * *

F. R. Romack wrote:

"As I have been called to the service of the counry, and as this October number of the Apostolic Faith may be the last issue of the paper we may be privileged to get out before being called to the camp, I wish to express my appreciation to the many and dear friends whom I have met and with whom I have had fellowship these last seven years that I have been in the work.

"Some have thought it rather strange that I have held to this work so long—and there have been a great many discouragements along the way—but that was my consecration to God, that I would fill any place that I saw opened to work for Him.

"I did not take up this work through any desire for worldly gain, or through the influence of a message, dream or vision, but just that a place was opened where I saw it was possible to work for God. And God has blessed,. as many letters testify to the blessings received through reading the messages sent all over the world.

"Time, at the longest, is short in which to serve God, but it is possible that the Lord will provide some other way for the continuation of the publishing of the paper, that the truth may continue to go forth for these last days."

* * * * *

Mr. Parham wrote: "No one in this movement has shown a deeper consecration to the work of God than Rolland Romack and not one whose life has been more above reproach. He has the most considerate respect for his sterling Christian personality, not only in his home town, but abroad.

"For over twenty years we have seen these present wars coming and it has been as real to us as it is now. All this time we have taught that true Christians must not fight for 'he that taketh the sword shall perish with the sword.' This is true, for you invite some to kill you or you will kill some one, if you take the sword.

"It is hard for those who sincerely believe that we are nearing the end of this age and the shedding of blood to be of no avail, to fight for the perpetuation of these nations, which we know will fall as the Gentile age will close and the millennium come, when the nations of the world shall become the kingdom of our Lord and Savior, Jesus Christ.

"The very forces that caused the fall of all other nations and civilizations are rampant in our own land, and (leaving God and the Bible prophecies out) this civilization cannot survive the same forces that overthrew all those gone before.

"Prophecy states that near the time of the end the nation will become lifted up and forget God and spread itself abroad in power and self glory and sorely oppress the laborers in their hire.

"For these things God will bring the nation to a close and the whole body of the eagle will be burned, as Washington, in his vision of the close of this nation's history, saw the cities laid waste from coast to coast. This will surely come true in the struggle between capital and labor.

"It has been our teaching for the last twenty years, that this country will end with a dictator and a final fall in a great struggle in which the government, the rich and the churches will be on one side and the masses on the other.

"After many calls, and earnest prayer, I feel it my duty to make a trip to the west and south and will start about the 10th of November for California. On my return trip I will stop at Houston and other places near there and many points on the Frisco from there to Baxter Springs, Kansas as I want to aid and help all I can."

Chapter XXVII

MARRIAGES AND DEATHS

 ORROWS' and war-clouds were settling down heavily on hearts and homes, training camps were rapidly being filled and at any time now the call might come for Fred Campbell and Rolland Romack to go, who seemed to Mr. Parham as his own sons and a part of the family.

It appeared to us rather an unsuitable time now to think of marriage but it is said that "love is as strong as death," and our oldest son Claude was trying to persuade us—though not quite of age— that he was old enough to take the responsibility of married life.

In the time of the creation, God said, "It is not good that man should be alone." In this point at least, man has always seemed to agree with his Creator. So now our minds are turned for a while from the troubles of war to the thought of welcoming into our home our first daughter-in-law.

·In spite of the old saying that "one roof is not large enough for two families," Claude showed confidence in his parents and his intended bride and decided to prove whether at least in their case, this could be made satisfactory. So he remodeled two rooms in our big, "old brewery" home and by February 20, 1918, his little home was ready, waiting to receive his bride, Lula Wene.

Mr. Parham, always said that he wished to marry all his children himself, and see that the knot was well tied, as he did not want any slip-knots. He performed the marriage ceremony at the home of the bride's parents, Mr. & Mrs. Wm. Wene of Baxter Springs, Kansas. Claude had said to us in his persuasive way, that we needed a daughter in the home and a real daughter Lula proved to be. She has been a blessing, not only to her husband but also to the rest of the family. As I write this, they are still living and are contented in the old home place.

In the spring, Fred Campbell was called to Camp Travis in Texas and Rolland Romack went to Camp Funston in Kansas, April 25, 1918. He belonged to Company G. 353rd Infantry, 89th Division. They were only in training about a month when they were both sent to France though they never saw each other. These were anxious days for relatives and friends all over the United States, as all watched eagerly for news from the boys "Over there"; our soldier boys "somewhere in France." Many hearts were sad when the news reached us that F. R. Romack had been killed in action, Sept. 19, 1918.

* * * * *

Mr. Parham wrote the following in a religious paper published at Wichita, Kansas by G. B. Winrod:

"To a host of friends and loved ones; we are made sad indeed to publish, the news of the early passing of our beloved brother and co-worker who for seven years stood by our side in the work of God as the efficient managing editor of the 'Apostolic Faith' paper.

"He came to the work as a lad consecrating his whole time and strength without money or price, to give all to the work of God with only his food and clothes as an earthly reward. No task was too great but what he was able to successfully accomplish it; no task too small or menial to which he would not give the most painstaking care. He was as noble and brave as he was kind and gentle. One of nature's noblemen, knighted by the grace of God.

"When the call of the draft came, he went forth as grandly to be a hero of the flag he loved, as he had been of the cross. Without reserve he laid his life upon the altar of his country; in France he paid the price of the great sacrifice on the fields of St. Mihiel. As did the Master; for those who compelled him to go the mile, he gladly went the twain.

"That 'he was obedient unto death' is an obituary that is carved to his memory upon the hearts of those near and dear to him, as it should be upon the little headstone that marks the dust of heroes that return to dust in far away France. In one of his last letters he said. "I have no fear in my heart for the things I am coming up against, and if sinners can gave their lives for their country and the world's freedom, I, prepared to meet my God—ought the more freely yield my life.'

"The city of Baxter Springs where he lived, was proud to have the honor of having in their midst a young man of such sterling qualities, and unitedly they mourn his early going on every side. Here and there, from ocean to ocean, comes the letters of consolation to loved ones, and unitedly the movement to which he gave his life so long, mourn for him we loved beyond all.

"I personally have dealt with hundreds of thousands and have yet to find a life so noble. For him no funeral service will be held and yet why should we, when his life was a service. His deeds full of music, add to his memory a lasting benediction.

"He was born near St. James, Ill., January 11, 1888. His relatives have our utmost sympathy in their bereavement for we loved him equally well."

*   *   *   *   *

While Fred Campbell was in France, Mr. Parham was assisted in his evangelistic work by other workers, but how grateful we were that through many dangers and narrow escapes his life was spared and he returned safely home. But he had been shell-shocked and his voice was injured so that he feared he would not be able to lead the singing again. But in answer to prayer his voice was restored and he continued to travel with Mr. Parham and lead the singing as he had done before he went to France.

Claude and Philip were now partners in a grocery business, but in the spring of 1921 Philip was taken very sick with rheumatism and heart trouble. I had written Mr. Parham about him being sick but had not told him how bad he really was, trusting he would soon be better. But instead he grew weaker, his suffering was intense and he was getting rapidly worse.

One day he asked me to telegraph his father to come home, saying, "If you don't send for father, I am going to die." As soon as Mr. Parham and Fred Campbell received the message, they started home at once from Colorado Springs driving day and night. They took it in turns to drive, and came through eating a lunch as they drove and only stopping to get gas for the car.

When they got home Philip was very low and suffering so that he could hardly bear to be touched, and we turned him in bed in a sheet. In answer to prayer, he soon began to recover and in two or three days, his father took him with them in the car to Nebraska and Colorado and he was restored to perfect health. They returned home for Mr. Parham's birthday meeting, the first Sunday in June.

During the summer, Mr. Parham held meetings in Texas and in August 1921, Ed. Durbin and others built a brush-arbor and made arrangements for him to hold a Camp Meeting at High Top, in a beautiful woods, near Gravette, Arkansas.

When the meetings were held near home, Mr. Parham always planned to have as many of his family attend them as possible, and this year we decided to arrange so that Robert could go with us.

Though he had been converted when quite young, in his school life, he had got his mind on other things and we hoped that the meeting would help to strengthen his faith in God. He enjoyed fishing and we told him that he could take his fishing tackle with him, as there would no doubt be some streams near where he could fish, and enjoy his vacation in the Ozarks. Paul said, "Being crafty, I caught you with guile," I guess this was what we used to get Robert interested in going to the Camp Meeting.

*   *   *   *   *

I have asked Robert to give you his testimony and tell you what he got out of his fishing trip in the Ozarks.

"In giving my testimony for what the Lord has really done for me and the joy that I felt in my soul, I don't believe words can express it. In coming to the High Top Camp Meeting, I had one suit case full of fishing tackle and was all ready to have a big time, but when I arrived on the Camp ground I found that only one small stream ran near there, and there was no hope of catching fish in it, so I turned my thoughts to hunting and began to try and find some one to hunt with me.

"Meanwhile different ones were praying for me, that I might be saved, so one morning I was in Brother Waterbury's tent and we were talking. He said to me, 'Robert, when are you going to be saved?' I told him I didn't know and he said he was going to pray for me. I answered, 'All right.' I know he did pray for me, also many others and very shortly I became convicted of my sins, and saw my need of God. I well remember the day that I went into the woods by myself to pray for help, and that night stayed in my tent, but I could hear the preaching, and the Holy Ghost was bringing the truth to my heart. When it was time for the altar call, I left my tent and went to the edge of the brush arbor, I was

surely seeing my need of God. Many were coming to the
Lord and I was ready to go, but needed a start. Brother B.
D. Coberly came by and said, 'Bob, it's time to go.' (I think
my father sent him to me.) I said, 'I know it,' and with a
moment's hesitation I went. Different ones of the dear
·people came and prayed for me, and their prayers went
through to glory, and the blessing of God flooded my soul,
and I was wonderfully saved. The power and presence of
the Lord was on the Camp Meeting from the very start, but
it had just come into my soul, and it was so good that I was
wanting more and more. The next day I fully consecrated
my life to the Lord, and He wonderfully sanctified me, with
a definite experience. I felt that I was not my own any
more; but I had been bought with a price, that was the precious blood of Jesus Christ. I was waiting upon Him for the
2nd Chapter of Acts experience, and the Holy Ghost was made
real in my life, with speaking in other tongues as the Spirit
gave utterance. I surely had much to thank the Lord for,
and I worked through out the meeting helping others to get
the same experience in the Lord that I had.

"After the Camp Meeting was over, we left for home to
be there for Monday night, and lo and behold, the front
yard was full of people, I wondered what was up. I found
out that Dad had sent word on ahead, and it was announced
on the front page of the newspaper that I would give my
experience that night in the front yard of the home. Here
was where I felt weak, but waiting on the Lord in prayer, I
was glad to give my testimony for what He had done for me.

"My experience has been like Peter's I was fishing for fish,
but Jesus said, 'Follow me, and I will make you a fisher of
men.' I followed Him and I believe He has made me a
blessing to many people, and given me the privilege of seeing
them get the same real experience that I got."

It was a good meeting. Surrounded only by the beauty of nature we were hidden away from the worldy things, and forgetting the cares of life, our minds were stayed on God, Robert with many others, prayed through to the blessings they needed.

One day as Mr. Parham preached on healing, the power of God was present to heal; many were healed as they sat in their seats and listened to the Word of God.

I wish it were possible for me to tell you of the power and glory of the last night's meeting, which is still remembered and talked of by those who were present. Mr. Parham used for his text, "What shall I do then with Jesus, which is called Christ?" I am sure many who read this book have heard him preach this sermon under the anointing of the Holy Spirit but that night he seemed to be entirely lifted out of himself and words flowed from his lips as coals of living fire, and fell upon that vast audience as the voice of God.

The brush-arbor had long since failed to accommodate the crowds but that night the audience extended far out into the woods, many standing, others sitting in buggies, wagons and cars.

But a holy hush prevailed over all; his words sounded clearly on listening ears and sank deep into hungry hearts. As conviction settled down over the audience, many wept and others shouted for joy as the waves of glory rolled and all recognized the presence and power of the living God. At the close of the sermon, the people flocked to the altar and prayed through to victory.

Our hearts still burned within us, the next day as we returned home, longing to carry some of the glory to our loved ones who could not be with us.

Mr. Parham was seldom permitted to spend Christmas at home as he was usually engaged in meetings in distant states, but this year, as his work was near home, we were expecting him to be with us during the holidays. But he said he believed that he should divide his time between us and his parents saying that perhaps it might be the last Christmas that they would be together. So it was decided that he would be with us for our family gathering Christmas Eve, and then take the midnight train and be with his folks at Cheney, Kansas for Christmas Day.

They prepared a good Christmas dinner for him and when in the afternoon a number of his old friends came in to see him, he had a meeting and preached to them.

His parents were good church members, but in that afternoon meeting, his step-mother got a better understanding of his faith and teachings, her prejudice was broken down and her faith strengthened in the Word of God.

Mr. Parham returned to Baxter Springs, but had not been at home long before he received a telegram asking him to come to Cheney at once as his mother was very sick.

He went on the first train, and for weeks he stayed day and night near her bed-side, praying that God would restore unto her the joys of His salvation, which she felt that she had lost sight of in a formal church worship. She said, "I thought when I came to death, it would be all light, but it is so dark; God won't let me go out into the dark, will He?" Before her death she said that the light had come and she was not afraid to go for the fear of death had been taken away. While Mr. Parham held her hand, he sang,

> "My latest sun is sinking fast,
> My race is nearly run,
> My strongest trials now are passed,
> My triumph is begun."

She squeezed his hand in recognization and soon passed quietly away, Thursday night, February 2, 1922.

The funeral services were conducted at the home the following Sunday afternoon and an immense crowd of friends and neighbors bore witness to the high esteem in which the deceased was held. She was born near Lake View, Ind., and was a life time member of the M. E. Church. Her father was an early circuit rider for the church of north Indiana, and rode far and near in the service of the Master.

Rev. J. A. Holmes assisted Mr. Parham in the funeral service. Mr. Parham preached the sermon, and told with great affection and appreciation what she had been to him and the rest of the family.

During this time of sorrow, Mr. Parham had renewed the acquaintance of the friends of his boyhood days. They became better acquainted with his faith and teachings and wanted him to come to Cheney and hold a revival meeting. So in the spring, Mr. Parham put up a big tent, and in spite of opposition, held a victorious revival.

*   *   *   *   *

Mrs. Hattie Ostrander of Cheney, Kansas will tell you some of the results of this meeting:

"In the year of 1922, I was attending the M. E. Church of which I was a member. I had known my sins were forgiven for three years as I had been converted in a revival meeting in the Free Methodist Church at Junction City, Kansas, yet there was such a longing deep down in my heart to have the deeper truths of God wrought out in my life, but I knew of no one who could help me.

"One Sunday morning when I attended our church as usual, our pastor called on Rev. Chas F. Parham to lead in prayer. We were all attention as we saw a little man emerge from Wm. Parham's pew and walk forward. It seemed to me as though a halo of glory had swept over the large assembly gathered there that morning to worship God.

"In silence we waited only for a brief moment, then a deep, rich voice began to float out over the congregation— ireighted with the power of God—till it seemed we were as reeds, shaken in the wind. My limbs would no longer hold me and there I knelt as the words of love and adoration for his beloved Master pealed forth, and I asked God to make each one of us know Him as this man of God knew Him.

"God in His great love and mercy heard the cries of His children and in a few short months sent our beloved brother and spiritual father to our town, who erected a large tent; with him came Fred Campbell.

"Crowds came, packed the tent and stood outside, some-times clear across the street. Rains drenched the people but they only raised their umbrellas, so eager were they to drink in the truths of God; the Lord had visited His people at Cheney and it was too sacred and precious to even seek shelter in our homes from the drenching rain. Many mir-acles were wrought and the altars were filled; many souls were saved and sanctified, and many bodies were marvelously healed.

"In direct answer to prayer, God sent a fireman on the railroad home, who was working in Wyoming, hundreds of miles away, and he was saved and sanctified the second day of the meeting.

"Mrs. Jessie Dibbens who had not been able to raise her feet from the ground for several years, but dragged them as she walked, was wonderfully healed in answer to prayer.

"Mrs. Anna Dibbens Mahan was marvelously delivered from a nervous trouble which she had suffered with since childhood.

"I had never seen a well day since the birth of my son then twenty-years old. One day as Brother Parham was preaching, the Lord touched my body and healed me com-

pletely and sanctified my soul.   Blessed be the name of the
Lord.

"Many prayed through in their homes.   A man left the
meeting one night with conviction deep down in his heart.
He tried to sleep but could not so he sought an old fashioned
mourner's bench, a kitchen stool at his home, and there prayed through and found God.

"Brother Parham closed his meeting May 7, 1923 but the
revival never ended; for three years people prayed through
who got under conviction in that meeting.

"God had wonderfully heard and answered Brother Parham's prayers.   Ever since he had been called to the ministry,
a boy of fourteen, he had asked the Lord to give him his home
town for God.   Nights that he had spent with his parents in his
old home were wakeful nights.   With his east window raised,
through the night he looked over the little village of his childhood, and had many pleasant memories and also bitter heart-
aches. With a heart in tune with God, he sometimes prayed
all night for God to save his loved ones, his friends and the
surrounding country. How much it meant to us all, as we now
saw his prayers being answered."

Mrs. Philip Stoehr tells her experience:

"For about 20 years I was a wretched, miserable sufferer
with little hopes of ever finding relief.   Like the woman mentioned in the Bible who had an issue of blood, I sought to
many physicians and spent hundreds of dollars, but grew no
better.   At times I was able to drag around and attend to
my household duties, but most of the time I was far from
able to do anything and was never free from pain.   At times,
too, my mind refused to work, and a great fear of insanity
came upon me, so that I would cry unto God, 'Oh, don't let
me loose my mind.'   I often wished for death to end all my
suffering.

I was a strong Lutheran. Yet in my heart I longed for a
closer walk with God. One day, while in Cheney, Kansas, I
saw a large tent and as I passed by I read: 'Hear Chas. F.
Parham, Old time Salvation and Healing for the body.' I
said, that sounds good I believe I'll go in. The sermon impressed me as the most powerful one I had ever heard and
the minister emphasized the fact of an experience for every
one, witnessed to by the Holy Spirit; a freedom from sin by
who's stripes we are healed. I, church member tho I was, was
hungry for that experience and oh, how I needed healing!
So when the call was made for those who were sick to be
prayed for, according to James 5-14, I went forward, and
when the man of God laid his hands on my head and in a
few words prayed for me, I felt the healing touch of God.
But I was not perfectly healed at that time. I prayed nearly
all that night, and never before had I felt the reality of God
as on that blessed night. At the next meeting I went forward
again, and praise His Holy Name, I felt the healing power
go through and through my whole body and was wonderfully
healed from the crown of my head to the soles of my feet;
made every whit whole, Hallelujah! Oh, I cannot praise Him
enough. He fills my soul with His glory, and my greatest
delight is to tell to others the wonderful story."

*   *   *   *   *

Mrs. Stoehr endured much persecution and before the
courts at Wichita, Kansas was asked why she left her church?
She had told them of her healing and how they had said
that they could not fellowship her unless she gave up her
faith in healing and the baptism of the Holy Spirit.

Turning to the lawyer she said, "After what God has
wrought in my life, could I do it?" The lawyer frankly ad-
mitted that she could not.

The record of her healing was taken in the Wichita courts.
Oct. 15, 1925.

We persuaded Father Parham to make us a visit and he was with us on Mr. Parham's forty-ninth birthday. Many people came from far and near for an all day meeting. Father Parham listened to the prayers, singing, testimonies and preaching, drinking in every word. He was convinced that this was indeed the gospel that Christ and the Apostles left on record and that these people had a faith and a hold on God that he sorely lacked.

He was not well and very lonely but we did what we could to make him happy and contented to stay with us. One night as I went to the kitchen door, I saw him sitting in the dark. "Oh, Father Parham!" I exclaimed, "What are you doing out here in the dark all alone? I nearly threw this dish water on you." "Well, Eleanor," (he always called me by my middle name) "it seems impossible for me to give up my tobacco and I came out here for a little smoke, where I thought no one would see me." "Come in," I said, "You are perfectly welcome to smoke in the house. We all understand that it would be hard for you to give up tobacco after you have used it so long." "No," he said, "I would not smoke in my son's home, before my grandsons who don't use tobacco for any thing. I am glad they don't smoke and I don't want to set a bad example. I have never been ashamed of it till now, but now I would be glad if I could give up this dirty habit."

In August he went with us to the Camp Meeting at Beth-page, Mo. We had expected to find a nice shady place to camp, like we had at the camp meeting at High Top, but in-stead the big brush arbor had been built right out in the sun.

At first we could not conceal our disappointment and won-dered how we could ever stand the intense heat, but when we understood that this location was especially chosen to reach some souls that were interested, no one complained, and the thought of the comfort of shade was forgotten as the meeting grew in interest and power.

One day Mr. Parham found his father in the tent weeping under deep conviction. "Charlie," he said, "you know I have always been a good church member and thought I was a Christian till now, but I have not got what these people have. I wish I could really know that I am saved."

Mr. Parham plead with his father to meet the conditions and he could have a real assurance of salvation. He did not want to go to the altar that night as his heart was so weak he was afraid he could not stand the excitement, so Mr. Parham asked several of us to go to him and have prayer where he was, at one side of the brush-arbor.

His heart seemed to be especially touched, as Robert earnestly plead with God for his dear old grandfather's salvation. The burden was lifted, his soul satisfied with the assurance of real salvation and his life was changed from that time on. The Lord took away from him the desire for tobacco, which he had been unable to give up himself, and it was a wonderful testimony after he had used it for so long.

The remainder of his life he did all he could for the establishing of the full gospel which had become so dear to him. He donated the use of a large store building at Cheney which was seated and used as a mission.

*   *   *   *   *

Mrs. H. Ostrander wrote: "Bro. C. F. Parham came and dedicated our mission to the Lord Sept. 1, 1922. I shall never forget how the waves of glory swept the multitude as this man of God expounded the blessed Word of God and glory flooded our souls.

"The next morning as a number of God's children assembled for early morning worship, the blessed Holy Spirit fell in our midst. Four received the baptism of the Holy Spirit, some were saved and sanctified."

Mr. Parham held other meetings in this building and it was used as a mission until after his father's death, when a new mission was built.

* * * * *

Our second son, Philip, was married to Virginia Lee Stephens, Oct. 22, 1922, at the home of the bride's parents, Mr. and Mrs. J. C. Stephens of Baxter Springs, Kansas.

Mr. Parham performed the marriage ceremony and earnestly prayed that these two young lives might be so united that they would be a help to each other through life's journey. A wedding dinner was served and the young people had the best wishes of a host of friends.

Though Virgie did not know much about our faith at the time of their marriage, she has not only accepted the full gospel but is also preaching it, and telling others the story of this wonderful salvation.

I must now tell you of another wedding of interest, though quite different to the one just mentioned.

On March 4, 1923, Mr. Parham's father, Wm. Parham was united in marriage to Mrs. M. E. Walkenshaw of Joplin, Mo., at our home.

Our young people elaborately decorated the rooms in pink and white, and the refreshments of ice-cream and cake, which were to be served after the ceremony, were in the same colors. I remonstrated with them saying that I didn't think their grandfather would especially care for these things. But they insisted saying, "This is grandfather's third and last wedding and we want to show them a good time; and really they seemed to rather enjoy it.

Besides our family, Mrs. Walkenshaw's children and grandchildren were present which made quite a large company and Mr. Parham performed the marriage ceremony.

It was a touching scene as the son prayed so earnestly for his father: many tears were shed as Mr. Parham very reverently mentioned the two former wives and how much they had been to both the father and his sons. He then prayed for the devoted Christian woman, who we all loved, now standing by his father's side, ready to be a help and comfort to him in his declining years. While I reverently listened to Mr. Parham's prayer, I glanced at the company assembled, and thought how differently youth and old age regard life, and how often the sublime and the ridiculous meet together as I viewed the scene before me.

Our grandson was trying to patiently wait to shower the rice which he held in his hand, and one of our boys had promised himself that he would kiss the bride before his grandfather and was on the elert to do so.

Though the family showed their interest in different ways, all gave the new wife a hearty welcome in the Parham home, and their married life was a happy one, though of short duration.

Wilfred had been working in Aachs Dry Goods Store at Baxter Springs, and this spring went to St. Louis and took a course in window-trimming and card-writing to make his business career more successful, but the Lord had other work for him to do.

In May he went to a convention his father held at Perry-ton, Texas and this meeting was to him what the High Top Camp meeting had been to Robert. He consecrated his life to God, was sanctified and received the baptism of the Holy Spirit. Since that time, he has spent his life in evangelistic work, singing and preaching the gospel.

On July 4th, Father Parham had a paralytic stroke but was wonderfully healed and in August he camped in the beautiful grove at Wyandotte, Oklahoma, where Mr. Parham held a big camp meeting. This was only about twenty miles from Baxter Springs, Kansas so all our family could attend this meeting. Philip and his wife camped on the grounds, and Virgie was converted and accepted the full gospel.

People came from far and near and a large company camped on the ground. It was a very successful meeting and at the close, many were baptized in the clear stream of water that flowed by the camp-grounds.

It was a great joy to Mr. Parham to baptize his father and as he brought him up from the watery grave, he felt like saying as did Simeon of old, "Now let Thy servant depart in peace," as he had been granted the desire of his heart.

Soon after this meeting closed we started on our western trip.

A DARK CLOUD AND ITS SILVER LINING.

"In the Minister's morning sermon, he told of the primal fall,
And how, henceforth, the wrath of God rested on each and
   all;
And how, of His will and pleasure, all souls, save a chosen
   few,
Were doomed to eternal torture, and held in the way thereto.
Yet never, by Faith's unreason, a saintlier soul was tried,
And never the harsh old lesson a tenderer heart belied.
And after the painful service, on that pleasant, bright first
   day,
He walked with his little daughter thro' the apple bloom of
   May.
Sweet in the fresh green meadow sparrow and blackbird sung;
Above him its tinted petals the blossoming orchard hung.
Around, on wonderful glory, the minister looked and smiled;
"How good is the Lord, who gives us these gifts from His
   hand, my child."
"Behold in the bloom of apples, and the violets in the sward,
A hint of the old lost beauty of the garden of the·Lord."
Then upspake the little maiden, treading on snow and pink,
"O father! these pretty blossoms are very wicked I think.

Had there been no Garden of Eden, there never had been a
　　fall;
And if never a tree had blossomed, God would have loved
　　us all."
"Hush, child!" the father answered. "By His decree man fell;
His ways are in clouds and darkness, He doeth all things well.
"And whether by His ordaining to us cometh good or ill,
Joy or pain, or light or shadow, we must fear and love Him
　　still."
"Oh, I fear Him!" said the daughter, "and I try to love Him,
　　too;
But I wish He were kind and gentle—kind and loving as you."
The minister groaned in spirit, as the tremulous lips of pain,
And wide, wet eyes, uplifted, questioned his own in vain.
Bowing his head, he pondered the words of his little one,
Had he erred in his life -long teachings?　And wrong to His
　　Master done?
To what grim and dreadful idol had he lent the holiest name?
Did his own heart, loving tho' human, the God of his worship
　　shame?
And lo! from the bloom and greenness, from the tender skies
　　above,
And the face of his little daughter, he read a lesson of love.
No more as the cloudy terror of Sinai's mount of law,
But as Christ in the Syrian lilies the vision of God he saw.
And as when, in the clefts of Horeb, of old was his presence
　　known,
And dread, ineffable glory was infinite goodness alone.
Thereafter his hearers noted in his prayers a tenderer strain,
And never the message of hatred burned on his lips' again.
And the scoffing tongue was prayerful, and the blinded eyes
　　found sight,
And hearts, as flint aforetime, grew soft in his warmth and
　　light."—Selected from Mr. Parham's Scrap Book.

Chapter XXVIII

OUR TRIP TO CALIFORNIA

R. PARHAM, Fred Campbell, Wilfred, Robert and I left home September 1, 1923, in two cars for California.

The first night we stopped at a Tourist Camp at Sand Springs, Okla. The next morning went on to Oklahoma City, Okla., where we stayed with our friends, the Johnsons, and Mr. Parham preached on the street every night for a week, and prayed for the sick. He had a hungry crowd of eager listeners. One night, as he asked how many desired our prayers, fifty hands were raised.

Mrs. Martin joined us here, which made six in our company. Our next meeting was at Enid, Okla. Here we had a precious week of service, and the Lord wonderfully blessed.

We had left home with insufficient means to meet our expenses for very far on our journey, but as we held meetings from place to place and trusted the Lord, He wonderfully supplied our needs.

We camped out in the school-house yard at Vining, Okla., and in spite of terrible rains, the people came and souls were saved in the two nights of service.

As we left there, we drove through mud and water that looked impassable, but Mr. Parham said, "One car has been through before us and I am sure we can go through too." I thought of how often as we come to the hard places in our lives, they seem more than we can bear, but we remember "Jesus passed this way before" and we press forward, in "the footprints of Jesus," and are victorious.

We stopped for two or three nights meeting at many places in Oklahoma and Texas and everywhere Mr. Parham preached to large crowds, some coming for one hundred miles for just one night's service.

He held a two weeks meeting at Roswell, New Mexico. They irrigated here, but I guess the rain must have followed us for it rained most of the time we were there. The meeting was well attended, however, and a good interest shown, and there were five carloads drove from Lovington, New Mexico, and Polar, Texas to attend the meeting. We had some very interestng meetings at the jail, just across the street from our hall, where the revival was being held. How our prayers went up to God for the men there—the youngest about seventeen years old— as they earnestly asked us to pray for them. One young man was converted, and we gave him a Bible. He came in to the next service, bringing the Bible with him. He looked so changed as a new hope shown from his face and we believed he really found the Lord.

Nov. 6. We left Roswell, New Mexico, and before long we were in some beautiful mountains, tall pine trees, and snow several inches deep in places. We stopped and ate some snow. That night we camped in the Tourist Camp at El Paso, Texas, and the next day drove over to Juarez, Mexico. Here we saw the Mexicans in their adoby houses, and their stores and markets were very interesting. Mr. Parham had five dollars in Mexican money which had been given to him which he had hoped to spend but they told him it was out of date and of no value. We returned to El Paso, Texas, and that afternoon continued our journey camping that night at Deming, New Mexico.

Nov. 8. We started on our way again in a rain that made it very hard to drive. We went by a big sign "The Great Continental Divide." All east of this, we were told, the waters go to the Atlantic Ocean. We were driving on the west where the waters go to the Pacific Ocean.

This afternoon we had been traveling between two ranges of mountains and as the clouds hung low over the mountains it was a wonderful sight. Here we saw copper mines for the first time. The road was so fine coming down the mountains that we coasted for many miles. Here a rain caught us, but we soon drove out into the sunshine again, and looked back at a terrible storm in the mountains behind us. We soon bid farewell to New Mexico and welcomed Arizona, and appreciated the good road to Douglas. Then we came to Bisbee, a large copper mining town built between the mountains. Fred Campbell said it reminded him of a French town. There were great factories and business houses on the main streets, which were very narrow, but most of the residences were built up the mountains on each side. Mr. Parham remarked, "I would not like to be a delivery boy in this town."

We camped on the other side of this town and started on the next morning about five o'clock. We thought we had gone up mountains before but not like this: this was not a "gradual going up," but we were "going up right now." On we went, turned sharp curves and still up and up! We looked back and bid farewell to the quaint, foreign looking city of Bisbee, in the canyon beneath us.

We argued about over which mountain the sun would arise. How beautiful it looked, when at last it came up over the mountain on the west—according to my thinking. Here we were, "on the mountain tops of glory," above the clouds, which lay below us and looked like a great lake of water. In the distance, far away we could see other mountains which looked like the shore, and here and there the tops of mountains appeared, like little islands.

These mountain scenes were familiar to Mr. Parham, as he had been to California so many times, yet he enjoyed them with us, and nothing in the beauty of nature escaped his appreciation. I shall never forget our ride that morning as we drank in the fresh morning air. How we thanked God for the salvation purchased for us by the blood of Christ that makes us "more than conquerors through Him that loved us," which enables us to rise above the clouds of sin and sorrow.

It is said that "every cloud has a silver lining" and I believed it that morning as the clouds looked so beautiful with the sun shining down upon them. We can not see the silver lining of the clouds of our sorrows, until we overcome them, and view them in the glorious light of His love. The clouds of sin and sorrow are so dense and dark when we are going through them but when we take an "heir-ship" in Christ and soar above, and look down upon them, how different they look. We can then see the silver lining.

By the time we got to Phoenix, Ariz., it was raining, so we camped in the beautiful Tourist Camp, there to rest for a few days till the rain ceased.

A lady told us she had lived here five years and never seen such a rain, "But of course," she added laughingly "tourists are always finding the unusual weather, as we tell them."

But the rain at last was over, and we pulled open our tent one morning in time to see the sun-rise. As it shone through the palm trees, and the mist was rising from the pretty little lake of water just in front of our tent, it was a beautiful scene; not a cloud in the skies now.

Mrs. Martin and I read each others notes that we had taken on our trip. Though we had seen the same things it was rather amusing to see the difference in our discriptions. She had enlarged upon some things which I had either touched on very lightly or entirely left out, while I had gone into details about some things which she had not considered important enough to mention.

Our stories were so different that perhaps any one reading them might doubt whether either of them were correct. They were both true, though both incomplete.

We were both travelling the same way with the same hopes, plans and the same destiny in view but with our different natures different things along the way had appealed to us. Even the things that we both wrote about, we described a little differently.

Can we not get a thought out of this concerning spiritual things in the Christian life, on our "pilgrim's progress."

We who love God, have our names written in the Lamb's book of life, and are trusting in the atoning blood of Christ, and all have our faces set toward that heavenly city.

We are all "long on some truths, and short on something else," so let us not be surprised or quarrel with each other if we do not all tell the gospel story alike. It is so great, so grand and marvelous, "The half has never yet been told."

Let us not find fault with those who do not see as much of the great plan of salvation as we do, neither let us say what a fellow-traveler has seen is untrue because we have not seen it yet, but go prayerfully on, with our eyes fixed on Christ, the Captain of our salvation and ask Him to let the Holy Spirit anoint our eyes with eyesalve that we may see more of the length, and breadth, height and depth of God's great love, and know more of the great redemption that was purchased for us on Calvary.

We got our tents dried, packed up and were happy on our journey again. By night we reached Salome where a writer for funny papers owned the town, which consisted of a grocery store, filling station, lunch counter and post office all combined in one building; across the rail road track was a hotel.

He had a funny sheet, which he put in a mail-box out side every day, and above it was the sign, "Daily paper—put out daily—take one."He also gave away little maps with Salome, marked bigger than Los Angeles.

He had all kinds of jokes painted in black letters on his building. "Speed limit 147 miles per day," (you could scarely make this the way the roads were in that part of the country then) "Arizona roads are like Arizona people, good, bad and worse." "Free lot in the Salome cemetery for the first man found dead on the camp-grounds." "Smile, smile, smile, we have to live here, you don't," etc.

He had advertized this camp-ground as "the largest in the country, 1000 acres," and right indeed he was for as far as you could see in every directon, it was a great desert. The modern conveniences consisted of a brush-arbor dining room and an open fire place for cooking with wood furnished.

There were about fifty cars camped there that night, people from many different states and from Canada. We had met a number of the tourists at different places along the road, and they, like us, had hurried for the privilege of camping at "the largest camp-grounds in the country."

All took the joke good naturedly and after supper, our party got out their musical instruments and played some familiar pieces. The tourists gathered around and enjoyed the music, giving them the most applause when they played "Home, Sweet Home."

The next day we came to the Colorado River which we had to cross on a ferry. We crossed with six cars besides ours, and wondered what would happen if any thing broke, but we landed safely on the California side.

Truly we were thankful to God for His care over us, for we escaped several misfortunes which befell other travelers which came over the same road a little later.

After we got to Perris, California, we heard that the ferry was broken down, and a multitude of people had to camp at the other side in that desert country till repairs could be made.

After the usual inspection by the California authorities, we traveled on and before long the great desert lay before us. It did not look much different to the many deserts we had already crossed but more of it and the sand deeper, coming up to the hubs of the car in places. They told us it was ninety miles across this desert but added "desert miles are very long." We found this quite true.

There had been a rain in the desert, (unusual) a short time before and we found water standing in some places, which made the desert drive much better than it would have been otherwise. We reached "Desert Center" before dark which consisted of a filling station and grocery store.

Here again was an unlimited space for a camp-ground, and a great many cars camped here that night. We met again many of the tourists who had become our friends along the way. The next day we arrived at Riverside, California, where we got our mail and heard that Father Parham was very sick. Here we visited Ky Clark who had traveled with Mr. Parham in evangelistic work several years ago. He had married Edith Wilson of Webb City, who had been healed during Mr. Parham's revival meeting there. They have three sweet little girls. They gave us a hearty welcome, and how good it seemed to meet old friends again.

We then went out to Lewis Hunter's at Perris, where Mr. Parham always made his first stopping place in California and how we did appreciate their kindness and the good hot supper, after our long desert drive.

A trip to California is very different to this now. Cottage camps, new bridges, improved roads with pavement across the deserts, have taken away many of the thrills and dangers of the journey.

It is now a much easier trip to California than it was in 1923, but we enjoyed it very much, and the Lord blessed us all the way.

OUR TRUE FRIEND

"A man that hast friends must show himself friendly, and there is a Friend that sticketh closer than a brother." Prov. 18-24.

As the rose gives forth it's fragrance,
    As the sun sends rays of heat,
So is felt the power of friendship,
    When with kindred hearts we meet.

As we give so it is given,
    Kindly deeds will win a friend,
But there's One above all others,
    Who our cause will defend.

None so far from virtue fallen,
    But His love does still abide,
And tho' all our friends forsake us,
    He is ever at our side.

In His presence of that rapture,
    When the Sunlight of His grace,
Chases every gloomy shadow,
    And we almost see His face.

Then His Spirit so enthralls us,
    As we feel His love divine,
That we long for all God's creatures,
    That on them His light should shine.

Teach us, O Thou Holy Spirit,
    How to let Thy power prevail,
That we always give to others,
    Perfect love that ne'er can fail.
                Lilian T. Thistlethwaite.

Chapter XXIX

IN THE GOLDEN WEST

N O long rest was ever taken by Mr. Parham, without being in services and by Saturday he had a hall ready for meeting at Perris, Cal. The meeting lasted about two weeks and the Christians were encouraged and strengthened in the Lord.

Ky Clark and his family came over and helped in the meeting, and we also visited them at Riverside. They took us up to Mt. Rubidoux, which is just outside of Riverside, and we had a fine view of the beautiful city. At the top of the mountain there was a large cross and up here they held great Easter services each year. Thousands come from different places to hear the noted speakers and singers. Many camp there all night, to be there in time for the sun-rise service. Sunday, December 2, the meeting closed at Perris and Tuesday we bid farewell to our happy home at Hunter's and went to Compton, Cal., where Miss Hammond had invited Mr. Parham to come for a meeting. We visited old friends at Long Beach and Huntington Beach, invited them to the meeting. To some of us this was our first view of the Pacfic Ocean. In a hall way on the pier at Long Beach we saw the skeleton of a great whale on exhibition and we decided that Jonah could have been quite comfortable in a "great fish" like this.

Our hearts were now made sad by the news of Father Parham's death.

"On December 6, 1923, William M. Parham passed quietly away at his home at Cheney, Kansas, after six weeks of illness. He was 77 years, 11 months and 18 days old. The funeral service was conducted by H. Coberly at the home Dec. 8, and was attended by a host of relatives and friends.

"Many times, during his sickness, he talked of the love of the Master and how sweet His love was to him, and we saw fulfilled in his life, the words of the prophet, 'The path of the just is as a shining light that shineth more and more unto the perfect day.'

"He coveted only to trust in God, and in Him he fully trusted. He had the best of care and nursing; the watchful eye and ministering hand of the faithful wife who was as-sisted by others."

As we read this, how sad we felt that we could not have been at the funeral service, and have done something for him in his sickness. But it was a great comfort to Mr. Parham that his father had been in our home as much as he had, and that he had helped him to a real experience of salvation and knowledge of God which had sustained him in his last days.

On Monday (Dec. 10) Mr. Parham had not announced any night service, so he took us all to the "Midnight Mission" at Los Angeles. He always took a great interest in any work done for the poor and unemployed, and when ever he came to Los Angeles, he visited this mission, often going there after closing his own meeting, as the services there were held till midnight.

We got there about half past seven and found the hall nearly full of white men, negroes and Mexicans.

Some were of the class that Jesus spoke of when He said, "The poor ye have always with you," others you could see had known better days, had wandered from home, or in some way been unfortunate.

Mr. Parham always enjoyed preaching to these men and our party all helped in the service; Wilfred sang three solos during the evening.

T. Liddecoat, better known as "Uncle Tom" has charge of this great work. Between ten and eleven o'clock, he came in with a company of workers as he had held a meeting at some church that night.

He is a middle aged gentleman with a firm but very kind face, whose very presence seems to make every one feel a desire to live better lives and do more for God and humanity. When he came in and entered the platform, he had the attention of all. He gave such an earnest appeal to the men to come to the altar and give their hearts to God, that it almost made you feel like you wanted to be converted over again.

After prayer the service was closed by singing the Midnight Mission's favorite song, "Since Jesus came into my heart," and how they did sing! I don't believe this song can be sung anywhere as it is in the Midnight Mission.

It was now just twelve o'clock and they opened the dining room, where supper had been prepared for the men, and we enjoyed seeing this big crowd of hungry men sit down to a good hot supper.

Mr. Parham often ate with them, for he said, while enjoying the good eats, he had an opportunity to visit and get in touch with the men. After supper the men all went up stairs where a place was provided for them to sleep.

This certainly is a much needed work, and we feel sure if there were more missions like this, there would be less crime, and our jails and penitentaries would not be so crowded, as they are today.

Christmas night, we came again to the "Midnight Misson" and saw the men eat their Christmas dinner, and they had a good dinner with ice-cream and cake for dessert. Mr. Parham always enjoyed taking us to the "Midnight Mission," when ever he had the opportunity to do so, and we were always glad to go there. Things are rather different there now, and they have a new building and much better accommodations.

We had been holding cottage meetings at Compton, and

also at Long Beach which had been well attended, and we had met many old friends, who had moved here from the east, who greeted us as "home folks."

Miss Hammond had secured a small chapel, which she had moved on her lot, and it was now ready to be used, and Mr. Parham dedicated it to the service of the Lord, Sunday afternoon, December 30.

After he had served the sacrament he took some of the bread and placed it at each side of the front door, then he sprinkled some of the wine on the door posts, praying earnestly that those who entered this door might have the realities of the atonement wrought out in their lives, both for soul and body. We thought of the blood on the door posts in the olden days, and as we worshipped the Lord for the shed blood of the Lamb of God and what it means to us now, we felt His Presence in our midst. Mr. Parham said he had never held a dedication service like this before, but it was very impressive and sacred.

There were seven present who had been in the Bethel Bible School at Topeka, Kansas, where we first received the baptism of the Holy Spirit, which was very remarkable after so many years, and how glad we were to be together again. There was a good crowd, many coming from a distance. Lewis Hunter and family often drove from Perris to help in these meetings, and a large number of their relatives from other places.

A watch-night meeting was announced for the following night and though it was raining a good crowd came, some coming on the street cars from a distance. Mr. Parham told the audience as the weather was so bad we would close before midnight but as the meeting was so good, midnight came before we realized it. No one left till we welcomed in "1924" on our knees in earnest prayer and we then wished all a "Happy New Year."

The meeting grew in interest and several were saved, sanctified, and healed. We went to see a number of Mr. Parham's old friends among them Bishop J. H. Allen at Pasadena, Calif., who Mr. Parham had known for many years, and often visited when in California.

The meeting closed, January 20, with an all day meeting and a crowded house.

Mr. Parham rented the W. C. T. U. Temple at Los Angeles for two weeks, for his next meeting which began January 27.

It was in this building that Mr. Parham had held his meetings when he first came to Los Angeles, many years ago. The place was still held sacred in memory by many and they testified to how they had been saved, sanctified, healed or brought into the light of the full gospel in this building long ago, and God was still keeping them faithful.

Many came to the meetings who had been in Mr. Parham's meetings in different states, but we had no idea of seeing them here.

The interest grew, and the meetng met with such marked success that Mr. Parham decided to continue the meeting another week. The daily newspapers announced the subjects of his sermons from time to time, some of which were as follows:

"Where did Cain get his wife, or was there a pre-Adamite race?" "Mystery, Babylon, the great, the mother of Harlots and Abominations of the earth." Rev. 17 & 18 Chapters. "God's purpose in restoring divine healing to the church." "Signs of His Coming." "Hell—where—when— or are the wicked eternally tormented?" "The True Church." "Anglo—Israel—Where are the lost tribes and the scepter of David?" "The Jew in Prophecy and History, his present and future status." "What, then, shall I do with this Jesus who is called the Christ?" The afternoon services were generally given to Bible lessons, especially taken from the book of Revelation.

At the end of the third week, the interest was such that it seemed necessary for the meeting to continue and so the meeting went on for one more week, and as the paper stated truly "it had proven a source of great inspiration and blessing to hundreds at Los Angeles."

Beside the meetings at the hall, Mr. Parham held street meetings and great crowds attended. The meeting closed, February 24, and we spent several nights in meetings at different places.

March 2, we went to Long Beach where we ate dinner with Mr. & Mrs. James Davis and family, and then were to have a baptismal service. So in the afternoon we went down to the ocean, and as we stood on the shore, Mr. Parham preached on water baptism. The water looked very blue and the tide was coming in quite lively as Fred Campbell and our son, Wilfred, lead the candidates out into the water and baptized them and Mr. Parham offered prayer at the edge of the water.

A number of our faithful friends who had worked with us through the meeting at Los Angeles had come to be in this service, and had brought their lunch with them that they might stay for the night-meeting. How much we enjoyed the picnic lunch, served with hot coffee, which our friends had prepared for us, and the sweet Christian fellowship, yet we realized with sadness that this would no doubt be our last supper together. It seems that our joys and sorrows must ever be so closely linked together in this life.

The Davis large home was well filled that night. Every heart was touched as Mrs. Bigger, who was going to the Bible School at Los Angeles, was especially anointed to tell her experience which has been given in this book.

The Spirit of God rested on the service, and after Mr. Parham's fare-well sermon, we bid our friends good-bye. To some present that night, this was our last fare-well, this side of eternity.

After holding a few other meetings at different places, on March 11, we bid fare-well to our comfortable little home in Los Angeles, and went over the wonderful Ridge Route, that beautiful mountain drive to Bakersfield. We made our head-quarters with friends at Oildale, and spent one week in a meeting at Fellows. We then returned for one week's meet-ing at Oildale in the Congregational Church, but a larger building was secured for the last night's service. Some of our friends came from Riverside and Los Angeles to be with us for the last day of the meeting.

With grateful hearts we thanked God for His Presence with us in these services and the kindness shown us by our friends while there.

We left here March 24, for Modesto, where we visited old friends, and then went on to Sacramento, where we secured some light-house-keeping rooms across the street from the Capitol Building. The California people can justly be proud of their Capitol Building and park surrounding it; words would fail to describe its beauty.

The people of the Full Gospel Church here knew we were coming and wanted Mr. Parham to hold a meeting but did not understand that we would get here as soon as we did, so arrangments had not been made for the meeting. We went to their mission and Mr. Parham preached.

It was not a large mission, yet they had a wonderful zeal and faith. They were very anxious for the meeting and wanted to get a big tent to hold several thousand, and begin a real revival campaign for the city.

W. Yeoman, the leader of the mission said, "I have never seen Mr. Parham till now, but by reading his books, I have known him for ten years, and believe he is the one to hold a meeting here."

Though there was no special means on hand to begin the meeting, one by one the people arose, and said they would be willing to sacrifice the comforts and even the necessities of life to help to furnish the means for the meeting. As we witnessed their earnestness we felt surely God would supply the means, and by faith we saw "victory ahead."

It was a Catholic city, and there had not been a big Protestant revival here as the evangelists seemed to consider it too hard a place.

After overcoming many objections with the officers of the city, and Catholics, we got a permit to locate the tent in the center of the city on a vacant lot at 11th and J. Strs., which they rented to us for one hundred dollars.

A large tabernacle was then ordered from San Francisco which would seat three thousand, five hundred people. This was a very busy week for the men but how they did work, and by the next Sunday the big tent was seated and ready for service, and the meeting began with good interest. Bills were printed and distributed as far as a hundred miles around. Conviction began to fall on the service and souls began to pray through to salvation till the tent rang with real old-fashioned shouts of victory.

The interest increased, and the altars continued to be filled with souls seeking salvation, and many came asking prayer for their healing.

Wednesday night (April 23) it was decided to let the Democrats have the use of the tent for Mr. McAdoo to speak in, as they could secure no other place large enough.

The paper stated that there were five thousand present and perhaps there were, as the big tent was packed. The meeting was expected to close April 28, but the interest was so great that it was continued for another week.

The meeting had met with bitter opposition, and some had declared that the wonderful healings which had occured in the meeting were by the power of hypnotism.

* * * * *

I will quote some pieces from the daily papers regarding the meeting:

"Charles F. Parham, last night denied that his meetings were charged with hypnotism in the tent at Eleventh and J Streets.

" 'These meetings are for the good of the souls in Sacramento,' he said, 'there is no power but God. All the good thinking and hypnotism can not cure any organic disease or real sin. Repentance and the new birth only will save. Theory and good thinking will not get you redeemed, Christianity brings repentance and humility.' "

* * * * *

"Enormous crowds are attending the revival services in the big tent at 11th and J streets. These meetings are being conducted by Chas. F. Parham, of Kansas, assisted by his party of five. Mr. Parham is an evangelist of great merit, and also a Bible Student of over 25 years.

"The campaign is inter-denominational and all the Protestant ministers of the city have been called upon to assist in this large campaign.

"The meetings are held every day at 2:30 P. M. The afternoon meetings are given over mostly to the Bible lessons and instruction and prayer for the sick and afflicted, although Mr. Parham prays for the sick at every meeting held. The afternoon meetings are very instructive and helpful.

"In the evening are regular evangelistic services. Mr. Turner of Los Angeles is director of a la_ _e choir and orchestra and these assist the congregation in a song service at the opening of the meeting. Besides the 'big sing' by the congregation there are several special solos and duets. Mr. and Mrs. Turner often render duets of an unusual nature, and the audience always shows its appreciation.

"W. S. Yeomans, a talented musician, who has been with Dr. Chas. S. Price and Aimee Semple McPherson in their campaigns, is the campaign pianist here. Occasionally he delights the audience with his singing. Mr. Yeomans is unusually gifted, having a double voice, as he sings either baritone or high soprano. This always delights the audience."

*   *   *   *   *

Mr. Parham preached on "Demonology" and he was asked to preach it again. Many received the truth, and accepted deliverance from evil forces, by prayer, and faith in the power of God.

The large tent, which some feared would be too big for the crowds, was well filled before the meeting closed. The last day of the meeting was a wonderful day, and "everybody happy" in the victory that the Lord had given over every opposing force.

In the morning Mr. Parham preached at a "Full Gospel Mission" whose pastor had been coming to the meeting.

He preached at the tent in the afternoon on water baptism, to a large crowd. After the service, the crowd gathered on the banks of the American River where thirty-six were bapitzed. Some real old people were baptized, some whole families, and one crippled woman in a chair. There was a large crowd present and many said there had never been such a wonderful baptismal service in Sacramento. They had never seen anything like it and thought it was fine to see husbands, and wives enter the water, and be baptized together.

The place where they were baptized is reported to be the place where gold was first discovered in this part of California.

At night after Mr. Parham had preached his fare-well sermon to an immense crowd, he gave the sacrament. There were about five hundred came forward, knelt at the long altar, and chairs at the front, and partook of the bread and the wine; while many wept their way through to salvation.

It was a wonderful sight to see so many from the different churches and missions come together in unity where there had been so much division.

We left Sacramento (May 4) feeling, though the battle had been hard, it had made the victory all the sweeter. When we came to the Capitol City, we only knew one family, this morning we were leaving a host of kind friends.

We were now returning to southern California, and our next meeting was to be at Fullerton. We had a wonderful drive, but were very tired when we got to Fullerton and thankful for the cosy little furnished cottage the folks there had ready for us, with flowers decorating each room and we did justice to the good hot supper.

They had a tent up for the meeting and different preachers had come to preach to get the meeting started. There was a good interest in the meeting each night and the all day Sunday services were well attended; our friends coming from Los Angeles, Long Beach, Compton, Riverside, Perris, and many other places. At nights the tent was full and extra chairs were carried in. Several raised their hands for prayer for salvation, and a number came for prayer for healing.

One night during the meeting the pretty young lady pastor of the Four Square Church of Pomona came to the service, bringing a number of her members with her. Mr. Parham invited them to join the choir and when we were introduced to the pastor Miss Alice Wilson, little did we know that she would become our daughter-in-law.

It was a good meeting and from here Mr. Parham went to Home Gardens for a week's meeting before going to Texas on the train.

We had all expected to drive to Texas, but could not go the southern route in the cars as there was a quarantine placed on the southern states on account of "the foot and mouth disease," so we had to return home by the northern route.

Mr. Parham arrived safely in Texas, and on June 1, 1924, he dedicated the Beasley Mission, which is located on the East Bernard road, midway between Beasley and East Bernard. My son, Robert, his wife and I had the privilege of being in a service there last summer, and it certainly is a very nice little building.

When Mr. Parham held the dedication service, he hung his picture on the wall saying he hoped it would remind them to pray for him. They still had his picture there in loving remembrance of him.

*   *   *   *   *

After dedicating the Beasley Mission, Mr. Parham held a meeting at Hempstead, Texas, of which the newspaper gave this announcement.

Crowds Attend Camp Meeting.

Hempstead, Texas. "Much interest is being displayed by the people of this section in the big camp meeting held here by Rev. Chas. F. Parham.

"Large crowds are attending each service as the people are hearing the Gospel preached and the call of the lowly Nazerene is being sent out from this pulpit, and not politics as are heard from many pulpits today.

"Come out, friend, if you have not been, you will be welcome, and too, you will hear a real message."

*   *   *   *   *

A report from the Hempstead Mission.

"On June 5, 1924, Brother Parham came to hold his first revival meeting at Hempstead, Texas.

"Although his party could not come with him, he did not lack for help for old friends and converts of former years came from the north and south, east and west.

"Many that had been in this movement for years came from Katy, Beasley, Houston, Waco, Temple and other places that they might enjoy the meeting and assist Brother Parham once more in a great campaign for God and souls.

"Bro. J. E. Cabaniss and others brought a tent and erected it on the vacant lot by the house we used for meeting purposes, an old dance hall which had been consecrated to the Lord's service and truly it was hallowed ground.

"We dined and feasted on the Lord's good things for the whole twenty-one days. There were many saved, sanctified and some received the baptism of the Holy Spirit. Several real miracles of healing were wrought by the power of God in answer to prayer.

"A girl came that was possessed with a demon of epilepsy, and was delivered and is still free from that evil power. Oh, praise God forever!

"We loved and respected Brother Parham as the father in Israel of this movement and always welcomed him back in our midst when he felt lead to come."

*   *   *   *   *

We reached home from our northern route some time before Mr. Parham returned, from his meetings in Texas, but he came home in time to prepare for the camp meeting which he held in Joplin, Mo.

"HE KNOWETH OUR FRAME"

"Like as a father pitieth his children, so the Lord pitieth them that fear Him. For He knoweth our frame; He remembereth that we are dust." Psa. 103; 13, 14.

O wondrous thought, so full of consolation,
    When pressed with pain and overwhelming woe,
That He, the God and author of creation,
    Doth every fiber of our being know.

He planned and wrought our fearful mechanism,
    United it with spirit and with soul;
And tempered all together, that no schism
    Should mar the perfect union of the whole.

He knows our frame: each muscle, joint and bearing,
  Was fashioned from a heavenly design,
And for each member He so much was caring
  He wrote it in His book with Hand divine.

We stumble, grope and faint, with hearts despairing,
  And sadly fail His tender love to trust;
Yet, for us still, He faithfully is caring,
  He knows our frame, remembers we are dust.

Oh, lift us, Lord, up to the heights of blessing,
  Into a heavenly atmosphere so clear,
That pains and trials, howsoe'er distressing,
  Can never cause our hearts to faint with fear.

Quicken our broken bodies by Thy Spirit,
  And clear our tear blind eyes to plainly see
That Christ's atoning sacrifice hath merit,
  From sickness, as well as sin to free.

That we may honor Thee in our whole being
  As 'neath the shadow of Thy wings we trust;
Secure and sure in Thy compassion, seeing
  Thou knowest our frame, rememberest we are dust.

        —Emma Varney Robinson, La Habra, Cal.

Chapter XXX

CAMP-MEETINGS AND EVANGELIST WORK FROM
COAST TO COAST.

HE Joplin, Missouri, Camp Meeting was a great success and God blessed the crowds who attended. There were preachers on the grounds from California to Michigan; many states were represented. The beautiful grove was well filled with tents: a large crowd camped on the grounds, while others occupied furnished rooms. The Word of God was preached in power by several preachers, as Mr. Parham always planned so as to give each one a part in the service.

In September Mr. Parham with his son Wilfred and Fred Campbell started on another evangelistic tour of the west.

Their first revival meeting was held at Kellogg, Idaho, September 20, to Oct. 5.

Notes from newspaper clippings.

Many Attend Revival Services

"The revival meeting at the Apostolic Faith Mission in this city, conducted by Chas. F. Parham is attracting considerable interest and large crowds have greeted the evangelist at his opening sessions.

"Besides the company with him, he is being assisted in the campaign by Mrs. May Hinkley, pastor of the local church and other local workers."

*   *   *   *   *

"The revival at the Apostolic Mission increases in interest daily. Souls are being saved at every service and many people of all classes are coming, full of interest in the messages.

"Tonight there will be a question box. This will be one of

the most interesting meetings of the series as there will be such a variety of things discussed."

*   *   *   *   *

"The meeting now being held in the Apostolic Mission will conclude Sunday night after which Mr. Parham and party will begin a month's campaign in Monterey Hall at Spokane, Washington.

"The house has been full continually and altars full of earnest seekers; many have been saved during the meetings.

"Baptismal services will be held before the evangelist leaves the city. Any person wishing such rights, who really know they are converted will be immersed by application at the meetings, regardless of faith or church affiliations."

Evangelist to hold Service at Spokane, Wash.

The Reverend Charles F. Parham has engaged Monterey Hall for a month.

The Spokane Press. Oct. 9, "What do you mean by, 'Speaking in tongues'?

"That is the question the Press reporter asked the Reverend Chas. F. Parham, founder of the Apostolic Faith, who had announced that he believed in divine healing and speaking in tongues.

" 'Speaking in tongues means to speak, under the influence of the Holy Spirit a language of which the speaker has no knowledge. Many times our converts, while under the power of the Spirit, speak fluently in many languages.'

" 'Do you mean to tell me that a person without knowledge of German, say, can—while under the influence of the Holy Spirit— speak in German?' the amazed reporter asked.

" 'Certainly,' replied Parham, 'not only in German, but in any language. Is God not the Father of languages? Can He not make you speak in any language He wishes? Nothing is impossible with God.' "

*   *   *   *   *

Oct. 24. "Crowds of 800 to 1000 are nightly attending the Parham revival meetings in Monterey Hall. 'Numbers are seeking and finding the real old, know so salvation,' said Parham, Friday. 'Some are pressing through into sanctification, while still others are finding Hebrews 13, 8 to be true, indeed for in their own bodies is being demonstrated that Christ is the Healer still; the same yesterday, today and forever.' "

"Mr. Parham has spent his life in giving these glorious truths back to the world and is now teaching, preaching and demonstrating in Spokane a real second chapter of Acts baptism in the Holy Spirit in all its dignity and power. A full gospel to a full house, given from a full heart, salvation full and free for who-so-ever will; light and understanding; present possession as well as profession of the life more abundant; that's the message from this messenger of the Lord.

"The gospel message in song with orchestra accompaniment add zest and sweetness to the meetings. Solos, duets, quartets or full choir renditions are given at every service with charm and spirit.

"So the salvation of the Lord flows like a stream and who-so-ever will may come. Few men have lived to see the fruitation of their life's work as has Mr. Parham, all Apostolic missions, Pentecostal missions and Assemblies of God, have their beginning, (directly or indirectly) from Parham's Bible School at Topeka, Kansas. 1900—1901.

"Parham is described as a powerful speaker, a hard hitter, who is both humorous and pathetic. His meetings in Spokane will include an exposition of prophecy relating to the end of the age."

*   *   *   *   *

Nov. 3. "Mr. Parham will conclude his work here Wednesday night with the communion service to which all are invited to partake in Christian unity.

"Miss Alice L. Wilson will continue the meeting in Monterey Hall over next Sunday and Mr. Parham and his party will hold their next meeting at Portland, Ore."

* * * * *

Mr. Parham began his series of revival meetings at the "Church of Portland," November 9, and continued till December 7.

Although it is a good sized church the interest was so great that partitions were taken down to accommodate the crowds. But still this was not sufficient for the Sunday services, so they secured the large Odd Fellows Auditorium.

It was a wonderful meeting; billows of God's blessings rolled over the services, prayer was answered and God met the needs of His people.

The meeting closed Sunday Dec. 7 at the Odd Fellows Auditorium. In the afternoon Mr. Parham preached on the Lord's supper, and then served the communion of bread and wine, to which all the ministers and congregations of the city were invited.

At night hundreds testified to the marvelous benefits derived from this campaign and Mr. Parham preached his farewell sermon.

Mr. Parham then went to Sacramento (where he had held the big tent meeting in the spring) and held a meeting there from December 14 to December 30. He was not a stranger here now but was greeted by a host of friends.

January 4, Mr. Parham held an all-day meeting at the Bible Standard Church at Eugene, Ore., of which Fred L. Hornshuh is pastor. This Sunday service was to open a revival which they were to hold there. The all-day meeting was well advertized, well attended and a great blessing to the people.

They have a beautiful church there now called the "Light House Temple." Last summer (July 1929) when we were in the west, we visited their camp-meeting. Our hearts were refreshed by the cordial welcome and non-sectarian spirit manifest by the pastor, and my son, Robert, showed his father's pictures of Palestine in the big tent.

After Mr. Parham and party left here they went north into Canada, holding meetings at different places on the way. From Jan. 11 to Feb. 1, they held a meeting at Victoria, B. C.

Their next big meeting was at Lindsay, California, at the Full Gospel Tabernacle.

* * * * *

Mrs. O. G. Cannon's report of the meeting:

"The Lindsay revival campaign began Feb. 14, and was to continue till Feb. 28, but owing to the great interest it lasted longer than the date announced and is still going on in the hearts of the people. How the joy of it rings through my soul even now.

"Rev. Chas. F. Parham was truly a man with a message. Wilfred C. Parham, choir leader and soloist, was a great inspiration to the meeting and Fred A. Campbell, musician and soloist, was a blessing in God's hands.

"Beside the party, other preachers and workers came at different times and helped in the meeting. Miss Alice Wilson and her party—who were booked for a meeting at Tulare, Cal.,—were in attendance at the meeting, and their presence was very helpful.

"Mr. Ky Clark's high soprano swept the audience with tremendous cheers and his wife's voice was also appreciated. The Rex Qualls quartet received a mighty ovation; there were quartets, duets or solos at every service and all ministers, musicians and singers of the town were invited to join in this campaign for God and souls.

"The day services were wonderful to say the least and whether night or day, the meetings can not be described. As you stepped in the services we felt the divine Presence, which lifts and inspires one to a holy life.

"There was something inspiring about the bills. As we posted a number near our house, we would see scores of people stop and read them, then re-read them. They would then ask us about the meeting, come to the next meeting and continue to come. The people came like bees to the meeting, for the Spirit drew them. Some of the preachers did not like their members to come, but come they did almost emptying some of the churches.

"Hundreds came the first night and the crowd increased nightly until the building was packed and standing outside in spite of the unusually cold nights. A tent was put up by the side of the large tabernacle to accommodate the over-flow, but some nights hundreds were turned away for lack of room.

"Brother Parham preached nightly from one to two hours to a hushed audience. Wave after wave of divine power would sweep over the people, and as he became more and more endured with the mighty power of God, it seemed that heaven bent low to indorse what was being said.

"Sometimes as that vast audience would be swayed by the mighty power of God, you could feel the wave of power. Tears would flow, then a wave of power and holy joy and laughter.

"Allow me to say here for the benefit of any who might think that there was not opposition to the meeting, that when the saints of God meet together satan comes also, but we went on to victory through much prayer and fasting. God was able, and the walls of Jericho fell.

"Brother Parham did not white-wash sin, and we never heard anyone preach so clearly the whole Word of God. God worked mightily in this meeting and many were saved, sanctified, healed and baptized with the Holy Spirit.

"The baptismal services for this meeting were held at Portersville, Calif., and many cars lined the high-way going to that service. As they went down into the water and Brother

Parham said, 'I baptize thee in the name of the Father, and of the Son and of the Holy Ghost,' the glory of God rested on that vast audience, and shouts of praise ascended from those who came up out of the water and who were received with joy by loved ones on the bank.

"We then returned to Lindsay for the night service with the glory of God still resting on His anointed servant. Only eternity will reveal the results of this meeting. How many times we have heard Brother Parham say, 'I want to die on the battlefield.' He did, and his works will follow him."

*   *   *   *   *

Mr. O. G. Cannon wrote: "I had been healed in answer to prayer, but my faith was greatly strengthened by hearing the sermons on healing, and seeing the power of God manifest in the Lindsay meeting. Mr. Parham's sermons on healing were printed in the Lindsay Gazette, covering a whole page. The following evening, a man attended the meeting testified to being healed of a double rupture by reading this sermon.

"Later we returned to Idaho.

"In January 1926, the year after the meeting at Lindsay, California, a growth started on the upper part of my right tonsil. Five doctors diagnosed the case and pronounced it an incurable case of cancer. My father died with a cancer on his tonsil, and a great fear tormented me, that I had inherited the same disease, which might also prove fatal. The cancer had become so large that it interfered with my speech and swallowing food, crowding the palate out of its place. I watched its growth, and thought of it continually.

"I believed God was able to heal, and finally put my case in His Hands and requested prayer of several who believed in healing but still I was not healed.

"How I desired to have Brother Parham pray for me!

"Then I remembered how he had said distance did not make any difference with God, and he, like Paul, Acts 19-11-12, had blessed handkerchiefs and sent to the sick and scores had been healed. So I wrote Brother Parham, asking him to pray for me, and to send a blessed handkerchief.

"Sooner, than I thought it possible, I received the hand-kerchief and a letter saying that he was praying nightly that God would cast every demon of disease out of my body. I placed the handkerchief on my throat that night and in about 36 hours the cancer had so diminished in size, and left the palate that I had no more inconvenience. About seven days later, my wife asked me to let her look at the cancer. I said, 'You may look but you wont see anything for it is entirely gone.'

"I received a letter from Bro. Parham saying how he re-joiced when I wrote him of my healing. It is now about four years since I was so wonderfully delivered, and I have had no return of the disease. How I do praise God that I ever met Bro. Parham and for the blessing he has been to me."

*   *   *   *   *

From Lindsay, Mr. Parham went to Bakersfield for a revival meeting beginning March 27 in a big tent.

Miss Alice Wilson and her party were now holding a meet-ing at Taft, California, and I have asked her to tell you of a very important event which took place, April 2, 1925.

Alice writes; "While I was pastor of the Four Square Gospel Church in Pomona, Cal., in 1924, I received a letter from a friend in Sacramento, Calif., saying, 'If you want to hear a man with a message, go to Fullerton, Calif., (which was 23 miles from Pomona) and hear Rev. Charles F. Parham, of Baxter Springs, Kansas.'

"I announced to my congregation we would all go over on a certain night, the date was all set, so the night came when we loaded our cars and went over. At that time, Mr. Parham was holding a revival in a large tent. After they had learned we were all from the Pomona Church, we were invited to come to the platform.

"There was a rousing song service conducted by Brother Parham's son, one I was to become a little more acquainted with later on. Some very interesting testimonies were given and the splendid orchestra led by Bro. Fred Campbell surely did their part.

"I was anxious for the preacher to start preaching. At last he rose to his feet, and I must say I never heard a more eloquent sermon nor one more impressive than the one he delivered on, 'What are you going to do with Jesus, which is called the Christ?'

"The Saviour was pictured so vividly before that great audience that the altar was filled with hungry hearts seeking the Master. But during the course of the message I laughed till my sides ached; one moment he would have you crying and the next moment convulsed in laughter. His comical sayings were all so original and yet all had a deep meaning. Later I heard him say, he did that for a purpose, to get their mouths open so he could administer a 'Gospel Pill.'

"After the service was over, I was introduced to the song leader, whom they called Wilfred, and he seemed to take a special interest in the preacher of the Pomona Church. I extended an invitation to him to attend one of my meetings, which he did a few nights later and sufficient to say—we were married in Bakersfield, Calif., in the big tent where Brother Parham was holding one of his big campaigns. Mr. Parham married us, and Wilfred joined me in the campaign at Taft, Calif. The meeting at Bakersfield proved to be a great success, for out of that meeting, they were able to erect a beautiful house of worship, and revival services are being held in it continually.

"Wilfred (who was now my husband) and I travelled from coast to coast holding revival campaigns and God bless-

ed in a very precious way.   Many souls were saved, sealed
and filled with the Holy Spirit, and we made so many friends.
Many times we would cross Dad and his party in campaigns,
and their meetings were always a wonderful success.

"Now a little about Dad Parham.   If any one were to ask
me what kind of a minister Dad Parham was, I would say he
had a ministry all his own.   Truly he was one of God's
anointed, and his messages were all orginal and very unique
and very impressive; messages you would not forget in a
hurry.   He preached straight from the shoulder and those
who were converted under his ministry were converted to
stay converted and they, from the moment they were saved,
were his staunch friends.   Never have I met a minister that
had so many friends that followed him from place to place,
and the thing that puzzled me was the fact they were just
as interested as though they were in the meeting for the first
time; hundreds came from many miles around to hear him
that their souls might be fed and they never went away
disappointed."

* * * * *

Mr. Parham wrote home saying he missed Wilfred so much,
as he had become used to depending on his help in the meeting, but he was glad for their happiness and very proud of
his new daughter-in-law.   He always took a great pleasure
in their work for God.

Mr. Parham and Fred Campbell returned home from their
nine months tour on the coast, and on June 7 we celebrated
Mr. Parham's fifty-third birthday in the Library Park at
Baxter Springs.

In writing about his birthday, Mr. Parham said, "June 4,
I passed another milestone.   Fifty-three years have rolled by
in my very eventful life, thirty-five of which have been spent
in almost constant service for the Master in preaching the
gospel.   It seems impossible to think that the zenith of life

has come; the glorious triumph of His grace seems only to have begun."

Though most of Mr. Parham's time was spent away from home in evangelistic work, he always tried to be with his family at this time each year, and meet with other ministers, workers and friends, in an all-day service of praise and worship.

A multitude of friends came from far and near; and all the surrounding missions were well represented.We gathered together as one family in the Lord, and thanked God for the battles fought and the victories won in the past year, and covered our mistakes and failures with His precious blood.

After a good meeting in Wichita, Mr. Parham went east, and wrote of wonderful meetings in Michigan. One week each in Port Huron and Detroit, and then to Lansing.

Our Return From Michigan Campaigns

"The last week at Lansing was one of great victory and we left them in fine shape for future work, the healings were most wonderful there; about fifty were saved. God bless the dear people there, how we learned to love them all.

"Then we hastened on to Battle Creek where dear Brother and Sister Branch have a great work for God and the full Gospel. We had a most gracious meeting with them and prayed for many sick and were refreshed by their great faith in God and His dealings with them.

"The next night found us in the dear old chapel in Three Rivers where we had fought many battles for God. The people were so kind to us there. Some came from towns about. With great joy we met and parted with our old-time friends; it was a time of refreshing and all about felt like a great freshet from the Lord, was due in Three Rivers.

"The next night found us in Mishawaka where we always meet our friends from South Bend, Elkhart and other towns. The hall was packed and my, my, how all did enjoy the flood of blessing and truth that fell about us that night. We were made to sit together in heavenly places in Christ Jesus. Brother Kirsh and wife have been in charge for many years, bless their true hearts.

"After a blessed time and a splendid lunch for our trip, we parted with the Bryer family, so dear after many years of making them a convenience on our journeys east. We came on to Monroe City, Mo., the first day. The next day brought us to the Brush Arbor, 22 miles northeast of Sedalia, where Brother W. E. McCorkle and wife were holding meetings in the neighborhood where he was raised.

"They had been having great crowds, they said. We could hardly believe people would come out like they did that night; it looked like a county fair, they had announced for our coming and a multitude were there. This was Saturday night but on Sunday they came with great lunches and such a time. In three services we prayed for about one hundred. In the afternoon meeting an M. E. preacher had dismissed and nearly all his people from a town 14 miles away were there; they brought their daughter and 8 others for healing. Three had been baptized in the Holy Spirit here; influential people and a mighty wave of conviction was on.

"From here we came swiftly to the great Brush Camp near Adrian, Mo. Here Brother Durbin had begun a meeting and Brother Waterbury was led to go to aid him, and they were giving the people some wonderful preaching. Here again a great multitude greeted us; they had been having fine crowds all along and we had a fine meeting with them and prayed for a great number for healing. Our surprise was beyond measure to find Bro. Cabaniss and his wife and many dear ones from different places."

Mr. Parham returned home in time to plan for the National Camp Meeting, which was to be held at Kingman, Kansas, September 5 to September 28.

FLASHES FROM BIG INTERSTATE CAMP MEETING. KINGMAN, KANSAS.

"Great interest was shown among the people of Kingman, Kans., and surrounding communities in the Big Interstate Camp Meeting, this year. About a dozen states was repre-sented among the people on the camp grounds and about 200 were camped.

"The campers were allowed the free use of a very nice little park, including lights, water, lumber for seats, etc., the city officials ordered the street closed a block in front of the camp grounds in order to keep the cars from disturbing the services.

"Many of the best workers and evangelists from different parts of the country were present to help in the campaign and to enjoy the wonderful Bible lessons given by Brother Parham and Brother Wm. Bacon of Chicago, noted cornetist and Bible teacher.

"A company of fine musicians and singers were present to assist in the musical program, and a 10 piece orchestra was enjoyed by all. Meetings continued with great interest in spite of the heavy rains over that section. A crowd of 1500 or more attended the Sunday night service, Sept. 20th, many driving from a distance of 50 and 75 miles to be in the all day services.

"Many were saved, sanctified and healed during the meet-ings and a number went through to the baptism of the Holy Spirit each one speaking a clear perfect language. It seemed to be the earnest desire of all the people to draw closer to God and deepen their experience, and become better equipped for the coming year of harvest.

"Several of the outside ministers were in to help in the campaign. A bishop of the Mennonite Church came in and while listening to our workers pray at one of the altar ser-vices, understood one of our workers, who was praying in the Hindu language. He has been a foreign missionary for over twenty years, gave a wonderful testimony and stated that both he and his daughter (who is also a missionary) had received the baptism of the Holy Spirit.

"Scores of Brother Parham's boyhood friends who knew him as a sickly and at times crippled child, came to wonder and accept the Full Gospel seeing what a miracle God had wrought in him and it was with great satisfaction that a meeting held at the door step nearly of where he was raised was such a success and that many old time neighbors paid tribute to him with faith in his gospel and asked prayer for their healing.

"A fine baptismal service was held Sunday afternoon Sept. 27, twenty-four people being baptized. The meeting closed Sunday night with great crowds present, and about 400 partaking of the sacrament of bread and wine.

"When Brother Parham went to thank the marshal for the kindnesses shown and ask him to convey to the city officials of Kingman the gratitude of the campers and the meeting for their splendid help to make the meeting a success, the marshal in return said, 'And we want to thank you for coming to our city and for the world of good you have done our town and community around.' God bless Kingman, many pleasant memories linger there.

"The plans are for the next State Camp Meeting, if the Lord tarries, to be in Cherryvale, Kansas.

"The next big revival campaign will be held in Roswell, New Mexico, starting October 11th, 1925."

Written for the Apostolic Faith by Dora Preston (now Campbell) who was Mr. Parham's private secretary.

* * * * *

Mr. Parham wrote; "The Roswell campaign,—which was announced from Oct. 4th to Oct. 25th—closed Nov. 1st.

Many of the church people were deeply interested and there were some remarkable cases of salvation and healing.

"From here we felt constrained to visit the Plains about Lovington, N. M., where four years ago we had such a wonderful meeting.

"At that time we made a whirlwind campaign in all the school houses in Lea Co., then held an immense campaign in the county seat, Lovington. After which we made another visitation of the school houses holding meetings with immense crowds and had planned to close with an all day service in Plainview, New Mexico, where a multitude of people gathered with their sick. But another preacher claimed the building for the day by previous appointment so at the noon hour when a vast throng had spread their dinners upon the grass, I called aloud to them telling them that I would preach to them while they ate, as I would rather preach to them than eat chicken any day.

"Brother Campbell backed the auto right up into the middle of the crowd who could scarcely eat as they wanted to hear the message, so hungry were the people for the gospel there. Catching sandwiches from the table they came about the auto for spiritual food. After eating their dinners I preached on for a half an hour and prayed for the sick in great numbers. Many had been brought in automobiles for 60 to 70 miles to be prayed for.

"A number from the audience cried out, 'Why can't you pray for rain,' 'WHY CAN'T YOU PRAY FOR RAIN?' Standing in the auto I beheld a line, of fleecy clouds along the western horizon about the height of a man's hand. The thought of Elijah's rain and Elijah's God swept thru me like a thrill of fire and I caught myself saying to the people, 'Since you have been so kind to God's messengers and accept the message they brought, the Lord His promise will bring to mind and bless your land with plenteous rain. The meetings are

over, the rain due any moment, everybody hurry home.'
The people obeyed, and within three hours a five inch rain
swept the plains convincing infidels and skeptics of the reality
of God.

"Among the remarkable conversions of that meeting was
that of an old cow man, who for years had only lived with
one thought in mind and that was to kill an enemy of his
who had often attempted his life. When under powerful
conviction after attending the meeting, he cried out to God
saying, 'Oh God, if you will forgive me of my sins, I will
forgive my enemy.' But the Spirit of the Lord said to him,
'You forgive your enemy first,' and with ease such as he never
dreamed possible he cried out to the Lord, 'Oh Lord, I do
forgive him, help thou me.' And the glory and power of
God flooded his soul in an old-time conversion.

"Since then several of our best evangelists have held meetings there. As soon as it was announced that we would come
to the city of Lovington the auditorium at the court house was
filled with an anxious crowd by six thirty o'clock.

"Never in thirty years of travel have we received a heartier
welcome by everyone. Merchants and cattlemen vied one
with another to express their gratitude for even a few days
meetings. They fed us almost to suffocation. We shall never
forget the many kindnesses and the many fine people we
have learned to know and love in Lea County, N.M. The
welcome of sinners, those who don't yet know the love of
God, will be a memory long to be enjoyed. From there we
came rapidly to Snyder, Texas. But that for a few days we
might conduct services at Polar, Texas, where for years there
has been a strong and splendid body of full gospel believers.

Many have been the remarkable conversions and healings
among the Polar people. The enemies of the full gospel
sought by many means to destroy the light of the gospel

planted there but, being good yeast, the more they walked on it the wider it spread."

*   *   *   *   *

They left Snyder, Texas, Nov. 13, to see D. Givens, who was very low with consumption, and then went on to California to begin a meeting at Lake Elsinore, Nov. 22.

The meeting there was a revival almost from the start, and many remarkable healings took place in this meeting.

From Elsinore the party went to Compton, Cal., where a very fine meeting was held in a big tent on Culver St. They were assisted in this meeting by Miss Anna Hammond, Rev. Cooper and others.

The attendance increased as the meeting progressed. People within a radius of one hundred miles attended the meeting, many of them old friends of Mr. Parham who had received the blessings of the full gospel through his ministry. Another year had passed away and now the year of 1926 was to be welcomed in at Compton; a great time was enjoyed by all and many made a deeper consecration for future service.

Many different nationalities attended this meeting and gave their testimonies, and the tent was crowded Sunday nights to its utmost seating capacity.

Mr. Parham preached one whole week on the coming of the Lord.

*   *   *   *   *

Mr. Parham wrote: "I asked God to open up a place in Los Angeles where I could meet with my friends and hold a week's campaign of Bible study and teachings on the deeper things of God.

"My prayer was so wonderfully answered by the opening up of the beautiful little Immanuel Chapel on 41st Drive. The chapel is in charge of Sister Jessie Stark, who has a fine work started in this community. We were invited to stay the second week and had a blessed time in the Thursday tarry meetings and evening Bible studies.

"Many of my old friends attended the meetings whom I have known for twenty-five and thirty years and the testimonies of the different ones who have so long enjoyed the wonderful salvation and keeping power of the Lord were of great benefit to all who attended. Communion services were held Sunday afternoon and we closed the campaign that night.

"After closing the evening service we all drove to the Midnight Mission to take charge of the services there from 10 p. m. until 12:30 a. m. The building was packed with poor unfortunates who were so eager to hear that there is a reality in salvation and healing.

"Many hands were raised for prayer for both soul and body, and that they might speedily find positions in the great city of Los Angeles where seemingly every man's hand is against them.

"We start our next campaign in Burbank, Calif., at 6th and Olive streets. A petition was circulated among the residents of Olive Street who were all in favor of having our tent pitched there and seemed so anxious for the meeting to start.

"While other meetings have largely resulted in healing this meeting has been specially freighted with salvation. The wonderful results will never be known until the unfolding of the Book in the great day of God.

"We are closing our part of the great meeting in Burbank, but the meetings continue under the splendid leadership of Wilfred and Alice Parham. The people of Burbank expect soon to build a beautiful chapel."

* * * * *

W. J. Alder wrote: "Let us rejoice together for God hath visited His people. Just as the gifts of the Spirit is ministered by the Spirit of God, so the Spirit of God, in His way, has ministered salvation in our community.

"Brother Parham landed into the battle for souls, with pick, shovel, and dynamite, exposing sin, hypocricy, and religious cheat of every kind, but this "acid test" proved to be the very thing that brought many out of their darkness, into real repentance and a "born again" experience.

"How we thank God for this wonderful Gospel that brings deliverance to our souls. It was repeatedly stated by Brother Parham that, 'We need new wine skins for the new wine, for God was doing a new thing in the earth.' How this Kingdom message has stirred our hearts, and brought action that will last, we believe, until Jesus comes."

*   *   *   *   *

Choosing Mt. Rubidoux as the romantic scene of their wedding, Fred A. Campbell and Dora E. Preston were united in marriage on the crest of the rugged old mountain on the morning of March 10, 1926.

The beautiful out-door ceremony was performed by Mr. Parham, and was witnessed only by members of the party and Mr. and Mrs. Harms.

I will quote a few verses which were written in honor of the occasion:

"O Rubidoux, Thou Mount of Rock,
With Cross uplifted high,
'Twas on thy crest, with hearts aflame
They stood beneath God's sky.

Below, the fields and orchards green,
And flowers blooming fair,
Whose fragrance reached to heights above,
Had filled the morning air.

Though years may come in endless flow
And cares and trials press,
May God in all His goodness great,
With love and mercies bless."

BUT WE SEE JESUS.

While we look, not at the things which are seen.—2 Cor. 4:18. But we see Jesus.—Heb. 2:9.

I don't look back; God knows the fruitless efforts,
The wasted hours, the sinning, the regrets;
I leave them all with Him who blots the record,
And mercifully forgives, and then forgets.

I don't look forward; God sees all the future,
The road that, short or long, will lead me home,
And He will face with me its every trial,
And bear for me the burdens that may come.

I don't look around me; then would fears assail me,
So wild the tumult of earth's restless seas;
So dark the world, so filled with woe and evil,
So vain the hope of comfort or of ease.

I don't look in, for then am I most wretched;
My self has naught on which to stay my trust.
Nothing I see save failures and shortcomings,
And weak endeavors crumbling into dust.

But I look up—into the face of Jesus,
For there my heart can rest, my fears are stilled;
And there is joy, and love, and light for darkness,
And perfect peace, and every hope fulfilled.

By Annie Johnson Flint

Chapter XXXI

SUCCESSFUL REVIVAL MEETINGS AND A
MARVELOUS ANSWER TO PRAYER.

RED CAMPBELL and his wife are now traveling with Mr. Parham, and she has given us a brief mention of their meetings from coast to coast.

"The work in California closed with a week of fine meetings in the Christian Advent Church of Colton, Calif. This meeting was a great blessing to many hungry hearts. After visiting other places we had a big farewell meeting at Burbank.

"From California, our party then went to Phoenix, Ariz., and had a big ten days meeting; hundreds stood to hear Bro. Parham's message and the big tent was filled with those seeking salvation and healing.

"After leaving Phoenix, we all joined Bro. Wilfred Parham and wife in a fine meeting in the First Baptist Church in Deming, New Mexico. Here we found them holding sunrise prayer meetings with good attendance. Several were saved, others healed and one man gave his life to the ministry. Several ministers of Deming attended this meeting. The Methodist preacher's wife had been healed years ago, and the Baptist preacher, Wiley Wilkerson, had been saved in Bro. Parham's meeting at Temple, Texas.

"We then started on our journey to Kansas, stopping off for one or two nights in Roswell, New Mexico, Lovington, New Mex., Amarillo, Tex., Polar, Tex., Perryton, Tex., Gray, Okla., Buffalo, Okla., then on to Kingman, Kan., and Cheney, Kan., Bro. Parham's home town, where he dedicated their new mission.

"Wilfred and Alice Parham, also her mother, Mrs. Wilson, arrived at Baxter Springs, in time to be with us for Bro.

Parham's birthday meeting, which was held in the Baxter Springs Park. Many musicians and singers took part in the fine musical program. Bro. Parham preached and other preachers and workers spoke during the day's service. A great feast was spread on the grass in the beautiful park.

"At night, the theatre was filled to its utmost capacity to hear Wilfred C. Parham and his wife, Alice W. Parham, the lady evangelist. They received a hearty welcome from an appreciative audience.

"The Great National Convention was then held in Cherry-vale, Kans., with hundreds attending and many were wonder-fully saved and blessed in this meeting.

"At the close of the convention our party left for San Saba, Texas, for a few days meeting. A flaming revival swept the whole place and many were saved, healed and filled with the Holy Spirit; about 30 were baptized in water. After we left, Sister M. E. Daley continued the meeting to great victory.

"We then spent two nights in Temple, Texas; the City Park had been secured, and a goodly crowd was out the first night, and the second night a revival flame swept the audience. Many raised their hands, desiring prayer for salvation, and a long line came by for prayer for healing.

"Two nights at Gay Hill, Texas, with great crowds attend-ing and wonderful services. Then on to Bellville, Texas, where we secured the opera house, the owner deferring the moving pictures that we might use the building. Then over Sat. and Sunday at Hempstead, Tex., to this meeting came a large number of people from Houston and towns about for many miles. It was indeed a feast of fat things; several were saved and some wonderfully healed. Then on to Waller, Texas where a number came forward for salvation and healing. We then went to Katy, Texas, for a two days meeting; at this place the life of Bro. Parham was threatened many times, but the Lord always wonderfully protected.

A snap-shot taken of Mr. and Mrs.
Parham at the Cherryvale Camp
Meeting.

"From here we went to Houston for two nights. Here every available standing room in and about the building was packed. Old time converts of twenty years ago thronged the place; after ringing testimonies, Bro. Parham was wonderfully inspired to preach.

"Then to Alvin, Texas, then on to Angleton, Tex., where they had secured the High School Auditorium for us; the second night twenty-one hands were raised for prayer and many thronged the altar, and numbers came for healing. We then left for Galveston, Texas, for a one night meeting.

"The big convention was then held in Houston, Texas; many souls were saved and many healed. About fifty missions of the state were represented in this meeting. An orchestra of about fifteen pieces rendered special music through this meeting.

"The next campaign was held in Hempstead, Texas; many people were saved who had been living in the churches as Christians. We were assisted by the Presbyterian and Methodist ministers.

"After bidding farewell to the south land, we left for the State of Michigan where a number of campaigns were held. The first was in Charlotte with dear Mother Lang, where a number were blessed and healed including Mother Lang's grand-daughter, Miss Beatrice Lang, who was wonderfully healed of heart trouble. Then on to Port Huron and Detroit then a convention in Lansing where many were wonderfully blessed.

"We then opened a campaign in the beautiful little chapel at Grand Rapids in charge of Brother and Sister B. M. David. Brother David is from Persia and has been in the gospel work for over twenty years. Several marvelous healings took place. One man was healed who had been blind in one eye for 12 years. He was also delivered from the tobacco habit in the Charlotte, Mich. meeting. A lady was healed of a cancer.

"The State Watch Night Meeting was then held in Battle Creek with Brother and Sister Branch, who have charge of the work there. Preparatory meetings were held in their regular hall, but the watch-night meeting, which was to bring many from other towns, was billed for the G. A. R. Hall, which was packed to its utmost capacity.

"This was the 26th anniversary of the outpouring of the Holy Spirit in these later days, and we had a most wonderful time. The evening passed so quickly without any intermission that we could scarcely believe it, when someone announced that it was nearly midnight.

"As the old year went out and the new one came in, we partook of the bread and wine with all its marvelous meaning to full gospel believers. On bended knees, we radioed a prayer around by the throne to the many thousands who knew of this meeting and had promised to meet us at the throne. At Brother Parham's home in Baxter Springs, they were also having a watch-night meeting, and they telegraphed us New Year's greetings.

"Then on to Kalamazoo, Mich., with Bro. Bliss in Victory Tabernacle for one week's meeting. A two weeks meeting was then held in Alma, Mich., Jan. 16 to Jan. 30, with good interest in spite of the terrible cold weather and ice and snow underfoot. We also held services in the K. K. K. Hall in Saginaw, Mich., before leaving for the East. Brother Parham said, 'I have been convinced that no reform for man's betterment will be of any lasting use to the human race unless it shall begin with an old-fashioned conversion and a real change of heart.'

"Some old time friends of Brother Parham's wrote from New York, N. J., asking for a campaign, so we held the next meeting in a hall in West New York, N. J., with Brother and Sister Boyle. The crowds soon overflowed the building, and we were able to secure Trinity Reform Church, the largest

in West N. Y., (thru the courtesy of Dr. Hopper, their pastor) for Sunday services.

"At this time we attended a big union meeting in the 5th
Ave., Presbyterian church, where many ministers of different
churches had gathered to hear the girl evangelist, Uldine
Utley, who had taken New York City by storm with her
simple message of old time salvation.

"Feb. 11, we held a healing service in Glad Tidings Tabernacle, one of the largest gospel tabernacles in the U. S., in
charge of Brother and Sister Robert Brown.

"This work was started by workers sent here by Brother
Parham during his meetings in Zion City, Ill., in 1906-1907;
he came later and assisted them in the work.

"From small, side-street missions, this work has grown, under
the splendid care of Sister Marie Burgess Brown, and her
husband, Robert Brown, until they have one of the most
progressive works known to the Pentecostal world.

"Many were wonderfully saved in the New York meeting,
different nationalities were present including a Jewish lady
who brought an afflicted child for prayer and said she believed in Jesus Christ and that He could heal her child."

*   *   *   *   *

Mr. Parham and his evangelistic party left New York,
March 9th for their return trip home.

Mr. and Mrs. Fred Campbell went to Wichita, Kansas, and
Mr. Parham returned to his home at Baxter Springs, Kansas.

When Rolland Romack was killed in France we gave up
printing the Apostolic Faith paper as we could find no one to
take his place but in the spring of 1925 we began to publish
it again, getting it printed at the newspaper office in Baxter
Springs, Kansas.

Mr. Parham wrote the following for the Apostolic Faith:

"On returning home from our refreshing trip to New York,
we devoted almost day and night to the visitation of the hos-

pitals, where either at the request of individuals or of the whole wards, we went to pray with the afflicted, seeing gracious results.

"A great rally filled the largest theater in Baxter Springs, then one at the Market Square Auditorium in Joplin, Mo., followed by two big meetings in Webb City and Prosperity, Mo. We then held an all day meeting at Stella, Mo., where people came for many miles.

"Then we headed westward to cheer and bless the people as God might lead. One week was spent in my old home town, Cheney, Kansas.

"Well, here they came, many had been my childhood playmates and school chums; but the last Sunday was the crowning day with such crowds and wonderful blessings on the people.

"Dates for meetings had been made in western Oklahoma and Texas, so leaving Brother and Sister Campbell in Wichita for a rest, I pressed on to the west and found big crowds awaiting at Olive Meeting House (near Beaver, Okla.,) then two nights at Gray, Okla., and Perryton, Texas.

"No sooner was it noised about that I had entered that section than the people of Booker, Texas, where they had lately bought a double roomed school-house and dedicated it, wanted at least one night, so I decided to give them an all day rally. Sunday came and what crowds filled the spacious auditorium all day.

"Bro. McCorkle had started a meeting at Dessaurette, Texas, and begged for a boost, so I went for two nights. The principle of the High School lead the singing and asked me to speak to the school in chapel service and use all the time I wanted. He afterward said that for sixty-nine minutes hardly a child or High-school student 'batted an eye' as I told them of the errors and dangers of evolution.

"He begged me to stay long enough for one more talk the next morning; that day at least two hours were consumed in out-lining the present location of the Ten Lost Tribes of Israel and locating the Gentiles and the heathen. The whole school was very much interested.

"Having promised to dedicate the new and beautiful Light House Temple which had been built in Burbank, Calif., they claimed my time. Then, too, I had received two telegrams from Reuben Davis, asking me to hasten on to California, as his father had lost his mind and they wanted me to come and pray for him.

"So I headed on alone in my Ford for the western coast. I stopped for one night meeting at Spearman, Texas, then to Amarillo, Texas.

"Hereford, Texas came the next night, and it being Saturday, I spoke on the street to a multitude of people. At night the large auditorium of the Court House was jammed.

"At Roswell, a large crowd awaited me, and I had great joy in ministering to them here. From here I hastened on to California.

"I had announced a two weeks meeting at Corona, and on arriving in California, I found all ready for the meeting, and the Lord greatly blessed me in giving out the Word. Many old timers were refreshed and others added to the faith. Bishop Allen was with us for the week-end and gave much fine and valuable help.

"One night a young man from a town many miles away came to ask that we pray for his father, who was dying; we immediately did so, and he was healed and his son reclaimed.

"A man came all braced up with pillows from Glendale, Calif., (70 miles), who had been sick a long time, had eaten no solid foods for two weeks. He was healed and is doing fine.

"Then we went to Burbank, May 12, where we dedicated their fine new church and held a two weeks meeting. After the meetings here I visited several places as calls came begging for meetings for one or two nights in many places in southern California. My, what blessings fell on many hearts as we went from mission to mission. So many were healed, for as they heard of the mighty miracle of deliverance wrought in Bro. Davis of Long Beach, Calif., (who was delivered from the incurable ward of the Sanitarium,) they had faith for healing too.

"I came to California especially to pray for my old-time friend, Bro. James Davis, (who used to live in Verona, Mo.), when I heard of his helpless plight and confinement.

"He began to hear a voice that said he was God talking to him telling him in a very seducing way that if he would yield fully, he would not only give him great light, but would make him a mighty worker in the vineyard.

"Well, the thing was just what our brother wanted to be and do, so he was led to yield more and more to this spirit, believing it to be of God. This spirit told him many truths. and lead him along religious lines of thought and activity until it got his confidence entirely. Later he felt a hand laid on his head, and from that time on, there was sort of a weight there; but still being deceived that it was God, he felt blessed even by the weight.

"Then it gained full ascendancy and he became a raving, cursing maniac; threatening and so violent that the officers had to come for him. The family in sore distress, wired me to pray and again wired me telling me of his pitiful condition; he had to be shackled.

"I was in west Okla., so I wired them I would drive right out there, as I always answered the call of distress of any of my people. He was about to be committed to the state institution as an utter incurable, when they got my wire. They were able to get him a place in a private Sanitarium at quite an expense till I should get there.

"In three days he was delivered, and on the fourth day attended an all-day meeting at Corona, and was then released from the asylum, entirely delivered so that there is not a sign of the disorder. After doctors said he never would be any better, God did the work.

"I am closing my campaign here preparatory to going to Polar, Texas, (twenty-four miles north of Snyder, Texas), for a big brush arbor meeting. Bro. Davis and his family are accompanying me to be in this meeting and also at the National Camp Meeting at Baxter Springs, Kansas.

"From the first day the meeting at Polar rose in power and blessing. Two altar services the first day resulted in about twenty conversions and many sanctified and healed. With only one night's exception, each night witnessed a double altar, thirty feet long, filled with earnest seekers, and praying such as can only be seen and heard in Polar; several nights men's prayer meetings were held all night in the canyons.

"The church people of other denominations joined heartily in the meetings, and great unity prevailed, and all declared this to be the greatest meeting this country ever knew. The testimony of Bro. Davis, so lately delivered from insanity, convinced the most skeptical that the day of miracles had not ceased. Five received the baptism of the Holy Spirit one day, followed by others throughout the meeting.

"Many evangelists and workers were here from other points and people came from a radius of fifty miles. As we left, all rejoiced over the mighty work done, as the fame of Jesus went abroad.

"We stopped for one night meetings at many places in Texas and Okla., and spent two nights, (July 3rd and 4th,) at Buffalo, where we dedicated their new tabernacle.

"Stopping at other places, we arrived at home and dedicated the new mission at Baxter, July 10th.

"Now all is set for the National Camp Meeting here, July 16th to Aug. 16th."

*   *   *   *   *

I have asked Mr. Davis to tell his experience.

"As the people want to know about a crazy or insane person I will write a few things. I felt like a drunk man and many times I would put my hand on my head; my head was so hot, it would almost burn my hands.

"When I was getting better this demon that controlled me said, I had high blood pressure, that was the devil himself. So I pleaded the blood of Jesus and the devil moved his traps at once.

"At the hospital they gave me an examination and blood test and my blood was 100 per cent pure and they could see nothing wrong with my head. Other people can't see demons in you, but insane people can both see and hear them talk. Lots of people say there is no devil but there is a personal devil as well as there is a God. This devil that controlled me showed me many wonderful truths about the Bible; he did that to deceive me.

"This spirit passed himself off as the Holy Spirit and told me things that happened when I was a boy that I had forgot until he named them to me. This spirit told me all about my dead relatives and friends. He told me about my brother's wife that had been dead thirty or thirty-five years.

"We may say that the devil does not know anything but I heard the voice of a school girl that I went to school with. She had been dead twenty-five or thirty years, but she and I talked about things that happened forty years ago. That devil could talk like a dead person for he talked and laughed like this girl. Spiritualism is of the devil for when people think they are talking to their dead folks they are talking to a devil and we ought to be careful what we are doing.

"The devil knows about us too for when I was first put in the hospital they put me in a cell, hand-cuffed me and tied my feet to the bed. This demon said to me, 'Just be quiet, I will turn you loose.' As soon as they were gone, he told where to put my hand and to push on the key and I felt the key slip then he said, 'Now on the front,' then it came loose and I took it off, then untied my feet and got up. Then the demon says, 'Now you whip that fellow that tied you, hit him with your hand cuffs,' and I did. Some people will say the devil can't talk but he surely talked to me and told me what to do. There are lots of these sayings, 'The Lord told me,' so and so or showed me this or that. Lots of this is the devil talking to people.

"We know that the devil can surely talk whether he tells the truth or not. He doesn't care how much you know, if he can only deceive you. He will tell you some truth to get you to believe lots of lies.

"It was twenty-two days from the time I left home, until I was back home. The Lord shut the demons voices off and stopped them talking, as quick as you could shut off your radio.

"As much as I always loved Brother Parham before, you would think I would be glad to see him when he came to pray with me, but oh no, the devil didn't want me to have anything to do with God's true children.

"When I got so bad my folks had wired Bro. Parham. He was in a small town in Texas. He wired back at once he was coming out to pray for me. All alone he started west. God was surely with him. He said to his Ford, (which he called Bill,) 'Billy, you will have to stand up and let's get to California in a hurry, Bro. Davis is sick and needs us.'

"God had began to answer his prayers before he got there. My folks were keeping me in a private hospital, (knowing God was going to deliver me) though they had heavy expenses.   Four days after Bro. Parham first came to see me, my folks took me to Corona, California, for an all day's meeting, promising to get me back by 6 o'clock.   The following Wednesday I was released to go home to my folks.

"A few days later with our daughter Pearl driving our Dodge touring car, and our son, Reuben driving for Bro. Parham, the five of us started east stopping each night for a meeting.   The Lord wonderfully blessed me in each service.

"We stopped in Roswell, New Mexico for meetings over Sunday then on to Polar, Texas where Bro. Parham was announced for a two week's meeting.   There we could hear prayers echo all over the canyon.   Each one of my family got closer to God.   Pearl received her baptism, Reuben renewing his experience and wife and I were rejoicing for what God had done.

"Leaving there going through Amarillo, Texas, we were to stop with friends who Bro. Parham always stopped with and had made arrangements for us to stop with while having meeting in the mission in Amarillo.   My wife was embarrassed as this had been our dustiest day of travel and we were so dusty.   She complained and asked to go to an Auto Camp or some place to clean up but to our great surprise the friends happened to be wife's own cousin, Mrs. J. Means, who we had not heard from in years.   Though she had been an unbeliever of this faith she had been healed and was now one of God's true children.   Bro. Parham was so pleased to see the cousins meet, he told about this several places we went.

"From there we stopped at Buffalo, Oklahoma over the 4th of July.   Bro. Parham seemed to be feeling fine and preached some of the most wonderful sermons on our trip.   Many souls were saved and healed at each service.

"Then on to Cheney, Kansas stopping at Mother Walkenshaw Parham's, and holding services in their mission.   The last service on our trip was where we met Fred Campbell in

Wichita, Kansas who Bro. Parham loved so much after their years of service together.

"We arrived in Baxter where we enjoyed the great National Camp Meeting."

*   *   *   *   *

It had been several years since there had been a camp-meeting at Baxter Springs, and none that was any better attended, perhaps than this one, and many came from far and near and camped on the grounds.

From the start a holy hush, and the presence of the Holy Spirit was noted; perfect unity throughout the whole four weeks. Great altar services filled the hours between public services: many fasted often, and all night prayer was common. Mighty healings took place. One man came to the altar crippled on crutches, was mightily saved and healed; leaving his crutches at the altar he went everywhere leaping and praising God. During the last two weeks, some received the baptism of the Holy Spirit nearly every day, while every night many were saved.

Many ministers were here from all over the United States, among them Abbie Morrow Brown, of Los Angeles, Cal., whose visit to the convention was a blessed benediction, to all. She said she had never seen such a wonderful communion service, when hundreds partook of the bread and the wine, in the afternoon of the last Sunday's meeting; nor had she ever seen such a mighty service as the last night's meeting in all her fifty years in the ministry.

For some time, Mr. Parham had been feeling that he should take a trip to the Holy Land, and now was expecting to do so, after holding a few meetings he had planned.

Beginning Aug. 21st., and lasting two weeks, he conducted a meeting in the High School grove at Nelson, Mo. He held a meeting at Colorado Springs in September and one at Moorefield, Neb., in October.   By this time he had fully decided to sail for Palestine, Dec. 3rd, so stopped at Wichita, where Mack Wyatt was holding a meeting, and had a farewell meeting with his friends there, and also many of his old friends coming from Cheney.   He then returned home to make his final arrangements.

CONSECRATION

I beseech you therefore, brethren, by the mercies of God, that ye present your bodies a living sacrifice.   Rom.   12:1.

"While we choose, we are not willing;
   Consecration yieldeth all;
Consecration means obedience
   To the Spirit's every call.

Meaneth dying, meaneth living—
   Death to self, and life in God;
Meaneth work, or patient waiting,
   Or submission 'neath the rod.

Meaneth such a full surrender
   We shall never dare to ask
Why God gives our faith such testing,
   Or assigns so hard a task.

We are here to be perfected;
   Only God our needs can see;
Rarest gems bear hardest grinding;
   God's own workmanship are we."

This picture was taken of the Parhaf family just before Mr. Parham left for New York. Beside Mr. Parham on the front row are the three daughters-in-law, Mrs Parham and her sister Lilian and her sister Lilian Thistlewaite. The top row from left to right, the grandson, Charles; the son-in-law, Ernest E. Rardin, and the daughter, Esther Rardin. The four sons, Claude, Wilfred, Phillip and Robert.

Chapter XXXII

MR. PARHAM'S TRIP TO PALESTINE.

R. PARHAM'S farewell meeting at Baxter Springs, Kansas, November 6th, was well attended by a host of friends from far and near, some coming over 200 miles to spend the day with him in these services and bid him God's speed on his journey to the Holy Land.

The morning service was mostly spent in testimony, after which Mr. Parham told of his plans in the foreign fields. The afternoon was especially given for a healing service, and a host of sick ones were prayed for. At night Mr. Parham's sermon was on the subject of prophecy and the presence and power of God was felt throughout the day.

The solos and duets sung by Mr. and Mrs. Wilfred Parham, who have just returned home from the west, were enjoyed very much, also the music which was furnished by the "Gospel Orchestra" of Baxter Springs, Kansas. All felt rejoiced that God has made it possible for Mr. Parham to soon do what he has so long desired, to tread the land our Saviour trod. But there was sadness, also in saying good-bye to the one who had lead so many of them to the Christ and deeper experiences in God. Tears filled many eyes as they promised to pray for him during his absence.

Though Mr. Parham did not complain, I knew he was not very well, and it seemed hard for me to see him take this long trip alone, but there seemed to be no one who was free to go with him, who had the means to do so.

I told him that I hated to think of him being alone among strangers and foreigners, but he said he did not think it would be any harder than to face the lies and slander in this country which he had done for years for the sake of this gospel.

Mr. Parham left November 8th, for Tonganoxie, Kansas, where he held a farewell meeting Tuesday night. He left Kansas City Wednesday for New York with Wilfred and Alice Parham who drove through to help him with his meeting there.

They arrived in New York, Saturday 10:30 p. m., where they found a warm reception awaiting them.

*   *   *   *   *

Alice Parham wrote: "For several years Wilfred and I had travelled in evangelistic work. He had much training in the work, for he travelled with his father for several years before we were married. We often heard Dad say, he hoped before the Lord called him home, he would make it possible for him to take a trip to the Holy Land, as it has been the dream of his life. In October 19, 1927, we received word from Dad, that his many friends had made it possible for him to take this long looked for trip, and at last the dream of his life would be realized.

"He expected to leave before Christmas, so Wilfred and I said we would have to hasten back and see him before he left. At the close of our campaign, and after cancelling all other campaigns on the western coast, we started for Baxter Springs, Kansas. On arriving there we found Dad and all the rest of the family busy as bees getting ready and planning for this great trip. At last everything was in readiness and the day arrived when Dad was to leave for New York, every one was happy and yet on the other hand we were sad, as many realized their leader was going away, and there was no other to take his place, at least they all felt that way.

"Wilfred and I decided to take him to Kansas City, and put him on the train, so after all the tender goodbyes were spoken the old Studebaker started away with its load. We arrived in Kansas City and after holding a few nights meetings in the Friend's Church in Tonganoxie, where Mother

Parham's relatives lived, we thought we would like to take Dad all the way to New York, and see him off on the boat.

"After praying about it definitely, we started for New York, where Dad was booked for a campaign at Rev. and Mrs. Robert Boyle's church in West New York. We made the trip as hurriedly as we could, as the time for the campaign was drawing near, but we enjoyed the drive immensely, and Dad thought nothing was too good for us. After several days of good driving we arrived in West New York.

"The meeting was well advertised and as Dad had been there the year previous, all of his old friends were there to greet him and scores of new ones. We had one month of glorious meetings, we will never forget them. The power of God fell in copious showers, and so many were saved and filled with the Spirit, and many sick bodies were healed. Praise the Lord. The church was indeed benefited by those meetings.

"The farewell night had come and the church was filled, everyone carried packages and flowers and a lovely shower was given to Dad, useful presents he could use on his voyage. Then we went down to the big boat he was to sail on and we had time to go all through it. It surely was a wonderful ship furnished so luxuriously, and so comfortable.

"At 12 o'clock we heard the command 'every body off!' And the loud gong sounded and we all hurriied down the gang way and stood on the pier and waved and shouted, and sang 'God Be With You Till We Meet Again,' till the boat pulled out, bound for the land of Palestine. We will not forget in a hurry the 3rd. of December 1927 at midnight.

"We expected to return to Kansas and fill some of our dates for campaigns, but the Cumberland Mountains which we had to pass over were covered with snow and they were impassible, so we prayed for God to lead us definitely. He answered prayer in a way which we never expected, He laid it upon our hearts to open a work in the Bronx in New York. There was no other Full Gospel work any where near there, so we opened a church and started the work. The Lord blessed in a very precious way giving us many friends and making it possible for the work to grow. We labored there for six months, and while there we realized more and more the coming of the Lord was drawing nigh, for New York is certainly the dumping ground for every country.

"We received letters constantly from Dad telling us of the wonderful times he was having, which we will know by the letters received by his loved ones, parts of which are printed in this book."

NOTES FROM MR. PARHAM'S DIARY

Written on Board the Ship Carinthia.

I thought I would keep sort of a diary of what happened each day on boat and then mail all at the first stop in France so that you might know the routine of boat life.

Dec. 3rd. Last night a lot of folks came down to the boat with me and stayed to wave good bye and sing, "God be with you till we meet again." At last we were on the way! The great ship slipped out into the night. I stayed out on deck till we passed the "Goddess of Liberty," then came in and went to bed. I was surprised to find in my room a letter from Fred Campbell and his wife. They had addressed it in care of the ship.

Three fourths of the passengers are foreigners going over for a visit so I don't have much chance to talk as they are of all languages, but I am getting used to this so it won't seem so awful when I land.

I have not been sick yet. My, we get all we want to eat, and fine things too. We have every luxury of a first class hotel. We have just had a life belt drill, and showed our boats in case of need. The weather is cool.

Chas. F. Parham, with Wilfred and Alice Parham, on the deck of the ship
Carinthia, before he sailed for the Holy Land, Dec. 3, 1'27

Leaving at midnight by noon today we had safely passed all the shipping in New York harbor and made 170 miles due east by south toward Gibraltar.   If you will get a map of the Atlantic and draw a line direct from New York to Gibraltar you will have the line we are taking.

Sunday, Dec. 4th.   At eleven o'clock we were called by bugle to church.   The chaplin conducted an Episcopalian service, it was all very nice, and good singing.

The service was read, the prayer likewise but he prayed for all our friends and relations scattered all the wide world over and that sounded good, and that we might have a safe journey and all arrive without harm or danger to our desired haven.

Dec. 6 I went to bed at 8 p. m. and arose at 7 a. m., and got the morning news at breakfast.   I will enclose a Daily News.   I will send a radio-gram today as we are nearing mid-ocean.   The message home cost me $1.26.   That was not so bad, was it?

I have been invited to visit a very wealthy Jew in Tel-Aviv right near Joppa and also to visit my cabin-mate in Zaleh near Damascus, who will take me to see the greatest ruins in the world at Balbesk.   I have always wanted to see them as they are the largest stones ever placed in temples in the world. No one knows who built them.

He says that autos go everywhere in Palestine and Syria and travel is safe and luxurious. I feel like a new man already.

Dec. 7.   We had such a wind this morning that the waves were dashing on deck.   It was a wonderful sight and I got in a protected place with my chair.

I just read in the morning paper of a terrible storm in N.Y. and thought Wilfred would be worried about me.   I sure sleep and eat lots and enjoy the ocean every minute.

My, old Columbus was a great man to venture all this way on unknown seas!   They say it's three thousand miles from N. Y. to Gibraltar.   We had a few rough jolts in the night but this morning it's calmer. They promise us better things for the morrow. I guess that is what keeps us going, is the promise of better things.

My two Syrians, who had part of my room were good fellows but awfully noisy, so I gave my bed steward a small tip and he went to the purser and they moved me into a cabin by myself; a room all to myself, isn't that fine?

Dec. 8. Last night I had a hot bath in sea water; we can have one every day, they get the water from the ocean and heat it and my, they are fine. I wrote till after ten then went to bed and slept till 8:30 a. m. Today the sun is shining for the first time and the sea is beautifully calm. It is just too grand to stay off deck very long but I am in for some writing for the paper.

I met a fine minister the other day and he is going up the Nile to Central Africa to visit some missionaries. This morning I met a couple who used to come to my meetings in the W. C. T. U. Temple in Los Angeles and they are going to Jerusalem. Well the world is not so large after all. The day has been a dream but now it is clouded over and looks like a mist coming up. We are now south of the Azore Islands, too far to see them. We will go between them and the Madiearas on to Gibraltar. 10:30 p. m. Well, the clouds that threatened us this afternoon soon broke away and gave us one of the most ideal nights I have ever experienced! Beautiful floating clouds, drifted across the sky behind which the full moon played hide and seek. When it came out in all its glory, as only a tropical moon can shine, silver sheens spread far across the waters. Only artists could imitate the loveliness of the scenes! I am in love with the sea.

Dec. 9. As I went on deck 6:30 a. m. the boat was rolling from side to side. They said it was because there had been a storm and the seas were heavy but there was not much ruffling of the surface. Our morning paper said there was a terrible storm at Gibraltar and in Spain, hail ruining orange groves, and derailing a train but its two days till we pass there so it will be over by then.

We have been on sea one week tonight, and are over 2000 miles from N. Y. One thing we don't have any dust and have good hot sea water baths whenever we want them. I saw a sea gull and one porpoise today, that's the first life I have seen since leaving New York.

Dec. 11, Sunday. This morning the ocean has turned from blue-black to a lovely pea-green and varied coloring to melt into it, the most beautiful of all the days. Two vessels were passing and a school of porpoise were playing and lots of sea gulls flying about. Most all were watching the ships pass, but I kept my eyes on the horizon as I knew the coast of Algeria, Africa must be near. Direct thru the mist, I caught the outline of coast and mountains. I ran over to the other side and loudly announced, "Land!" Here they came, two hundred of them! Many said, "Oh no, that's only heavy clouds along the horizon." I laughed and said, "You wait." Finally they broke out into cheers and then in 20 minutes the coast of Spain appeared thru the mists on the other side and we have been having a sight for sore eyes, as we feasted on lands and mountains. 2 p. m. We have passed many ships as we entered the straits of Gibraltar, between showers, we saw wonderful sights. After 8 days on sea, land was a great sight to "land lubbers." On the one side Tangiers, Africa, the beautiful, appeared in sight; most all the buildings were white. On the other side was Alcazar, Spain; my, it was beautiful too and then the hills and mountains of Spain with many castles and all so lovely and green. At last the most awe inspiring and magnificent sight burst on our view; out of a great shower came the great Mt. of Gibraltar all so marvelously fortified. It staggers imagination to give you a word picture of it. All my life I have wanted to see it, for I have often said our faith was as solid as the rock of Gibraltar. Gibraltar is 3,269 miles from New York, the way we came.

I was so glad for my field glasses as it brought it all so near. We shall not be out of sight of land now for 7 days, skirting Spain, France, Italy, passing between Italy and Sicily then up the east coast to Greece, then loosing from there we will be out of sight of land till we come in sight of Egypt, ten days more, and it will all pass too soon. We had a song ser-vice led by a minister from Toronto but no one is allowed to preach on the boat, only the Church of England service read. There are many lights along the shore now and we feel safer inside the Mediterranean.

Dec. 12. They are running about 7 miles an hour, as we ran ahead of our schedule on the ocean and must not get in ahead of time. We are passing thru the straits between the Baleric Islands and the southeast coast of Spain. I saw the most wonderful sunset tonight I have ever seen and the sea in the Mediterranean is the most beautiful of all we have passed thru! We have not been out of sight of land all day; tomorrow we will see France.

Dec. 13. I knew before getting up that we had a wild sea today, it has proved the worst of the trip and yet was all so grand and boisterous that I enjoyed it immensely. I wanted to see the water when it went wild. We are crossing the Bay of Lyons, and a terrible wind is blowing off the coast of France. The waves are breaking over the lower deck and spraying the upper one. You can hardly stay on deck but I got in a sheltered place and watched it all. I will have to close my letter today and get it ready for mail as we lay in for Villa, France, don't dock but boats come out and take the passengers ashore. You will see by our daily news I am mailing you, that we have not been lost to the world, as each paper kept us in touch with it. I have just gone up to the wireless and paid for a cable to be sent in the early morning

from Villa, France so that you all will know where I am. I
wish I had asked you to wire me once on the trip as it would
have been quite a novelty to get it away out in mid Atlantic.
I could have sent a wireless every day if I had wanted to
spend the money.

Villa, France. Dec. 14. I mailed the letter, so will have
to start anew. We scarcely moved all night as we were so
near to this port and could not enter till daylight owing to
custom regulations. We anchored off shore and soon the
official boats came out to look over the passengers who were
to disembark. We are not losing many here, but get three
hours to feast our eyes on the beauty of the scenery.

2 p. m. We have passed the great place, Monte Carlo,
and other points and came to the Italian shores where even
the Italians joked about smelling the garlic. The Mts. tower-
ed one above the other till the Italian Alps, snow capped,
pierce the clouds. It is one of the grandest sights of my life.
We are now entering the gulf and will soon stop at Genoa,
Italy for three hours.

4 p. m. We are anchored off Genoa. My, what a beautiful city. As early as the 13th century this was a great ship
building town, and is still one of the greatest ship building
cities and specializes in war vessels. Away back on the
mountain one can see what is said to be the finest cemetery
of the world, most of the walls and many of the tombs and
tombstones are carved out of native rock found right on the
spot.

9 p. m. We stayed in Genoa till 7 p. m., then headed south
from the great city where Columbus was born toward Naples.
325 miles; will arrive there at 5 p. m. the 15th. It was truly a
wonderful sight as we passed out of the mooring in Genoa;
the city is built on say 7 or 8 great hills or Mts. and when
all lighted up as they know how to light them over here, it
looked like a city of a million lights as they say of Portland,

Ore.   There they can show you the house where Columbus was born.

Naples, called by the Italians Napoli.   Dec. 15.   We are heading toward Naples.   We came into port very slowly that gave us a magnificent view of this wonderful city, one of Italy's greatest.   I expect to go out into the city tonight for awhile.   A dozen of us made up a party and went for a stroll in the city.   There was one Englishman, one Canadian, two Americans, one Zealander, Greeks and Syrians, well that was some crowd, wasn't it?

Dec. 16.   Well, we have a most wonderful day.   We secured from Cook's Agency tickets for a trip to Pompeii, a city built before Christ's time and shaken by an earthquake in Nero's time about 69 A. D., then destroyed by the ashes and fire from Vesuvius in 87 A. D., entirely covered with ashes and fire so that 25 to 30 thousand perished in less than five minutes.   The ruins have all been dug out and the town as it was then, though in ruins, all brought to sight.   We have been in sight of old Vesuvius all day with her volume of smoke rising from the crater and forming real clouds for many miles away. The street cars are a pocket edition of our American cars, they call them "Trams."   The railway coaches are very small as are the freight cars.   The houses, most of them built right out to the sidewalk, are one to three stories high, some of them very old, have been here since the days of Christ.   Pompeii is about 40 miles around back of Vesuvius.   In connection with our ticket for the round trip, they give us a great Italian dinner at the entrance to the city of the dead.   Tonight we are sailing south to the straits separating Italy from Sicily.

Dec. 18.   We are entering the harbor of Greece and will soon have lunch and go ashore for 4 hours, it's a twenty minutes drive to Athens.   When we arrived on shore they were waiting for us with about 20 automobiles, Dodges, Buicks and our party had a big Cadillac.   We were soon away from the street facing the water and on a fine boulevard, very wide and all paved. Here we saw every faze of life in this beautiful city. On and on we went at terrific speed, no traffic rules here. We went up to Mars Hill and stood where Paul did when he told the Greeks of that unknown God they ignorantly worshipped. Well, it was wonderful to stand there, you could just about tell where a speaker would stand so that I know my feet have stood on the same rocks Paul stood on. When we came back to the boat they had moved our boat owing to rough seas to an inner bay and so we got miles of more rides thru the city.

We get into the Bay at Alexandria tonight but can't go off till we are passed quarantine tomorrow morning. I must get this ready as the mail will soon close for Alexandria.

Dec. 22. Here I am still in Egypt's sands, but "old Pharaoh" says I can go to the "Promised Land" today.

When we left Greece, I tried to hold my head up and write you all I saw, but the waters were rough and I was so sick and dizzy. I had got so warm climbing the Acropolis in Athens, and then rode twenty-five miles in an open car and about the same out to where our boat was anchored, that I took a terrible cold and just escaped having pneumonia.

When we got to the Bay of Alexandria our boat could not enter, so we stayed outside the harbor twenty-four hours. That caused many to miss their out-going boats and have to stay here a week or lose their money by taking another boat. They nearly mobbed the officials, I wish you could see this bunch quarrel!

My trunk went up to Cario in the rush. As this made it impossible for me to leave Jerusalem, I asked him where I could find a decent hotel, and he sent me here, right off Main Street. It is the fine French quarters and everything beautifully clean.

I had not eaten anything for three days, and was very weak and sick.   In the night the Lord touched my body, and I am so much better this morning.   When I booked at this hotel I found my Los Angeles friends, who had been so good to me on the ship, were here too; across the street my Jewish friends are located.

I wish you could see how they fight over satchels. If the agitators for labor would come over here, they would think the U. S. A. was a workman's paradise.   I saw nearly naked natives almost running with two hundred pound sacks of grain from the store room to the train.   They are very strong but get only a few pennies a day; they can live on about five cents a day, mostly eating rice.   But like the old Hebrews said, when they got in the wilderness, remember we not the leeks, and onions, melons and fish we had in Egypt; they have some of this too.

I saw men who almost ran from daylight till dark carrying dirt in a sort of bushel basket on their shoulders to fill up great holes.   In all places, like in days of old, if they don't hurry the boss either slaps them or gives them a good kick and they slip along the faster, each one looking as though he deserved to be kicked for not speeding up.

When we left Alexandria we entered garden lands, the flat Delta country of the Nile.   Vegetables of all kinds grow here.   You would not believe me if I told you I saw cauliflower as big as a little tub.   Well, it's true.   The farmers are, most of them, very poor.   Many of them have a water buffalo, a donkey, and may have one camel.   The water buffalo is a funny blue looking animal with very little hair, much like an elephant.   They milk them too.   With them they plow up their acres, many or few and plant to wheat, alfalfa or rye and they have plenty of water to irrigate.   They have a well and they hitch up a camel or buffalo and all day he walks about in a circle to turn that wheel, and it is wonderful the amount of water they can pull in this primitive way. I saw something about fourteen feet long, round like a log and hollow, with a circular doings running up the inside of it and two men or women sit all day turning this up the side of the irrigation ditch to get the water over. The plow has but one pointed share like a cultivator and the men and women literally rake and rerake their fields with hand rakes and they make very little garden in order to get their grain in. The larger farmers have some machinery.

These farmers all live in mud houses, all grouped, which is the way they all do in these countries. They have all their winter fodders stacked about their houses. The manure is on top to keep it safe, and near night as I came through they were coming in processions from their fields with wives, children, donkeys, camels, buffaloes, all bringing green feed with them. They pile a load of alfalfa on a donkey, then climb on too. I saw camels carrying as much fodder as a wagon could in America.

The people, animals and chickens all live together here. I saw many places like this close to the railroad.

We changed cars as we were on the regular road to Cairo at Benka station and waited one hour for the Kantarah train, which took us to the Red Sea border. We arrived there about 9:00 at night, but was glad that "Cox and Son" had sent their agent word to have my trunk there. They were waiting to help me across the Canal to the Customs.

Something seems to bubble up inside of me, "Are you not glad you live in America?" I tell you, America for me!

I will arrive in Jerusalem, Decemebr 23, 8:30 A. M. about midnight with you.

THE WILL OF GOD

These lines, surely the loveliest ever written on the will of God, were found among the papers of an African Missionary after his death.

"Laid on Thine altar, O my Lord divine,
Accept my gift this day, for Jesus' sake:
I have no jewels to adorn Thy Shrine,
Nor any world famed sacrifice to make;
But here I bring within my trembling hands,
This will of mine, a thing that seemeth small,
Yet Thou alone, O Lord, canst understand
How, when I yield Thee this, I yield Thee all.

Hidden herein, Thy searching gaze can see
Struggles of passion, visions of delight,
All that I have, or am, or fain would be,
Deep loves, fond hopes, and longings infinite;
It hath been wet with tears, and dimmed with sighs,
Clenched in my grasp, till beauty hath it none,
Now from Thy foot-stool, where it vanguish'd lies,
The prayer ascendeth, "May Thy will be done."

Take it, O Father, ere my courage fail,
And merge it so into Thine own that e'en
If in some desperate hour my cries prevail,
And Thou gives back my gift, it may have been
So changed, so purified, so fair have grown,
So one with Thee, so filled with love divine,
I may not know or feel it as my own,
But gaining back my will, may find it Thine."

Chapter XXXIII

NOTES FROM HOMELETTERS WRITTEN
IN PALESTINE

Jerusalem, Palestine
December 23, 1928

URRAH, I got here at last and found my trunk awaiting me at Kantarah, the place where you pass from Egypt to Palestine. It was in the hands of one of Cox's and King's men, whose instructions from their Agency in Alexandria were to see me across the head of the Red Sea, and get my baggage and person on the train for the Holy City. He did it all for me so nicely. As I was so worn out with this cold, and not over sea sickness I never could have gotten through alone.

It was midnight when the train left there and all through the night we crossed the great desert. By morning we had entered the land of new development, of many fine orchards of oranges, figs, lemons, and olives. About 8:30 we arrived at the town of Lydda. Here, all Jerusalem bound got off and changed trains. My, there were many of them.

Thousands came here for the big time in Bethlehem. We came up through rugged old barren mountains for many miles, and saw little vegetation until we neared the city. At last we pulled into the station, and I was in the "City of the living God."

Well, I felt rather weak for some time, but I called a policeman and asked him to call a taxi, who drove me to the American Consulate for my mail. I got your Christmas Greetings you cabled, but no letter from anyone.

I had written to the Christian Missionary Alliance to see if they had any rooms, and have just received the secretary's reply, saying since they would have a three weeks convention in January they would be full up, but recommended me to a place. I went to see the Y. M. C. A. but they don't have roomers, so I told them about the place to which I had been recommended.

They said it is a fine place, and is called the "Almasie Pension," and is across from the immense Rothchild's Hospital. This is an old-fashioned place, an old time Inn, run by a Swiss lady and her husband. The place is clean, the linens spotless, and the whole place has been renovated and remodelled. There are mighty nice people stop here, mostly religious. It is cheap too considering it has such good eats. Most places like this are double that, and more as you get up in the hotel class. Well, so far I like it.

I'll tell you one thing I can do. I can go out on the second story porch here any minute and see the whole of Mt. Olivet, not a thing to hinder. I ran over there and I got a glimpse of the City, David's Tower, and some of the old wall, but I have not been near the inside of the old City. I'm going to rest and be ready for Bethlehem.

Dec. 24. I am going to write a bit and try again to get a cable message off to you for fear you didn't get the cable from Alexandria. Wilfred could have gotten daily reports of our vessel from the office in New York, and could have known where I was each day, if he had known it.

The thing you are confronted with here is, most of the places you want to see have been claimed by two or three different denominations, each claiming theirs is the one, but Jacob's well and a few other places are real and sure.

Dec. 28. I got my first envelope of mail yesterday. It sometimes takes about five weeks to get mail from home, but this came through in three weeks.

In spite of my feelings, I went to Bethlehem and got a donkey ride to Emmaus and it did me good.

I have been to the Consulate, which is about a mile away, and back by the Post Office every day. Then by Damascus Gate, and Joppa Gate, and today ventured to go farther and see the new Assembly of God Church, which has just been dedicated.

My window opens on a flower garden. I am on the first floor and my door opens into a sort of court. I am very comfort-able. The house is full of missionaries, either going home for a rest or to their fields of labor, and they have been very kind to me, and I am well cared for.

Half of the people dress in American clothes, but the rest are of every description, from very clean priests to most filthy rags.

Most all the donkeys and horses and some of the cars have blue beads on their necks and radiators to ward off evil spirits. They have bells on the horses and blow their horns on the cars almost continuously. There are literally hundreds of taxis to take you anywhere in Palestine, and very reasonable if you know how to deal with them. The new Ford will be on ex-hibition here January 5, and they are about as excited over the new car as New York was when I left there.

Most all the store-keepers speak a little English. I get along pretty well with the Arabic.

You are beset on every hand by beggars, solicitors and would-be guides who inquire about your business, where you are going and when, and a thousand other questions. They all talk at the top of their voices, and the one who can talk the loudest thinks he has got the best of the argument.

It is almost impossible to do anything religious here as most of the church work is captured by Catholics and they are unapproachable, the Arabs worse, and the Jews impos-sible. The only Protestant work is, first, the Episcopalians, next the Christian and Missionary Alliance, called the Ameri-can Church, then the Assembly of God, a small Mennonite work and little else. As the orthodox Jews gain, the work of the Protestants grows harder. The orthodox Jew, young and old, wear curls down to their necks in front of each ear.

It looks funny to see the people here walking the streets, prayer book in hand and reading their prayers. Others sitting on mats on the street. Here is a Mohammedan, and people who are too busy to pray drop him a few pennies to pray for them.

The Brimsons, my friends from Los Angeles, got a furnished room for light housekeeping yesterday, so I went round that way to see them this morning. You know in life I have had to adapt myself to many things, pleasant and otherwise, but here we have no daily paper and no news, which seems strange to me.

Tomorrow I think I'll take a lunch and make my way through the Jaffa Gate and across the old city to the Temple grounds. I can rest anywhere, and can take the whole day for it. It is only a little over a mile. I want to put my hand on the rock on which old Abraham laid Issac when he offered him up, and see the hill where God has chosen to set His name. I'll get a donkey and ride around the City the next day and to the top of Mt. Olivet, I guess.

Well, it all seems like a dream, yet I go up on the roof and look all over Mt. Olivet. I come down and walk down to Damascus Gate and go inside and watch the parade of humans, camels and donkeys. I come back and go over to the Consulate and back to the P. O., and stroll down to Jaffa Gate and watch it all, sit down and take a look around. Yes, there is David's Tower. I've seen it often in pictures, but there it is. Yet it's all like a dream. From the roof I can see the Mountains of Moab across the Jordan, yet it all seems I'll awake yet and find myself not here.

I don't know whether I told you about this or not. The farmer class live in small villages and farm the land around for miles, and many of these villages don't have water so the women take a five gallon jar on their heads and often a baby in their arms, and go three hours journey for water and three hours back. Everywhere the women seem to be the slaves of the men and do most of the work.

Just now three long lines of camels went by the door laden with heavy loads. I guess they are going to Jaffa. They all looked well fed and were well togged out, compared with some of the hard workers I see. But under whatever circumstances you find them they carry themselves with such superior dignity that they seem to be far above their position in life, real aristocrats.

I wanted to tell you that the vegetables here are unsurpassed, while from the banana plantations come the most tasty fruit. The orange groves from which come the sweetest oranges, equal anything I have ever seen in California. Many of them are thick skinned. They have but few seeds and my, my, they are certainly juicy. They were shipped in great loads to Europe, for Christmas, yet the trees are still loaded.

Jan. 7. We are making up a party to go to Nazareth and Galilee and Tiberious and other northern points Monday. We will see the ruined marble palace of Herod, and stand on the same floor before his throne where Salome danced for the head of John the Baptist. I shall walk along the lake, see the Mountains of Hermon with perpetual snow, and the Valley of Esdraelon where the last fight of the ages will take place.

I am eatng a Tangerine Orange while writing this letter. They are about as large again as the ones in the United States.

The Mohammedans here keep Friday, the Jews Saturday, and the Christians Sunday, so when a man is employed he must state what day he wants off. The Postmaster and the Manager of the Cable and Telegraph Board tell us amusing things about what a time they have getting along with their various employees over their religion.

Don't fuss about the narrow streets there. If you ever come here inside the old city you will have to stoop and crouch when a camel passes and get in a doorway for a laden donkey. In the new city they have good streets and most of the leading highways over the country are good for autos.

Well, this is Sunday. I went to the American Church this morning and this afternoon I am going to the Y. M. C. A., to hear the Professor from Chicago University speak on "Brains and Religion." I don't see how he can mix them, but will see.

Jan. 13. As I was feeling quite well today, I went down to the American Colony Store. This Store is just inside the Jaffa Gate in the old City. I spent an hour at the Wailing Place of the Jews. Well, it is a sight. They beat the Holy Rollers in their performances.

Jan. 15. I had a good dinner and went to hear the Russian Choir from the Cathedral sing their New Year's carols. There were four priests and six nuns. It was about the best singing I have ever heard. You ought to have been here. It was heavenly. We'll have to have that group in heaven to lead the singing.

I then went to hear the Y. M. C. A. Secretary speak at 3:30. One of the things he said was that many at home had asked him to describe this Judean wilderness and at last he told them if you were to have a mighty storm on the ocean and roll the billows high and sink the trough of the sea and then roll the waves higher and the trough lower, and suddenly petrify the whole thing you would have the Judean wilderness. Well, it was so true that we all applauded. In closing he said the man who finds the true spiritual life in Jesus Christ finds the law of Jehovah written on his soul and with the gladness that springs in his soul, feels that the river of heaven had broken its bounds and flooded his soul. It was fine indeed.

Chas. F. Parham, with Mr. and Mrs. G. J. Brimson, near Jacob's Well

Mr. Parham in the flower garden back of the hotel where he stayed while in Jerusalem. Taken Feb. 25, 1928

Chas. F. Parham bidding good-by to his guide and the Mosque of Omar.

Chas. F. Parham with his guide, at the fountain in the temple area at Jerusalem

Chas. F. Parham on the roof of the house of Simon, the tanner.

Chas. F. Parham on the steps leading to the roof of the house of Simon the tanner.

Chas. F. Parham on Main Street at Beersheba.

Chas. F. Parham, dressed as Elijah, at the top of the canyon at Brook Cherith, where Elijah was fed by ravens.

Chas. F. Parham dressed as a shepherd, in the gate of a thorn-bush sheepfold.

One day this week we will have our baptismal service down at the Jordan.   Brother Feuterer thinks he knows about where Christ was baptized so we are going there.   I'll baptize Mrs. Brimson and her husband is going to take the picture.   Won't that be fine to baptize some one in the Jordan?   This is something that I have always desired to do.   It is always warm down there as it is so far below sea level.   We shall spend the day along the Jordan, Dead Sea and Jericho and have a picnic dinner.

Jan. 20.   One day some people stopping here asked me to go with them to Ain Fara on donkeys.   While there is a good auto road we took part way through most unlikely trails, a donkey boy always running along to whip up the donkeys. It is about twelve miles and way down in a mighty canyon. This is the spot where David got his inspiration to write the 23rd Psalm.   I'll tell you about it.   They pump 200,000 gallons of water from this mighty spring into Jerusalem every 24 hours, yet never lower it.   I've seen the "little Davids" tending their flocks and "the sower going forth to sow," and all these things of Bible material, first hand.

I baptized Mrs. Brimson in the Jordan and I was glad they asked me to do it.   It was a great Catholic day and thousands of people were there.   Many people had cameras and one movie man took the whole baptizing.   We had a fine dinner on the banks of the Jordan in a place where we could see Mt. Nebo through the trees in the distance.   We saw the Dead Sea and lots of people bathing.   Also the wonderful tropical fruits of the Jericho Valley.   My, that's a great sight! Such a Paradise!   Also we saw the place where Elisha made the waters sweet and a mighty gushing spring which waters hundreds of acres.   There we saw the ruins of old Jericho and some of the walls that fell when they shouted, saw where they crossed the Jordan.

I am going to Nazareth and Capernaum, Mt. Carmel and the Valley of Armageddon. I am going by invitation on another trip to Bethlehem and the surrounding country. They all laugh here at the Hotel because I get so many free trips. They don't know what to make of it, but I just say, "I trust the Lord and live by faith. I am the Lord's pet. He looks after poor me."

Well, I could write for a week and not tell you what I would like to. God bless you.

Jan. 20. Tomorrow the guide who takes most of the parties from here has asked me to go with a party of people to see Bethlehem again and adjacent country. This is a compliment from the Guide Agency as I have sent them several people who wanted guides. When not on a long trip I wander about this great city all day long. I know so many people now and feel so much at home. I sure am having a great time. The weather here beats California. My, my, it is fine. We even get to hear the world's speakers as they pass through here. There are many missionaries who stop here going to and from their work. Next month one of my old College mates will stop on his way from India to see me here. It is such a little old world after all, and this is the center too.

Jan. 24. Yesterday I rode on a donkey to Mt. Franck and to the Cave of Adullam where David used to hide with four hundred men. The Franck Mountain is where the Crusaders made their last stand against the Turks 1100 years ago, and there Herod built another mountain on the top of a high one and on top of all built his palace and was buried there in great pomp. On the northern side of the mountain he built a beautiful city. Only a few ruins remain called Herodius. He called the mountain Herodium. He built an artifical lake in the garden of the city, which is now planted to wheat, but in that sea of green wheat there is still a lake.

I have just received the Joplin Globe. That account of the Christmas services at Bethlehem could not be better. It is all very correct. I was there you see and know all about each thing mentioned, and happen to know the young man from Yale University who sent it over to the Associated Press of America.

There is a terrible noise in the street. They are loading a camel and he is sure growling and taking on as though they are about to kill him.

Jan. 26. I guess I'll go to Gethsemane today and stay a couple of hours looking around. It is only a twenty minutes walk from here and I am feeling fine these days.

There will be five hundred tourists in today in one body. They are on a cruise and all came at once. They expect over forty thousand tourists here in the next two months, which will make board and room much higher. I meet lots of people, most of whom are old, and many are preachers, missionaries and professors.

Jan. 28. Now to tell you about what I am doing this morning. I got up early and the air was cold, the sun was fine. I had breakfast and soon was on my way down Prophets Road past the Damascus Gate, then the Stone quarries from which Solomon got the Temple stone. To my left appeared Calvary and soon I was walking along the northern side of the old walls of the city. These walls are 2 1-2 miles around the City and the City within the walls contains 210 acres of which 35 are in the old Temple area. I left the wall and passed down the Tyropean Valley into the Keddron. It is hardly running now, but a good paved road runs across it and after going away down I began the ascent to the Garden of Gethsemane. An old priest let me in, and showed me about. There are many very old trees here, cared for like babies.

After staying quite a while I came up the hill and entered St. Stephen's Temple grounds. No doubt many times Jesus

came this way too. There are many small Moslem buildings
in this area, but the main buildings are the Mosque of Omar
and the grand Mosque of El Aksa, which was once a Christian
Church built by the Crusaders. I passed out one of the west
gates and came through David's Street to Jaffa Gate. The
street is about 12 feet wide and full to suffocation of people
of all nations. Little holes in the walls on either side are
stores where you can buy anything in the world you might
want, eats, wonderful vegetables and all kinds of goods. Struggling through the mass I came at last to the American Colony
Stores near the Jaffa Gate and there had a rest. Then I went
on up the Manila road to the American Consulate where
your good letter awaited me. Tomorrow I am going to Mt.
Carmel, Haifi, Tiberias, Nazareth, Capernaum and Galilee. I
will be gone two days. Won't it be wonderful to see all the
places He saw, His towns, His hills, and His lakes?

I am praying God to let me have enough money to buy
200 slides. Then with a good lantern I can show and tell the
people over there all I have seen and do it geographically and
in an interesting way. One young man had 86 new ones.
They were just the ones I wanted. I bought them. Pray
that means may come in to help me get the rest, and I will
get the lantern in New York. Then I will give two nights at
Wilfred's and Alice's mission and the Boyles two nights.
There will be no charges.

I shall try to stay here until March 25th, then get to New
York about April 12. I hope to have a fine outfit and can
tell the people many grand things about this wonderful country.

I have made many friends here, but there is little chance
to work for God. This is the greatest place for petrified religion in the world. Millions upon millions have been spent
here in churches, homes, hospitals and all such.

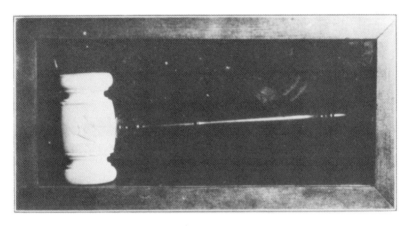

The gavel Mr. Parham brought back from Palestine and presented to the
Masonic Lodge at Baxter Springs, Kansas.

I have been many places on donkeys as they can go up or down canyons, mountains, and other places where one can hardly walk. However, it costs like everything to stay here, pray for me.

Feb. 1. I received your letter and one from Alice before going north. They seem to be nicely located in New York.

I have had the greatest trip of my life up north. My friends, Mr. and Mrs. Brimson, and Brother Doty went with me. When I got home the guide asked me to take a free trip to Jericho, the Dead Sea, and Jordan once more, so I did that yesterday. I got so much more out of this trip as I was not feeling well the other time. Mr. Beardmore went to the Jordan with me.

I am to preach at the Nazarene Church February 12th. The longer I stay the more real everything becomes and I am really feeling that I am here, and the country and places are all outlining in my mind. Now I can see each thing as it comes to me from the Bible, where it happened, the mountains, the lay of the land and towns. It makes the Bible all new.

I am going to bring a gavel home with me. The handle is made of olive wood but the mallet part comes from the stones in the innermost part of Solomon's quarrys where the Masons come to hold their lodge. I am going to present it to the Masonic lodge in Baxter Springs with my respects. I have been 1000 feet back under the old City in the most wonderful quarrys.

Feb. 2. I have just returned from a trip to the south of Palestine, to the land of Abraham, the fields of Mamre, and on to Beersheba. I am quite tired as it was a long trip. I saw many wonderful things including the Pools of Solomon from whence the city gets water, and the place where Philip baptized the Eunich, etc.

Then our party went through Hebron and on for many miles to Beersheba. This country is barren now, but must have been very fertile at one time. The mountains show they have been terraced and the valleys still are full of wheat fields. Wherever a few feet of ground can be found they sow it to wheat, which is still cut with a hand cycle.

We found the finest sturdiest children in Beersheba I have seen in all Palestine, and Professor Adams got down in the street and played marbles with some of them. They knew all the tricks he knew. We had our lunches in the new Municipal Park there, and sat right under General Allenby's Monument. While there we found some deep wide wells older than Abraham's time, and still in use. My, what wonders we see at all of these places!

In Hebron nearly all the women wear veils, a custom which has been discarded by most every other place. There we saw what is called Abraham's oak where he entertained the angels who had come to tell him he was to have a son. I have an acorn from that oak. I am going to send it to you and a little minature crown of thorns, like they put on the head of Jesus.

I am quite tired tonight as I have been two days to the north of Palestine and one day to the Jordan, and now away to the south and back. I'll have to figure it all out with the Bible now.

The Brimsons are leaving tomorrow for New York. They are going to stop and preach for Wilfred 'and Alice.

I was out to Hebron yesterday, but people staying here have asked me to go along again today to tell them the interesting things along the way, thus fixing them more firmly in my own mind.

Feb. 7. I have been all over the old and new city the last two days. Here the almonds are blooming, and there are many indications of spring, but very little rain.

I cannot see much difference in this city and some of our towns near Mexico. You can buy everything you can in other countries. We really have good stores, and can get all sorts of things here.

Today is the "Jewish Feast of Fruits" and great parades of Jewish children waving banners and tree switches, passed by. I went out to the place they had their exercises and there were thousands of Jews there.

I walked about David's tomb this morning and saw the "Upper Room" where He ate the Passover and where Pentecost fell. Then I saw where He was judged in the Hall of Caiaphas the high priest and where Peter denied Him, and saw the wall on which the rooster sat, with only the rooster missing.

I get some mighty good oranges to eat here. My, they are sweet! Tomorrow I shall see the great orange groves of Jaffa and the green wheat fields over the Valley of Sharon. You ought to see the lily of the valley and rose of sharon in bloom. The calla lilies are growing along the way amid the rocks, in vale and mountain side.

Feb. 8. I am going to Jaffa tomorrow and will see all the places there including the big Jewish town of Tel-Aviv, the most modern city in Palestine. It has a population of 10,000 people. I will drive through many thousands of acres of oranges, and many ship loads leave Jaffa for other countries. They shipped honey by the ton from there this year. While at Jaffa I am going to climb where Peter did when he saw the vision on the top of the house of Simon, the tanner.

Yesterday I walked all over the new City, and outside the gates. It sure is a fine town with many fine apartment houses. Today I wandered through the narrow streets within the walls, and there the stores are mere holes in the wall beside the streets, and yet they have everything you can think of for sale. They get gasoline and kerosene here in large cans using them for water cans later after putting handles on them, and today I saw a tin shop where they were converting them into many kinds of tin cups and tin ware for the kitchen. They don't lose anything here, it is all carefully saved and used in some way.

There are fine roads in every direction, and the country is only fifty by one hundred and fifty miles, so one can get over it well, but every time I go out I see something new and have to stop and think of old Bible times and pinch myself to see if I'm not living 2,000 or 3,000 years ago. The incoming Jews bring all modern machinery, yet the old settlers here keep on plodding along with old tools.

Feb. 15. I shall try to spend some time in Egypt before sailing, and want to spend a few days in Galilee too. I had another free ride to the Jordan and the Dead Sea and Jericho yesterday. The ladies, (one quite an old lady and two old maid daughters who have spent all their lives in Africa near the equator living by faith after having gone out independent forty-two years ago) were going. Mr. Shell, a fine Christian gentleman, told them he would send around a car for them, and if they could get me to go along and show them the sights, I would be better than a guide. So that is the third trip I have had free down that way, and it gets better all the time. While in Jericho I pried a large brick out of the old walls of the city that fell to Joshua nearly 4000 years ago and brought it home with me. I found it imbedded in the mortor between a little rock that had lain there all this time.

Feb. 17. As I am going to Galilee for the week-end and for a part of next week I will write today. I have just been out to 4 o'clock tea with a nice Turkish family. He is a fine Christian and an elder in the church here. They had tea and three kinds of cake, one made of nuts, and very rich.

He gave me a fine picture of Jerusalem taken from an airship by the Germans just five weeks before the English occupation of the City. I treasure it very highly.

Feb. 24. I had a great time at Galilee going all over the holy places. The old ruins of the synagogue of Capernaum where he preached is still there and being rebuilt, but the steps leading up and the door sills are all in place so I know I have stood on the same rocks He stood on.

I met my Jewish friends who came over on the same boat with me and we had a good time . They were so glad to see me again. I'm going down to Tel-Aviv to see them soon on a big Jewish feast day.

A party of six of us were going over to Jordan for a few days, were to go today, but last night while eating supper there came a real earthquake. I had wanted to feel one and this was a good one; the table jumped two inches and the house swayed back and forth. After it was over and we had partly recovered our surprise, they all told how they felt. One lady said, "I got so full in my chest." One man said, "I felt like running out." I said, "I did too, but my limbs were too weak and I felt creepy like." I was not scared in my mind, only my limbs "hesitated" as the colored man said. This morning we had word that the Allenby bridge was so damaged it would be impossible to cross now so we will have to wait a few days. Many walls and buildings were cracked and some houses fell in different towns, as well as here but no one was killed.

I got to preach in a nice church on the shores of Lake Galilee, saw again the ruins of Capernaum and Bethsaida and Magdala, and had a good time.

Feb. 25. It has been snowing all night, and this morning the snow is about one half foot deep. I could scarcely get to the Consulate for the snow, and the young people playing snow ball.

Well, this is quite a modern town or I have become adjusted to it. It seemed like home when we came through the terrible storm from the capitol of Moab last night, 50 miles beyond the Jordan.

I had my picture taken this A. M. in the flower garden with one half foot of snow on the flower beds and roses, and will send you one when they are ready. The snow is fast going for the rain has set in and is washing it away.

Yesterday a "prominent party" of us went over the Jordan to see Moab and all the great ruins over there. It is now called Tranjorania, and ruled by Emir Abdullah under British protection. The capitol is Amman, a town of about twenty-five thousand. It was called Philadelphia by the Romans and was the town of Moab where Joab went to destroy, took the springs and starved out the garrison and David had him put Uriah in front to get killed so that he, (David) could get his wife; read up on that point in the Bible. Well, the old walls are there, and many other ruins, especially a great Roman theatre, called an amphitheatre.

We had scarcely gotten into our hotel when we heard a great noise of Scottish bagpipes and drums and the hotel man said the Emir was going to pray as it was Friday so sent these with soldiers ahead to protect his entrance into the Mosque. So we all went to the Mosque and there was the band and soldiers already. Promptly, a few minutes to twelve, he came in a fine red Studebaker car with other soldiers. While the band played the national anthem, everyone bowed to the ground and he went in to pray. As he entered the Mosque cannons were fired on the mountains and soon a thousand Moslems were kneeling in and around the Mosque, some right in the mud and rain.

After half an hour the soldiers lined up and the band got ready. Two of our ladies wanted a photo of the King so the chauffer let them stand right at the back wheel of the car. I was near, and the mounted soldiers drove all the natives back but left us. Then the band played and a long line of soldiers lined the pathway to the door of the Mosque and stood in rigid attention. When from the door the King emerged, he was preceded by a servant in fine linen, and the lady with the kodak, not used to King's costumes, took the servant instead of the King who followed. Seeing their confusion, he bowed most graciously to them, and turning, kissed the high priest on both cheeks, and as the servant opened the car, entered and was driven rapidly away. It was so funny. He had a fine driver who spoke perfect English.

While visiting the ruins a terrible storm broke and they told us there was snow in the mountains between us and Jerusalem. Last year a party of tourists had been delayed eighteen days, owing to four feet of snow. So I rallied our forces and told them we had better beat it to the Holy City, as it was late in the afternoon and we were a hundred miles from home. We got the driver and he said he would make it. It was all pretty hard graveled roads with a little soft mud now and then. We started, with six besides the driver. My, what a storm was on in the mountains! The snow was already a half foot deep. We knew we could not visit other towns next day but glad we were on our way home. As we left the wonderful mountains of Moab and came down into the Jordan Valley the snow ceased, but it was raining hard.

Soon we had reached the Allenby Bridge and passed the customs and were in Jericho and soon climbing the Judean mountains. The wilderness of Judea was surely a howling rain storm last night. The driver told us he was sure it was snowing in the mountains about Jerusalem and so it was.

But after a warm supper, we all laughed at nature and felt good to be in our warm rooms for the rest of the storm. This morning we had good laughs at our experiences and felt it was worth all we had paid out on the trip for what we saw, and it was quite as warm coming home in the storm in a closed Hudson Super Six as in that great roomy hotel in the eastern plains of Moab.

I have been in all parts of this country two or three times. Since I have been here so long people coming to our hotel are told about me in Egypt and other countries, and told if they can get me to go along I will be better than the guides. So they invite me to go with them and pay all my bills. I learn more each time as I tell them about it all.

I got to preach in a church on the very shores of Galilee where we could hear the waves as we talked.

March 2. I have a few more places to look over once more, then I am going to Jaffa and Tel-aviv for a week. I shall return for my mail and go on to Egypt for a week before sailing.

After the snow it has cleared up and looks fine again. We are planning a donkey ride to Michmash where Johathan and his armor—bearer whipped the whole army of Philistines. We will see the hill they climbed and the rocks they passed through. Won't that be fine? I have a slide of the place to show you. I had planned the party, so we left at eight in the morning by auto for Ramallah. Mr. Jones, Secretary of the school, had three donkeys and one horse for us. The horse fell to me and the secretary not only sent a donkey boy along, but sent their native Bible woman too. She knew all the places and villages along the route and it has been hard work to visit them and get the women together and tell them the story of Jesus. She goes alone in three wild vil-lages among Moslems and takes with her some eyedrops and other little remedies for the people and they are so grateful for her seeming kindness that soon she has a house full. Then she tells them of Christ and His love.

All the time we ate our lunch yesterday she recounted her experiences among the villages and tents of the Bedouins where she said she often had to sleep with lambs and kids climbing

over her.   Yet her great love and tact in dealing with them
all has won their love and now she visits about twenty villages
where she is more than welcome.

Now to return to the trip. We started out over great mountains with only a miserable rocky trail, yet the sure footed
donkeys never missed their footing.   On past Ai on the north,
then Bethel came in sight away to the north. From one height
we see the Dead Sea and we had also seen both the Dead
Sea and the Mediterranean from the heights of Ramallah.
Well on we went, up and down until Gibeah of Saul came in
sight.   'Twas on a very high mountain that Saul had his
camp under the shade of the trees and from there he could
easily look about three miles right over into the camp of the
enemy, yet their camp was on a high mountain too.   Climbing very high we passed the outskirts of Michmash, then
down a precipitous mountain where we and the donkeys had
to slide part of the way, passing into a mighty gorge.   Going
on down we came at last to the two rocks through which
Jonathan and his helper passed.   We then found what must
have been the only place of ascent, where one if used to
mountains, could climb on hands and knees and toe nails.
There we had our lunch and took a few pictures.

On our way back our path was lined with flowers, the lily
of the fields, daisies, calla lilies and many others among the
rocks.   From the sheer mountain side the donkey boy brought
me the most gorgeous red tulips.

I was out to Ramallah yesterday where the Quakers have
their headquarters for Palestine and Arabia.   They sure have
fine schools for the boys and for the girls, and a good church.
It is by far the best work I have seen among the natives in
Palestine.

March 10.   Last week I went one day to see the parade
from the Judgment Hall of Pilate to the Church of the Holy
Sepulcher.   It was about the hour that Christ made His way,

bearing the cross. Hundreds of priests and nuns and others began the long way kneeling in fourteen special places along the way where certain things are supposed to have taken place in the way of the cross bearing and there they pray and kiss the stones, and then go on. It is all very wonderful, and yet it is so full of form that one is disgusted.

Today I was at the lower and upper pools of Gihon and Monday I am going to Siloam and Bethesda. That will about finish my explorations in and around the Holy City.

I have had the privilege of meeting and associating with the world's greatest intellectual men, and it has been quite refreshing to meet and brighten up one's own learning.

March 12. I went to see the pools of Bethesda and Siloam, and look around once more before leaving for Egypt. The guide took me to see the whole Temple Area today. My, it was some sight! One of the most beautiful edifices in the world was built on the sight of Solomon's Temple, by the Moslems. Its beauty is indescribable. The Mosque of El Aksa is built on the same grounds by the Crusaders, and is the largest church in the world. Now carpets costing a fortune cover the large area in each Mosque. We visited Solomon's stables which are underground, and which cover about three acres, having great arches supporting the roof which in turn is part of the Temple area. The Temple area covers thirty-five acres all together.

March 14. The train leaves at 8:30 in the morning and gets to Cairo, Egypt at 10:30 at night. I have already wired for a room and have had reply so I will go at once to my room.

I am leaving with some regrets as I have seen many happy days here and some very sick ones, but altogether it has been very wonderful and I have many friends, and learned many things.

MR. FAREED IMAM

"A splendid young man who knows the country well and who accompanied me on many of my excursions in the Holy Land. The way to see Palestine is thru the eyes of this thoroughly competent and highly cultured Arabian guide."—Mr. Parham.

MY ARABIAN FRIEND AND GUIDE MR. FAREED IMAM

In coming to Palestine, the first thing to be considered is, how can I see the country in the best and most economical way and get the most out of it? Well, it is a foregone conclusion here with those who have had experience, that a good guide is indispensible, and in the long run, the cheapest. There are many places where exorbitant prices and tips are required and anyone, not initiated, will be paying far more than guide fees, beside having to quarrel with the tip hunters and beggars, who swarm all tourists, all this is very annoying. Then again to find a good guide is a problem. If you are contemplating a trip to Palestine, you cannot afford to miss seeing, knowing and consulting our friend before going further.

Mr. Fareed Imam is a young man of exceptional character, highly cultured, a Moslem of splendid moral uprightness, neither smokes, chews or drinks. He is especially qualified to escourt ministers, missionaries and college or university professors about. Being highly recommended by the Y. M. C. A., the Chamber of Commerce and the Suisse Pension; he is also a student of Archaeology himself.

Anyone can secure his service by calling on him or addressing Mr. Fareed Imam. Suisse Pension Almasie, Jerusalem, Palestine.

WHILE IN THE HOLY LAND

"It was a great pleasure to meet Mr. Parham in Jerusalem and in addition to the pleasure it was a great honour for me to have served him or conducted him while visiting places of interest.

"My friend was not a tourist to the Holy Land but a real hard working scholar. In short, I am sure that Mr. Parham's time and money both were spent wisely and profitably.

"I would like to say more about my friend but I am sure

that I cannot speak enough of his kindness, thoughtfulness and his real friendship.

"Please allow me to express my sincere appreciation and many thanks more than my words can convey for putting my name and picture in the book.

"I consider what my friend wrote about my services in his paper under my picture, was the best recommendation I ever heard of, so please put this article in the book under my picture and I shall appreciate it very much and will never forget your kindness in my life.

With kindest regards, I remain, always

Most respectfully yours," Fareed J. Imam.

MRS. G. J. BRIMSON'S EXPERIENCE IN PALESTINE

"I want to say just a few words about our Bro. Charles F. Parham who has gone to his home that Jesus went to prepare for them that love Him and look for His returning. All that knew our dear Bro. Parham, knew that it was his heart's desire to live and he looked for His returning but God called him home to rest with Him in glory.

"I met Bro. Parham on the ship Carinthia on our way to the Holy Lands, December 19, 1928, on that beautiful ship sailing so smoothly.

"All on board were up and seemed so happy. From the upper deck, I was going to my state room and just behind me I heard a sweet voice, singing, 'Throw out the Life Line' as I turned to see, and knowing no one could sing like that but 'one who had the new song and a ring on his finger.' I said, 'that sounds good,' knowing I was not speaking to a stranger but a brother in Christ. He smiled and came near me and said, 'Where are you from?' and I said, 'Los Angeles, Calif.' 'Well, very likely you have heard me preach.' Then I remembered hearing him preach many times at the W. C. T. U. Temple in Los Angeles. I went to hear him

Charles F. Parham baptizing Mrs. G. J. Brimson of Los Angeles, Calif., in the Jordan River. January, 1928.

every time he preached for he knew God and His Word.

"Oh, what a wonderful visit we had on the ship as we got acquainted. With his human nature and freedom, he never forgot to tell all he talked to about Jesus and there were Jews Italians, Greeks, and Mohammedans. He and my dear hus-band preached every day to some one and told them about Jesus and His blood that saved the worst sinner, bless His Name.

"We left Brother Parham in Egypt and arrived in Jerusalem Christmas morning. One day, at Jaffa Gate, we saw Brother Parham and it was like meeting a dear father. We were so glad to see him, but he said he was not very well. Not thinking of his condition, I said, 'Now, Brother Parham, I have come all the way to Jerusalem to be baptized in the River Jordan and I want you to baptize me. There is no one else in the whole world that I would rather be baptized by than you. He smiled and said he would be glad to do it, as he was always so willing to do what he could, not only for me, but all who asked him. So we made an agreement for Sunday for the baptism. We rented a lovely car and left Jerusalem early by the Dead Sea on to the Jordan. I am so sorry about the robe I wore. It was just one of my little gingham dresses, for I thought there would be no one there; but to our great surprise there were over 3,000 there, as the Greek Catholics were having a baptismal service for three days. Oh, what a crowd! I soon got ready and was the first one who was baptized. Oh, but the cameras and moving picture machines that were turned on us! Brother Parham found a good place after trying out many places. The old Jordan is deep and muddy and swift but I felt safe, as he knew just how to handle one in swift water. I was so happy to know I was baptized where Jesus was and where Joshua led the children of Israel across. I am so thankful to God that

He opened a way for me to go and made all things possible, and all glory be to Him. It was such a beautiful January day. We had our lunch with us and on the dear old banks of the Jordan we sat and ate. Many wonderful things happened on that day I will never forget.

"It was a beautiful morning, January 30, that Brother Parham, Brother Notie, my dear husband and myself left the Clock Tower for Galilee. We had our car rented the night before and an Arab chauffeur. My, but these Arab boys are wonderful drivers! We always rented a good sedan for there were always four in the party; and we went 50-50 on the expense and took our lunch. We left the Clock Tower, at 6:30.

"Just the break of day, we went past Jesus' tomb and how still we were. I thought of Mary Magdalene, for it must of been about that hour she went to Jesus' tomb. After leaving the city over the mountain, we could look back to the City and see the sun rising and its glory shone on Mount Olivet and many of the steeples of the cathedrals and even to Bethlehem. How I wish I could show it to you as we saw it! We never said one word to each other; we all had our thoughts and I am sure they were much the same.

"On a little farther we saw the shepherds taking their little flocks out from the villages to the fields, oh, how beautiful they were! Then we met at the place they loaded camels trains. Some were loaded with honey and some with oranges. Then up and around the high mountains; our chauffeur was a good guide and when we came to historical places he told us, and then Brother Parham and my husband would preach to us what they both knew of the Bible and their God; so those places were not strange.

"It was 10 o'clock when we got to Jacob's well, where all got out and went down the steps to the well. Brother Parham with his wonderful personality and kind voice made friends with the door keeper and the priest' so they were exceedingly nice to us. We drew water and had a drink and took with us a bottle of water. I have mine yet. Then on to the north, where we had lunch at Mary's well where Jesus had played just like other little boys. We had our pictures taken in all those places; then on to Galilee.

"Oh, I almost forgot to say, coming into Galilee there is a range of mountains which we went up and down and around and around, and all that time we could see dear old Galilee. Saw the fishermen out in their sail boats and Brother Parham suggested we have fish for supper.

"The place where we stayed all night and got our meals, was kept by an Assyrian woman who had a wooden leg. How it did squeak when she walked! We thought we were fortunate that our rooms joined and were so large and clean and over-looking the sea. We sat on the porch and saw the sunset: how wonderful! No wonder Jesus loved Galilee; it is the most beautiful place in all Palestine.

"The bell rang for supper and we went, thinking we would have fish, but she said the sea was too rough and the fishermen did not get any; and not one of us ate goat meat. On the little table was goat meat cooked in rice, and some native bread and some goat's milk cheese.

"I asked if we could have some tea and the woman said, 'Sure;' it was good tea and my husband asked the blessing. I was so amused to see us go after the rice and tea, and when I looked at Brother Parham I just laughed right in my plate. My husband, being an Englishman and very conventional, never smiled. I said to Brother Parham I thought I would die if I couldn't laugh and he thought I was laughing at the woman's squeaky wooden leg, but it was at the rice.

"The next morning we had a little wade in the sea and it was a lovely morning. I just went out as far as I could, knowing that on this same sea Jesus walked. I thank God for having seen dear old Galilee.

"Then we went to Capernaum, leaving there at noon for Jerusalem. We arrived at sun down. We went many other places while there and were always together. I shall never forget my trip and the pleasant times we had, and I thank God for Brother Parham and for my baptism in the River Jordan.

"Every word is just as true as when it happened. We looked forward to the time of meeting again, in the dear old U. S. A., with dear Brother Parham and rehearsing our experiences, but that was in the Father's hands: He took him home. I can never tell how sorry, so sorry we felt. I shall always see that smiling face the morning our train pulled out of the depot at Jerusalem. It was a long wave, and the last one till He beckons me over. I want to see him over there and if I live as our brother did, I know I will.

"Mrs Parham, I am sending the following piece for your book. I think it is so beautiful and fits you. Much of this work we have done.

"'Lord of all pots and pans and things, since I've no time to be
A saint by doing lovely things or watching late with thee.
Or dreaming in the dawnlight, or storming Heaven's gates.
Make me a saint by getting meals and washing up the plates.
Altho I must have Martha's hands, I have a Mary's mind;
And when I black the boots and shoes, Thy sandals Lord
        I find.
I think of how they trod the earth, what time I scrub the
        floor;
Accept this meditation Lord, I haven't time for more.
Warm all the kitchen with Thy love and light it with Thy
        peace;
Forgive me all my worrying and make all grumbling cease.
Thou who didst love to give men food, in room or by the
        sea,
Accept this service that I do, I do it unto Thee.'"

Chapter XXXIV

GOING DOWN TO EGYPT AND "HOME SWEET HOME."

AIRO, Egypt, March 16, 1928—Here I am in the land of the Pharaoh, the land of perpetual sunshine, and I feel so much better than in Palestine. It is tropically warm here while in Jerusalem it is so cold most of the time.

This town is said to be hard for newcomers to get straightened in, but I got here after dark and before I got up I saw where the sun came up and got it straight so North is North. I have been all over the town this morning and easily found my way back. This is a great town, the second Paris of the world, a wonderful dream of a town, so many grand buildings, dreams of architectural beauty. Tomorrow I am going out to see the "old lady Sphinx" and the great Py-ramid. Can you believe it that I'm here in the midst of the world!

I try to think of the maps and where I am, but it is all so wonderful, yet I thought this morning and yesterday coming through the desert where I could see the Mediterranean, it is 7, 000 miles home over that way.

I enjoyed coming out of Palestine although there was a touch of sadness in leaving the places and people I had enjoyed for three months. I have been all over it so often and when I came out I knew all the villages and mountains by name, and the interesting things that were all so strange to me when I came in. All the way down to Ashdod, Escalon and Gaza there were many thrills as memories came swift and fast; of the plains of Philistia and old Samson setting the wheat fields afire and carrying off the gates and thousands of acres of wheat, covering all the great plain as well as the plains of Sharon and farther north where Esdralon stretches her vast sea of green wheat to Carmel Heights. So all was sad, but bitter sweet to me in leaving. I gave all the servants tips and had quite a leave taking of the home like place where I have been stopping.

March 18. Here I am enjoying the warmth of the Nile Valley. I had a trip to the Pyramids yesterday and am going to spend the day out there again tomorrow.

I have been over the city a good deal by tram and find it a good cheap way to see the city. This is a city of one million and reminds one of Houston, Texas or Mobile, Alabama. There are so many fine mansions of the very old native part.

There are lots of negro servants here which makes it seem like the south.

I'll be going to Alexandria on the 22nd and go on ship, after which I will visit the city until I sail. I shall see the Island of Cypress and shall spend one day at Naples and another at Gibraltar to see both that place and Tangi, Africa, right across. May God bless you all.

Ever your loving Husband and Father
Charles F. Parham.

I had ten days of most interesting days in Egypt, seeing all the wonderful sights of this age old land, especially the Pyramids and the Sphinx and the museums and many of the old timey mummies living in the days of Hebrew slavery and the exodus. I saw all the great treasures of King Tut's tomb. You could not conceive this wealth and the wonderful things they found there, it is impossible for experts to estimate the wealth of these treasures. Then I had five days in Italy and saw the great sights of Naples and the museums of wonderful paintings and all the things dug from old Pompeii and other things. Then many days of happy home going sea travel. When I was 1500 miles from land I got a wireless from home. One morning about ten o'clock, as I was sitting on an upper deck, the bell boy came up and said, "Excuse me, a Marconi

for you." Here it was, unbelievable—a message from away
across the waters and about 2000 miles off land: "Welcome
Home," from the Parham family.

MY LAST EXPERIENCE, GLORY!

I am going to try to tell the readers of my paper something,
if possible, of the wonderful experience the Lord has revealed
to me by His Presence.

Many of you have known that during the last national camp
meeting I so over worked that my heart gave way until I
was useless or nearly so. Before leaving for the Holy Land
I had a sort of stroke of paralysis but I felt I must go as
many would have said, had I failed to go, that I had planned
a trip to get money and then used it myself; so I boarded
the steamer for the Orient.

After a terrible experience with a dreadful cold in Athens,
Greece, I landed in Jerusalem in a very serious condition, and
one day I had a very bad heart attack; my strenuous life has
worn out my heart action. I have no assurance of tomorrow
nor of even crossing that room. Of course, personally, it was
good news if all the battles and strife of life were over, I
was glad. But when I thought of the distress of loved ones
in the home land if I should pass in a far off strange land, I
felt I must live on to at least come home where loving hands
might lay away the dust of human form.

Day by day, hour by hour, moment by moment I went on,
yet each moment I had a touch of weakness that warned me
that I lived only for the moment. Every one was kindness itself.
Guides assisted me up steep places; tourists took my arm. In
going only a few blocks I had to rest many times.

At last having done Palestine as few people are permitted
to, I went on to Egypt. There my case was even worse, yet
I saw the wonders of that age old land and got on my boat.
I felt then some assurance I might again see loved ones and
then lay me down to rest.

Many nights I awoke early and lay there meditating, oh so hungry for a touch of the Lord! I felt like the one who had sought Him till my locks were wet with the dew of the morning, yet I felt not His Presence. Then one morning 3:30 A. M. in mid-ocean, He came to me. It was the Presence of my Beloved. "Leaping upon the mountains, skipping upon the hills."

How can I explain it to you? Perhaps it was thus He was manifest to me. He and the Father came and took up their abode with me. He came in to sup with me, yea "He brought me into His banqueting chamber and His banner over me was love." I saw no vision of His personality, but knew He was there. I was in the aura of His Presence; all was peace, perfect peace. There was life and that life more abundantly. All darkness vanished; all thought of sin and disease, real or unreal, disappeared. "In His Presence"—then I knew the power of that virtue that went out from Him destroying disease, and I knew there was no sin, no disease in the light of His Presence.

Well, words fail me to explain this wonderful experience! I had read how Christian Science affirmed there was no disease, no sin but I knew there was. But I did not have to affirm or deny. I had found the real of which they perhaps have grasped, that in His Presence, in the radius of His influence, sin and disease does not exist. It was like the light of the morning that drives the darkness and shadows all away. You know that at night the darkness in your room is real, but touch the electric button and where is that darkness? It is gone. So is all sin and disease when faith touches the button and the light appears; darkness is simply not there. Darkness is the absence of light, so sin and disease is the absence of His Presence.

When His divine Presence became so real to me, all sin and disease ceased to exist. Glory to our God. I have had many

blessings, He has been my Staff and Stay.   I have loved Him
and knew He was mine, but now it is no longer the blessing,
it's the Blesser in manifest reality.   For years I have heard
people testify, "I am crucified with Christ; nevertheless I live;
yet not I, but Christ liveth in me; and the life which I now
live in the flesh, I live by the faith of the Son of God."

Well, I knew they were not there.   But listen—softly—if
this wonderful experience lasts, and the aura of His Presence
remains, I will be tempted to testify that, "The life I now
live in the flesh, I live by the faith of the Son ofGod."All
struggling is past; I rest after a weary way.

There was no struggle when I came into this or when He
came softly and made Himself real by His Presence; just that
I felt Him slip into my bower of love and clasp me in His
arms and I was comforted and rested.   Bless His holy name.
I have a full assurance of the life that now is and the life that
is to come.

I am living on the border land.   Immortality is as real as the
life that now is, there seems only a line drawn between, only
a vale intervenes.   This side is loving service, just across is
the land of eternal praise and worship.   I would rather stay
awhile here than cross, but I can reach across and feel the
full reality of the other side.   Oh, it is all so real!   For many
years I have said to many, "I am not worthy of heaven, I have
been such a weak, unprofitable servant, so quick of tongue, so
full of faults and weaknesses.   Like Moses, who for some
few hasty words, was not permitted to enter the Promised
Land; or like Paul 'after having preached to others, I might
myself become a cast-away.' "

I said to the Lord many times, with tears flowing down my
cheeks, "Oh Lord, if you will only let me love Thee, and
serve faithfully my fellowmen and feel the joy of service and
the joy of following in Thy gleaming footsteps, wet with
the dew of Thy blood o'er weary miles of service, and then

give me one look of love, one smile of approval on my labor, I will gladly take any sentence Thy lips might frame, as my just deserts for all eternity."

Well, that is all gone, vanished like the shadows of the night when the morning dawns. I have assurance of the life that is and a glorious assurance of that which is to come. If I could explain it, I have it now. I seem to dwell in the seventh heaven already, or rather feel I have been transfigured in His Presence, as Jesus was upon that exceeding high mountain. For He has promised that He and the Father would manifest themselves to us and take up their abode with us.

Well, now some may say, maybe so, he never was converted. But I was and sanctified as a second definite work of grace. And twenty eight years ago, baptized in the Holy Ghost and scarcely a day since that, I have not spoken in tongues. My dear friends of many years will know that I have served faithfully thru days of indefatigable toil and nights of blackness and storm. No days were so cold and terrible or nights so frightful but what it .was joy to run His errand; ever on the wing on errands of mercy and missions of love. The mighty deserts or rugged mountains, or distances long, but what it was joy to me to rush to help, feed or comfort my loved ones in the Lord.

And I thought if ever I was privileged to enter into His glory, it would be thru the gate of faithfulness. I don't have to enter, He has taken me to Himself; and in His Presence it is heaven here, all longing for that sometime place is gone for I walk and talk with the King. My beloved is mine and I am His, He feedeth among the lilies. He has inclosed me in His garden and sealed all my fountains and surrounded me with the flowers of fragrance and the trees of all spices. I long only that the north winds may blow and the south winds come and blow upon this garden that the sweet perfumes may flow out and that all my dear friends may come and enjoy with me the glorious bower of His loving Presence.

Well, all of us have had our special trials; we have all had things, some more than others, to fight in our lives. We have dealt with most of them and conquered but perhaps one thing, the thing that we have struggled with, dealt with and some times conquered, sometimes not. Fought and then gave in and said, "Well it is natural for one to be thus and so; or it is a birthmark with me; or it is my besetting sin, or it is "my thorn in the flesh etc."—It may have been temper, habit, passion or lust. But all have had their fights and won or lost thru the years. I too have fought on; but oh, it was so easy when He came and took up His abode with me and I was brought into His Presence.

All this faded like mist before the morning sun; it simply can't or don't exist in His Presence. Oftimes when camped in the open, creatures of the night prowl about your camp and oft frighten you and terror seizes you, but they all vanish with the morning light. Sometimes the insects of the night are heard in your room or creatures crawl or scratch about your room, and you wonder if a cricket or mouse may not suddenly leap upon you, and thus frightened you are sore afraid to rest in peace. Softly you reach over and touch the electric button and they scamper away.

Did they exist? Oh yes, all affirming or denying or mental process could not have destroyed them. I wonder if this will help my Christian Science friends, who seek by mental processes to dissipate sin and disease, and show them the real of which they have the counterfeit; that if He comes in His Presence, disease cannot, does not exist. Praise the Lord, all fear is gone. I dwell in His Presence and sin and disease and that one thing is gone, as flees the creatures of night when the morning dawns.

I seem to have been caught forward into the age to come and feel the power of the fullness of His Presence in the effulgent life and health of the Millenium Sabbath. Glorious rest, fullness of peace, joy unspeakable.

Had I the power this morning I would gather the mountains and carve them into a throne and there enshrine my Beloved. Then would I place the sun as a crown upon His head: catch the moon from her throne and place it like a great jewel sapphire upon His bosom, catch the veil of heaven's blue and ensnare the stars and wind them about His shoulders emblazoned with the jeweled stars of night; gather all clouds and weave them about His body for a garment and into this I would throw all fires to emblazen all with effulgent glory. Before Him, would stretch all lands as the floor of a mighty temple and gather all waters and cast them about this land that none should ever or could ever more go out.

And then would gather all peoples into this temple and call all the host of heaven to encircle above it and call upon all nature, animate and inanimate to worship Him the King of Kings, the Bridegroom of my soul. For He is my Beloved, the fairest of all.

*   *   *   *   *

I had a fine voyage, fine sunny weather till the last day when a light rain set in.

I arrived in New York City April 11th. No one knows except those of travel, what it feels like to see happy faces of loved ones when you dock at the home port. My son and his wife, Wilfred and Alice, were there when the boat came in with happy loving smiles of welcome. Soon the customs were passed and some duty on my slides, and we were speeding to their mission.

I have been able to buy 200 photo slides of Palestine, showing its people, costumes, customs and many of the holy places. This will allow me to give two lectures on the Holy land,

and with all I shall be able to tell you, it will be of special interest to every one. I wish all to have the benefit of my months of travel in the Holy Land and of many trips over the whole of it.

Wilfred and Alice had me billed for my two lectures with the slides on the Holy Land and a week's revival. The Lord filled the hall till people really fought their way in. Many other places begged for revivals and the lectures; the people wanted to get a large auditorium and have a regular campaign. One big Methodist church in the heart of the city, begged for a meeting. I preached the second day I was here at the "Glad Tidings Mission," the largest Pentecostal church in the east. I also preached there April 24. This work is the result of work that I was instrumental in doing with workers from Zion City about twenty-two years ago and one of the workers, Sister Marie Burgess-Brown, is still with her husband in charge, so it was like visiting my spiritual children in the Lord.

My son and his wife felt their work in New York was done for the present, so they came west with me and will fill some of their pressing calls in the evangelistic field.

*   *   *   *   *

Wilfred and Alice Parham express kind greetings to all the readers of this book.

"After Dad had spent three months in Palestine in research work, we received word he was returning. He cabled us the boat he was to take and the date of his arrival so without asking him we booked him for a campaign in our church in New York, feeling that his messages on prophecy and deeper teaching would greatly benefit our church.

"The day came for his arrival. We were at the pier to see him leave and we were glad to be there to see him arrive. Although he thoroughly enjoyed his trip, he was glad to be back on American soil, and he said when he saw the dear old

Statue of Liberty, he threw his hat in the air and shouted "Hurrah for America," so did many others.

"Later in telling some of his experiences and feelings about the trip, said that everywhere in the foreign countries, the atmosphere seemed to bespeak war; every body was on tiptoe expecting at any moment something to happen, and when a stranger came within their gates they were watched from the time they entered until they left.

"Our party received him with open arms; some were there who had known him when in Zion City, years before and heard he was to be in New York. They brought him beautiful bouquets of flowers and fruits, and from every pocket he brought forth souvenirs from the Holy Land. He brought me an orange that he had picked from the tree himself, just before leaving; so after unloading all of his treasures from his pockets and hiding places he said he felt several pounds lighter.

"We informed him of the coming campaign the first thing. telling him it was well advertised and every body was expecting great things. Imagine his surprise he could hardly believe it, but said, "Well if it was any one else, I don't know what I would do, as I am anxious to get home, it seems years since I left, but I will stay," and he did.

"Needless to say, we had a splendid campaign. The church was packed nightly and many times standing room was at a premium. The meeting continued three weeks with God's blessing upon it and it was said of many, that never was the truths of prophecy made so plain to them before, and he made a warm spot in the hearts of many for himself.

"At the close of the campaign we both left with Dad for Kansas to see that he got safely home, coming by way of Niagara Falls and we enjoyed the trip very much. Arriving home once more, every one breathed a 'praise the Lord.' When we stepped into the door, friends who came to see him leave were there to welcome him home, and they had an old fashioned prayer meeting in thanksgiving to God for his safe return.

"Now, dear readers, the following chapters will tell you of events that took place before God called His servant Home to be with Him. How he went from place to place showing those wonderful pictures which every one enjoyed, and how he died at his post, and as was said by one who knew him, 'surely a Prince has fallen.' But his word and work will live forever in the hearts of all who knew him and loved·him."

＊　＊　＊　＊　＊

It was indeed a happy day (May 10, 1928) when the Parham family was united again. How we thanked God, and still do thank Him, that Mr. Parham's life was spared to come home and be with us again, though we did not know that it was to be for such a short time.

Though the travelers were tired from their day's journey, we were all happy and talked till a late hour; then before retiring Mr. Parham hung a sheet upon the wall, and showed us some of his Jerusalem pictures, among them the twenty-third Psalm, which were all very beautiful.

All were interested in knowing what his future plans were, but he only said, "I am not planning very far ahead these days, but expect to show the pictures and give my lectures in missions and near by towns till after my birthday meeting."

The birthday meeting was well attended. Many ministers and friends came to the all-day meeting from different states and the crowd filled the mission for the morning service. Mr. Parham received a number of useful presents, and many congratulations on his safe return. Our friends then brought their baskets, and eat a picnic dinner under the trees in our front yard.

The afternoon and night services were held in "The Baxter Theatre" and the people of his home town showed their appreciation by attending in great crowds and they truly gave him a hearty welcome home.

In the afternoon Mr. Parham spoke especially to the ministers present and at night he gave an address upon Palestine enlarging upon the message which he had given over the radio in the early morning at Picher, Okla. Mr. Parham also used the same theater when he showed the pictures of the Holy Land to a crowded house. Everywhere he showed the pictures they were very much enjoyed.

Another very important event was soon to take place. Our youngest son, Robert was to be married to Miss Pauline Holman, of Picher, Okla., on June 17th. As they wished to invite all their friends, the wedding was to be at the Baxter Mission, which was beautifully decorated with flowers. The chief floral offerings were the gift of the Wm. Johnson Art Shop of Oklahoma City. A musical program was given and Mr. Parham performed the wedding ceremony for his youngest son. A host of friends witnessed the beautiful and sacred service, and the young couple received their congratulations and best wishes and were also presented with many nice and useful presents.

Unlike some parents, we have not had much to do in trying to help our children in the very important matter of choosing their life companions, believing that they should decide this for themselves, but we prayed much for them, that God would be with them in all things.

Truly God has answered prayer and those who have married into our family have filled their places in the home circle in a blessed way and were all very dear to Mr. Parham as well as myself.

As the last camp-meeting had been such a strain on Mr. Parham's strength, he was not planning to have one this year. He talked about going to Portland to see his brother Harry who had been sick; also of going to California to show the pic-

MR. AND MRS. ROBERT L. PARHAM

tures of the Holy Land to a host of friends there who were writing to him from different places about coming.

But such an extraordinary desire on the part of the ministry and laity all over the country, expressed in urgent appeals by letter, compelled him to surrender and promise to lead the National Camp Meeting, which was held at Baxter Springs, Kansas, Aug. 11 to 26.

Instead of taking a much needed rest, Mr. Parham planned meetings which kept him busy up to the date of the Camp-meeting. He went to Cave Springs, Ark., then to Wichita, and Cheney, Kansas. Stopping two nights at many places, in Oklahoma and Texas, he went to Houston, Texas. Beside many places in Texas, he stopped at Fayetteville, Ark., on his return home, showing the pictures of the Holy Land.

Where Mr. Parham had showed the pictures the largest halls and auditoriums were packed into the streets. As the great audiences listened to these lectures they were swept into tears or lifted into shouting as they saw the scenes—pictured so wonderfully before them—connected with the life and work of our Lord and Savior, and many who had before had no interest in religion, now raised their hands for prayer for salvation. At the close of these meetings, Mr. Parham prayed for the sick and many were healed.

REPORT OF THE GREAT NATIONAL CAMP
MEETING

We decided to again have the Camp Meeting in Baxter, and knew it was the Lord's will as the place where we had held so many good old Camp Meetings in years past, right across from our home, was secured again. A mammoth tent was brought from Joplin and pitched with the help of many delegates who had already come to enjoy the feast of good things. The opening service on Saturday night started off with great victory and the air was soon rent with praises and hallelujahs. All day Sunday the people came from every direction and by Sunday night a great crowd was in attendance. The big orchestra and choir furnished splendid music, and solos, duets, trios, quartettes and instrumentals were rendered each evening by the singers and musicians.

All during the meetings as the ministers and workers came in they were asked to give a report of their work for the past year, and it was surprising yet pleasing to hear many of them report that this last year was the best they had ever had and they witnessed the greatest miracles and saw more souls saved than ever before; everyone rejoiced with them.

All who attended the Camp Meeting considered this to be the best Camp Meeting we have held in years. There were delegates who came from many states to stay for the entire meeting which lasted two weeks, and over week-ends hundreds came from the adjoining districts and cities.

The second Sunday and Monday nights of the meeting, Mr. Parham showed his two hundred pictures which he brought from the Holy Land, showing one hundred each night, and lecturing with each picture. It was said that at these two meetings was assembled the largest crowds that Baxter had ever seen. The pictures and lectures were thoroughly enjoyed by everyone. These picutres made Christ and the Bible more real to those who saw them and many said to him after he was through, that they intended to live better and more useful lives in the future.

Brother Bacon gave a Bible lesson each day and so many derived such benefits from these as he would take them from one passage of Scripture to another explaining it thoroughly and making each Scripture very clear. The children's meeting was followed by the afternoon service, and this was a time when all of the ministers had an opportunity to preach: Our hearts were made to rejoice as they arose and without fear or favor, preached this fuller Gospel. It was noticed that a number of the ministers who had attended the Camp Meeting the year previous to this one had been digging into the deeper things of God, and the Bible and were able to bring out the truths of the Word of God so much better than before.

Salvation, prophecy and healing were the messages for the evening services. The altars were filled every night with hungry hearts seeking salvation, sanctification, and the Holy Spirit and healing and pleading to be made ready for the coming of the Lord. Many hundreds were prayed for. Many wonderful healings were much in evidence.

We are privileged to have with us again for two days, dear little Abbie Morrow Brown of Los Angeles, California. She was with us last year for several days and we were glad to welcome her back again. She brought two messages to us which were immensely enjoyed; a few of her thoughts I think I will pass on to you. She has traveled around the world three times, and of course has had much experience. She said, "In praying for many people for healing, I have found that some do not get healed because they have been criticising the preacher and one another. Now when you go to these earthly doctors the first thing they ask you to do is, 'Show me your tongue,' and of course they stick out their tongue, and I believe when we come to our Lord, and He knows we have been talking about our neighbors; He says, 'Show me your tongue'." Many were struck with this illustration, so a word to the wise is sufficient.

A baptismal service was also held and a good number were taken out to the waters and buried with their Lord and Master.

Without taking collections or begging for funds to carry on this meeting sufficient money came in to pay all expenses and give to every preacher and worker that came expense money and gas to get them safely to their next appointments. For this we truly praise the Lord. His promises are yea and amen, and He has promised to provide for all who put their trust in Him.

The meeting came to a close Sunday night the 26th, and communion was served. My, what a sight, from many churches in Baxter and other places, came people to partake of this sacred ordinance! For three quarters of an hour three lines passed by each taking a sip of wine and breaking off a little piece of bread. It was a time of weeping and praising God and shouting, and getting back to God; this will be one service that will not be forgotten by all who partook.

All the ministers and workers left the camp with a greater determination than ever to do the whole will of God, and all said they received exactly what they came after, an infilling and a blessing to send them forth with renewed victory.

The Apostolic Faith, September, 1928.

"Oh to be nothing, nothing
Only to lie at His feet
A broken and emptied vessel
For the Master's use made meet.
Emptied—that He might fill me
As forth to His service I go;
Broken—that so unhindered
His life through me might flow.

Oh to be nothing, nothing
Only as led by His hand
A messenger at His gateway
Only waiting for His command
Only an instrument ready
His praises to sound at His will
Willing, should He not require me
In silence to wait on Him still."

Chapter XXXV

HE FOUGHT A GOOD FIGHT AND FINISHED HIS COURSE.

 AM thankful that the Lord permitted Mr. Parham once more to have such a successful camp meeting again on the old camp grounds, which brought back to many, sacred memories of the past wonderful meetings which he had held there, and enabled him to meet again with old friends, from far and near and be with them in a camp meeting for the last time.

He seemed to enjoy the meeting and never complained of feeling over-taxed though he was constantly busy. But some said they had seen him stop to rest, even when walking a short distance, when he thought no one was noticing him.

During the meeting one of the brothers put his hand on his shoulder and said, "Brother Parham, I love you." He smiled and asked, "Why do you love me?" The minister replied, "I love you, not only for yourself but for your work's sake, and because God chose you and gave you a mighty message and work, and you have been faithful." To which Mr. Parham replied, "Yes, but I feel that it has been nearly accomplished and my work is about done." We also have heard that he had made similar remarks while in Texas, as well as after this time.

Mr. Parham had received word that his brother Frank, who lived at Topeka, Kansas, was sick and we had asked him to come to the camp-meeting, but as he did not come, Mr. Parham decided that he would drive up in the car and see him and bring him back to make us a visit if he was able to come.

So they returned together, and we are so glad that he came, and for the week that he spent with us. The brothers had not had an opportunity to be together much since their boyhood days; and when he left he had a better understanding of our faith, and was feeling very much better, being strengthened both physically and spiritually.

When Mr. Parham took his brother home, they stopped one night at Sedalia, Mo., where Wilfred and Alice Parham were having a revival. How glad they were to have their uncle visit their meeting, and he said he enjoyed it very much.

Wm. Yeakel was now going with Mr. Parham to help him in showing the pictures, and they went through west Oklahoma, Texas, and Colorado to Roswell, New Mexico, stopping for two nights meeting at many towns in these states.

From Roswell, New Mexico, he returned to Wichita, Kansas, to hold a meeting there from December 13 to 23. They filled several dates for meetings on their way back to Wichita, but were unable to go to all the places they had planned on account of the bad weather, that had made the roads impassable.

Driving through mud and snow was a severe strain on Mr. Parham's strength, and he took a severe cold, so by the time he got to Wichita he was far from being well.

During the meeting at Wichita he told them about his experience on the ship and said, "Now don't be surprised if I slip away, and go almost anytime, there seems such a thin veil between. I am thankful that God revealed His presence and made me to know that my life pleased Him."

He wrote a letter home to Philip and Virgie in which he said, "I am glad for every move my children make for God and souls and the blessing of humanity for its only what we sacrifice and do for others that is worth while in this old world.

"I am living on the edge of the Glory Land these days and it's all so real on the other side of the curtain that I feel mightily tempted to cross over.

"My, my, I've had such a glory and peace in my soul since my experience on the sea that I can scarcely stay here. 'Tis, heaven below, my Redeemer to know.   Some day I may slip over.   The Lord bless you all."

For his last sermon in Wichita, he used for his text, "Greater love hath no man than this, that a man lay down his life for his friends."   John 15:13.   He likened the parent's love as being wonderful and then pictured the love of the Savior as far surpassing anything in this world.

He spoke words of encouragement to the Christians and urged all to press on for God and be melted together in one bond of love.   These messages were a blessing and sank deep into many hearts.   This was his last revival meeting.

While at Wichita he told the friends there that he had not spent a Christmas at home for many years, but he had promised the children that he would this year, and he was looking forward to spending this Christmas with his family.

We were looking forward very much to this also, and the young people wanted to do something more than usual to celebrate his coming, had got a little Christmas tree on which to put our little tokens of love, which were to be distributed Christmas Eve.

He got home about the middle of the afternoon December 24 with Gail Schultz and Wm. Yeakel with him, and was quite worn out with driving from Wichita, but he was ever thinking of others.   Seeing our little Christmas celebration and not knowing that we had included his company in our Christmas remembrances, he went up town to get something for them, that they might feel included in the family circle.

While our grandson passed our Christmas gifts, and we were thankful for Mr. Parham's home coming, we telegraphed Christmas greetings to Wilfred and Alice at Los Angeles, California, that they might know they were not forgotten.

Mr. Parham had a big stack of letters waiting for him when he got home and he spent most of the holiday week answering his correspondence.   He was so pleased that so many of his friends had remembered him this Christmas with a Christmas card, word of cheer or some token of love. Though hardly able to go, he visited a few sick ones in Baxter, who he thought would not be out to the Watch Night Meeting.

It had been a long time also, since Mr. Parham had held a Watch Night Meeting in Baxter Springs, and we were looking forward to this very much expecting a good crowd, and many were coming from a distance. But it had been very cold and began to snow and by New Year's Eve had turned into a terrible blizzard. However, Floyd Durham and a number of others came from Stella, Mo., driving about fifty miles through the storm, and there was a very good crowd considering the weather.

Several testified and preached, and when Mr. Parham preached his main thought was as it had been at Wichita, telling about his experience on the ship, and how near the Lord had been to him. He said that it had made him feel homesick to go, and he might go on before the rest of us.

Mr. Parham had announced to show the pictures of Palestine at Temple, Texas, January 4th and 5th, Moran, Texas, Sunday Jan. 6th afternoon and night, and San Saba, Texas, Jan. 7th and 8th.

He was hardly able to be up, and unfit for such a long drive, especially as it was very cold, and a heavy snow on the ground and we tried to persuade him to cancel his engagements. But it had been such a strong principle, all through his ministry, never to disappoint his people that even now, unable for the trip, he did not feel that he could do so. He left home January 2nd with Wm. Yeakel and Roy Reed of Houston, Texas, driving for him.

The following Monday we received word from Keet Reeds at Temple, Texas, that he was very sick, and I immediately went to him. I found him in a very serious condition, his heart bad and unable to eat.

He had become unconscious while showing the pictures Saturday night. So anxious was he that the people might not be disappointed that several times, as he partly regained consciousness, he asked that they would continue the pictures and show the 23rd Psalm.

Keet Reed and his wife were caring for him, as they would one of the family, and everything possible was done for his comfort; but it was agreed when I left home, that if I found him no better that I would send word home and either Claude or Robert would come and help to care for him.

I telegraphed them but instead of one of the boys coming the whole family in two cars, came to see him; driving all night they got there early in the morning.

He seemed some better that day and was able to be dressed, and the family decided that it was best to get him home, and that he would be able to return on the train by getting a Pullman.

It was not without difficulty, however, that he was at last persuaded to cancel his dates and do this. After his meetings at San Saba, Texas, he had planned to go to Horace Watkins at Sabinal, Texas, who had been laboring in meetings there in a new field, and had made dates for Mr. Parham to have some meetings near there. It seemed to hurt him very much to give up these meetings. He said it was disappointing them the second time, as he had planned to go there when he was at Roswell, New Mexico, but could not on account of the muddy roads.

By night, however, all arrangements were made and Mr. Parham accompanied by his daughter, Esther Rardin, returned home on the eight o'clock train, the rest of us going home in the three cars; Robert driving his father's car.

While we had all been planning for his comfort, even though he was so sick, he had been planning for us, so that we might all have a comfortable place to sleep and rest that night, as he knew the family were all tired after driving all night.

However, this was not our intention for we wanted to get home and be with him there as soon as possible. We left Temple, Texas, about eight o'clock, and got to Baxter about the same time the following night. We found that he had stood the trip very well and many friends had done all they could to assist Esther in making him comfortable.

His family were all with him now except Wilfred and Alice, who were in Los Angeles, California, and his thoughts now turned to them. If Wilfred would come home, he still had hopes with his careful driving, he would be able to make the trip to California.

When Wilfred received the message he took the first train for Baxter Springs sending his father telegrams to be of good cheer, that he was on his way home. Mr. Parham was rapidly growing worse, but it now seemed to be his one desire and and constant prayer to live to see Wilfred again. How much he loved his boy who he trained in evangelistic work, and who was spending his life in the service of the Master.

Though none of us had been doing much eating, one day Robert went to his room to spend the day in fasting and prayer after which he had a talk with his father. When I entered the room a little later though he was so weak he could only say a few words at a time, he told me that Robert had consecrated his life to preach the gospel and serve the Lord in any way He wanted him to.

I shall never forget the expression on his face. Tired, worn and suffering yet lit up with a joy and a look of peaceful satisfacton that his prayer for many years was answered, and that now another one of his sons was going to preach this gospel which was still so dear to him, and for which he had so gladly spent his life.

During the meeting at Lindsay, California, in 1925, Mr. Parham had told some friends that he expected some day that Robert, his youngest son, would be preaching this gospel. Robert was then working in a Dry Goods Store and his father was proud of his success in business, saying that it was giving him a good opportunity to learn to meet the public, as it would be a help to him to know how to meet people of all classes when he went into the work of the ministry.

Robert was interested in his business; getting married, and preparing his little home, had taken his time and thought.

His wife had been raised to believe in the full gospel, as her mother had acceped this faith at Prosperity, Mo., during the meetings held there in 1916, and had been an earnest worker ever since. Though a believer, Pauline had never experienced a real know—so salvation until after they were married, during the last camp-meeting.

Mr. Parham had talked to them about giving their lives to the service of God, but in their young married life, with all their hopes and plans for the future, they seemed unable to make the consecration.

> "I walked a mile with pleasure,
>   She chatted all the way,
> But she left me none the wiser
>   For all she had to say.
> I walked a mile with sorrow
>   And ne'er a word said she,
> But, oh, the things I learned from her
>   When sorrow walked with me."

Sorrow will sometimes accomplish a work in lives, which seemingly cannot be wrought out in any other way. As Robert now saw his father's life, worn out in the Master's service and seemingly so near its close, he felt that he must make the consecration to preach this gospel.

Not that he could take his father's place, or do his father's work, none could do this, for his work had been faithfully done, but that he might tell to others the precious truths that his father had so firmly established in his heart and life.

Wilfred was due to arrive on the early morning train. All that night, Mr. Parham's life seemed to hang, as it were by a tender cord, which might at any moment be broken, and only God could strengthen and hold the brittle thread of life. But his prayer was answered when the early morning train from Wichita brought Wilfred accompanied by Fred Campbell, who had for so many years been Mr. Parham's traveling companion in evangelistic work.

Mr. Parham rallied and Wilfred had the privilege of being with his father for sometime and helping to take care of him. Twice he was relieved from all pain and suffering and apparently was really healed, but it seemed as though the Lord was just keeping him lingering on the Border Land till we could say more willingly, "Thy will be done."

One day he told Claude he wanted to talk to him. Claude tried to persuade him not to talk, as he was so weak that he could only say a few words at a time.

He said he was not feeling any worse, but wanted to tell him that life had been worth while, and wanted him to know about some of the wonderful healings which God had wrought through his ministry. Among them he told Claude about Mrs. Stoehr's healing at Cheney, Kansas, and it being recorded in the courts at Wichita, Kansas.

One day I quoted the Scripture that Jesus learned obedience by the things that he suffered, and Mr. Parham said, "Yes, but Jesus never suffered with sickness. He suffered by being despised and rejected by those He loved and gave His life for."

He never doubted God's healing power. The Great Physician had been his health and strength ever since he had consecrated his life to the ministry, but now at times he seemed to doubt whether or not the Lord required him to keep up the fight any longer.

He said though he knew he was not old, yet going night and day, he felt that he had already spent seventy-five years in the service of the Master, and that he was so tired he wanted to go home, but we were holding him here by our prayers. Yet he wanted us all to pray for him and often called us together for prayer and as too many came to the house to admit to his room, prayer meetings were held in other rooms in the house.   But he seemed to feel like Paul, who said, "I am in a strait betwixt two, having a desire to depart, and to be with Christ, which is far better."

He said he was glad he had fought for God all these years and that now multitudes had come into the truth of the restoration of Pentecost for these last days.   His interest continued in the work of God to the last.   He believed the evangelistic work would go through a terrible testing time, but that there would be a sweeping revival before the second coming of Christ.

The last day he was with us, he quoted many times, "Peace, peace, like a river," adding, "that is what I have been thinking of all day."   During that night he sang a part of the chorus of "Power in the Blood," and asked us to finish it for him, which we did.   Then he said "Sing it again," so we sang two verses.

On the afternoon of the following day Jan. 29, 1929 he went to sleep in Jesus, leaving a broken-hearted family.

> "A precious one from us is gone,
> A voice we loved is stilled.
> A place is vacant in our home
> Which never can be filled."

As I write June 27, 1930, the sorrow still remains fresh in our hearts but I can see that this sorrow has drawn us closer to God and to one another.   It has perhaps given us an experience which we could of had in no other way except by the taking away of the one who (perhaps too much) we had always leaned on and looked to for help and comfort.   But we feel that his prayers are still being answered for his family.

As we can not tell all that has been accomplished by his life, neither can we know the purpose and plan of God, which may (unseen to our blinded eyes) be carried out for His glory by his death.

The problem now confronted us, how were we to let his many friends from coast to coast, know of his death.   Many of them loved him as one of their own family and would no doubt come to the funeral, could they know it in time, yet it was impossible to send telegrams to all and multitudes who were so dear to him were strangers to us.

It was now Tuesday and the funeral was to be on Sunday, so it was decided to send a personal letter to all his friends of whom we had the address, so by very rapid work, and the assistance of many friends by Wednesday night, 2000 letters were mailed out.   We telegraphed Alice Parham at Los Angeles, Calif., who came at once, and others would have come from California had they known it sooner.

Many who had planned to drive from a distance could not come on account of a blizzard; the roads were so slippery with snow and ice, they were almost impassable.   But in spite of the weather, great crowds came to the funeral.

One car coming from Perryton, Texas, drove day and night to get here which was a very dangerous drive, considering the condition of the highways.   They arrived at the funeral just before the casket was closed, but said they were glad that they had made the drive.

Words fail to describe the beautiful flowers, which were sent by friends from coast to coast, and came from far and near.

The following is in part an account of the funeral which was published in the Baxter Citizen:

Hundreds Attend Funeral Service of Chas. F. Parham

The funeral services for Rev. Charles F. Parham at the Baxter Theatre at 2 o'clock Sunday afternoon packed the building long before that hour and at least a thousand persons were unable to get inside until the casket was opened for the last view of the famous evangelist. It was more than an hour from the time when the first person passed the casket until the last group, the members of the bereaved family, looked for the last time at the face of the deceased husband and father.

Inside and out of the building the crowd was estimated at 2500 despite the fact that snow fell for some time before the hour of the services and during the time they were being held. Flowers came from many places, some of them from thousands of miles, and hundreds who lived far away were prevented from attending on account of the weather conditions.

Using the theatre, (which had the largest seating capacity in the city) for the funeral services was in keeping with the activities of Rev. Parham during his ministry, as he often held services in other buildings besides church buildings. His first sermon in Baxter Springs was preached in a pool hall, his followers say, and many services were held in the open air.

A chorus of fifty persons occupied the spacious stage, as did also a number of ministers from different sections of the country. The Psalm Mr. Parham loved best, the 23rd, was read and the songs he often called for were sung. Even one hymn he tried to sing when he was near death, "There is power in the Blood," was completed with lips trembling from emotion. The Rev. Mrs. Lou Love of Galena was in charge.

* * * * *

Over his casket, persons who had been healed under the ministration of the fallen leader, mingled their tears.

"When a soldier of the cross falls, close up the ranks and press the battle to the gates," Rev. Parham often urged and his followers insisted that the work would be carried on as he had directed.

At the Baxter Springs cemetery where Mrs. M. E. Daley of Oklahoma City, Okla., read a poem written by Rev. Parham on the death of a friend, "A Loved One Is Sleeping," a verse of "Sweet Bye and Bye" was sung; Mrs. Love spoke a few words and Mrs. Alice Parham dismissed the audience.

Rev. Parham is survived by his widow, four sons, Claude W., Philip A., Rev. Wilfred C., and Robert L. and one daughter, Mrs. Ernest Rardin; one grandson, Charles Ernest Rardin. The four sons, Ernest Rardin, son-in-law, Charles Rardin, grandson were pallbearers.

*   *   *   *   *

Many letters, long distance calls and telegrams were received daily offering assistance during Mr. Parham's sickness and many friends had helped in every possible way. Among them Mrs. N. Patton, our next door neighbor, who although she had been a trained nursed, was a strong believer in prayer, and had her sight restored when going blind. Her letter will tell you something of Mr. Parham's sickness from a nurse's standpoint.

Dear Mrs. Parham:

"May I offer this as a theme from the last chapter of Brother Parham's life? I feel like it was his last sermon and should be listed as, 'Yield not to temptation.'

"I admire loyalty and faith, friendship or ideals and I do so admire Brother Parham's loyalty to his faith. He practiced what he preached for he was certainly loyal under circumstances most of us would not have had the courage to be.

"I do not mean to offer my ideas as an excuse for my part in this but only that you might know that it was my desire to

Blessed are the dead which die in the Lord from henceforth: Yea, saith the Spirit, that they may rest from their labours; and their works do follow them. Rev. 14:13

give him rest from pain for a little while. I am a Baptist by faith and believe in Christian doctors when and where they are needed. I also believe in divine healing for I have seen His wonders worked. I have heard doctors pray over their cases and I have seen hopeless cases cured by prayers of loved ones after doctors had given up the case. I know God answers prayer.

"I think Brother Parham believed in good nursing, but did not believe in a lot of the modern ideas of doctors. No one had told me his ideas of doctors, but my thoughts are taken entire from being in the home, as a neighbor and friend, the last few weeks of his life.

"As God is my judge, I say to you, my friend, no man ever had better care or more loving attention and service than did he during his last illness. May I also say, few suffered more than he and **none could be more patient.**

"I have been asked, 'Did he have a doctor?' and my answer to these 'doubting Thomases' may seem rude, for it has been thus; 'Would it be any of your business if he had, but he did **not.**' Would they blame me for my seemingly abrupt answer, if they knew as I did how he suffered holding to his faith and ideals, when science offered rest in pills, hipo and other forms.

"One morning when Brother Parham was suffering more than usual, I felt I just must do something to relieve him. Unless God wrought a miracle in his life, in his condition I knew that he could not live long, so relief from pain was all I could offer. I vowed if he would accept a tablet or hippo I would certainly give it to him and the world would never know, for I would not destroy the faith, he gave his life to establish. Had he accepted relief this letter would have never been written and perhaps my answer to inquiries would have been more kind. Yes, if you wish to call it so, I would have cheated to bring relief to my fellow man.

"But listen this was his answer, 'Oh, Mrs. Patton, tempt me not. Jesus suffered more than I, and if it is God's will that I drink of this bitter cup, than let it not pass. I thank you for you mean well, but I must not fail my belief, thus, so pray for me now.' What a loving rebuke, then thanks, and then pointing to the light, and may I say, forgiveness.

"Now you who follow this or any other denomination, whatever your choicec may be, won't you read between the lines and carry on God's work to the best of your ability. Oh, for more Christians who are loyal even in suffering and trial. Oh, you pastors, I beg of you, 'Practice what you preach.'

"Words seem shallow in expressing what is in my heart, but the loyalty to my ideas, strengthened by association with Brother Parham during his last days has helped me so much. So if I, a friend, can gather Christian courage from my acquaintance with him for so short a time, what a privilege has been your's by knowing him and his Christian life for years.

He lived to a ripe old age seemingly in the short life he lived. Where anytime there was an opportunity to help others, it can be said of him—he took bricks from his earthly temple to help others build their altar. No sermon he ever preached could send a more direct lesson to his listeners than that last short sermon of 'Loyalty,' manifest in the experience I have just told you about. Can't you, won't you, understand what from my heart I am trying to convey? I believe Robert and Pauline have this loyalty and can tell it better than I, so I will close saying, God is God, even if the suffering or glimmer of this world sometimes hides His blessed face. I know he is there and I too will be loyal."

Your friend, Mrs. Nellie G. Patton.

* * * * *

Offerings were being sent from all over the United States to help to purchase a monument, which we selected before Wil-

HIS LIFE THE MUSIC
HIS DEEDS THE SERMON
HIS MEMORY A LASTING BENEDICTION

fred and Alice returned to California.   It was a pulpit made of granite with an open Bible on the top on which we had carved. John 15:13, which was his last sermon preached at Wichita, Kansas.   We thought the pulpit very appropriate to his life work and it will be easy for his friends to locate when visiting the Baxter Cemetery.   But to me the most real and lasting monument is the Full Gospel Message, which he was used of God to establish in a multitude of lives, and his name engraved in the hearts to which he had been a blessing.

I am sure as many of his friends read this book, you will know of many meetings of interest which have not been mentioned, but I have tried to condense it as much as possible and also earnestly endeavored to make my statement correct.   If however, I have made any mistake, I trust you will pardon them.   I pray that it may be a blessing to all who may read it, and that it will seem to you like his voice "calling back," to encourage you to be faithful and true till we receive that crown of life, that fadeth not away.

* * * * *

He is not dead. He's just gone on before.
Just slipped away to yonder golden shore.
He passed from death to life, he still lives on-
While here we wait the coming of the dawn.
He traveled far, and steadily he went-
Going: Not caring whither he was sent.
Filling the ranks so well, until at last-
One day he realized that he had gone too fast.
Could go no further now, and tho't it best
To rest awhile, ah yes, he needed rest.
He lay down by the way side for a while
With such a little tired weary smile.
And bade them "carry on" to let him lie.
"I'm so tired, I'll meet you by-and-by."

Mrs. Alice A. Wilson.

A LOVED ONE IS SLEEPING

A loved one now is sleeping,
Just gone on before;
Another link to bind us
To that eternal shore.

The waters threatened deep,
And, seeming widely rolled;
But weary limbs and tired feet
Soon pressed the sands of gold.

We loved thee well 'tis true,
But Jesus loved thee best;
So lay thy tired head upon
Thy Savior's loving breast.

World's trials and temptations
Thy soul again shall never test;
Beyond their power victor,
Thou hast entered into rest.

Over death and grave a conqueror,
A victor's crown is thine
While we around thy memory
A laurel wreath will twine.

Now looking for the Savior,
With those who've gone before,
To come again rejoicing
We'll meet to part no more.

United then a family
To sing His praise, His name adore;
Joining tender thoughts and memories
Of these then happy days of yore.

Composed by Charles F. Parham at the death of a friend.

Chapter XXXVI

IN LOVING REMEMBRANCE,

Written By Friends.

CHARLES F. PARHAM

C. Christ first, last and all the time with

H. hope of His second coming, the

A. Alpha and Omega of his faith.

R. Redemption the message of

L. love to fallen man and

E. eternal life offered to those who accepted;

S. Salvation for the whole man, through the blood of Christ.

F. Faith the wings that lifted him above,

P. Persecutions, testings and trials.

A. Answered prayers a monument for the

R. royal service he rendered to his Lord.

H. Home he quietly went for a season of rest to

A. await the sounding of the

M. Master's trumpet "arise thou that sleepeth in the Lord."

—Mabel E. Daley, Oklahoma City, Okla.

* * * * *

I first met our Brother Parham, when he was a young preacher and unmarried. He then being pastor of the Methodist Episcopal Church at Eudora, Kan., at which time I was holding the Blue Mound Holiness Camp Meeting.

Bro. Parham came into the service a little late, his congregation having come to the Camp Meeting. I had announced previously that I would preach on our Anglo-Saxon identity with the house of Joseph of "the ten lost tribes of Israel." The theme was new to him as it was also to the entire congregation.

The inspiration of the Holy Spirit was upon me, and I preached for two hours and a half, and no one left or thought of dinner. After looking at my watch, I told the people to get some dinner and that I would continue the subject at the afternoon service. I did and preached for one hour and a half.

During that morning service, I was especially drawn to that young boyish looking brother who came in late and sat in the rear of the tabernacle, and I went to him. After the introduction and first greetings were over I said, "Brother, do you know that these are the last days, and that Jesus is coming soon?" His reply was, "Every sanctified man knows that."

That melted our dawning fellowship and brotherhood, which remained unbroken and which, I am sure will now remain unbroken throughout the eternity of God. Yours in that marvelous love and inheritance of the saints.

Bishop J. H. Allen, Pasadena, California.

Note: This is our last communication with Mr. Parham's dear friend, Bishop Allen. He fell asleep in Jesus, May 14, 1930, but his influence and teachings will ever live in the hearts of his many friends.

* * * * *

Over twenty-five years ago into the little mining town of Galena, Kansas, came the wonderful story and the fulness of the old-tme gospel.

Although but a little child at that time, how well I remember how God swept that little town with a mighty revival and how He anointed our beloved friend and brother, Charles F. Parham, with the Spirit of the Living God and indeed "His minster was a flaming fire."

Then on down through the weary years how he labored, toiled, suffered and rejoiced, endured afflictions, did the work of an evangelist, made full proof of his ministry, fought the good fight, kept the faith and finished his course.   Surely like Paul of old we can hear him say: "Henceforth there is laid up for me a crown of righteousness which the Lord, the right-eous Judge, shall give me at that day."

Truly Brother Parham's life was a life of sacrifice for his fellow men.   Yes, he gave more than "reasonable service," he gave his life.   John 15:13—Greater love hath no man than this, that a man lay down his life for his friends.

This was the text he used for his last sermon in his meeting at Wichita, Kansas before coming home for Christmas.

He likened the parents love as being wonderful and then pictured the love of the Savior as far surpassing anything in this world.

What a comfort it will be to the friends of the Southland to know that he loved them well enough to make the last long drive through mud and snow to keep that last appointment.

How he loved the people of the plains and the ones up through the hills where we used to gather in the little school-houses, where shouts of praise and tears of the repentant mingled together with the joy of souls born anew.

Never a day too dreary or a night too cold and dark for Brother Parham to answer a call.   Yes, even across the deserts of Arizona he drove to reach the bedside of a dying friend and again I recall how he drove night and day from California to Kansas to visit a home where a much loved son was dying and as he entered the home in the night how the parents were comforted by his prayers.

Then again I recall our visit to the slums of "Hell's Half Acre" where we sometimes held four hour services for the men who were without God and hope.

Then across the continent through winds, rain, sleet and snow to the snow clad cities of Michigan telling the glad Gos-pel story, then on through the vast mountains stretches to that great turbulent city of New York, just to tell the same old story.

Surely no one led a busier life than our friend and brother; never an hour of idleness. Even when his thoughts were given to dictating his sermons or answering his great load of letters, he was always busy walking back and forth across the room.

I have so often marveled at his wonderous intellect and his power to concentrate his thoughts upon his work; the vast amount of prophecy, history, etc., that seemed to be stored back in his excellent memory.

Brother Parham never lost sight of the handiwork of God and the beauties of nature; he loved the hills, the valleys, the snow capped mountains and the great surging sea. He loved all flowers from the tiny delicate yellow blossoms he one day found on the desert road through Arizona to the roses and stately poinsettias of California. And only God alone knows how his soul delighted in music and song. The song of a little yellow bird with its head lifted toward God and its golden voice untrained by man and unspoiled by flattery, held a foremost place in his heart.

I can scarcely realize while I write that Brother Parham is not somewhere in this world walking with hurried steps through the multitudes.

Precious in the sight of the Lord is the death of his saints. —Psa. 116:15. May God bless and comfort dear Sister Parham who has been so faithful and true to God through all these years. May her children be a blessing to her and to all they come in contact with.

And to our beloved brother, may he rest and stand in his lot at the end of days and at that time, Michael shall stand up, the great Prince, and many of them that sleep in the dust of the earth shall awake, some to life everlasting. "And they

that be wise shall shine as the brightness of the firmament and
they that turn many to righteousness as the stars, forever and
ever." Dan. 12:3.

These beautiful words are from Rev. Oatman's song:

"When I've gone the last mile of the way,
I shall rest at the close of the day
And I know there are joys that await me,
When I've gone the last mile of the way."

Dora Preston Campbell, Wichita Kansas.

*   *   *   *   *

May I speak in honor of our beloved Brother Parham, a man
honored and loved by the thousands who knew him, in his
world wide acquaintance. Speaking of the most cardinal vir-
tues of the man, I would say his deep piety and Christ-like
charity, toward all man kind. A love that was unfeigned and
true to his friends; a love that heard the heart cry of the poor
and needy, and ministered to their needs; a love that seemed
to be burnished and brightened by the foul attacks of his enemies, who often sought his downfall and destruction; a love
and enduring patience through it all, that seemed to speak
amidst the most firey trials saying as did the Master of old;
"Father forgive them, they know not what they do."

Another great virtue, his faith—which like the morning
star, rose upon his life, to lift him out of an almost helpless
state on invalidism, paved the way to an entire consecration,
of spirit, soul and body; laid as a living sacrifice for life or
death, for weal or woe.

The Holy Spirit led him on and on, bestowing upon him
the holy honor, as leader and founder of the wonderful Latter
Rain Apostolic Faith Movement, fought with the mighty out
pouring of the baptism of the Holy Ghost, like as it was on
the day of Pentecost Acts. 2. So it was also seen and heard
in Bethel College in the New Year of 1901 at Topeka, Kan.,
the students speaking in other tongues (languages) as the
Spirit gave them utterance.

Then like the beacon star, his faith transcended and in mighty revivals he preached the kingdom of God, to unnumbered thousands, a primitive Christianity Jude 1-3. A salvation for soul, body and spirit manifested in a full salvation. The Lord confirming the Word in mighty power, with signs and wonders and gifts of the Holy Ghost. Demons were cast out, and healing streams flowed through the bodies of many who were sick and afflicted, so that scores have risen up and called him blessed, who was able to pray the prayer of faith. Again in Bible Schools, at Camp Meetings, in many states his wonderful prophecies and Bible instructions to workers and ministers have gone forth to the world.

Altho our beloved brother sleepeth and his voice is stilled, he still speaks through a host of ministers and will speak, until this age closes, and the Kingdom of God is ushered in, the mighty prophetic truths of God's Word.

Speaking of our brother's ambition or zeal—moved by the unseen dynamic forces, and power of God—his activities and zeal was marvelous. One week in observation of his labors in Camp or field was enough to chase the lazy worker back to the brush or to real pep and action. He set the pace for ministers and laymen, that but few could keep pace with. His zeal and activities were a most wonderful part of the man. His God-given, super-human strength allowing him to double over the labors of men of his class, so that through the grace of God, he was able to bring to monumental completeness a work and service for the Master which all might envy, but which none but one called, Charles F. Parham, could fulfill; anointed of God, elect and precious.

The crowning and golden sheaf of his life was in his Palestine trip. He was there for over three months and was blessed with the privilege of traveling to the shrine of many places made sacred by Bible lore, visiting the places of Christ; His birth place, the Garden of Gethsemane, the beautiful Mount of Olives and Golgotha. These, and many other scenes, numbering over two hundred slides our beloved brother brought back with him that he might show his friends what he had seen of the land our Savior trod. The most beautiful of these scenes to me were "Sunrise over the Sea of Galilee" and "Jerusalem at sunset". No wonder it was called the "Golden City!"

This was his last sweet service and sacrifice to us his people and to all mankind. The beautiful pictures of the Holy Land, together with his wonderful Bible lectures, will always bring sweet memories, especially to those who have known him so long and loved him so dearly. His was the life of a prophet, like Moses of old, who was taken up into the Mount and saw over into the Promised Land and has prophesied and told us of the holy and redeemed people and City of God, the land where the saints shall dwell.

For some reason, we know not why—God knoweth—He hath called our brother to rest. He has fallen asleep in Jesus, to await the glorious morn of the first resurrection. A prophet, a priest of God, laid to rest. Your brother and servant in Christ.

S. E. Waterbury, Cave Springs, Arkansas.

* * * * *

Emanuel—God With Us.—This was a meaningless word to me, until coming into contact with the meetings held by Brother Parham, in 1903, at Galena, Kansas. When I heard of the wonderful works of God, it seemed too great to be true. But the first time my husband and I attended one of these meetings we were convincd that God was there; for the evidence wrought by the Holy Spirit could come from no other source than the Omnipotent.

Many times after the evil one tempted me to doubt the reality of the work; but when I sought the Lord for light, He showed me so clearly that the work was of Him and that this messenger was His apostle to bring these wonderful truths to a world, reduced to religious forms, and darkness, and doubt. I often asked the question, "How can I know that I will be saved?" but no one to answer, until Bro. Parham taught us the full gospel.

I wish to say emphatically that I stand for all that Brother Parham taught. Not because it was Brother Parham, or a personal matter, but because God showed me again and again, that the work was of Him, and that Brother Parham was just His meek, humble and consecrated servant, willing to do His will at any cost. We loved our brother, not for himself alone, but for the God within him, and all the fruits of the Spirit.

There are many counterfeits in the world today, which are doing more harm, and causing greater unbelief than dead churches; but those who were in this faith, and received these precious blessings for twenty-five years after these meetings, and came in contact with Brother Parham's work and life, could not doubt the presence of Emanuel, or be deceived by the counterfeit. Yours contending for the faith.

Isabelle M. Whitney, San Francisco, Calif.

* * * * *

My good friend, Charles F. Parham, I had known for twenty-five years, a quarter of a century. He was a man of courage, a good speaker, and did much good in the world. He was the first who preached the baptism of the Holy Spirit in these last days, and he labored from city to city and in the highways and hedges compelling men and women to get right with God. He labored in the Midnight Mission on every visit to California. He loved—with that love that God speaks of— the poor, fallen human wrecks and showed them the way of righteousness and pointed them to the "city not made with hands, eternal in the heavens."

We will meet again. God help us all to be true until we hear Him say, "Well done."

"Brother Tom" T. H. W. Lidecoat, Los Angeles, Calif.

CHARLES F. PARHAM

One year ago he went to be
In that rare Land of Liberty,
Where every one in Christ is free,
And faith melts into certainty.

Bold messenger of Pentecost;
Which to the world had long been lost.
In human fields of thirsting grain.
He spread news of the Latter Rain.

His message foiled each critics probe
And won adherents round the globe.
By constant toil he cleaned his slate,
Then knocked at God's eternal gate.

To this remarkable man alone, belongs the distinctive honor of presenting to the world anew, The Pentecostal Movement.

I met him a quarter of a century ago at Orchard, Texas, where he was conducting the FIRST Pentecostal meeting ever held in this great state.

I was with him in his second meeting held at Houston, in Bryan Hall. This was a famous effort, and was the nucleus of a marvelous work in the Lone Star State.

I seldom praise men, but I will say for Bro. Parham that never in church, auditorium or the halls of learning, have I heard such volumes of truth and eloquence flow from the lips of any other man. But his voice is now hushed by the cruel monster of mocking silence, and I shall never hear it again until my own voice is silent too.

Ah! I err, for I hear him now in the echoes of sweet memory.

In our last conversation together, while he was in Texas in July, 1928, he told me seriously, that he was crossing the Border Land. I could not believe that his Border Land was so narrow, but I could believe that when this charitable, unselfish Christian nobleman reached life's western shore, viewed its golden sunset, and tarried for a moment in the twilight, he saw beacons of royal welcome on the farther shore, as well as Some One near him, walking on the water.

Day and night without cessation he labored in white harvest fields of wasting grain. He never lost any time or neglected his work, but scored daily for the Master.

For 35 years he labored strenuously declaring a fuller gospel to the world, and establishing numerous missions throughout the land.

He also encountered continuously, buffeting waves of persecution, scandal and criticism set in motion by selfish usurpers and evil designers.

One of his last remarks was "Now I am tired and want to go Home."

Is it any wonder he was weary? Is it strange that he desired to accept God's invitation to take his well earned vacation?

What a wonderful light disappeared on earth, and what a brilliant star appeared in Heaven when Brother Parham went home to cash this promise:—"The wise shall shine as the brightness of the firmament; and they that turn many to righteousness as the stars forever and ever."

> "I cannot say and I will not say
>   That he is dead. He is just away.
> With a cheery smile, and a wave of the hand,
>   He has wandered into an unknown land,
> And left us dreaming how very fair
>   It needs must be, for he lingers there."
>   W. M. Gray, Houston, Texas.

*   *   *   *   *

In the year 1905 I met Evangelist Charles F. Parham in East Bernard, Texas, who preached a message that was convincing, convicting, and converting. It stirred the country around about and many hundreds were saved, sanctified and baptized with the Holy Ghost.

Never before had the people known such a revival as when Brother Parham came to south Texas and the Lord visited people with His mighty presence and convicting power as in the days of old.

People came to the meetings and repented of their sins and it was reported that in their homes, fields and different places souls prayed and cried unto the Lord for mercy and He changed their lives from darkness to light, and from the power of satan to serve the living God.

I was only a little girl then, and did not know much about sin, but when I came in the presence of Brother Parham I got homesick for Jesus. Every day I prayed and when I awoke in the night, I cried and prayed until God made me to know that I was really converted.

My trials were so great in my childhood days and Pharaoh's host followed me to bring me back into Egyptian bondage. But I was determined to live for the Lord and my trials only drew me closer to Him.

I consecrated my life to God, presenting my body a living sacrifice. (Romans 12:1-3).

The Lord gladly accepted my offering and sanctified the gift, and I am so thankful for the teaching Brother Parham brought us of sanctification, as a second work of grace. I had crossed the River Jordan and entered the land of Canaan to receive my inheritance thru faith in Christ. Acts 26:18.

I surely enjoyed the good things of God. The honey and the wine of the Promised Land, which He has purchased for me on Calvary. One night I prayed to the Lord and He graciously sent the Comforter and baptized me with the Holy Ghost and I spoke with another tongue as recorded in Acts 2:4.

As Brother Parham used to say; at one time he had a one story house, salvation. Then the Lord lead him to consecrate his life and added the second story, sanctification. He thought surely now the building was complete, but one day a rushing mighty wind came and lifted the roof and added a Pentecostal tower, and filled the whole building with His Presence and power. Now this was my experience.

I want to tell you more about Brother Parham who became dearer to me as I learned more about him. He preached the Gospel without fear or favor, and when he was persecuted he was faithful and went on about the Master's business. He was a man of great intelligence and ability, but like Jesus he chose the humble way and his life and ministry became a blessing to many thousands. In later years I had the privilage of making my home with Brother and Sister Parham and their family for about three years. They were as daddy and mother to me, and I was at home in the house of a prophet of God.

The consecration and sacrifice that they made for the sake of the gospel and humanity was wonderful and it made a great impression on me. Brother Parham was so busy for the Lord he often did not have time to eat or sleep. No wonder the Lord blessed them with a family of children that loved and respected them. I often heard the boys say, "Dad, whatever you say goes."

The whole family accepted his faith and teaching and backed him up in his work and I have never seen parents who had a better influence over their children. While I was with the Parham family, I attended three camp-meetings; held at High Top near Gravette, Ark., Bethpage, Mo., and Wyandotte,

Okla., and many other meetings near Baxter Springs, Kansas.

The fame of Jesus went abroad, as when He walked the shores of Galilee. The great "I AM" is still working miracles through His children.

Though Brother Parham is gone, he is not forgotten, and he still speaks, for his influence will go on and bless humanity, as he rests from his labors, his works will follow him.

I have heard him say that he was homesick for heaven, and had a desire to depart and be with the Lord. Brother Parham lived among us as a beautiful rich flower, which when crushed, you smell the sweet odor and see the good quality. When his enemies said all manner of evil against him falsely, he prayed for them who despitefully used him. But God has said, "It is enough;" he will never be wounded and crushed by his enemies anymore. His friends everywhere often called him "Daddy," and I am sure he was the greatest daddy in the world, for he was a father to the fatherless, and a friend to the widows.

He was a great hero of the cross who brought light and truth to the world, and was brave and true in the battle for the King.

Though he got many scars from the enemy, he did not shrink or shirk: there was no retreat or surrender, his life was an example of faith that will stand as a monument of righteousness. He fell in the battle for God, and loved not his life unto death. Truly he could say like Paul. (2 Tim. 4:7) I have fought a good fight, I have finished my course, I have kept the faith.

I was praying that the Lord would comfort me in my sorrow, and Brother Parham appeared to me in a dream. He was preaching in a mission about the resurrection from I Thess 4:13-18.

What a comfort this was to me and I trust that Christ will pray for us as He did for Peter, that our faith fail not, till the great resurrection morning when we shall all meet again.

I am praying for all of God's children everywhere and I am looking for Christ's soon coming.   Your sister in Him.

Ida Drachenberg, Beasley, Texas

*   *   *   *   *

And the numbers can never be known until "the books and the book" are opened that can say "He cleared a pathway and became my guide, and let the sunlight of life shine into my soul where it had long sought to penetrate, but could not."

He came as my neighbor when I lay bleeding and wounded from sin upon the battle field, he "poured in the oil and the wine" and it touched "the silent chord" that for two score years had brought forth no response and I lived again, and a gloomy world became cheerful and the cold was dispelled by the new fires that burned upon my hearth.

He never knew defeat, though at times, when they murmured his soul grew vexed and like Moses he cried out to God, "Yet, now, if thou wilt forgive their sin; and if not, blot me, I pray Thee, out of Thy book which Thou hast written."   Exodus 32-32.

No night too cold, no storm too fierce, that he would not go to the call of the sick, helpless, brier-torn, bleeding lambs of his flock—or another's.

He had wished to die a martyr, and he did; all battle scarred, his burden grew heavy and he became tired, and a hero, one of God's noble generals, closed his eyes in restful sleep, to see no more, the blood stained battle field of worldly strife and carnage—brought on by sin—for his old sense of hearing was no more, but the new quickened ear had caught the sweet strains of the blended voice of angels, as they sang, "Jesus is tenderly calling today, calling today."

Though the sacrifice he made in obedience to his call so often, against his own will, kept him from home and loved ones: but "Greater love hath no man than this that a man lay down his life for his friends." The principles he taught his sons and daughters will enable them to meet the crisis when it comes in their lives.

I expect to meet my brother in his next "Big Camp Meeting."Brothers and sisters, let us all strive to be there.

                                    Jesse M. Barnes, Carthage, Mo.

*   *   *   *   *

My nearly four years with Charles F. Parham were years full of sunshine and happiness and memories of those days will live in my heart forever.

I think it was the latter part of 1915 or the early part of 1916, that I first joined him in Houston, Texas. I know I was nearing my 14th birthday, and was with him until I was almost 17.

I always called him "Dad" for he was a father to me since the day he took me from the streets of Houston, Texas as a newsboy. With his love he taught me the things of life and guided me in the way of truth and trained me in evangelistic work which enabled me to give and preach the full gospel to thousands of people.

The greatest shock of my life was when I learned of his death; it was hard to believe and realize. I wondered why he should have to leave us, he was not so far up in years and always full of life. He was so comforting to the faith all over the country, that never failed to hear him for they not only loved him but his powerful lectures and sermons were food to their souls. They, like myself, feel lost without his dictations.

Then it occured to me how forcibly he used to bring out in his sermons that the time would come and is upon us, when like in war the captain in the deadliest fight of the battle gave command "every man for himself."

It is thus that God has called "Dad" in the thickest of the battle, and he fought to the last for the truth and salvation of souls. He is not here. in body to guide us and help us and keep us encouraged, and direct the battle now, so the warning that he has rang out time and again is upon us, and if we are to be saved it means that every one must individually depend on God alone, and follow the teachings of the Apostolic Faith which the late Charles F. Parham first brought to us.

Charles F. Parham was indeed the greatest evangelist and Bible student of our times. He never used the Scripture for a money-making scheme; he was content with what the Lord let him have. Nor did he use the Scriptures to gain fame. He never submitted to publicity schemes to reach the multitudes. He never failed at any time to ring out the truth whether it hurt or not. He used the Scripture for the only purpose it should be used, and that is for the salvation of souls, and the thousands that were saved in his meetings were taught how to walk in the right path.

He never failed to preach anywhere that he felt he could do good. He has appeared in some of the finest places of the land, and also on street corners. He has preached before thousands at one gathering, and also preached to the few.

One of the most enjoyable times of his life, (when I was with him) was the time he and a party including myself, left Baxter Springs, Kansas in two cars and headed to Nebraska, and Colorado holding meetings on the streets of towns and cities that we went through. People would come and sit on the curbing hours before meeting time, waiting to hear his message. In Denver, Colorado it was estimated over two thousand people lined the sidewalk and streets to hear him. After his lecture he would give the invitation for people to come up for prayer. Hundreds came and he would pray for them by laying on of hands. Many remarkable healings took

place and many were saved.   Many old men came up with
tears streaming down their cheeks to be prayed for that they
might be even convicted of their sins.

I could tell of hundreds of things I have witnessed the Lord
do through Daddy Parham, and I am thankful to God that
he permitted me to be with him, as I don't know what my
life would have been without that four years with him.   I
only hope that we may all be true to God and some day we
will meet Dad Parham on that great day when the dead in
Christ shall arise and live during the Millennium where we
will be known as we are known; where there will be no more
sting of death; where there will be no more burning heat or
bitter cold.   Then we all can sing the praises of the Lamb and
be thankful that we, like Dad Parham, fought the fight of
faith and won.

Clarence Heckendorn, Houston, Texas.

*   *   *   *   *

It seems incredible that we shall not hear Brother Parham's
voice again in this life.   I had counted on it so much, fully
expecting to hear of some announcement of services in this
vicinity at the time I received the sad notice of his death.

I first heard him preach in Los Angeles, California in 1906
and his message was so wonderful.   I had received the truth
of healing by the Lord through the Dowie movement four
years before.   Here was something which seemed to me greater and grander, as he taught us that the baptism of the Holy
Spirit was for us today as it was given on the day of Pentecost.   He was preaching on the Heavenl City once and the
rostrum shone with the glory of God and I got my first
glimpse of the towers and streets of that City.   Oh, I know
that there are towers there!   Somehow from that time, I have
lost the desire for an earthly home for heaven became so real

and beautiful! How beautiful upon the mountain are the feet
of him that bringeth good tidings, that publisheth peace; Isa.
52:7.   I have written the following:

In Memory Of My Dear Friend
Chas. F. Parham

How beautiful the feet that tread
   O'er Zion's rugged mountain trail.
That pathway made by One who said,
"I am the Way, the Living Bread,
   And the Waters that never fail."

Stained footprints mark the lonely height,
   And thorn-bruised feet that follow on
To yonder summit of delight
Are changed to beauty, thru the night,
   And grief is swallowed up by song.

Who follow Christ the upward way
   Thru storm, thru lair, where darts are hurled
Past doubts and darkness and dismay
Will reach the mountain peak of day
   And hear God's message for the world.

And thus our brother came and went
   Preaching the gospel God had given
That every sinner should repent
And live in God's grace-convenant
   And have the Holy Ghost from Heaven.

He told of mansions in the sky
   And lo, the Spirit brought to view
Yon city's streets, and towers high!
Resplendent homes for you and I!
   Thus, God had sealed the message true.

He preached, "The Sun of Righteousness
　　Shall rise with healing in His wings."
He prayed, and many in distress
Felt virtue from Christ's seamless dress
　　Flow thru and heal them from their stings.

He told of balm that could be found
　　In Gilead, and there alone
A balsam leaf for every wound
To sooth distress the world around
　　Is found in Jesus on the throne.

How beautiful upon the mount
　　The feet of him who bringeth near
The tidings of an open fount.
Where sinners lose their dark account,
　　And find eternal life and cheer.
　　　　　　—Mrs. Dell Reed, Long Beach, Calif.

*　　*　　*　　*　　*

In the death of Rev. Charles F. Parham, of Baxter Springs,
Kansas, the cause of Christ has lost a valuable and fearless
preacher. During a two week's sojourn in my home I found
him a congenial, warm-hearted Christian minister.

Because he dared to preach a full gospel and because of his
unabated zeal, those who know him will always remember him
kindly. On the mount of revelation and prophecy his life
often seemed transfigured before the large congregations he
addressed.

Long linger in our memories the life's work of this great
apostle of the full gospel movement.

　　　　　　　　A. B. Stanberry, Wichita, Kansas.

Note. His son, Bennie Stanberry, traveled with Mr. Parham
on several evangelistic trips, and sang in the meetings.

I believe I heard him preach for the first time in the spring of 1919. The message he brought, as I listened, convinced me I was a sinner, and that Jesus Christ came to save me from my sins.

He told how all the gifts that the early Christians enjoyed were ours today if we make the consecration and believe as they did. This was good news to me.

One thing I especially noticed was his humble life. He seemed to preach because he had love in his heart for God and souls. He was willing to suffer, willing to go hungry, willing for his name to be a reproach, just for the gospel. I thought that was walking in the footprints of Jesus.

Many others in our community were saved through his message, and were sanctified, and baptized with the Holy Ghost of promise according to Acts 2:4.

He never was afraid to tell a person the truth if it made enemies or if it made friends. At first his prophesies were too much of the Scriptures for me to grasp, but they gave me a greater love for the Bible.

I shall never forget the example he gave in one of his sermons. He told how he had seen dogs follow their master until they starved to death, and he said if a dog was willing to die for his master how much more ought we to be willing to die for our Master. I always appreciated Brother Parham because he practiced what he preached, and counted this life as nothing that he might win Christ.

His passing away out of our midst does not cause us to doubt any of the Bible truths he preached but causes us to press on to the mark of the high calling in Christ Jesus. I thank the Lord for the message of salvation that came to our country first in 1905, at Orchard, Texas preached by Brother Parham, and for the clean, consecrated life he lived.

Mr. & Mrs. E. T. Buls, East Bernard, Texas.

*   *   *   *   *

In the summer of 1921, while at Mineral Wells, Texas, where I had gone for my health, I heard of the meeting at Wichita Falls, Texas, which was being conducted by Chas. F. Parham. At the request of my wife, I consented to attend.

I had just fasted eight days, meanwhile drinking the mineral waters, but on our way to Wichita Falls I got sick, and in the following twelve days I ate only two meals, losing fourteen pounds. I was in a terrible condition, and it seemed to me that I would surely die.

During this time the brethren were praying conviction on me, and an overload of sin-sickness added to my other troubles made my condition unbearable. It seemed to me that every sermon Bro. Parham preached was hurled at me; and oh, how I thank God that those words of truth sank deep into my heart, and in my distress I cried unto the Lord and he heard me.

In the summer of 1905, while operating an irrigation plant on a rice farm in South Texas, a pulley bursted, a piece of it striking me in the face, bursting the eyeball in five places, tearing the iris loose and folding it over the pupil, and turning the eyeball to one side, causing a partial paralysis of one side of my face. Trusting in the arm of flesh, I went to the hospital and had an operation, suffering excruciating pain. About six months later the other eye developed an intense inflammation, and again I went to the hospital for an operation, and a few months later I went the third time. At this time I was given some very strong medicine to reduce the inflammation; the doctor forgot to tell the nurse not to give this more than three days, and the result was that the lining of my stomach and digestive tract was destroyed.

From that time on my troubles were multiplied, and for sixteen years I had to exist on the things I hated, and was sick all the time, suffering intensely. I had what is known as auto-intoxication, or self-poisoning. During this time I tried mineral waters, patent medicines, mountain air, sweat baths of various kinds, electrical treatments, chiropractic treatments, had more than two hundred osteopathic treatments, and regular medical treatments, and all to no avail. As a last resort, I came to the Lord, and as He saved my soul, He healed me of this dreadful stomach disorder. Praise the Lord, forever! He did more for me in a minute than all of these things that I had tried for sixteen years had done. How much better it would have been had I come to God first, and thus escaped those sixteen years of living hell.

During the Wichita Falls meeting a number of people were saved, healed and sanctified. I remember one little woman who for three days prayed, "Oh, Lord, give me faith." The Lord answered this prayer; she made restitution, went to her mother-in-law to whom she had not spoken for years and they came to meeting arm in arm. She then went out and brought others to the Lord, one after another, having faith that God would save them.

One man was saved and paid a grocery bill that he had dodged. We went to the factories at the noon hour; also went to the prison with the message of hope, comfort and cheer. So the good work spread and we had a glorious meeting, finishing with a baptismal service, when several were buried with Christ in baptism, including myself.

Since that time I have been walking in the light as I understand it, and have received sanctification, the second definite work of grace; then later the baptism of the Holy Spirit according to Acts. 2; and am still saved and healed, and enjoying the presence of the Lord.

To me, Chas. F. Parham was the greatest preacher that ever graced a pulpit, excepting only Jesus Christ Himself. In loving memory of the message I received from his lips I dedicate this article. He sacrificed and endured hardships that he might bring a message of deliverance to poor suffering humanity like myself. May the Lord bless every one that reads this article, and may the words of our Lord become spirit and life to you. — C. H. Stockdick, Katy, Texas.

*   *   *   *   *

My impressions of Chas. F. Parham:

H's was the stamp of an individuality that stood out as stands the dawn at daybreak, mimicking no one, emulating no other preacher or modeling his brief phrases after none who had gone before. He was always himself, ready to eject some ridiculing barb to prick the heart that had hardened, melt the callous soul that seemed beyond redemption or set afire a careless one that pretty speeches could not win.

His witticisms were as victory's flush upon his cheeks, kindly, yet with but one purpose in mind-souls, souls, souls! His hatred for evil was always evident, and one had to be able to understand a little the silent symbols of heaven to read the liquid sign language of his accusing eyes when he preached to sinners. It was then that hidden springs in his nature welled to the surface, that fervors of unbridled enthusiasm shook through him and under the fusillade of such strong preaching sinners were won to Christ.

He could make God so big that He gleamed and shone forth like a star in the gray skies of the listeners' existence and all else paled into insignificance, and with their harvest of barren regrets gathered could kindle a new fire reaching God toward and starting anew. His emotions played around the risen Christ with a slavish devotion and love, his ever-reaching goal, the harbor he ever anchored in.

Smiling, laughing, his was a face of joy that ever looks beyond the mists, the narrow view, to where the visioning makes golden stairways to the skies. He seemed untouched by life's deep throbbing woes, wearing a shiny countenance, perhaps that others might be more easily won to the Master he was serving.

I shall carry the sweet memory of him as one who had fought for Christ well and true.

And he built with his life and service a structure that the elements of time can not destroy. Some day we shall see him again.   Mrs. A. L. Wallace, Oregon City, Ore.

* * * * *

The first time we met Bro. Parham was in the spring of 1922 when he came to Waka, Texas where we were living at that time.   Never can we forget those days of meeting and the wonderful messages he brought us under the anointing of the Holy Spirit.   It seemed that the very presence of God was in every service and we felt to say with those of old "never man spake like this."   Some of those messages are still lingering in our hearts, stirring our souls to go on with God. The influence of this meeting reached for miles and scores were saved, sanctified and healed.

Bro. Parham's next visit to the plains of Texas was in May, 1923 when he conducted a Convention at Perryton, Texas; here again God's presence was felt over that section of the country.   The sick were brought for miles and many were healed before going home, also many were saved, sanctified and received the baptism of the Holy Ghost.   The influence of this meeting is still going on as some fifteen preachers are in the field today as a result of this meeting.

Bro. Parham was always an inspiration and help to us because of the life of sacrifice he lived and his willingness to serve whether in the large cities or in the small country school houses; where ever he thought he could be a blessing to humanity. Never was the road too long or too rough if he felt God was leading him to be a blessing to some one.

We remember one time when we were in a meeting at Kibby, Okla., a small country school district, how he refused an opportunity of a night's service at Enid, Okla., where he could have spoken to hundreds, to give us that night because he felt that God was leading, and always his message would be in harmony with the meetings. That night he preached on "Divine Healing" and at the close of the service he prayed for about forty people suffering from different diseases, and to my knowledge many were healed and are to this day, who had never heard the message of healing before that meeting.

Another time when the work on the plains had been somewhat hindered, he turned back as he was on his way to Denver, Colo., to help us, having two nights meeting at each of the missions and established them in the things of God.

And then again when he was making that last trip home that he might spend Christmas with his loved ones, how he stopped with us for one night in our meeting at Perryton, Texas. I am sure many will remember that last message there on "The Commandments of Jesus" how he exorted us to a life of sacrifice to help others and by serving others thereby serving Christ saying, "In as much as ye have done it unto one of the least of these my brethern, ye have done it unto Me."

The memory of Chas. F. Parham will always be a help to inspire us on to stand for the truths he gave his life to bring to the world. Yours in Him.

Evangelist Chester Jackson and wife, Perryton, Tex.

* * * * *

Brother Parham had a strong and wonderful personality. His many friends declared that his had no equal, and just to know him was to both admire and respect him, and I am glad that I had the pleasure of knowing him.

The first time I met him, I knew him, even before I had been introduced to him. In a crowded hall of hundreds of people I singled him out, because of his unmistakeable personality, and jovial disposition.

He was a man of rare intellect and ability and noted for his keen insight in human character, and well do I remember how, with his delightful sense of humour, he would portray some odd character so well, but without the least bit of unkind ridicule, that he would have us all doubled up with laughter and merriment.

I also knew Bro. Parham as a preacher and he nobly excelled himself along this line, his sermons being always interesting and inspiring. There was never a dull moment in Brother Parham's meetings from start to finish. I have seen him many times sway large and mighty congregations, and saw them weep and laugh by turns, as they sat listening to this great and elegant speaker as he expounded, exhorted, and ridiculed each in his own immutable way.

When at the close of one of these sermons, he would give the altar call, the altar would be filled with seekers. Many there are today who can rise up and call him blessed, for he surely pointed out the way of salvation in a way that could not be mistaken.

But if I knew Bro. Parham as a preacher, I knew him much better as a host, for upon entering his home in Baxter Springs, a perfect stranger to the other members of his family, I was entertained right royally and was soon made to feel like one of them, and indeed it is with much pleasure that I now look back to those days that I spent in the Parham home.

"The house of the open door" I call it, for it was surely
like home to me, and there were always visitors coming and
going at all hours of the day and night, and all were welcome.
That large, commodious house of twenty rooms was almost
always filled, and many times some member of the family had
to camp on the floor that they might give their room to some
unexpected guest.

I remember that on the bureau in my room was a little framed verse which I used to read often, and which gave me freedom of the whole house, and I remember Bro. Parham, one
day, asking me if I had seen and read it.

I assured him I had, and he told me that he himself had suggested putting that little "homey" verse there, and that they
all wished me to understand that it was not merely to fill up
space on my table, but that I was to accept their hospitality as
freely as it was given, and I did, for never have I been in a
home where I felt more at home than I did while there.

The motto which Brother Parham had framed reads as follows:

> "Hello, Guest and howdeedo!
> This small room belongs to you,
> And our house and all that's in it
> Make yourself at home each minute,
> If the temperature displeases,
> Take a couple of our breezes;
> And if that should chill you later,
> Sit upon our radiator.
>
> If a hungry pang is twitchin'
> Make a raid upon our kitchen,
> Help yourself to book or blotter,
> Easy chair or teeter-totter;
> All is yours that you like best.
> You're at home now!
> Welcome, Guest."

Both Brother and Sister Parham were remarkable in many ways. Their home life was very beautiful, and harmony prevailed everywhere. Not because I am, in a way, more closely related to them than some others, do I say this, but because being thus related, I was enabled to see the "inside" life of the Parham family. Strangers were made equally welcome and can say with me that "it was good to be there."

Knowing Brother Parham as a preacher, as a host, I can say that I also knew him as a gentleman, a man of high intergrity, ever displaying a fine spirit of generosity, always handing out to some one not so well off financially as he was, and I believe with all my heart that he died a poor man, for he was always giving. He received a great deal of money from his many friends, but he gave it away as fast as he got it, and no need for the Master to say to Brother Parham that it is easier for a camel to go through the eye of a needle than for a rich man to enter the kingdom of heaven, for truly he left his riches behind him. He might have been a rich man with wealth at his command, but he preferred the kingdom of heaven, and many a life has been made brighter, many a home made happier, many souls born again because our brother lived.

His own home was an example of what a real home should be. His dear wife, Mrs. Parham, was all that a wife and mother should be, and surely kept up her share of the burden and task of caring for, and bringing up their nice and beautiful family, one of which happens to be my dear son-in-law, Wilfred Parham, and of whom I am vastly proud.

But it is not because of this fact that I write this article, which I feel is far below the standard which Bro. Parham had reached, but because I feel it incumbent on me to submit it, that I might add my tribute to the memory of one who has contributed so much to the comfort and happiness of so many others, and also for comfort and solace to the noble wife and family he has left behind, but who will ere long join him over on that golden shore where no parting days will ever come, where there will be no more goodbyes.

"They shall hunger no more, neither thirst any more; neither shall the sun light on them nor any heat; For the Lamb, which is in the midst of the throne, shall feed them, and shall lead them unto living fountains of waters: and God shall wipe away all tears from their eyes. Rev. 7: 16-17.

He lived his life for others
And he lived it not in vain.
He labored in the vineyard;
Away over hill and plain.

He preached the precious gospel
Yes, preached it far and wide,
The same sweet gospel message,
Of a Savior crucified.

He spent his life for others
His time and talents gave.
That souls might grasp the gospel;
That sinners might be saved.

He lost no opportunity
He never sought for rest.
He served the Master faithfully
He did his very best.

"Salvation" was his slogan.
"Redemption" was his creed.
He showed the Blood stained banner
To souls who were in need.

He gave his life for others,
T'was all he had to give.
He showed to all the way of life,
That all might look and live.

Mrs. Alice A. Wilson, Los Angeles, California.

*   *   *   *   *

CHARLES F. PARHAM AND HIS WORK RECORDED
IN HISTORY

I have not written this book in the form of a regular history, but just told you of my husband's life, in the form of
a story, in my own simple way; trusting that it will be enjoyed and kept as a sovenir in the homes where his life and
message have been a blessing and that his influence and memory may still be a power for the glory of God. The preceding
articles, written by some of his friends, show that his name
is engraved on hearts and held in loving remembrance.

But his name and work has already been recorded. A history of Kansas published in five volumes, has the following
to say of Mr. Parham:

Rev. Chas. F. Parham.—The attractive little city of Baxter
Springs, Cherokee County, claims as one of its honored and
influential citizens the distinguished and world-famed evangelist whose name introduces this paragraph and who was
the originator of the Apostolic Faith movement, for the restoration of primitive Christianity. Mr. Parham has maintained his home at Baxter Springs nearly a quarter of a century,
and here his spacious and attractive residence had its nucleus
in the brewery building that he purchased and transformed
to its present uses. Instead of being a place for the manufacturing of intoxicating beverages, the building now figures
as a center from which has gone forth a great and noble influence in bringing humanity back to the simple and uphold-
ing faith of primitive Christianity. A New York statistician
has given Mr. Parham credit for the conversion of fully 2,000,-
000 persons, through his personal appeals and through the me-
dium of ministers who have loyally followed his teachings
and examples. Charles F. Parham was born at Muscatine,
Iowa, June 4, 1873, and is the son of William M. and Ann
Marie (Eckel) Parham, both natives of Pennsylvania, where
the former was born in Philadelphia and the latter at German-

town, the Parham family having been founded in the old Key-
stone State in the Colonial period of American history. Chas.
F. Parham was a lad of five years when, in 1878, his parents
came from Iowa to Kansas and numbered themselves among
the pioneer settlers in Sedgwick County, where the father
instituted the reclamation and development of a productive
farm; the home having been one in which luxuries were few
but in which was a prevading spirit of gracious Christian faith
and practice that the son, who was to become a distinguished
evangelist, can look back with satisfaction to the benignant influence of the home of his boyhood and youth.

After profiting by the advantages of the Kansas graded
schools Chas. F. Parham attended the Methodist Episcopal
College at Winfield, this state, where he prepared himself
for the ministry of the Methodist Church. After his ordination as a clergyman he served as pastor of the Methodist
Church in Eudora, Kansas, as successor of Rev. Dr. Davis, the
founder of Baker University, this state. He entered evangelistic service in 1894, and during the long intervening years
his work of zealous consecration has been splendidly fruitful.
As an evangelist he has labored faithfully and with great success in all parts of the United States and Canada, and has
often addressed audiences of 7,000 persons. Each year during the past 20 years his birthday anniversary has been celebrated by great assemblies of his followers and other friends
at his home in Baxter Springs, and from an article that appeared in the Baxter Springs Citizen of June 2, 1928 are taken,
with minor paraphrase the following extracts:

"The Rev. Chas. F. Parham, senior minister of the Apostolic Faith and original preacher and teacher and of all Full Gospel movements, will be honored here next Sunday for the
twentieth year in celebration of his birthday anniversary.
Similar affairs held in past years drew crowds of from 1,000
2,000 people, and the evangelist has been showered with letters

and telegrams of congratulations, as well as with gifts of all kinds."

From another newspaper are gleaned the following statements in which minor changes are made in reproduction: "Mr. Parham says that he was moved to bring out the new doctrine through his experience as a young minister when he preached two years with only one conversion for his work. His conviction that the people wanted the old-time religion resulted in his organizing the Apostolic Band, and his conviction and deductions have been amply confirmed, as he has preached to audiences varying from 2,000 to 7,000 persons during the intervening years, while thousands have been saved through his earnest ministrations."

It was thirty years ago that Mr. Parham felt that the world needed the restoration of primitive Christianity, with all its gifts and graces, and he was moved to leave the narrow confines of the modern pulpit to preach everywhere the "New-Old Way." Mr. Parham has been signally blessed and favored in his great work as an apostle of righteousness and his rewards have been on a parity with his consecrated zeal. In connection with his work he founded the paper known as The Apostolic Faith, and which is issued in his home city of Baxter Springs.

On the 31st of December, 1895, was solemnized the marriage of Mr. Parham and Miss Sarah E. Thistlethwaite, who was reared in Kansas, of English ancestry, her parents having been birthright members of the Society of Friends. Mr. and Mrs. Parham have four sons and one daughter, and all reside at Baxter Springs, except Rev. Wilfred C. who is a traveling evangelist in the Apostolic Faith. Claude W. is engaged in the grocery business at Baxter Springs; Philip A. is engaged with his older brother in the grocery business; Esther is the wife of Ernest Rardin; Robert L., remains at the parental home.—History of Kansas State and People. Compiled by Wm. E. Connelly, 1928 Edition, Volume III, page 1324.

"Conclusion"

"THE AMERICAN COLONY AND PICTURES
OF THE TWENTY-THIRD PSALM"

OST of our readers know that with the pictures Mr. Parham brought back with him from Palestine was a series of thirteen pictures illustrating the twenty - third Psalm.

He especially loved this wonderful Psalm, and always took great pleasure in showing the beautiful pictures representing it. Everywhere these pictures have been shown they have been very much appreciated. Christ said, He was the "Good Shepherd,' and as we look at the pictures of the well - cared for sheep, our hearts are lifted up in praise and worship to the tender Shepherd for His watchful care over our lives.

As Mr. Parham enjoyed these pictures so much, I thought it would be a real monument in memory of his three months spent in Palestine, if we could secure these pictures to put in this book for truly this Psalm was made real in his life. The Lord was his Shepherd and we did not want, and how often the Lord prepared "a table before him in the presence of his enemies," and kept him from harm and dangers, seen and unseen. God "anointed his head with oil" when He bestowed upon him the baptism of the Holy Spirit in 1901 and gave him this message to give to the world. When at last he passed "through the valley, and the shadow of death" we know God was with him, and "His rod and staff ' did comfort.

I decided to write to Jerusalem and see if it would be possible to obtain these pictures, and it is through the kindness and courtesy of the American Colony Stores—Vester and Co.—that I have the pleasure of adding these beautiful pictures to this book.

I consider this a rare treat, as I understand, they have only been reproduced [a few times before in the United States. It was at these stores that Mr. Parham brought over two hundred slides, (beautiful pictures of the Holy Land) which since his death, my son, Robert, has been showing from coast to coast.

Mr. Parham also bought a number of nice souvenirs of different kinds at these stores, beside a large number of postal cards (various views of Palestine) that he mailed to many of his friends in the United States. As Rev. G. J Brimson is so familiar with the American Colony Stores, I have asked him to tell you more about them.

"The American Colony was established in Jerusalem in the year 1881, and composed of various nationalities among whose first members were Mr. and Mrs. H. G. Spafford of Chicago, Illinois. It is a small community, patterned after the first Christian Church of Jerusalem, which now numbers about eighty to a hundred souls. Service to their fellow man, as emphasized in the Bible, being the guiding principles.   ....

"It was in front of the American Colony Stores just inside the city wall of dear old Jerusalem, (on David's Street opposite David's Tower) that Bro. Charles F. Parham loved to sit and watch the people go by. When we wanted to find him we would just go to these stores and we would see his jolly, broad smiles, talking to the natives or watching them.

"Several times we came to the stores when one of the clerks would be interpreting something for Brother Parham and it would make you laugh to see him laugh. He had the time of his life. Pilgrims from all over the world, passed by these stores. I am sure the friends of the American Colony Stores miss our dear Brother Parham as they so much enjoyed his genial company. He also was a godly inspiration to them and to all the people he came in contact with, for he always had a word for the goodness of our blessed Lord.

"Many curious events transpired at the doorway of the American Colony Stores. I was present at many of these occasions. Many of the Arabs and Jews learned to know him. At this moment, I can imagine myself listening to some queer thing that would make Brother Parham laugh, and his laugh won its way into the hearts of the people.

"Wife and I went to Jerusalem on the same ship with him. We were all interested in research work for the furtherance of the gospel and had many trips to places of interest, and spent many happy days together. We all miss our brother, for to know him was to love him. Though we are now separated for a little while by the grace of God, we shall be united forever. Amen"

"Regarding the American Colony Stores, I can truly say any one wishing anything on these lines, can make no mistake in the purchases from them.

"American Branch."

"The American Colony Stores (Vester and Company) 559 Madison Ave., New York City, New York, U. S. A. The people connected with the American Company are real courteous Christian men and women, and all manners of beautiful souvenirs can be purchased from them."

Shepherd Life In Palestine

 ASTORAL life in Palestine flows on in the same channels today as it did in the time of David, and in the open region to the northeast of Jerusalem, the flocks are still taken down the rough and winding paths, into the picturesque gorge, in the bed of which winds the silvery stream of Ain Farah. This is still the popular gathering place of the shepherds of the surrounding hill country of Judea, and is generally accepted as the scene of David's boyhood experiences in shepherd life, which in his riper age he recals and uses in this "Sweet Psalm of Trust," to illustrate the Father's protecting care over His people. To aid in portraying the scene, we will imagine ourselves going down to this valley, where most of our studies were made.

As we walk down some early morning, (it is only six or seven miles from Jerusalem) when every blade of grass sparkles, and the dewdrops glisten on the mountain-sides, we see the shepherds from the neighbouring villages, (it may be from old Anathoth close by, the home of Jeremiah), leading their flocks out in search of pasture. Near noon, we see the flocks on the hillsides making their way down the slopes, toward the watering places in the valley. Here the flocks assemble, and after "restoring their souls" at the mint-bordered stream, they rest for a few hours "in the shadow of a great rock."

while the shepherds gather in groups for their lively chats, which usually center on the welfare and care of their sheep, or similar subjects, and to partake of their frugal noonday meal.

After resting during the heat of the noon hours, the many flock swhich have congregated, separate as if by magic, when each shepherd goes off in a different direction calling his flock. A good shepherd "knows his sheep and is known of them," and to him the sheep hearken. Shepherds often call each of their sheep by a special name, which the sheep learn to know, and to which they respond. These names are usually suggested by some particular trait of the sheep, or perhaps, by a peculiarity in colour. The large congregation of flocks has now broken up into several smaller groups, moving slowly up the hill. The tinkling of the bells carried by one or more of the sheep in the flocks, blends with the wild cadence of the shepherds' flutes, as they wend their way toward their respective sheepfolds. Shepherds are always equipped with a rod, staff or both. "Thy rod and thy staff" is quoted in a figurative sense, and both words may mean one and the same thing, denoting a shepherd's stick, which varies in form and size, and which is usually carried for protection, it may be against the attack of wild animals. If night overtakes the shepherd before he reaches the fold (which he usually does by sunset) he uses his staff as a sounding rod, striking the ground with it as he goes along, producing a ringing sound for which the tired sheep listen; for by it, they can follow in the path picked out for them by their shepherd, in whose guidance and protection they are reassured; hence David's poetic words "thy rod and thy staff they comfort me.'

In spring this whole valley of Ain Farah is ablaze with the rich yellow of the wild Chrysanthemums, splashed over with scarlet patches of the Anemone or the "Lily of the Field," as well as numerous other flowers, and the rocky sides of the high precipitous walls of the valley are decked with rosy bunches of Cyclamens. A little later in the year, the stream itself is bordered with a fragrant hedge of green and purple Mint. To this beautiful and restful valley, one may well imagine that the "sweet Psalmist of Israel" resorted with his flock. The shepherd life seen there today, moves smoothly along, as does the stream that flows through it, in the same channels as it did in his day. It was in fact right here, that David often led his flocks of sheep and goats,—

> And here, in nature's soothing calm,
> He oft composed a thoughtful psalm;
> And in his shepherd life he learned
> Deep truths for which his soul had yearned:
> The flock required his guiding care,
> And all their woes twas his to bear;
> The sheep he likened to God's flock,—
> The shepherd, to man s Refuge Rock.

The Psalmist concludes with the beautiful theme, "And I will dwell in the House of the Lord forever." David dreamed of building "an House of the Lord," and prepared the site on Mount Moriah, where his son Solomon erected the wonderful Temple. This hill-top, the Rock Moriah, has been revered by all peoples from that day to this, and is now crowned with the impressive monument known as the Noble Sanctuary. American Colony Stores

"*American Colony Pictures*"

The Lord is my shepherd; I shall not want.

"American Colony Pictures"

He maketh me to lie down in green pastures;

"*American Colony Pictures*"

He leadeth me beside the still waters.

"American Colony Pictures"

He restoreth my soul.

He leadeth me in the paths of righteousness for His name's sake.

Yea, though I walk through the valley of the shadow of death.

I will fear no evil for Thou art with me;

Thy rod and Thy staff they comfort me.

Thou preparest a table before me in the presence of mine enemies.

Thou anointest my head with oil:

"American Colony Pictures"

My cup runneth over.

Surely goodness and mercy shall follow me all the days of my life.

And I will dwell in the house of the Lord forever.

"American Colony Pictures"

TITLES in THIS SERIES

1. THE HIGHER CHRISTIAN LIFE; A BIBLIOGRAPHICAL OVERVIEW. Donald W. Dayton, *THE AMERICAN HOLINESS MOVEMENT: A BIBLIOGRAPHICAL INTRODUCTION.* (Wilmore, Ky., 1971) *bound with* David W. Faupel, *THE AMERICAN PENTECOSTAL MOVEMENT: A BIBLIOGRAPHICAL ESSAY.* (Wilmore, Ky., 1972) *bound with* David D. Bundy, *Keswick: A BIBLIOGRAPHIC INTRODUCTION TO THE HIGHER LIFE MOVEMENTS.* (Wilmore, Ky., 1975)

2. *ACCOUNT OF THE UNION MEETING FOR THE PROMOTION OF SCRIPTURAL HOLINESS, HELD AT OXFORD, AUGUST 29 TO SEPTEMBER 7, 1874.* (Boston, n. d.)

3. Baker, Elizabeth V., and Co-workers, *CHRONICLES OF A FAITH LIFE.*

4. THE WORK OF T. B. BARRATT. T. B. Barratt, *IN THE DAYS OF THE LATTER RAIN.* (London, 1909) *WHEN THE FIRE FELL AND AN OUTLINE OF MY LIFE,* (Oslo, 1927)

5. WITNESS TO PENTECOST: THE LIFE OF FRANK BARTLEMAN. Frank Bartleman, *FROM PLOW TO PULPIT—FROM MAINE TO CALIFORNIA* (Los Angeles, n. d.), *HOW PENTECOST CAME TO LOS ANGELES* (Los Angeles, 1925), *AROUND THE WORLD BY FAITH, WITH SIX WEEKS IN THE HOLY LAND* (Los Angeles, n. d.), *TWO YEARS MISSION WORK IN EUROPE JUST BEFORE THE WORLD WAR, 1912-14* (Los Angeles, [1926])

6. Boardman, W. E., *THE HIGHER CHRISTIAN LIFE* (Boston, 1858)

7. Girvin, E. A., *PHINEAS F. BRESEE: A PRINCE IN ISRAEL* (Kansas City, Mo., [1916])

8. Brooks, John P., *THE DIVINE CHURCH* (Columbia, Mo., 1891)

9. RUSSELL KELSO CARTER ON "FAITH HEALING." R. Kelso Carter, *THE ATONEMENT FOR SIN AND SICKNESS* (Boston, 1884) *"FAITH HEALING" REVIEWED AFTER TWENTY YEARS* (Boston, 1897)

10. Daniels, W. H., *DR. CULLIS AND HIS WORK* (Boston, [1885])

11. HOLINESS TRACTS DEFENDING THE MINISTRY OF WOMEN. Luther Lee, *"WOMAN'S RIGHT TO PREACH THE GOSPEL; A SERMON, AT THE ORDINATION OF REV. MISS ANTOINETTE L. BROWN, AT SOUTH BUTLER, WAYNE COUNTY, N. Y., SEPT. 15, 1853"* (Syracuse, 1853) *bound with* B. T. Roberts, *ORDAINING WOMEN* (Rochester, 1891) *bound with* Catherine (Mumford) Booth, *"FEMALE MINISTRY; OR, WOMAN'S RIGHT TO PREACH THE GOSPEL . . ."* (London, n. d.) *bound with* Fannie (McDowell) Hunter, *WOMEN PREACHERS* (Dallas, 1905)

12. LATE NINETEENTH CENTURY REVIVALIST TEACHINGS ON THE HOLY SPIRIT. D. L. Moody, *SECRET POWER OR THE SECRET OF SUCCESS IN CHRISTIAN LIFE AND WORK* (New York, [1881]) *bound with* J. Wilbur Chapman, *RECEIVED YE THE HOLY GHOST?* (New York, [1894]) *bound with* R. A. Torrey, *THE BAPTISM WITH THE HOLY SPIRIT* (New York, 1895 & 1897)

13. SEVEN "JESUS ONLY" TRACTS. Andrew D. Urshan, *THE DOCTRINE OF THE NEW BIRTH, OR, THE PERFECT WAY TO ETERNAL LIFE* (Cochrane, Wis., 1921) *bound with* Andrew Urshan, *THE ALMIGHTY GOD IN THE LORD JESUS CHRIST* (Los Angeles, 1919) *bound with* Frank J. Ewart, *THE REVELATION OF JESUS CHRIST* (St. Louis, n. d.) *bound with* G. T. Haywood, *THE BIRTH OF THE SPIRIT IN THE DAYS OF THE APOSTLES* (Indianapolis, n. d.) *DIVINE NAMES AND TITLES OF JEHOVAH* (Indianapolis, n. d.) *THE FINEST OF THE WHEAT* (Indianapolis, n. d.) *THE VICTIM OF THE FLAMING SWORD* (Indianapolis, n. d.)

14. THREE EARLY PENTECOSTAL TRACTS. D. Wesley Myland, *THE LATTER RAIN COVENANT AND PENTECOSTAL POWER* (Chicago, 1910) *bound with* G. F. Taylor, *THE SPIRIT AND THE BRIDE* (n. p., [1907?]) *bound with* B. F. Laurence, *THE APOSTOLIC FAITH RESTORED* (St. Louis, 1916)

15. Fairchild, James H., *OBERLIN: THE COLONY AND THE COLLEGE, 1833-1883* (Oberlin, 1883)

16. Figgis, John B., *KESWICK FROM WITHIN* (London, [1914])

17. Finney, Charles G., *Lectures to Professing Christians* (New York, 1837)

18. Fleisch, Paul, *Die Moderne Gemeinschaftsbewegung in Deutschland* (Leipzig, 1912)

19. *Six Tracts by W. B. Godbey. Spiritual Gifts and Graces* (Cincinnati, [1895]) *The Return of Jesus* (Cincinnati, [1899?]) *Work of the Holy Spirit* (Louisville, [1902]) *Church—Bride—Kingdom* (Cincinnati, [1905]) *Divine Healing* (Greensboro, [1909]) *Tongue Movement, Satanic* (Zarephath, N. J., 1918)

20. Gordon, Earnest B., *Adoniram Judson Gordon* (New York, [1896])

21. Hills, A. M., *Holiness and Power for the Church and the Ministry* (Cincinnati, [1897])

22. Horner, Ralph C., *From the Altar to the Upper Room* (Toronto, [1891])

23. McDonald, William and John E. Searles, *The Life of Rev. John S. Inskip* (Boston, [1885])

24. LaBerge, Agnes N. O., *What God Hath Wrought* (Chicago, n. d.)

25. Lee, Luther, *Autobiography of the Rev. Luther Lee* (New York, 1882)

26. McLean, A. and J. W. Easton, *Penuel; or, Face to Face with God* (New York, 1869)

27. McPherson, Aimee Semple, *This Is That: Personal Experiences Sermons and Writings* (Los Angeles, [1919])

28. Mahan, Asa, *Out of Darkness into Light* (London, 1877)

29. *The Life and Teaching of Carrie Judd Montgomery* Carrie Judd Montgomery, *"Under His Wings": The Story of My Life* (Oakland, [1936]) Carrie F. Judd, *The Prayer of Faith* (New York, 1880)

30. *The Devotional Writings of Phoebe Palmer* Phoebe Palmer, *The Way of Holiness* (52nd ed., New York, 1867) *Faith and Its Effects* (27th ed., New York, n. d., orig. pub. 1854)

31. Wheatley, Richard, THE LIFE AND LETTERS OF MRS. PHOEBE PALMER (New York, 1881)

32. Palmer, Phoebe, ed., PIONEER EXPERIENCES (New York, 1868)

33. Palmer, Phoebe, THE PROMISE OF THE FATHER (Boston, 1859)

34. Pardington, G. P., TWENTY-FIVE WONDERFUL YEARS, 1889-1914: A POPULAR SKETCH OF THE CHRISTIAN AND MISSIONARY ALLIANCE (New York, [1914])

35. Parham, Sarah E., THE LIFE OF CHARLES F. PARHAM, FOUNDER OF THE APOSTOLIC FAITH MOVEMENT (Joplin, [1930])

36. THE SERMONS OF CHARLES F. PARHAM. Charles F. Parham, A VOICE CRYING IN THE WILDERNESS (4th ed., Baxter Springs, Kan., 1944, orig. pub. 1902) THE EVERLASTING GOSPEL (n.p., n.d., orig. pub. 1911)

37. Pierson, Arthur Tappan, FORWARD MOVEMENTS OF THE LAST HALF CENTURY (New York, 1905)

38. PROCEEDINGS OF HOLINESS CONFERENCES, HELD AT CINCINNATI, NOVEMBER 26TH, 1877, AND AT NEW YORK, DECEMBER 17TH, 1877 (Philadelphia, 1878)

39. RECORD OF THE CONVENTION FOR THE PROMOTION OF SCRIPTURAL HOLINESS HELD AT BRIGHTON, MAY 29TH, TO JUNE 7TH, 1875 (Brighton, [1896?])

40. Rees, Seth Cook, MIRACLES IN THE SLUMS (Chicago, [1905?])

41. Roberts, B. T., WHY ANOTHER SECT (Rochester, 1879)

42. Shaw, S. B., ed., ECHOES OF THE GENERAL HOLINESS ASSEMBLY (Chicago, [1901])

43. THE DEVOTIONAL WRITINGS OF ROBERT PEARSALL SMITH AND HANNAH WHITALL SMITH. [R]obert [P]earsall [S]mith, HOLINESS THROUGH FAITH: LIGHT ON THE WAY OF HOLINESS (New York, [1870]) [H]annah [W]hitall [S]mith, THE CHRISTIAN'S SECRET OF A HAPPY LIFE, (Boston and Chicago, [1885])

44. [S]mith, [H]annah [W]hitall, *The Unselfishness of God and How I Discovered It* (New York, [1903])

45. Steele, Daniel, *A Substitute for Holiness; or, Antinomianism Revived* (Chicago and Boston, [1899])

46. Tomlinson, A. J., *The Last Great Conflict* (Cleveland, 1913)

47. Upham, Thomas C., *The Life of Faith* (Boston, 1845)

48. Washburn, Josephine M., *History and Reminiscences of the Holiness Church Work in Southern California and Arizona* (South Pasadena, [1912?])